D0721997

Dictionary of Hindu
Lore and Legend

Dictionary of Hindu Lore and Legend

ANNA L. DALLAPICCOLA

With 243 illustrations

Acknowledgments

The author wishes to express particular thanks
to Professor J. L. Brockington for his valuable
suggestions, to Mr T. R. Blurton for his
continuous encouragement and support,
and to Mr A. Korner for his timely rescue.

Dedication

To Duncan Shaw and Sushie Abbasciano

© 2002 Thames & Hudson Ltd, London

All Rights Reserved. No part of this publication may be reproduced
or transmitted in any form or by any means, electronic or mechanical,
including photocopy, recording or any other information storage and
retrieval system, without prior permission in writing from the publisher.

First published in hardcover in the United States of America in 2002 by
Thames & Hudson Inc., 500 Fifth Avenue, New York, New York 10110

thamesandhudsonusa.com

Library of Congress Catalog Card Number 2001099690
ISBN 0-500-51088-1

Printed and bound in Singapore by Star Standard Industries

On the title page: Ramanuja.
Southern India. Copper,
18th–19th century. *See p. 162*

Contents

Introduction

'Unity in diversity' or 'diversity and continuity' are two of the many catchphrases applied to India. Although commonplace, they contain more than a grain of truth. India is so vast – roughly the size of Europe from the Atlantic Ocean to the Urals – that each region is a land in its own right, with its particular language, customs, religious and cultural traditions. Yet shared social systems, firmly grounded in religious beliefs, provide the cohesive force that unites over a billion people of very different backgrounds.

The land

The Indian subcontinent is severed from the rest of Asia by the mighty range of the Himalayas, the 'Abode of Snow', which, according to Hindu mythology, is the dwelling place of the gods. Shaped like an inverted triangle, measuring *c.* 3,200 kilometres from north to south, and almost the same from east to west, it extends into the Indian Ocean. A variety of physical features determine the different climatic zones, ranging from the inhospitable, windswept terrains of the northernmost parts of the country, to the subtropical, fertile regions of the south.

A number of imposing fluvial systems cross the land. In the northern part of the country flows the Indus (*Sindhu*), from which India derives its name. From its source in the Himalayas it journeys through an arid desert waste, westwards to the Arabian Sea. Its five tributaries gave the name to the Panjab or 'five waters' region. Also in the Himalayas lie the sources of the two most

important sacred rivers of the subcontinent, the Ganges and Jumna (the goddesses Ganga and Yamuna), which flow eastwards, merging at Allahabad (Prayaga) and eventually joining the Brahmaputra. They traverse a vast expanse of flat land and enter the Bay of Bengal in the mighty Ganges delta, an extremely wet and fertile area. Central India, a hilly region, is bounded by the wooded Vindhya hills in the north and by the westward- flowing Tapti and the Narmada in the south. The arid Deccan plateau, characterized by a dramatic landscape of granite and sandstone outcrops, the centre and possibly oldest part of the subcontinent, is skirted both on the east and the west front by a range of forested mountains, known respectively as the Eastern and Western Ghats. The two most relevant rivers of the Deccan are the eastward-flowing Godavari and Krishna, both ending in a fertile delta. In the south the principal river is the Kaveri, the Ganga of the south, which springs from the mountains of Kodagu (Coorg), nestled in the Western Ghats, on the border between the states of Karnataka and Kerala, and flows eastwards for some 785 kilometres, fanning out in a delta along the Coromandel coast. On the shores of the Arabian Sea, the Malabar coast, a narrow strip of land, blessed by abundant rainfall and lush vegetation, is delimited in the east by the Western Ghats. Kanyakumari (Cape Comorin) is the southernmost tip of India, where the Malabar and Coromandel coasts meet.

India has six seasons, the most important being the monsoon, which is expected in the summer months from June to September, and is vital for the survival of the population. An additional, albeit lighter monsoon occurs in the winter months in southern India.

Regional languages and cultures

In the course of its long history, the northern part of India was repeatedly overrun by waves of invaders, coming from the north-west. The first identified were the Aryans, who appeared in the middle of the 2nd millennium BCE; they were followed between the 1st century BCE and the 1st century CE by the Shakas, the Parthians and the Kushanas, by the Huns in the 6th century, and finally, by successive waves of Muslims from the 12th century onwards. Among the most important Islamic dynasties to rule India were the Mughals (1526–1858), world-renowned for their splendid artistic achievements. Cultural, ethnic and religious differences notwithstanding, the invading peoples gradually became integrated.

The local population, belonging to different ethnic groups, was as diverse as the foreign invaders. Most of them were settled along the rivers and in the fertile areas, and were often separated from other groups by arid tracts, hills or forested mountains. Each community developed its own distinctive language, cultural, religious and artistic traditions, some of which still survive.

In modern India, there are eighteen official languages, most of which have their own script. The inhabitants of northern, western, central and eastern India, as well as those inhabiting the northern part of the Deccan, speak languages that evolved from Sanskrit, probably the oldest among the languages of the Indo-Aryan group. Southern India is the home of the Dravidian languages. In 1956, when the British system of provinces was abandoned in favour of the formation of states based on linguistic principles, the languages gave their name to states such as Maharashtra, Bengal, Tamil Nadu, Karnataka. A range of northern Indian languages, spoken from Bihar to Rajasthan, coalesced in the course of the last thousand years to form modern Hindi, the official language of India. The second most important is Urdu, derived from the Turkish word for camp. It is a refined language, strongly influenced by Persian, Arabic and Hindi, which originated in northern India probably during the 13th and 14th centuries. It is mainly used in Islamic cultural and religious milieux. Both Hindi and Urdu have spread all over the subcontinent and serve, along with English, as a common language among Indians. Apart from the official eighteen languages, most of which have a sizeable literary output, there are hundreds of dialects, some of which are spoken by only a small number of people.

As varied as the languages are India's textile patterns, dress, ornaments and dietary habits. In the same region, these may vary from community to community and, until recently, before the introduction of the ubiquitous jeans, trainers and baseball cap worn by fashion-conscious youths, the pattern – or the absence of it – on a *lungi* (an ankle-length cloth tightly drawn around the waist) or the way a *dhoti* was draped, would immediately indicate the native place, caste and religion of the wearer. The same applies to the complex tying of turbans and other styles of headgear. In the last decade or so, young women have discarded the sari of everyday wear, in favour of the *salvar-kamiz*, loose trousers and a long tunic, and the *dupatta*, or scarf, thrown over the chest or draped over the head, which was once worn only in the northern part of the country, and generally by Muslim women. The older generation, however, still wears the age-old sari of traditional hues and designs, draped in various ways, proudly proclaiming their background and social status. A determining factor in the choice of fabric colours is the surrounding landscape: in the barren and arid tracts of Kutch and Rajasthan, women wear colourful dresses profusely embroidered with intricate mirror work, while in Kerala, one of the most verdant regions of India, both men and women wear white garments, occasionally set off by a narrow gold border.

As well as dress, dietary habits vary throughout India according to each region. The northern Indian diet is based on wheat products and unleavened bread, while southern India concentrates on rice. Fish plays an important part in the people's fare in the coastal regions of India such as Bengal, Orissa and Kerala. Each region can boast a vast array of vegetarian and non-vegetarian dishes, as well an innumerable variety of sweets; noteworthy are the culinary specialities of individual communities and particular religious groups.

Also dependent on communities are the local religious festivals, some of which are rooted in tribal traditions and deities. A number of ceremonies are linked to specific locales, either the site of some miraculous event, or connected with a saint or ascetic, or characterized by a particular natural feature, such as a spring, mountain, cave or tree.

The climatic, religious and cultural diversity of the various regions is mirrored in their art. Building materials, technique and styles differ dramatically in the north, west, east and southern parts of the country, following the local religious traditions and the impact of the climate. The same applies to the various styles of sculpture and painting. The performing arts have proved as rich and diverse as the visual arts, ranging from the sensuous *Kathak* dance of northern India, to the martial dance drama of Kerala and south Karnataka.

India boasts one of the largest film industries in the world, as films, some of them inspired by Hindu myths, are produced in almost all regional languages, and cinemas are still filled with enthusiastic audiences. One of the most renowned centres of film production is Mumbai (Bombay), which is home to the Bollywood-style films, vividly described in Shashi Tharoor's novel *Show Business* (London, 1994).

Such a diversity of traditions, in language, diet, dress, art and customs, is held together by a religious and social structure, which provides the extraordinary cohesive force around which Hindu culture gravitates.

Religions of India

Although Hinduism is the main religion in India, there are other faiths that continue to have an impact on the life of the subcontinent, such as Islam, with *c.* 120 million followers, approximately one tenth of the total population. Islam played an important cultural and political role in the history of India, and a constant interchange of ideas between Islamic and Hindu culture has left an enduring legacy in thought, arts and literature.

Other religions to shape India include Sikhism, a 16th-century religion founded by Guru Nanak, which is followed by around fifteen million people in India. Sikhism has borrowed elements from Hinduism as well as from Islam. Jainism and Buddhism, older faiths dating from around the 6th century BCE, were instrumental in the development of Hindu thought. Jainism is now followed by around three million people and Buddhism, after having practically disappeared for about a millennium, is now experiencing a revival.

Minority religions include the Jews, who arrived on the west coast of India in the 2nd century BCE and established communities mainly in Mumbai and Kochi (Cochin), and the Christians (*c.* 23 million), some of whom claim to descend from those converted by the apostle Thomas. The latter arrived in India in 52 CE, settled in Kerala and there established a Christian community. Later European missions founded various Christian denominations. Finally, a tiny, but prominent group of approximately one hundred thousand people are the Parsis and Zoroastrians who, in the wake of the spreading of Islam, migrated to India in 936 CE. They are concentrated mainly in and around Mumbai.

The development of Hinduism

A vast, undetermined number of deities, saints, ascetics, seers, mythical beings and deified heroes, along with devotional cults and local beliefs, constitute what is loosely termed Hinduism. Although some scholars look for the origins of Hinduism in the religious traditions of the Harappan civilization, which flourished between the 3rd and 2nd millennia BCE, contemporary Hinduism is not so ancient. The movements of devotional theism (*bhakti*) and the worship of a personal deity (*ishtadevata*), a 'chosen god or goddess', on which Hinduism is grounded, date from the centuries immediately preceding the common era. The message given by these cults is that only *bhakti*, the path of love and complete surrender to a deity, can help the devotees to achieve their goals and attain release from the bonds of death and re-birth (*samsara*).

The deities of early Hinduism mainly derive from those of the Vedic religion, the prevailing religious system between *c.* 1500 and 900 BCE, which were transformed by local traditions and folk cults and are scantily, if at all, recorded in early literature. Among these non-Vedic deities, first and foremost are the *yakshas* and *yakshis* (nature spirits), *nagas* (snakes), *vrikshadevatas* (tree spirits), associated with mountains, springs, lakes, caves, trees and plants; others include the *grahas* or seizers, responsible for mental illnesses, and a number of goddesses who, if not duly propitiated, will unleash plagues, droughts and famine. Eventually, the cult of the deified heroes, whose deeds are celebrated in the classic epic poems such as the *Ramayana*, the *Mahabharata* and numerous local folk epics, entered the Hindu pantheon, thus increasing its already considerable number of deities. This catholic approach to the divine lies at the core of Hinduism; even today its remarkable elasticity is demonstrated by the creation of new deities such as Santoshi Mata in the 1950s and early 1960s.

By the beginning of the common era, the most important Hindu cults, which were to mould belief, practices and the culture of India up to the present day, were established. Minor divinities and spirits, however, were not forgotten, but incorporated as attendant deities and semi-divine beings into the Hindu fold. Moreover, in the Hindu holistic conception of the universe, there is no essential difference between human beings, animals and plants. The bull, the peacock, the tiger, the owl, the eagle and many other animals, which were probably connected with tribal cults, became the *vahanas*, or mounts of the classic Hindu deities, each reflecting the character of its master. Every deity has its favourite tree or flower, so these were also incorporated into the Hindu pantheon. The most popular among the flowers is the lotus (*padma*), which serves as the throne or pedestal for the majority of heavenly beings.

Various species of fig trees play a pivotal role in many sacred myths and legends, as well as in folk tales. Plants, such as *haldi* (turmeric), still form the basis of traditional Indian medicine and are also widely used in worship.

Hinduism's two thousand years of continuous interaction with Buddhism and Jainism has resulted in a number of shared philosophical notions and religious practices. These three faiths are particularly rich in myths and legends, providing an inexhaustible source of inspiration for the arts.

Cults of Hinduism

Despite the multitude of gods, goddesses and other semi-divine beings populating the Hindu pantheon, the major cults of Hinduism focus on three main deities: Shiva, Vishnu and the great goddess Shakti, in her multifarious aspects. In urban communities, Devi generally appears in connection with a male god, but in rural communities she is often worshipped on her own.

The personalities of Shiva, Vishnu and Shakti are extremely complex, comprising diverse and often contrasting elements which coalesced in the course of the centuries. The various aspects under which these deities are worshipped bear testimony to this process. Each of them possesses a wide range of powers, but their worship is not mutually exclusive. A devotee of Shiva will also worship Vishnu, albeit as an ancillary divinity, and vice versa. However, for a follower of Shakti, all male deities will be of secondary importance.

A striking feature of Hinduism is the notion that, immaterial of whether they focus on Shiva, Vishnu or Shakti, a worshipper will reach the ultimate goal. This has defused the potential for sectarian rivalry among these three cults. Some schools of thought see these various deities as mere aspects of the transcendent divine, an attitude that encourages tolerance. The concept of a trinity consisting of Brahma, Vishnu and Shiva has also been introduced. Brahma, called the 'Creator', is the pivot between a centripetal and a centrifugal force, represented respectively by Vishnu, the 'Preserver', and by Shiva, the 'Destroyer'. All major Hindu gods are surrounded by a posse of deities, some of which are recent introductions (such as the already mentioned Santoshi Mata), others of local importance, such as Vithoba of Pandharpur, or Minakshi of Madurai. Many of them are believed to be aspects of, or to be associated with the 'family' of the main deities, and some, such as Dattatreya, may result from the combination of two or more gods. Deities can attain great popularity in a particular region, but after being worshipped for a time, may disappear altogether, while others, who seemed to be forgotten, can suddenly make a comeback. Far from being a dogmatic religion, Hinduism has the remarkable capacity to accommodate practically any facet of the divine. Beliefs and religious practices of Hinduism do not have a unique doctrinal basis, as the unifying factor lies in the acknowledgment of the authority of the four *Vedas* and other Vedic scriptures.

Sacred literature

Sanskrit is the language of Hindu sacred literature, including the *Vedas*, the *Brahmanas* and the *Upanishads*, which are regarded as the basis of Hindu religion and ethics. However, the most important source for understanding popular Hinduism are the epics, *Ramayana* and *Mahabharata*, the *Puranas*, 'stories from old times', as well as the *Dharmashastras* or Law Books, containing the rules that govern the life of an individual from birth to death. This vast literary output was first transmitted orally, and only committed to writing during the early centuries CE. There is no way of ascertaining the correct date of composition of these works; the chronology is approximate and is steadily subjected to revision in the light of new philological and archaeological research.

Parallel to Sanskrit literature, there exists a substantial literary output in the various regional languages of India, in which both the epics and a number of the stories drawn from the *Puranas* are reworked following local traditions. A particularly important literary genre is the *sthalapurana* or *mahatmya*, the celebration of a single place where a deity appeared or where a mythological incident occurred. Most of the *sthalapuranas* are composed in regional languages or in corrupt Sanskrit. These are vital for appreciating some of the sculpted or painted narratives in temples.

Before the advent of cinema in the early 1930s and of television in the mid-1960s, sacred lore was disseminated among the rural population, the majority being illiterate, by professionals reciting episodes drawn from the epics, the *Puranas* and occasionally, folk ballads. They would embellish their presentation either with painted scrolls, or with sets of paintings on paper. This was later replaced by films, the subjects of which were drawn from the epics and the *Puranas*. Eventually, the same themes were adapted for the television screen, suffice to mention the comparatively recent productions of the *Ramayana* and *Mahabarata*.

Pilgrimage

Preoccupation with the divine in its most different aspects had as a consequence the creation of a sacred geography. The potential sanctity of landscape elements, such as mountains, caves, pools, rivers and trees, has already been mentioned. These are the places in which deities, spirits and other semi-divine beings manifest themselves as incarnations of the powers of nature.

Some sites are connected with mythical events or with the life of a holy person. A complex network of holy places encompasses the whole of the subcontinent from the Himalayan shrines at Kedarnath and Badrinath, to Rameswaram and Kanyakumari in the extreme south, and from Puri in the east, to Dwarka in the west. At another level, sites of local importance form part of a regional sacred geography which connects one place with another, and thus creates pilgrimage circuits. Particularly popular in southern India are the six places sacred to the god Murugan, or the five great temples enshrining the five elemental *lingas*. Some particular sites, such as Girnar in western India and Sravana Belgola in Karnataka, are specifically Jaina pilgrimage sites, whereas Gaya and the neighbouring Bodh Gaya are visited by both Hindu and Buddhists. Most of the *dargahs* (tombs) of the Muslim *pirs* (holy men) are visited by both Muslims and Hindus. The fact that generally the *dargahs* are placed in the shade of an old tree, shows a connection, perhaps subconscious, with the age-revered Hindu and Buddhist tree worship. This is corroborated by the number of votive offerings, such as pieces of cloth, small cradles, etc., that hang from its branches. Interestingly enough, the recently built Roman Catholic basilica of Our Lady of Health at Velankanni, in Tamil Nadu, increasingly attracts visitors of all faiths.

Hindu myths

Day and night, light and darkness, creation and destruction, good and evil are the main themes around which Hindu mythology revolves. In Buddhist, Jaina and Hindu thought, creation is a cyclical process. The universe is created with four eras (*yugas*) in which creation undergoes a gradual moral and physical decay until it is destroyed in a great conflagration at the end of the Kali *yuga*. However, this is not the end, for after a period of sleep, the creative process starts anew. All deities, even the most benign, have a dark side which occasionally emerges, as for instance the Devi or Shakti, who appears in benign and awesome aspects, as Parvati and Kali respectively. The same applies to Shiva and Vishnu in their multifarious aspects as protectors of their devotees and as destroyers of the negative forces threatening creation. Because of the cyclical conception of time, the balance between good and evil is constantly shifting, the gods and their adversaries are locked in an eternal conflict. This dynamic relationship between gods and anti-gods is illustrated in a number of myths, in which both parties try to outwit each other. Sometimes it is the gods who are forced to acknowledge defeat, other times their adversaries: there is no final victory. Myths still provide a constant source of artistic inspiration, as amply testified by the vast number of images and narratives carved and painted on temple walls, book illustrations, theatre, dance and in modern times, cinema.

Mythology and art

Since its earliest period, as shown by the small statuettes, votive figurines and seals found at the Harappan sites of the 3rd millennium BCE, Indian art centres on human and animal figures. Many of the main Hindu deities appear for the first time in the art of the Kushana rulers of central India (1st–3rd centuries CE). However, earlier isolated sculptures dating to the 1st century BCE, suggest that there was already a specifically Hindu artistic production.

Images of saviours and deities, as the objects of devotion, were located in sacred precincts. They appear occasionally with their *vahana*, their consorts and attendant deities. Immaterial of whether they are painted or sculpted, the images obey a canon of conventions, which are established in the *shilpashastras*, or art treatises, which serve as a guide to image making, detailing iconography, emblems, dress, headgear, number of arms, attributes and the stance of an image. Only images fashioned according to the canonic prescriptions of the *shilpashastras* are deemed fit to be worshipped. This resulted in an overall standardization of forms, but it did not hamper in the least the lively imagination of the Indian artist. Morever, numerous regional *shilpashastras* existed, serving to dictate the rules for local art production. However, it has been demonstrated that the codified rules were followed up to a point, and that the intuition of the artist was the decisive factor.

Indian art depicts a number of hybrid creatures, as seen in representation of Vishnu as a man with the lower body of either a fish or a tortoise. This order is reversed in the Varaha and Narasimha *avataras*, in which the head of the god is shown to be that of a boar and a lion respectively. A number of semi-divine creatures also take on hybrid forms. Paramount among them are the *nagas*, human figures with the lower body and hood of a snake, *kinnaras* and *kinnaris*, human figures with foliated tails and bird claws, and finally, Garuda, a youth with wings and a hooked nose. Attributes, *vahanas* and elements of costume, are endowed with symbolic meaning and help to identify these various figures.

Narratives drawn from the *Ramayana*, *Mahabharata*, the *Puranas* – especially popular among these are the stories of Krishna – and the local *sthalapuranas*, appear prominently on sculpted friezes, murals, paintings on cloth, and book illustrations.

Along with mythological themes, sensuous depictions of young maidens and loving couples appear frequently in Indian art. Youthful female figures with full breasts and hips, gently kick tree trunks to encourage them to burst into flower, or clutch creepers, thus transferring their life-giving forces to nature. The same notion is expressed in the representations of the river goddesses Ganga and Yamuna, whose waters are imbued with life. The heavenly courtesans and dancers (*apsaras*), symbols of sensual pleasures, often mix with humans and seduce them. Enticing maidens play with a pet parrot, are disrobed by a mischievous monkey, or coyly stand looking out from a half-open door. Couples tenderly embrace under three canopies, and in flowering bowers others copulate in a variety of acrobatic positions. This all-pervading sensuality contains a magical purpose, celebrating and reinforcing the life-energy of nature.

This celebration of the senses, along with the depiction of hybrid creatures, baffled and shocked 19th-century Western scholars and visitors alike, who were accustomed to thinking along the Judaeo-Christian lines, in which there is a clear dichotomy between the flesh and the soul, as well as between humans and beasts. One of the great achievements of Hinduism is the acknowledgment and integration of all opposites inherent in human life. Human life, in turn, integrates with the natural world and the rhythm of the universe.

Social structure

Another great achievement for India as a whole lies in the cohesiveness provided by the social system, founded on religious beliefs. An elaborate, hierarchically structured social order renders it possible for each person to feel part of a greater whole, to which he or she can contribute, however modestly. The first record of a social order is to be found in the *Rigveda* (*c.* 1500 BCE), where in Hymn 90, *Mandala* X, v. 12, one reads that 'The brahmin was his [the Creator's] mouth, the *kshatriya* [warrior class] his arms, the *vaishya* [mercantile class] his thighs and the *shudra* [peasants and labourers] his feet.' This passage may be a later interpolation, but it legitimated the brahmins' claim to regard themselves as the privileged class. There have been movements, such as Buddhism, Jainism (6th century BCE) and later Virashaivism (*c.* 12th century CE) and Sikhism (16th century), as well as those initiated by individual saintly figures, which strongly opposed the caste system, but without success. To this day, a clearly structured caste system prevails, in which the different groups each have their own assigned duty.

Hinduism abroad

Although, in theory, orthodox Hindus are prevented from travelling abroad by the strict rules of purity governing their life, in the early centuries CE, at the request of local rulers, some brahmins travelled to Cambodia, Thailand and Bali, settled there, married local women and propagated Hinduism, introducing a number of Hindu customs, some of which are still observed. This, for instance, accounts for the popularity of the *Ramayana* and the *Mahabharata* in Southeast Asia, as well a number of strong Indian influences in art, architecture and the performing arts. Important trade connections existed between the west coast of India and Africa, as demonstrated by fragments of 9th-century cloth from Gujarat found in Egypt.

The migration of traders and businessmen in the 19th and 20th centuries was completely different: the Chettyars, a Tamil banking community, migrated to Burma, Malaysia, Mauritius and other parts of Southeast Asia, where they established themselves as successful businessmen. They periodically visited their Indian homes in Chettinadu and elsewhere in southern India, where they built magnificent mansions. At the beginning of the 20th century a number of migrants, mainly artisans and petty traders from Gujarat and Punjab, not necessarily Hindus, but also Sikhs and Muslims, settled in East Africa working for the British administration or setting up their own businesses. Once they had established themselves, they started to promote social and educational institutions and supported religious activities. New temples were built, gurus came from India and the traditional religious beliefs and practices received a new impetus. As East Africa and India formed part of the British Empire during that period, migrants could easily maintain links with their native countries.

It was a different situation for those who were indentured by the British and the Dutch, after the abolition of slavery in the mid-19th century. They were transported to Trinidad, British Guiana (Guyana), Dutch Guiana (Suriname), Fiji, Mauritius and South Africa. Although they were given the hope to be able, eventually, to return to India, only a small minority did so. Most of them settled in the new countries, gained their independence and were able to acquire land. The situation of the Hindu communities abroad changed from place to place.

In Trinidad, where the first Indians arrived in 1845, Hinduism is now well established, and a vivid description of Hindu Trinidad is conveyed in the writings of Sir V. S. Naipaul. The situation of the Indians in Britain, North America and Australia developed dramatically after they arrived and settled in the new countries, particularly after the end of World War II. In the wake of the new political developments in East Africa in the 1960s and 1970s, the majority of Indians holding a British passport emigrated to Britain and further afield. Highly educated Indians migrated directly from India to the USA as professionals, and took up jobs in electronics, science and healthcare. Despite being surrounded by values so different from those upheld by Hinduism, Hindus abroad continue to follow their ancestral practices. Brahmins are invited from India to care for the religious life of the community, caste marriage is still practised and life-cycle ceremonies are duly performed. The financial and numerical strength of Indians in Britain allowed temples to be established, first in makeshift premises, such as desecrated churches or halls, then new Hindu temples were built with attached educational institutions, conference and banquet halls and exhibition spaces. An example is the celebrated Neasden temple in London, which was funded mainly by the Gujarati community and completed in 1995, while many more such projects are in progress. All this testifies to the resilience and vitality of Hindu religion, traditions and institutions.

This *Dictionary of Hindu Lore and Legend* is aimed at all those who are interested in Things Indian and curious to explore another facet of human civilization. A list of English subjects with their Sanskrit equivalents, a brief profile of India's most important dynasties, a chronology, and two maps of India have been included for easy reference. This book does not, of course, cover every one of the countless aspects of Indian culture, which would be an impossible task, but seeks to provide a clear and scholarly introduction to the myths, beliefs, practices and arts of India.

Note on fonts and pronunciation

Within the dictionary, cross-references to other entries are printed in small capitals, e.g. AMRITA, VISHNU. Entries in Indian languages are italicized and followed by their literal meaning in quotation marks.

Transcribing Indian languages in roman script has always been a problematic task. Early on in the production of this book it was decided to avoid diacritical marks, which, if useful to the specialist, confuse the non-initiated; 'sh' and 'ch' are used where appropriate to indicate the correct pronunciation. Thus, *shakti* and *chakra* instead of *śakti* and *cakra*. Long and short vowels can result in a word having different meanings. In such cases, the entry has been repeated, e.g.: Sagara. Place names conform to the usual norms in roman script, although this may result in inconsistencies such as Sri Lanka, rather than Shri Lanka, Nathdwara rather than Nathdvara. In the last decade, some towns have reverted to their original name: Bombay to Mumbai, Madras to Chennai, Allahabad to Prayaga, to mention a few. In this case, care was taken to mention both names and to provide cross-references.

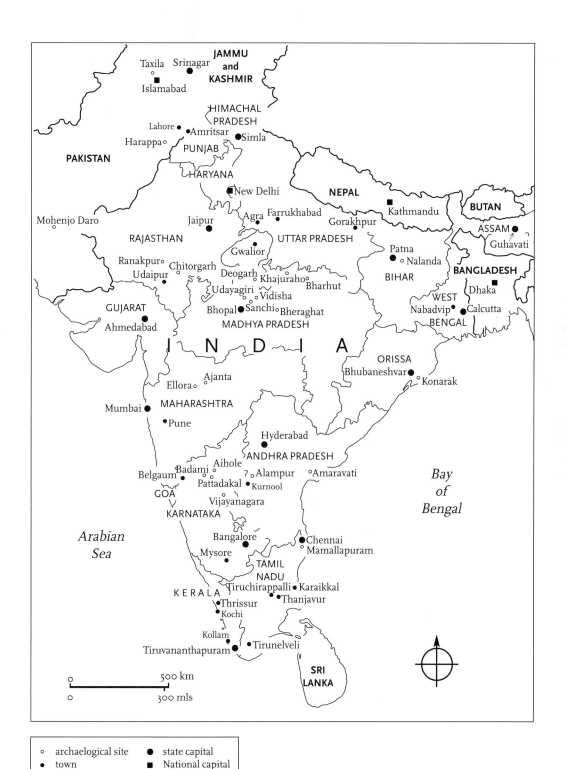

Taxila ○ ● Srinagar
■ Islamabad

JAMMU
and
KASHMIR

HIMACHAL
PRADESH

Lahore ● ● Simla
● Amritsar

Harappa ○

PAKISTAN

PUNJAB

HARYANA

● New Delhi

NEPAL

■ Kathmandu

BUTAN

Mohenjo Daro ○

Jaipur ●

Agra ● Farrukhabad

Gorakhpur ●

ASSAM ●
Guhavati ↗

RAJASTHAN

UTTAR PRADESH

Patna ●
○ Nalanda

BANGLADESH

Gwalior ●

BIHAR

Dhaka ■

Ranakpur ○ Chitorgarh
Udaipur ○ ○

Deogarh ○ ○ Khajuraho
Udayagiri ○ ○ Bharhut
○ Vidisha

WEST

Nabadvip ● ● Calcutta

Bhopal ● Sanchi ○ Bheraghat ○

BENGAL

GUJARAT

MADHYA PRADESH

Ahmedabad ●

I N D I A

ORISSA

Bhubaneshvar ●
○ Konarak

Ajanta
Ellora ○ ○

MAHARASHTRA

Mumbai ●

● Pune

Hyderabad ●

ANDHRA PRADESH

Aihole
Belgaum ● Badami ○ ○ Alampur ○ Amaravati
Pattadakal ● ● Kurnool

Bay
of
Bengal

GOA

Vijayanagara ○

KARNATAKA

Arabian
Sea

Bangalore ● ● Chennai
Mysore ● ○ Mamallapuram

TAMIL
NADU

KERALA

Tiruchirappalli ○ ● Karaikkal
● Thanjavur

Thrissur ●
Kochi ●

Kollam ● ● Tirunelveli
Tiruvananthapuram ●

SRI
LANKA

○
——————— 500 km
○
——————— 300 mls

○ archaelogical site	● state capital
● town	■ National capital

17

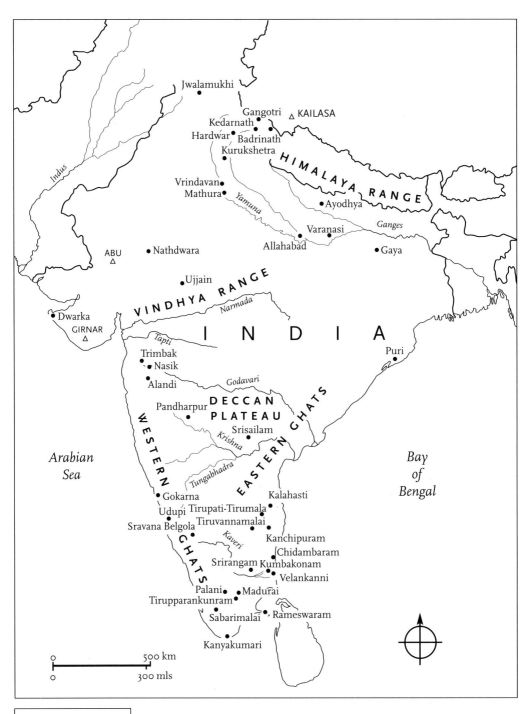

place of pilgrimage
mountain

THE DICTIONARY

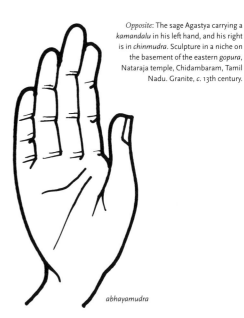

Opposite: The sage Agastya carrying a *kamandalu* in his left hand, and his right is in *chinmudra*. Sculpture in a niche on the basement of the eastern *gopura*, Nataraja temple, Chidambaram, Tamil Nadu. Granite, *c.* 13th century.

abhayamudra

abhayamudra 'gesture of reassurance, safety'. This hand pose is said to dispel fear and give divine protection to the devotee. The right hand is held upright, palm facing outwards. This is one of the earliest and most frequent MUDRAS depicted on Hindu, BUDDHIST and JAINA images.

Abhimanyu Son of ARJUNA and Subhadra and a brilliant warrior, who was killed in battle. Shortly after his death, his wife UTTARA gave birth to a still-born, premature child, PARIKSHIT, who was revived by KRISHNA and eventually succeeded YUDHISHTHIRA to the throne of HASTINAPURA.

Abhinavagupta (10th century). One of the most authoritative philosophers of the Kashmiri school of SHAIVISM and a writer on aesthetics.

abhisheka 'consecration (by sprinkling water); ritual bathing'. The ceremonial lustration of a sacred image with water, milk, honey, curds, saffron, etc.

acharya(s) 1. Spiritual guide or teacher within a particular tradition. 2. A class of VAISHNAVA teachers who based their teachings on both SANSKRIT and Tamil scriptures. They regarded the ALVARS as worthy of worship and considered them to be incarnations of VISHNU's attributes. The first of the *alvars*, Nathamuni (824?–924?), was responsible for assembling the hymns of the *alvars* in the NALAYIRA DIVYA PRABANDHAM ('four thousand holy hymns'), one of the most important canonical works of SHRIVAISHNAVISM.
Bhandarkar, R.G., 1982

Aditi 'unlimited, free, unbounded'. The Vedic goddess of space, the mother of all creatures and the gods. Her first children were the ADITYAS. She is said to be both mother and daughter of one of them, DAKSHA. In later mythology she appears as the wife of the seer KASHYAPA, by whom she became the mother of VISHNU, in his VAMANA AVATARA, and of INDRA.

Aditya(s) The sons of ADITI, each of whom represents a particular aspect of natural phenomena. There are, however, inconsistencies both in their number, as well as in their individual functions. In early Vedic times there were six, or more frequently, seven *Adityas*, of whom VARUNA was the first. Later, their number increased to eight, then to twelve, personifying the sun in the twelve months of the year. They are called by different names, many of which are epithets of the sun. The *Adityas* represent aspects of light and are collectively identified with Aditya, the sun.

Adishesha 'the primeval Shesha'. *See* SHESHA

Advaita Vedanta 'Non-dual' view of reality derived from the UPANISHADS and elaborated by SHANKARACHARYA (788–820), founder of the Advaita school of VEDANTA, according to whom the self (ATMAN) and the supreme entity of the universe (BRAHMAN) are identical.

Agama(s) 'that which has come down'. A body of works composed of mythological, ritual and philosophic material, not contained in Vedic texts. The *Agamas*, unlike the VEDAS, are accessible to women and non-BRAHMINS and are regarded by their followers as the 'fifth Veda', that is as divine revelation. The word *Agama* appears in the title of the early texts of the SHAIVAS; the texts of the VAISHNAVAS are called *Samhitas*, and those of the SHAKTAS, TANTRAS.

Right: Three-headed fire-god Agni, guardian of the south-east. He carries a spear and a fan. Caption in Telugu. Probably Thanjavur, *c.* 1830. From an album of paintings on European paper watermarked 1820.

Agastya 'mover of mountains'. A famous sage, especially revered in southern India, where he is said to have introduced the Vedic tradition and to have been instrumental in the formation of the Tamil language and literature. Tamilians believe that Agastya still dwells on the sacred mountain Agastya Malai (Tamil Nadu). Agastya was born, with VASISHTHA, from a pot into which MITRA and Varuna's semen fell at the sight of URVASHI. Agastya is reputedly the author of a Rig Vedic hymn and appears frequently in Vedic mythology. The puranic and epic traditions have magnified Agastya's achievements and he is credited with many miracles, such as forcing the Vindhya MOUNTAINS to prostrate themselves before him, hence his epithet *Vindhyakuta*, 'Subduer of the Vindhyas'. In another story, he is said to have swallowed the ocean to help the gods in their conflict against the DAITYAS, who had fled to the water, hence his name, *Samudrachuluka*, 'Ocean drinker'. It is however, in the RAMAYANA that Agastya appears most famously as friend, adviser and protector of RAMA, who visited him in his exile. Agastya, like other legendary seers, has been identified with a star, Canopus, the brightest star in the southern Indian sky.

agaru, agar (*Aquilaria agallocha*). The branches and trunk of the aloeswood tree yield a dark aromatic juice, which has been used since ancient times, both in India and China, for making incense, perfume and medicine. The Hindi word for incense, *agarbati*, or 'lighted aloeswood', is derived from its name. Powdered aloeswood is used in Ayurvedic medicine in cases of wounds, poisoning and fever.

Aghora, Aghoramurti 'non-terrifying'. 1. Euphemistic epithet of SHIVA. The name denotes the southern face of Shiva, which represents DHARMA, the eternal law. 2. Aghoramurti is an awe-inspiring aspect of Shiva, who is depicted standing naked in a warlike pose. He has eight, ten or thirty-two arms and carries a variety of attributes, such as a trident, drum, skull and noose. Occasionally, he wears an ELEPHANT hide or a lion skin, a garland of skulls, ORNAMENTS of snakes and scorpions. His body is smeared with ash from a cremation ground and his hair stands on end. The ferocity of his expression is heightened by two small tusks protruding from the corners of his mouth.

Agni 'fire'. An important Vedic deity, along with INDRA and SURYA. Agni acts as bearer of offerings to the gods and thus as mediator between the gods and men. The production of FIRE, by rubbing two fire sticks (*aranis*) together, is likened to the act of procreation: the lower stick is regarded as the mother, the upper as the father and Agni as the offspring. There are ten main forms of Agni, of which the first five are natural and the others ritual: 1. ordinary fire either visible or under the form of fuel; 2. lightning; 3. the sun; 4. the fire of the digestive process; 5. the fire of destruction, dormant until the end of the age, when it will devour the world; 6. the fire produced by the fire sticks during a sacrifice; 7. the fire given to a student at the time of his investiture with the sacred thread; 8. the fire of the hearth, centre of domestic rituals; 9. the southern fire of the ancestors used in exorcisms; 10. the funeral fire. Agni may be represented with one, two or three heads crowned by flames, four-armed, riding on a ram or a goat. He may carry a fan, a ladle, a waterpot and prayer beads. His occasionally portly figure suggests his creative and productive powers. He is one of the ASHTADIKPALAS, guardian of the south-east and one of the five ELEMENTS constituting the universe.

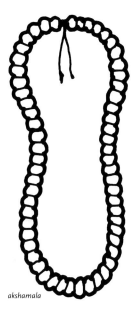

akshamala

Right: Processional image of the 8th-century *alvar* Tirumangai. He was a robber, hence he carries sword and shield, who eventually changed his life and became a devotee of Vishnu. Southern India. Bronze, 18th–19th century.

Agni Purana see PURANA(S)

agnihotra the 'oblation to AGNI'. A daily household ritual consisting in oblations of milk, oil and sour gruel poured into the fire at dawn and at twilight.

Ahalya The wife of the seer Gautama, who was seduced by INDRA disguised as Gautama, while the latter was performing his early morning rituals. Gautama cursed Ahalya who was transformed into a heap of rocks and took revenge on Indra by inflicting him with a skin disease consisting of marks resembling female genitalia. Later literature changes these marks to eyes, hence Indra's epithet *Sahasraksha*, 'thousand-eyed'. The story of Ahalya appears prominently in the RAMAYANA. Here, Ahalya is restored to her previous form by RAMA, who reconciles her with Gautama. Ahalya subsequently became the epitome of the chaste wife, unjustly accused of adultery, and her proverbial loyalty to her husband makes her one of the five exemplary chaste women daily invoked by Hindu wives.

ahimsa 'non injury' (in words, deeds and thoughts). Initiated by ascetics outside the Vedic tradition, *ahimsa* became an integral part of JAINA and BUDDHIST ethics and later influenced Hinduism, leading to vegetarianism and the abolition of ANIMAL sacrifices.

Airavata, Airavana or **Iravata** 'arisen from the ocean'. Name of the white, four-tusked ELEPHANT that emerged from the CHURNING OF THE OCEAN and which INDRA took as his vehicle.

Aiyanar or **Iyenar** 'Lord, master'. Of martial appearance, mounted on a horse, Aiyanar is regarded as the night-watchman of the villages in Tamil Nadu.

Accompanied by warriors and DOGS, he rides along village boundaries chasing away evil spirits. Clay figures of ELEPHANTS and horses of various sizes, donated by devotees, are housed in his shrines. *See also* AYYAPPAN
Whitehead, H., 1921

akasha 'ether'. The fifth ELEMENT of the universe.

akshamala 'garland of beads'. Made of pearls, bones, dried seeds, berries or skulls, the *akshamala* is the attribute of many gods. Generally, it comprises fifty beads, corresponding to the characters of the SANSKRIT alphabet. However, the number of beads may vary: 81 or 108.

Alakshmi *see* JYESHTHA(DEVI)

Allahabad *see* PRAYAGA

alvar(s) 'drowning, immersed, lost' in God. Southern Indian VAISHNAVA poet saints, traditionally ten or twelve in number, active between the 6th and 9th centuries. Their soul-stirring devotional songs in classical Tamil were collected in the NALAYIRA DIVYA PRABANDHAM by Nathamuni, the first of the Vaishnava ACHARYAS. The *alvars* are considered incarnations of VISHNU's attributes and worshipped as minor deities. *See also* ANDAL; NAMMALVAR
Dehejia, V., 1988

amalaka (*Emblica officinalis*). 1. Small tree with leathery leaves and fleshy fruits associated with VISHNU. The fruit (Indian gooseberry) is one of the richest sources of vitamin C and is used fresh or dried in Ayurvedic medicine. 2. The fluted, cushion-shaped stone crowning the spire of northern Indian TEMPLES.

Left: Ambika seated beneath a mango tree with her child and her lion *vahana* crouching beneath the throne. The smiling countenance and voluptuous forms, stress her caring and nurturing aspect. Orissa. Grey chlorite, 12th century.

Right: Anantashayana floating on the cosmic ocean. Seated on a lotus is Brahma. The six figures in the foreground are the four gods' personified weapons and the *danavas* Madhu and Kaitabha. Dashavatara temple, Deogarh, Madhya Pradesh. Sandstone, early 6th century.

Amaravati 'abode of immortality'. 1. Capital of INDRA's paradise. 2. An ancient city, now a village near Guntur in Andhra Pradesh, on the south bank of the RIVER Krishna. A centre of BUDDHIST learning since the 3rd century BCE, it is noted for its great STUPA, one of the finest examples of ARCHITECTURE and SCULPTURE of the first two centuries.
Knox, R., 1992

Ambika 'Mother'. Name of a goddess who, together with PARVATI, DURGA and KALI, is the focus of the SHAKTA cult.

amrita 'immortal'. The nectar of immortality in Vedic and Hindu mythology. According to a later myth, DHANVANTARI, the physician of the gods, emerged from the CHURNING OF THE OCEAN carrying *amrita* in a vessel, the AMRITAKALASHA.

amritakalasha, amritaghata 1. 'vessel [containing] the nectar of immortality'. Attribute of deities, such as BRAHMA, DHANVANTARI, LAKSHMI. 2. The pot-shaped finial placed on the AMALAKA of a TEMPLE.

Ananga 'bodiless'. An epithet of KAMA, the god of love, whom SHIVA reduced to ashes with a single look from his third eye for attempting to distract him from his austerities by arousing his love for PARVATI.

Ananta 'endless, infinite'. One of the names given to the king of the snakes, whose coils and hoods form a couch and a canopy for VISHNU. Ananta symbolizes both the cosmic waters out of which the new creation will eventually emerge and the endless cycles of time. Often identified with SHESHA.

Anantashayana 'reclining on ANANTA'. Aspect of VISHNU reclining on the coils of Ananta, beneath

the canopy formed by the snake's seven hoods. Ananta floats on the waters of the shoreless cosmic ocean and represents the three cosmic functions of creator, preserver and destroyer. Creation begins the moment Vishnu emerges from his yogic sleep (YOGANIDRA), when a lotus stalk sprouts from his navel revealing in its flower BRAHMA, the creator of the new world. The cycle progresses until, at the end of time, creation dissolves in a huge conflagration, and its ash, potentially containing all forms of life, disappears into the cosmic ocean. After a period of rest, the cycle is once again set in motion.

Andal, Antal or **Kodai** A 9th-century poetess and VAISHNAVA devotee from southern India. Abandoned as a baby, she was found and adopted by Periyalvar, a Vaishnava priest, who named her Kodai. Andal thought of herself as the bride of VISHNU, and at the age of sixteen she approached the IMAGE of the reclining Vishnu at SRIRANGAM and merged with it. She is the only woman among the ALVARS and is revered as an incarnation of Vishnu's consort BHUDEVI. There exists a large shrine dedicated to her in her home town, Srivilliputtur (Tamil Nadu). Her poetic works are recited on special occasions.
Dehejia, V., 1990

Andhakasura The ASURA who symbolizes darkness or spiritual blindness. He tried to abduct PARVATI from KAILASA, but was killed by SHIVA.

animals Various classifications of the animal kingdom are given in the UPANISHADS, the PURANAS and in a number of other works. They are first classified according to how they are generated (e.g. mammalian, oviparous, etc.) and are further distinguished by attributes (such as the number of legs), anatomy, mode of locomotion, diet,

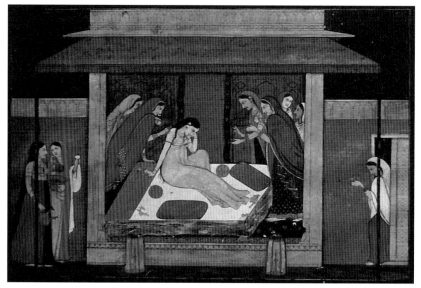

Usha dreams of a passionate encounter with a youth she has never met, who later turns out to be Aniruddha. This scene depicts the troubled awakening of the princess, surrounded by her friends. Folio from an *Usha-Aniruddha* series. Guler, Panjab Hills. Opaque watercolour on paper, c. 1785–90.

particularities (poisonous or non poisonous) and habitat. Distinctions are made between domesticated animals, wild animals and game. The majority of Hindu gods are associated with animal VAHANAS (vehicles), which may be regarded as extensions of their personalities. VISHNU assumed animal form in order to redress the balance between good and evil in his AVATARAS as a fish (MATSYA), tortoise (KURMA), boar (VARAHA) and man-lion (NARASIMHA). Several ancient tribes, epic heroes and royal dynasties employed animals as totems.

The study of *Pashu-vidya* (animal science) covered the topic in its entirety, including the language of beasts and birds. Generally, the secrets of only one species were mastered. A section of the AYURVEDA is devoted to veterinary science. BUDDHISTS and Jains were particularly concerned with the welfare of animals and established hospitals for their care. Horses (ASHVA) and ELEPHANTS (*gaja*), valuable animals both in peace and in war time, were treated with great care and skill, as testified by the substantial literature on the subject. Molluscs and crabs were considered unclean, the shells, however, were highly valued as ORNAMENTS, as currency (the cowrie) and as musical instruments both in TEMPLE worship and on the battlefield. Epic heroes are distinguished by the distinctive shape of the conches that they possessed. The SHANKHA, or conch, is one of the attributes of Vishnu. Fish play a great role in Hindu tradition and Vishnu's first *avatara* was in the form of a fish. Two fish, *matsyayugma*, are among the eight auspicious objects, as symbols of fertility, happiness and success. Crocodiles figure in Hindu and tribal mythology. The MAKARA, a sea monster bearing the head of a crocodile, the body of a reptile and a tail ending in a lush cascade of foliage (or occasionally an elegant fishtail), represents the zodiacal sign of Capricorn. It figures on the banner

of the god of love, KAMA, and is the vehicle of both the river-goddess GANGA and the god VARUNA. The serpents, especially the NAGA (cobra), are greatly revered and the subjects of many myths and legends. Also important is the lizard, as its position on a wall and movements are interpreted as omens. The bee appears frequently in poetry; drunk with honey, it is a metaphor for divine or human love. Kama has a sugar-cane bow, the string of which is made of bees and symbolizes the sting of passion.

Of all the animals the COW is historically the most revered: everything that issued from it was held to be sacred, including the excreta. The bull, Shiva's *vahana*, received and still receives homage as a symbol of virility. The buffalo is the *vahana* of the god YAMA; a buffalo was sacrificed to commemorate DURGA's victory over the buffalo-demon, a practice that survives in tribal areas. Although DOGS were considered among the most unclean of animals, they too appear in Hindu mythology connected with BHAIRAVA, DATTATREYA and Yama. They are worshipped in Maharashtra and Karnataka by the followers of KHANDOBA. Monkeys (VANARA) are treated as sacred animals in the whole of India because of the part they played in the RAMA story.

Several species of mythical animals appear in Hindu legends and ART. The most arresting is the YALI, half-lion, half-elephant, frequently depicted on the piers of southern Indian temples. The *shardula* or tiger (actually a leogryph with a prominent hooked nose) is carved on temple walls (e.g. at Khajuraho). The representation of the *ihamriga* depends on artistic fancy and usually consists of parts of different BIRDS, beasts and reptiles. The SHARABHA is the ultimate mythical monster, having two or three horns, six to eight legs and sharp arrow-like spikes on its body instead of hair. Shiva appeared on one occasion under the guise of the *sharabha*.

Right: Anthill and *nagakals*, snake stones. The *nagini* carved on the slab to the right is armed with sword and shield. In the foreground, incense sticks and clay oil lamps. Panagal, Andhra Pradesh.

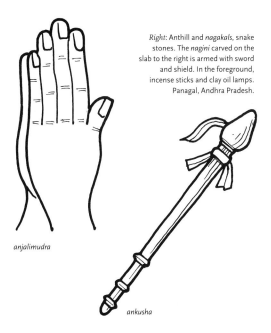

anjalimudra

ankusha

See also GANDABHERUNDA; MARJARA; MRIGA; MUSHA; SIMHA

Aniruddha 'unobstructed, unopposed'. Son of Pradyumna, grandson of KRISHNA, who became the focus of a minor cult and the subject of a romantic story. Usha, the daughter of the ASURA king, Bana, fell in love with Aniruddha, whom she had seen in a dream. Through the magic powers of her confidante Chitralekha, Aniruddha was conveyed to the princesses' apartments. When the king found out, he ordered his guards to seize him. Aniruddha defended himself and routed his assailants. Though Bana captured him by magical means, Krishna, BALARAMA and Pradyumna came to his rescue, defeated the king and the couple were married.

anjalimudra 'two handfuls'. A hand pose of respectful greeting and adoration in which both hands are clasped together, palms touching and held near the chest. It is characteristic of subordinate deities, attendants of the gods, RISHIS and devotees.

Anjaneya Name of HANUMAN. He was born from an illicit relationship between Anjana and the wind god VAYU.

ankusha 'goad, hook', especially an elephant driver's hook. One of the eight auspicious objects and an emblem of royalty. An attribute of many deities, including GANESHA.

Annapurna 'filled with (or giver of) food'. A benevolent form of PARVATI, who averts famine. Her main attributes are a bowl of rice and a ladle.

ants, anthills Ants, especially termites, are considered divine beings and are the subjects of a number of myths. They are believed to be the first beings ever created; in local traditions they play a pivotal role in the creation process. According to some, the world was created from their excreta, while others say that the first human beings were made from the clay of an anthill. Their liminal nature is expressed in the belief, common both in ancient and modern India, that the rainbow connecting the world of the living with that of ghosts, dark forces and the dead, originates in the anthills. Anthills are the haunt of snakes, providing access to the nether world which they inhabit and, as such, are inextricably connected with the NAGA myths and cult. In numerous texts, ants are associated with water and, according to the ATHARVAVEDA, they are able to locate water with healing properties. Anthills are regarded as living entities (hence classed with auspicious plants) and are reputed to have medicinal properties. It is believed that eating ants helps conception, and in southern India women wishing to conceive sleep near anthills, in which SUBRAHMANYA is said to reside. The earth of the anthill is scattered around the wedding dais to ensure the bride's fertility. Ants are regularly fed, as a meritorious act or to obtain a son.
König, D., 1984

anugrahamurti(s) Benign aspects of SHIVA, bestowing favours or grace to his devotees.

Apasmara or **Muyalaka(n)** A dwarf personifying ignorance or epilepsy. Apasmara is crushed by the right foot of SHIVA in his aspects as NATARAJA and, occasionally, as DAKSHINAMURTI. He is often shown with his hands in ANJALIMUDRA.

Appar (Tirunavukarasar). One of the four most important NAYANMARS, Appar lived in the 7th century and composed numerous poems in honour

The Shaiva saint Appar, with the hoe resting on his shoulder. This image, based on the set of the sixty-three *nayanmars* worshipped in the Mylapore temple in Chennai, is the work of a contemporary artist, Mohan *sthapati*. Copper alloy, early 1990s.

of SHIVA. He had an eventful life; in his youth he converted to JAINISM, then became a SHAIVA after being miraculously cured of a serious illness by Shiva. This caused the wrath of the Jaina community, who complained to the Pallava king Mahendra, himself a Jaina. Summoned to his presence, Appar sang the praises of Shiva. Despite having been tortured, the saint remained unscathed. Eventually, the king himself converted to Shaivism. Appar is generally represented with a shaven head, palms joined in ANJALIMUDRA and a hoe on his shoulder. The hoe represents his vow to remove all grass and weeds growing in TEMPLE areas.
Dehejia, V., 1988

apsara(s) 'essence of the waters, moving in or between the waters'. The *apsaras* are divine beauties, the dancers of the gods, who dwell in INDRA'S paradise, SVARGA. Mistresses of the GANDHARVAS and, occasionally, of men, they can assume any form at will. Generally they are believed to have originated from the CHURNING OF THE OCEAN, along with the wish-fulfilling PARIJATA, their favoured tree, and they are often sent by the gods to seduce RISHIS and ascetics. Heroes who fall in battle are swept away by the *apsaras* to *svarga*. They are reputed to dwell in the trees along with the *gandharvas*. The chief of the *apsaras* is URVASHI.

Aranyaka(s) 'forest books'. Composite works containing hymns, ritualistic and mythological material, written between *c.* 1000 and *c.* 800 BCE. As their name indicates, they were not for general circulation, but for study in the isolation of the forest, because of their dangerous mystical powers.

arati, arti or ***artipuja*** 'worship with *arati*'. A ceremony performed in honour of a deity.

The priest moves clockwise around the image, carrying a tray containing a lamp (usually with five wicks), camphor and other items, such as sacred ash, TULASI leaves, KUMKUM powder, flowers. Generally, an *arati* is performed on its own as a standard TEMPLE ritual. The climax of the worship is the burning of the camphor with its vivid light and strong fragrance. The flame symbolizes both the embodiment of the deity and the deity's transcendence of its bodily form, as camphor leaves no sooty residue. *Arati* is also performed on other occasions, such as the first visit of the bridegroom to the bride's house, the first entry of a married couple into their home and the birth of a child.

archa(bera) 'worshipping'. An IMAGE or icon of a deity, into which a deity is said to descend when the image is sanctified by special rites.

architecture *Vastuvidya*, or science of architecture, is believed to have been revealed to mankind by VISHVAKARMA, the architect of the universe. It was a highly specialized science, of which the tenets were orally transmitted from generation to generation. Eventually, the rules and rituals connected with building, especially TEMPLES, became so complex, that it was necessary to commit them to writing. A substantial literary production on architecture developed alongside temple building, from around the 4th or 5th century onwards. Some of the early texts were appended to the PURANAS, but in later centuries they became independent works, *vastushastras*, treatises on architecture, sculpture and painting. The majority focus on temple building and, to a certain extent, on town planning and private dwellings. They were generally composed by scholars and theologians, who did not have first-hand knowledge of the subject and were more

The Kailasanatha rock-cut temple at Ellora, Maharashtra, replicates the elevation of a structural temple in all its details. This magnificent basalt structure was hewn out of the rock in the 8th–9th century.

concerned with the symbolic and mystical interpretations of the various parts of the temple, than with the actual building process. The craftsmen in charge of construction had no need of scholarly prompting, since they relied on orally transmitted knowledge and practical experience.

Great attention is devoted to the choice of building material. From the *vastushastras* we learn that the material and its colour were directly related to the CASTE of the commissioner; some texts link material to gender, so that a brick temple is deemed suitable for a god, whereas a wooden one is reserved for a goddess. However, most of the texts recommend stone. As soon as the material is removed from its natural environment, it is purified by appropriate ceremonies, to render it fit to become part of the fabric of a temple. Despite the shastric injunction against reusing material from other temples, practice testifies to the contrary.

Vedic and later literature is filled with numerous references to buildings, both sacred and secular, but little remains of early Indian architecture. The earliest testimonies of building activity to have survived are a series of 3rd-and 2nd-century-BCE BUDDHIST sanctuaries cut into cliff faces, such as the Lomas Rishi cave in the Barabar Hills (Bihar). Their ribbed and vaulted ceilings, the reliefs depicting wooden façades and the shape of the pillars, reveal that the original architectural model of these caves was made of wood.

The earliest free-standing Hindu temples discovered so far, such as the Vishnu temple at Deogarh (Lalitpur district, Madhya Pradesh), renowned for its magnificent carvings, do not predate the 5th and 6th centuries. This, however, does not rule out the existence of earlier shrines, which were probably built of perishable materials and have since vanished. Alongside the free-

standing temples, rock-cut architecture continued to flourish, culminating in the splendid temples at Ellora (Aurangabad district, Maharashtra), the 8th-9th-century Kailasanatha in particular. This long tradition of rock architecture was to have an important influence on temple design. The notion of a MOUNTAIN cave is mirrored in the temple's sanctuary, which is conceived as a cave set beneath the towered superstructure, representing the profile of a mountain.

Generally, the architectural traditions of northern and southern India have retained their own styles, known respectively as *nagara* and *dravida*. In the Deccan, predictably, both styles are found at sites such as the 7th-century Pattadakal (Bijapur district, Karnataka). Contact between north and south resulted in borrowing and adaptation of ideas. The development of the northern style is difficult to trace, as a conspicuous number of monuments have been destroyed in warfare. It was distinguished by a number of features, the most notable being the tall and occasionally slightly convex shape of the tower (SHIKHARA) rising above the sanctuary. The virtuosity of the northern Indian mason is exemplified by the complex roof scheme of the 10th-century Khandariya Mahadeva temple at Khajuraho (Chhattarpur district, Madhya Pradesh). The main *shikhara* consists of a cluster of miniature towers obscuring the principal shaft. In the south the superstructure, called *vimana*, is smaller and pyramidal. The temple gateways in the north and the south display more radical differences; those in the north are not particularly elaborate, the most striking feature of the building being the *shikara*. In the south, however, the GOPURA (gateway) became the most important feature of the temple complex. From its humble beginnings in the 7th and 8th centuries, the *gopura* had a tower-like superstructure capped with a barrel-vaulted element.

Trishula bearing Ardhanarishvara
on the central prong, leaning on the
bull Nandi. Tamil Nadu. Bronze,
10th–11th century.

From the Vijayanagara period (14th–16th century) onwards, it continued to dominate the temple, revealing its surface encrusted with hundreds of vividly painted plaster figures. This development reached its most dramatic form in the Nayaka period, in the 16th and early 18th centuries. While northern Indian temples were generally modest in size, southern temples were enlarged over the centuries to become small cities. Apart from the *nagara* and *dravida* styles of architecture, regional styles can be found in the Himalayas, Kerala, Gujarat and Orissa.
Michell, G., 1977

Ardhanarishvara 'the Lord being half-woman'. Peaceful aspect of SHIVA in his androgynous form, which symbolizes the inseparability of the male and female principle, cause of creation. The right half of the image represents Shiva, the left PARVATI. Ardhanarishvara has been interpreted, among other meanings, as the union of the passive spirit (PURUSHA) and the active nature (PRAKRITI), or as the embodiment of the universe. The same notion is conveyed, in a more abstract form, by the LINGA emerging from the YONI.

Arjuna 'white'. The son of INDRA (through KUNTI, wife of PANDU), the third of the PANDAVA princes, and the chief hero of the MAHABHARATA. By his unmatched skill in archery Arjuna won DRAUPADI at her SVAYAMVARA (bride's choice), but, because of some words inadvertently uttered by Kunti, she became the joint wife of the five Pandavas. Though the brothers agreed that when one was with Draupadi none of the others could enter the chamber on pain of exile, Arjuna contravened this rule and was banished for twelve years. While in exile he did not lead a life of compulsory austerity, but married a number of distinguished princesses and entertained many mistresses and concubines. On a visit to his kinsman KRISHNA at DWARKA, he fell in love with Krishna's sister Subhadra, whom he eventually married and had a child, ABHIMANYU. In the course of his wanderings, Arjuna visited the great BRAHMIN warrior PARASHURAMA, who instructed him in the use of magical weapons. He later helped AGNI, the god of fire, and Krishna to burn down the Khandava forest, for which he was rewarded with a magical bow, the Gandiva.

Arjuna eventually returned home, but not for long. When YUDHISHTHIRA lost his kingdom to the KAURAVAS in a game of dice, Arjuna accompanied his brothers into a thirteen-year exile. In order to propitiate the gods and obtain weapons to rout the Kauravas, Arjuna left his brothers and resumed his solitary wanderings. Among the many adventures that befell him was the fight with a KIRATA, a hunter, who was none other than SHIVA in disguise. Arjuna eventually recognized his adversary, worshipped him, and received another magical weapon, the PASHUPATA. He then visited his father Indra at AMARAVATI, where he was again trained in the use of arms, and sent to fight the DAITYAS, DANAVAS and RAKSHASAS. In the last year of exile, he rejoined his brothers and with them entered the service of Virata, king of Matsya, under the guise of a eunuch. He taught music and dance to the ladies of the court, and was later instrumental in defeating Virata's enemies.

In the battle of KURUKSHETRA, Krishna acted as his charioteer. When Arjuna was plagued by doubts about fighting his own kin, Krishna expounded to him the doctrine of disinterested action, as contained in the BHAGAVADGITA, thereby helping him to overcome his scruples. During the preparations for the solemn ASHVAMEDHA ceremony, to mark the victory of the Pandavas,

Arjuna aims at the revolving fish target standing on two round devices and looking into a cauldron of boiling water. Draupadi and her father watch the scene in suspense. Detail from a late-18th- or early 19th-century ceiling painting. Virupaksha temple, Hampi, Karnataka.

Arjuna followed the sacrificial horse through various countries. He had many adventures and fought a number of kings, among whom was his own son Babhruvahana. The latter killed his father, but Arjuna was revived by one of his former lovers, the NAGA princess Ulupi, who had access to a magical life-restoring gem.

After witnessing the carnage among the YADAVAS and performing the FUNERAL RITES of Krishna – who had been killed inadvertently by a hunter – and those of Krishna's father VASUDEVA, Arjuna brought the survivors of the Yadava tribe and Krishna's HAREM back to HASTINAPURA. On the way, he was attacked and defeated by the Abhiras. Shortly afterwards, he joined his wife and brothers on their last journey to the Himalayas. Arjuna's other names include Aindri ('from Indra'), Gudakesha ('tufted hair'), Dhananjaya ('wealth winning'), Kapidhvaja ('with a monkey on his standard') and Partha ('descendant of Prithu').

arts There is no exact equivalent for the word 'art' in SANSKRIT. However, the two terms normally used are *kala* and *shilpa*. *Kala* means any practical, mechanical or fine art. The root of the word is probably *kal* which means 'to do, to make'. It is a word that is often used in literature, especially in the context of the education of noblemen or princes, who have to learn the 'sixty-four *kalas*'. Although the list may vary slightly according to the text, this standard expression refers to a range of skills that a cultivated person must master to prepare himself for life and to enrich his personality. The most detailed description of these occurs in the KAMASUTRA, a text on EROTICS, roughly datable between the 3rd and the 4th centuries. Knowledge of the sixty-four arts played an important part in the life of the cultivated elite, especially in that of the 'man of the world', as described in this work. Surprising entries among the

sixty-four include the creation of flower beds, prestidigitation and the art of colouring precious stones. Mastery of any of the *kalas* requires great skill. Neither inspiration nor talent are substitutes for practice, discipline and rigorous training. The idea that perserverance leads to perfection is pivotal to Indian artistic activity.

The etymology of *shilpa*, the second term for art, is unclear, but is usually translated as 'the art of colouring...decoration, ornament, artistic work; any manual art or craft' (M. Monier-Willams, *Sanskrit-English Dictionary*, s.v. *śilpa*). While *kala* deals with a range of activities based on skill, *shilpa* is widely used to describe art in general terms, covering a larger area, such as fine arts and the applied arts.

The VISHNUDHARMOTTARA PURANA, a treatise on the arts datable between the 7th and the 10th centuries, contains important information on the arts in general. These are clearly expressed in a dialogue between King Vajra and the sage MARKANDEYA, in which the king wishes to attain happiness in this and in the other world. The sage answers that the worship of the gods is conducive to happiness and for worship he stresses the importance of building TEMPLES and fashioning IMAGES, as mankind is no longer able to see the gods. Precise rules are given for the manufacture of sacred images. The messages contained in this legend are clear: the pursuit of happiness lies at the root of Indian sacred art, and the images must satisfy precise aesthetic criteria. This does not exclude the existence of a substantial number of non-religious motifs of equal importance in Indian art. In these cases artists have been free to represent them according to their own imagination. The dialogue proceeds with the king requesting the sage to teach him to make a sacred image. An illuminating passage reveals how, in the Indian

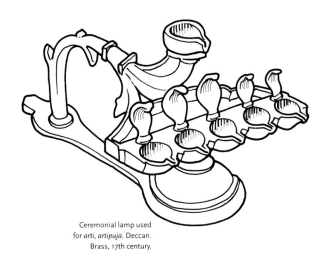

Ceremonial lamp used
for *arti*, *artipuja*. Deccan.
Brass, 17th century.

tradition, all the arts are interrelated. The person who does not know the canon of PAINTING, the sage states, cannot learn the rules of SCULPTURE. To know the rules of sculpture, one has to learn the canon of DANCE. Dance cannot be learnt without knowledge of instrumental music, which is impossible without first knowing the art of singing. According to Markandeya, he who masters the art of singing is the best of men and is all-knowing. But, the sage concludes, the art of singing is dependent on the various languages and their metrics. This way of considering the visual arts as part of the totality of artistic expression is borne out by a comparative study of ARCHITECTURE, sculpture and painting on the one hand, and of dance and drama on the other. Visual material serves to elucidate textual passages, and vice versa. The Hindu temple, often called 'the house of all arts', demonstrates this interrelationship. Architecture shapes the temple, sculptures and paintings adorn its walls, and music, dance, theatrical performances and recitations of sacred texts are performed in its halls. Architecture, sculpture, painting and iconography are all discussed in various SHILPASHASTRAS, or manuals on art, some of extreme antiquity.

The artists, or *shilpins*, were organized into guilds (SHRENI), generally based on CASTE; the ancient guilds of ivory carvers, silk weavers and metal workers were often wealthy and influential people in the community. The qualifications necessary to be a good craftsman, mentioned in a number of treatises, included self-control, power of concentration, the technical ability that comes from having been born into a particular artisan class, power of observation and knowledge of the canons of proportions (TALAMANA) and of forms divine, human, animal, etc.

Indian art has a wide geographical and ethnic range. Various influences reaching the subcontinent in the wake of political events brought a constant stream of new ideas from sources as disparate as Greece, China, the Islamic world and Europe, which in due course were 'Indianized' and merged into the vast repertoire of artistic motifs.

artha 'wealth, power, goal'. The pursuit of wealth and power, one of the four PURUSHARTHAS or aims of life. *See also* DHARMA; KAMA; MOKSHA

Arthashastra Treatise on politics attributed to Kautilya, or Chanakya, the minister of Chandragupta Maurya (*c.* 321–297 BCE). Accidentally discovered in 1904 by R. Shamasastry – chief librarian to the government of Mysore who translated it into English and published it in 1909 – it is the earliest surviving text of its kind. Critical analysis of the text suggests that it was probably compiled by various authors, and that the *Arhtashastra* in its present form dates only from the 2nd century CE. The fifteen sections of the work survey the whole range of government institutions: the duties of the ruler, the training of princes, the qualifications of the ministers of state, home and foreign offices, civil service, defence, the judiciary, civil and criminal law, corporations and guilds.
Kautilya, 1992

arti, artipuja *see* ARATI

Aruna 'Reddish One'. God of the morning, charioteer of SURYA. VINATA, one of the wives of the mythical seer KASHYAPA, bore two sons, ARUNA and GARUDA, both associated with solar mythology. They were born in the form of eggs, of which there were originally three, but in her impatience to hatch them, Vinata broke one, from which came a flash of lightning. When she broke another she found

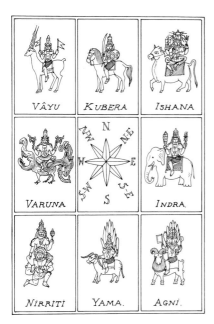

The eight *ashtadikpalas*.

Aruna, radiant as the morning sun, but lacking feet. Thus, he is represented seated without legs, driving Surya's chariot.

Arundhati 'fidelity'. The wife of the mythical seer VASISHTHA, identified with the morning star. Arundhati is invoked in marriage ceremonies, and represents the ideal wife.

Arya, Aryan 'noble, valid, trustworthy'. Name of the fair-skinned nomadic horse and cattle breeders, who arrived in India in the course of the second millennium BCE and established the Vedic civilization.

Arya-Samaj 'ARYAN, or noble society'. Hindu reform movement founded in 1875 by Svami Dayananda Sarasvati (1824–83), who aimed at reinstating the Vedic tradition, tempered by the introduction of European-style education and modern, liberal ideas. Dayananda respected CASTE distinctions, but denied their religious status and introduced the rite of purification (*shuddhi*)for re-admission of converts to other religions back into Hinduism. The *shuddhi* gave the opportunity to low-caste and outcaste communities to achieve an equal status with higher-caste Hindus in religious matters, a fact that was deeply resented by the latter and finally led to the marginalization of the movement.

asana(s) 'seat, throne, sitting position, posture'. In connection with MUDRAS, *asanas* indicate the different aspects of the deities. In YOGA the term signifies different modes of sitting, which are intended to help the devotee concentrate on the object of meditation. In iconography the term also covers riding, standing, reclining and a number of other positions.

ashoka (*Saraca indica*). An evergreen tree, of which the name means 'absence of sorrow' and is sacred to SHIVA. The *ashoka* is supposed to burst into flower when kicked by the foot of a chaste girl, a recurrent motif in Indian art. Garlands of red *ashoka* flowers are used in the worship of the god of love. Decoctions of the bark have medicinal properties.

ashrama(s) 'hermitage'. 1. Popular term for the abode of a holy man. 2. Designation of the four stages (*ashramas*) into which the life of a BRAHMIN is divided: BRAHMACHARI(N), 'student, disciple, apprentice', GRIHASTHA, 'householder', VANAPRASHTHA, 'forest dweller', and SANNYASI(N) 'homeless wanderer'.

ashtadikpala(s) or **dikpala(s)** 'eight guardians of the sky'. The guardians of the eight directions of space, whose images appear in the appropriate positions in most Hindu TEMPLES on outer walls and hall ceilings. Although the list may vary slightly, they are: INDRA (E), AGNI (SE), YAMA (S), NIRRITI (SW), VARUNA (W), VAYU (NW), KUBERA (N) and ISHANA (NE). *See also* PANCHANANA

Ashtadhyayi 'eight chapters'. *See* PANINI

ashtamangala 'eight auspicious objects' used in the course of important occasions, such as coronations, weddings, etc. The *ashtamangala* are repeatedly mentioned in Hindu, BUDDHIST and JAINA literature and are frequently found as decorative motifs in ART. The northern Indian tradition lists them as: a lion, bull, ELEPHANT, water jar or vessel filled with GEMS, fly-whisk, flag, trumpet and lamp. The southern Indian lists a fly-whisk, full vase, mirror, goad, drum, lamp, flag and pair of fishes. These may differ according to regions and communities.

A king and his retinue meet Arjuna's sacrificial horse which has wandered into their territory. Maharashtra(?). Opaque watercolour on paper, 19th century.

ashtamatrika(s) 'eight mothers'. *See* MATRIKA(S)

ashva 'horse'. The prototype of this animal, the divine UCHCHAIHSHRAVAS, emerged from the CHURNING OF THE OCEAN. It was white and endowed with wings. INDRA appropriated it and, after cutting its wings to ensure that it would remain on earth, donated it to mankind. It is believed that at the end of the present era, the KALI YUGA, VISHNU will appear on a white horse as KALKI, his last incarnation. Not indigenous to India, the horse was probably imported into the subcontinent in pre-Vedic times. There are a number of references to horses and horse-drawn war chariots in the RIGVEDA (*c.* 1500 BCE), but the warriors probably only used horses to travel to the battlefield, not in actual warfare. From the Epic (*c.* 900 BCE) period onwards, the horse occupied a prominent place in the army. In Mauryan times (*c.* 321–181 BCE) there was a State Superintendent of the Horses responsible for maintaining a register of the herds. No saddle was used, but the horse was controlled by means of reins leading from a ring of stitched rawhide fixed over the horse's mouth. The ring was studded with sharp metal points directed inwards. Metal bits came into use around the 4th or 3rd century BCE. It was customary to make the horse drink wine before a battle.

The horse played a pivotal role in establishing the supremacy of kings, as demonstrated, for instance, by the great horse sacrifice, the ASHVAMEDHA, which might have been established in the course of the Vedic period. Equestrian motifs appear prominently in Indian ART, for example in Orissan SCULPTURE of the 12th and 13th centuries, and in that of the late Vijayanagara and Nayaka periods (early 16th–early 18th century) in southern India. There is a branch of literature specializing in the breeding, care and training of horses, which contains detailed passages on colouring, proportions, gait, auspicious and inauspicious marks and lists of appropriate names for horses.

ashvamedha 'horse sacrifice'. The grandest among the royal ceremonies, the *ashvamedha* was a special rite for extending territory, obtaining male offspring, or atoning for a sin. The preparations for the actual ceremony lasted well over a year and were punctuated by subsidiary, complex ceremonies. Tradition credits BRAHMA with the institution of this ceremony at PRAYAGA (Allahabad), to solemnize the recovery of the VEDAS, which had been lost. The sacrificial horse was selected with great care: it had to be a male of white colour. It was bound, bathed, consecrated with FIRE and well fed for three days before being set free to wander about at will for one year, accompanied by a troop of noble retainers. The king and his army followed the horse; if it happened to cross over the boundary into another ruler's state, that ruler either had to submit to the invading king or establish his supremacy in battle. On the return of the horse, the last phase of the *ashvamedha* commenced, in which the chief queen, the MAHISHI, played a significant role. A number of ANIMALS, both domestic and wild, were sacrificed before the horse. It is not clear how the animal was killed, but it was usual for the king and the chief queen to assist in the procedure, which seems to have been hastened by strangling it. The chief queen then performed a further ceremony, in which she had intercourse with the dead animal. Eventually, it was dismembered, its flesh eaten by the participants in the ceremony, and the sacrifice concluded with the chanting of MANTRAS. A number of rulers have performed the *ashvamedha*, the last of them being Jai Singh, the ruler of Jaipur, in the mid-18th century.

Vishnu as Matsya kills the
demon Shankhasura and
rescues the Vedas, shown
here as four standing
male figures, who
were imprisoned
at the bottom of the
sea by the *asura*. Panjab
Hills, probably Mandi.
Opaque watercolour
on paper, *c*. 1760.

ashvattha*, *bodhi or ***pipal*** (*Ficus religiosa*). Tree sacred
to the Hindus, the eternal tree of life, of which the
roots are in heaven. The *ashvattha* is also revered by
the BUDDHISTS as the *bodhi* tree under which
BUDDHA meditated and finally reached the
Enlightenment. The fire sticks used to kindle
sacrificial fire were made out of *ashvattha* wood.

Ashvin(s) 'possessor of horses'. Pre-Vedic twin
deities, associated with the sun or the sky, knowing
all secrets of plant life. They are ever young,
handsome, agile and swift, riding a golden chariot
drawn by horses or BIRDS, as harbingers of the
goddess USHAS, the dawn. Their functions are
numerous, relating mainly to youth and beauty,
light and speed and, above all, healing powers. The
Ashvins became the physicians of the gods and
guarded the nectar of immortality. In later
mythology, they are the parents of the PANDAVA
twins, NAKULA and SAHADEVA, born of KUNTI. In
the rare depictions of the Ashvins, they are shown
as handsome young men with horses' heads.

asura(s) 'Lord, spiritual, divine'. In the oldest part
of the RIGVEDA *asura* refers to a supreme spirit,
indicating such deities as INDRA, AGNI and VARUNA.
By the time the later parts of the *Rigveda* were
written, it had acquired the meaning of demon or
antagonist of the gods, the sense also found in the
ATHARVAVEDA. It has been suggested that the term
derives from the root *-as*, 'to frighten away', thus
representing the dark side of the gods. There is an
eternal conflict between the gods and the *asuras*.
Both are the children of PRAJAPATI, the creator, the
asuras being the eldest. A number of other myths
also relate to the *asuras*. It is said that they inherited
speech, both true and false, but the gods rejected
untruth, while the *asuras* rejected truth, a fact that

led to their downfall. Another story states that since
they were equally powerful, their power was divided,
the gods exercising it during the day, the *asuras* at
night. There are, however, some *asuras* that are
devotees of the gods, such as RAVANA, a great
follower of SHIVA.

Atharvaveda 'The VEDA of Atharvan' or 'knowledge
of magic formulas'. Atharvan, the reputed author
of the *Atharvaveda*, was the priest who was the
first to kindle fire and to establish its worship. The
Atharvaveda, the fourth of the *Vedas*, reflects popular
beliefs ignored in the former *Vedas*. It depicts a world
in which malevolent spirits seek to injure those who
are not protected by magical rites (MANTRAS) and
spells. As a result, it was a long time before the
Atharvaveda was universally accepted and it is still
considered inferior by some. The *Atharvaveda* is of
particular importance for the AYURVEDA.

atman 'essence, principle of life'. Derived from the
Rigvedic term for breath, or 'animating principle',
atman developed into the Upanishadic 'inner self',
referring to the innermost essence of man, which is
identical with BRAHMAN, the transcendental divine
source of all reality.

AUM *see* OM

avatara 'descent'. An *avatara* occurs when a god,
or divine being descends to earth to protect the
righteous from evil and to re-establish virtue,
discipline, etc. The *avatara* doctrine was clearly
formulated for the first time in the BHAGAVADGITA,
and later elaborated upon in the PURANAS. It is
usually applied to the incarnations of VISHNU,
which are innumerable, according to the
VAISHNAVAS, though the main ones are, in

Group of personified weapons. From right to left: Gadadevi, (mace), Chakrapurusha (discus), Dhanuspurusha (bow) and Khadgapurusha (sword). Detail from the Vishnu Anantashayana panel, Dashavatara temple, Deogarh, Madhya Pradesh. Sandstone, 6th century.

mythological order: MATSYA (fish), KURMA (tortoise), VARAHA (boar), NARASIMHA (man-lion), VAMANA/TRIVIKRAMA (dwarf), PARASHURAMA, RAMA(CHANDRA), BALARAMA, KRISHNA, the historical BUDDHA and KALKI. The list of the ten *avataras* varies according to sectarian traditions, those that include Balarama omit Buddha, and vice versa. An *avatara* can be *purna*, meaning complete, when it covers the whole span of a human life – as for instance Rama – or *aveshavatara*, a temporary incarnation, as in the case of Parashurama.

Ayodhya 'invincible'. The capital of RAMA. Located on the RIVER Gogra (formerly known as Sharayu), four miles east of Faizabad (Uttar Pradesh), Ayodhya is one of the seven holy cities of Hinduism. To die there ensures eternal bliss.

ayudhapurusha or *shastradevata* A weapon of the gods represented in human form. Occasionally, the *ayudhapurushas* are regarded as partial incarnations of the deity to whom they belong. The *ayudhapurushas* are personified as two-armed figures wearing crowns, either emerging from the weapon they represent, or carrying it in their hands or on their head. One of the most common *ayudhapurusha* is VISHNU's *chakra* (discus), SUDARSHANA. The sex of the *ayudhapurushas* is determined by the gender of the word denoting them. The masculine weapons have the word *purusha* (man) added to their name, the female weapons have *devi* (goddess), e.g. Gadadevi or KAUMODAKI, the personified club of Vishnu.

Ayurveda 'knowledge of life, health, longevity'. Closely connected to the ATHARVAVEDA, the *Ayurveda* is a work on medicine attributed to the mythical DHANVANTARI, the physician of the gods. Empirical medicine was based on observation and experience in order to determine the causes of diseases and to find an appropriate treatment. The *Ayurveda* is a traditional and naturalistic system, based on the theory that ailments originate in an imbalance of the three HUMOURS, wind, bile and phlegm. Health can be restored through diet and treatments largely dependent on the use of water, herbs, minerals and other natural substances. In recent times, the *Ayurveda* system has successfully travelled to the West, where it has many adherents.
Zysk, K.G., 1993

Ayyappan The son of SHIVA and VISHNU in his female form as MOHINI. According to the myth current at Sabarimalai, Kerala, the main sanctuary of Ayyappan, the god transformed himself into a baby and was eventually found by the childless King Pandalam and adopted as his heir. Soon afterwards, the queen gave birth to a son and, jealous of Ayyappan, devised a scheme to get rid of him. She feigned illness and, claiming that only tiger's milk could save her, sent Ayyappan into the forest to fetch some. However, after numerous adventures, he returned riding on a tigress. During his time in the forest, he had been sent to heaven by Shiva to kill the demoness Mahishi, who was wreaking havoc among the gods. He had hurled her from heaven to earth, where she fell near Sabarimalai. Mahishi, thus freed from her demonic nature, asked Ayyappan to take her as his wife, but he refused, saying that he wanted to remain a BRAHMACHARI, a celibate. Instead, she was given a prominent position and is still worshipped at Sabarimalai. According to some scholars, Ayyappan is the Keralan form of the Tamil Aiyanar; their mythologies have many similarities, their iconographies, however, are different. Ayyappan now represents the ideal form of

Ayyappan

non-sectarian worship, all castes and creeds being permitted to enter his shrine at Sabarimalai. He is the 'lord of celibacy' and, as such, revered only by men; women in their fertile years are not allowed into the shrine. Since the 1950s, Ayyappan's appeal has spread to both Tamil Nadu and Andhra Pradesh. His other names include Hariharaputra, 'son of HARI and HARA' and Shasta, 'ruler of the country, teacher'.
Adiceam, M. E., 1967

Badrinath or **Badarinatha** 'Lord of the *badari*-tree' (*Zizyphus jujuba Lam.*). Name of one of the chief PILGRIMAGE places in India. Badrinath is situated in the Himalayas in Uttar Pradesh. The site is sacred to VISHNU in his dual form of NARA-NARAYANA.

bakula or *vakula* (*Mimusops elengi*). Name of SHIVA and of the tree with which he is identified. A legend reports that it flowers when sprinkled with water from the mouth of young women. These flowers begin to scent at twilight, exude their full fragrance at night, and fall to the ground at dawn. They are often collected by devotees who offer them to the deities. The flowers, fruit and bark of the *bakula* are used in Ayurvedic medicine in tonics, in lotions for wounds and ulcers, and as a remedy against gum disorders.
Patnaik, N., 1993

Baladeva *see* BALARAMA

Balakrishna 'child Krishna'. KRISHNA depicted dancing, or as a chubby child crawling on all fours. Sometimes he holds a ball of butter in one hand. Krishna is the only AVATARA of VISHNU to be worshipped in four different aspects: as a child, lover, friend and master.

Balarama 'Rama the strong' or **Baladeva** the 'god of strength'. The elder brother of KRISHNA, Balarama is an incarnation of VISHNU, or of ANANTA, and is rarely worshipped independently. He appears to have been a historical figure, who later became an agricultural deity associated with irrigation and viticulture. According to tradition, Balarama was the seventh child of DEVAKI. It was predicted that one of her children would kill KAMSA, the tyrannical king of MATHURA, and so six of her children were

Balarama carrying the ploughshare
and the staff. Caption in Telugu.
Probably Thanjavur, *c.* 1830. From
an album of paintings on European
paper watermarked 1820.

eliminated. In the course of her seventh pregnancy, the embryo was miraculously removed from her womb and transplanted into that of Rohini, who eventually gave birth to Balarama. Another legend states that Krishna and Balarama were born from a black and a white hair of Vishnu respectively. After an eventful life, Balarama felt death approaching and retired in meditation on the shore of the ocean. While he was thus engaged, the snake Ananta slithered out of his mouth into the ocean, and the god of the ocean welcomed him with offerings. This legend accounts for the belief that Balarama was an incarnation of Ananta, which led to the representation of Balarama either emerging from or leaning on a snake. Among his other names are Halayudha, 'having a plough as a weapon', and Samkarshana, 'the ploughing'.

Balasubrahmanya 'child SUBRAHMANYA'. This image is similar to that of BALAKRISHNA dancing, except that the left leg is raised, rather than the right. The god carries a lotus in one hand, and the other hand is in VARADAMUDRA.

Bali, *bali* 1. King of the ASURAS, who became extremely powerful through his valour and asceticism. To curb his might, VISHNU assumed his form as VAMANA (dwarf) and requested Bali to grant him the expanse of land that he could cover in three steps. Bali agreed and Vamana grew into TRIVIKRAMA: with the first step he covered the earth, with the second the sky, and with the third he trod on Bali's head sending him to the nether world, of which he became the ruler. 2. An offering of grain or rice to the household divinities, birds, animals, etc. The *bali* is part of the daily worship performed by the householder. The lotus-shaped stone altar on which the *bali* is placed is called *balipitha*.

Bali(n) *see* VALI(N)

bana 'reed, shaft, arrow'. A bow and arrow are attributes of numerous deities. They are, however, typical of RAMA, who is represented carrying a bow and arrow, and of KAMA, who is armed with five flower arrows, symbolizing the five senses.

banalinga Small, egg-shaped white stones found in the NARMADA RIVER, which are worshipped as the aniconic form of the LINGA. They are used either for domestic worship, or carried on the person as an amulet.

banyan or **nyagrodha** (*Ficus bengalensis*). The SANSKRIT name of this tree means 'down growing', as the roots sprout from its branches and trail down to the ground, forming a small forest around the main tree. The *nyagrodha*, also known as VATA, is sacred to VISHNU, as well as to other deities, such as SHIVA and CHAMUNDA.

Basava 'bull'. Southern Indian BRAHMIN (12th century) who, as a boy, refused to undergo the UPANAYANA ceremony, and later criticized the brahminical establishment, initiating the VIRASHAIVA doctrine. He became prime minister to the Kalachuri king, a JAINA, who ruled at Kalyana, and eventually took control of the state. With the help of his nephew Channabasava, Basava embarked on a vigorous campaign against adherents of VAISHNAVISM, Jainism and BUDDHISM. He invested public funds in the revival of SHAIVISM until the king accused him of embezzlement. Basava then arranged for the king's assassination and fled the country. When the king's son discovered his hideout, Basava threw himself into a well. According to the Virashaivas, Basava is an incarnation of SHIVA's bull, NANDI.

Despite her alluring aspect, the two tiny fangs at the corners of the mouth and the flame-like halo behind her head betray Bhadrakali's fierce character. Her attributes are the *damaru*, the noose, the skull cup and the *trishula*. Tamil Nadu. Copper alloy, 11th century.

bath In Hindu worship the *snana*, or bath, is an act of purification. Bathing in flowing water, preferably a RIVER or a spring, is the most satisfactory method of performing this ritual obligation. However, water from a tank, pond or fresh water from a bucket is also acceptable. Whatever the source of the water used in ablutions, it must be regarded as water from the Ganges. The most effective form of bathing is partial immersion in the river, accompanied by a series of rituals and ending with total immersion. Baths are also taken in fire – by jumping over one or sitting in front of it – and in ash, air and dust.

bel see BILVA

betel (*Piper betle*). Name of the betel vine, derived from Portuguese and originating from the Malayan word *vettila*. The fresh leaf of the betel vine is covered with lime and sprinkled with a variety of ingredients, such as areca nut and aromatic spices. The leaf is then folded, pinned with a clove and chewed whole, dyeing the saliva bright red. The areca nut, sometimes called betel nut, contains arecoline, a substance that is mildly intoxicating and leaves a feeling of contentment. The SANSKRIT word for the prepared leaf is *tambula*. However, the pan-Indian term used for betel (*pan*) and areca nut (*supari*) is the Hindi expression *pan-supari*. The ceremonial offering of *pan-supari* to an image of a god is a feature of worship; in private homes, the offering of *pan-supari* to a guest at the end of a meal is a standard form of hospitality. In the past, the preparation and offering of betel became a formal occasion requiring an elaborate etiquette and a special 'betel language' existed between lovers.

One of the most important functionaries of the court was the 'bearer of the betel purse', who was in charge of its preparation. The bearers were generally women who accompanied the king wherever he went, and placed the prepared leaf in the ruler's mouth. Apart from the standard ingredients, betel can contain other substances, such as opium, camphor, tobacco and aphrodisiacs. The betel vine was formerly grown in secluded *pan*-gardens, the *baras*, reserved for the elite and the royal HAREM. Betel culture has inspired an array of objects, such as perforated metal containers for the leaves, cutters, caskets, which are works of art in their own right.

Bhadrakali 'the auspicious KALI'. Brought into being by DEVI's wrath, when DAKSHA insulted SHIVA, Bhadrakali was probably a local goddess, eventually assimilated into SHAIVA mythology. She is one of the awesome forms of Devi, and is therefore represented with three eyes and four, twelve or eighteen hands carrying a number of weapons. Flames issue from her head and small tusks protrude at the corners of her mouth. She is the consort of VIRABHADRA.

Bhagavadgita '(the) Song of the Lord'. Embedded in the sixth book of the MAHABHARATA, the *Bhagavadgita* is one of the most famous religious texts in the world. It is couched in the form of a conversation between KRISHNA and ARJUNA, which takes place just before the great battle of KURUKSHETRA. Among the main messages conveyed by this work are the importance of performing one's duty disinterestedly, while still pursuing the way to salvation, the doctrine of periodical divine incarnations as a means of redressing the balance between good and evil, and finally, devotion (BHAKTI) to the Supreme Being (ISHVARA) and faith in his grace. The date of the *Bhagavadgita* has not been ascertained, some suggest the 4th century BCE, others later. However, the present form of the text suggests considerable revision.

Bhagavata 'related or coming from Bhagavan', i.e. VISHNU or KRISHNA. Name of a cult, in which the emphasis lay on worship rather than on sacrifice. Around 100 BCE, it developed into a sectarian movement, which later merged with the VAISHNAVA sect of the PANCHARATRAS.

Bhagavata Purana *see* PURANA(S)

Bhagiratha A descendant of SAGARA, a legendary king of AYODHYA, whose austerities induced SHIVA to let the GANGA descend to earth in order to bathe the ashes of the sixty thousand sons of Sagara, who had been burnt by the wrath of the sage Kapila. Bhagiratha, after leading the river over the earth to the sea, guided it to PATALA, the nether world, where the ashes of his ancestors were purified by its waters. On account of this myth, a part of the Ganga is also known as Bhagirathi.

Bhairava 'frightful, terrible'. 1. Name of an awesome aspect of SHIVA. There are eight different aspects of Bhairava. He is often shown accompanied by a DOG or riding one, and generally guards the entrance to SHAIVA TEMPLES; his rural counterpart is the village god Bhairon, the personification of a field spirit. 2. The Bhairavas, as a group of sixty-four, are the companions of RUDRA. 3. Name of the southern face of an IMAGE of the five-faced Shiva.

Bhairavi 'terror, or the power to cause terror'. Name of a goddess, one of the personifications of SHIVA's energy. Bhairavi represents decay and death, processes which begin at conception and last throughout the whole life-span.

bhakti 'devotion, worship'. *Bhakti* appears in the Hindu tradition as early as the BHAGAVADGITA;

however, it was not until the 6th or 7th century that it began to be an important movement. Beginning in southern India with the SHAIVA NAYANMARS and the VAISHNAVA ALVARS, an emotional, ecstatic kind of devotion became increasingly popular. In the *Bhagavadgita* devotion appears primarily as a disciplined way of life, which enables one to accommodate both social obligations and religious fulfilment. Later, *bhakti* became an emotional involvement between God and the devotee, in which the devotee is prepared to sacrifice everything for the love of God. *Bhakti* may assume many forms and the devotee may relate to God in various ways, as his slave, such as HANUMAN to RAMA; as friend or equal, such as ARJUNA to KRISHNA; as parent, such as YASHODA to Krishna; as lover such as RADHA to Krishna; and as enemy or hater, such as HIRANYAKASHIPU to VISHNU, the assumption being that the hatred implies a belief in the power of the deity. Anyone, immaterial of caste or class, is qualified for *bhakti-marga*, the path of devotion. The two attitudes required are to think of God constantly and to have a deep attachment to him. One of the most revealing examples of *bhakti* is the love of the GOPIS, who leave their husbands, families and domestic duties, in order to join their chosen god, Krishna.

bhang(a) or ***vijaya*** (*Cannabis sativa*). Hemp, a narcotic drug also called *bhang*. It is smoked, mixed with other ingredients or eaten as a sweetmeat (*majun*). Its leaves are also pounded and infused in cold water for their medicinal properties. Opium and *bhang* are consumed by the SHAKTAS. In southern Indian divinatory ceremonies *bhang* is taken to help reach a state of trance. It was regularly used in warfare to stimulate ELEPHANTS and soldiers before battle.

Far Left: Bhairava, accompanied by his dog, is depicted as an ascetic with conspicuous dreadlocks, a garland of skulls and a trident. Caption in Telugu. Probably Thanjavur, *c.* 1830. From an album of paintings on European paper watermarked 1820.

Opposite: Shiva as Bikshatana accompanied by a *gana* and a dog. Chidambaram, Tamil Nadu. Detail from a 17th-century painting on the ceiling of the Shivakamasundari shrine, in the Nataraja temple complex.

Right: Bhima, armed with two huge clubs, wreaks havoc on the battlefield. Maharashtra(?). Opaque watercolour on paper, 19th century.

Bharata 1. Name of a powerful tribe that took part in the great war described in the MAHABHARATA, to which it gave its name. 2. Name of RAMA's half-brother, sometimes believed to be the personification of VISHNU's CHAKRA. 3. Name of the mythical author of the Natyashastra. 4. The modern name of the Republic of India, Bharat.

Bharata-Natyam 'BHARATA's dance' is the modern version of a style of dance created in the Thanjavur region, which flourished under Chola (9th–13th century) patronage. The 108 classic *Bharata-Natyam* poses are sculpted on the walls of the eastern GOPURA passageway at the CHIDAMBARAM temple. Originally a temple dance, it was performed only by women, the DEVADASIS, for the benefit of the deities. Now generally presented by a soloist who plays more than one role, it requires masterly control of gestures, stances and facial expressions. Although some of the movements are forceful and dramatic, the dominant mood conveyed by the dance is *shringara*, or erotic sentiment. Because of its association with the *devadasis* and its vulgarization, *Bharata-Natyam* fell into disrepute, but since the twentieth century, much has been done to restore it to its former sophistication.

Bharatanatyashastra 'Bharata's treatise on dance'. This important treatise on drama, music and dance, was written between 100 and 300 CE by the legendary sage BHARATA. Its present form, however, dates from *c.* 500 CE. Bharata is regarded as the codifier of Indian drama and dance theory and as the first art critic. His encyclopaedic work expands on poetics, drama, dance, music and aesthetics. It contains the first attempts at codifying the theory of RASA (mood) and *bhava* (emotion), guidelines for dramatic writing, a description of gestures and

technical devices, which were further elaborated upon by his successors. In view of the close parallels between, on the one hand, the *Natyashastra* and its commentaries, and on the other, Aristotle's *Poetics* and Hellenistic dramatic theory, it has been suggested that Bharata and his editors may have been influenced by Greek culture.
Ghosh, M., 1950

bhasman 'ash'. *See* VIBHUTI

Bhauma or **Mangala** The planet Mars, one of the NAVAGRAHAS. Tuesday, Mangalvar, is named after him. Bhauma is generally represented with four hands and his VAHANA is a goat.

Bhikshatanamurti 'form as a mendicant'. Aspect of SHIVA as a wandering, naked mendicant, accompanied by a DOG and a dwarfish attendant carrying a begging bowl. Having cut off one of BRAHMA's heads, Shiva became guilty of the most heinous crime, brahminicide, and the skull stuck fast to his hand. After roaming the country for a long time, begging for alms, Bhikshatana arrived at VARANASI. There he atoned for his crime and the skull dropped from his hand.

Bhima 'fearful, terrible'. The second of the PANDAVA princes and the son of the wind god VAYU and PANDU's wife, KUNTI. Huge, coarse, violent and prodigiously greedy, he plays a conspicuous role in the MAHABHARATA. He had many adventures, one of which describes his fights against the ASURAS, his victory and subsequent marriage with Hidimba, the sister of their chiefs. His arch-enemy, was however, his cousin, the KAURAVA prince DURYODHANA. The latter, jealous of Bhima's strength, poisoned him and threw his body into the Ganges, where it sank to the

realm of the NAGAS. They attacked him, but their poison was neutralized by the one already in his blood and he recovered. The amazed *nagas* presented him with eight jars of nectar, which he proceed to drink, and gained the strength of a thousand ELEPHANTS. In his thirteenth year of exile, disguised as a cook, he worked with his brothers and their common wife DRAUPADI at the court of Virata. Here he killed Kichaka, brother-in law of Virata, who tried to rape her. It was only in the course of the *Mahabharata* war that Bhima fought with Duryodhana. Despite his strength, Bhima was on the verge of losing and struck Duryodhana's thigh with his club, thus disregarding the ancient rule forbidding blows below the navel, and he became known as Jihmayodhin, 'unfair fighter'. Eventually Bhima joined his bothers in their final journey to SVARGA, beyond the Himalayas. Some of his other names are Bhimasena, 'Bhima the fighter', Bahushalin, 'large-armed', Vrikodara, 'wolf's belly'.

Bhishma 'terrible'. One of the most prominent of the MAHABHARATA, Bhishma was the son of the GANGA and of Shantanu, a descendant of BHARATA. He is portrayed as a man of honour, exemplary loyalty and chivalrous behaviour and his personality dominates the whole epic. He was fatally wounded in battle, pierced by so many arrows that, when he fell from his chariot, he did not touch the earth, but lay on a couch of darts. He postponed his death for fifty-eight days, waiting for the sun to start its northern course, because it is believed that souls have an easier passage to the other world during this part of the year. While waiting for the appropriate moment to die, he delivered several long didactic discourses.

Bhringi(n) 'wanderer'. A RISHI and a great devotee of SHIVA, depicted as an emaciated person with three legs. The reason for his unconventional appearance is given in the following story: once the gods and the *rishis* were paying homage to Shiva and PARVATI, but Bhringi neglected Parvati. In her fury she reduced him to a skeleton, unable to stand on his weak legs. Thereupon, Shiva provided him with a third leg. To force Bhringi to worship both of them, Shiva assumed his androgynous form, Ardhanarishvara. However, the undaunted Bhringi transformed himself into a bee, bored his way through the body and continued to worship only Shiva. Bhringi generally appears beside him or dancing near NATARAJA.

Bhudevi or **Bhumidevi** The earth goddess (derived from the root -*bhu*, 'to be, exist'). Later, she was identified with Bhudevi or PRITHVI, the earth personified, but rarely worshipped as an independent deity. In his incarnation as a boar (VARAHA) Vishnu rescues the earth from the depths of the ocean. Vishnu is often shown flanked by both his consorts with Bhudevi generally standing on his left.

bhuta(s) Originally 'living beings', but later 'malevolent spirits, goblins, ghosts', who roam about and to whom a morning and evening offering (*bhutabali*) should be made. The *bhutas* were held responsible for harassing those who neglected to propitiate them and they were blamed for poor crops, contaminated wells, human and animal diseases and fatal illnesses in children. The cult of *bhutas*, accompanied by impressive ceremonies and dance performances, plays an important part in the rural life of southern Karnataka and northern Kerala.

Bhuteshvara 'Lord of the BHUTAS'. Epithet of SHIVA, VISHNU, BRAHMA, KUBERA and KRISHNA. In his

Opposite: Bhishma on a bed of arrows. Detail from a frieze on the basement of the Kedareshvara temple at Halebid, Karnataka. Soapstone, 12th–13th century.

Bhringi

Right: Part of a group of three, depicting Vishnu and consorts. Bhudevi, generally placed to the left of Vishnu, is shown as if carrying a flower in the right hand. Tamil Nadu. Bronze, *c.* 1000.

aspect as Bhuteshvara, Shiva inhabits the cremation grounds and is attended by a host of *bhutas*.

Bhuvaneshvara 'Lord of the world'. Epithet of SHIVA.

Bhuvaneshvari 'Mistress of the world'. She is the tutelary deity of Orissa. The epithet is shared by many goddesses.

bija 'seed syllable'. A *bija* is a mystic syllable that contains the essence of a MANTRA. *See also* OM

bijamantra 'seed *mantra*'. The main monosyllabic MANTRAS are called *bijamantras*. Each deity has its own *bijamantra*, which is said to be a manifestation of the deity evoked. *Bijamantras* are mostly used in TANTRISM.

bilva, **bel** (*Aegle marmelos*). The wood-apple tree, sacred to SHIVA and said to be the vegetal aspect of the god, who resides in its leaves. It is forbidden to break its branches and to use its wood for fuel.

bindu 'drop, dot'. The metaphysical point outside time and space, at which the manifested and the unmanifested meet. According to the philosophy of TANTRA, the *bindu* is the source of the universe.

birds Birds are believed to be messengers of the gods and their familiarity with the heavenly regions allows them access to secrets hidden from mankind. The crow knows the three greatest secrets: that of immortality, that pertaining to the origin of things – since it was the only bird to witness creation – and that of hell, because it dwelt for a long time in the infernal regions. For this reason, a whole mythology developed around the crow, and the *vayasa-vidya* ('science of the crow') became a popular study.

Omens were read in the cawing and flight of crows, though interpreting them required great skill, as crows were thought to be naturally inclined to mislead people. Other birds were also carefully studied and many treatises on divination have one or more chapters devoted to this subject.

A number of birds serve as mounts (VAHANAS) to deities. The most prominent in legend and literature are the peacock (the *vahana* of SARASVATI and KARTTIKEYA), KAMA's parrot, LAKSHMI's owl, SHANI's crow, VISHNU's eagle and BRAHMA's goose (HAMSA), around which a complex symbolism developed. The *hamsa* stands for detachment, because it swims on the surface of the water, but is not bound by it; it is a free, homeless wanderer, symbol of the emancipated soul. The vulture was once worshipped in the belief that the king of vultures, later identified with JATAYU, an ally of RAMA, was the ruler of the nether world. A number of birds are mentioned in poetry and other literary works as representing particular traits. Thus, the heron (*baka*) stood for hypocrisy and treachery, the cock for discrimination, the *chakravaka* (a kind of goose) for conjugal fidelity; the *chakora* (a partridge-like bird) is said to feed only on moonbeams.

blood The Ayurvedic system of medicine classes blood (*rakta*) among the basic constituents of the body. While the blood of women was considered impure, that of men was reputed to be life-giving. Continuity of life lies at the root of the blood offerings that were made to help the sun's movement through the heavens, to promote the fertility of the earth or of cattle, and to revitalize the gods. Some deities (e.g. the goddess KALI) have long been associated with human and ANIMAL sacrifices. Though these practices have been discontinued, a reminder of blood sacrifices is found in the rural

Brahma, whose fourth head is not visible, carries a water pot and prayer beads in his upper hands. The lower left is placed on the hip, and the lower right is damaged. Tamil Nadu. Granite, first half of the 11th century.

custom of daubing sacred IMAGES and the body or the forehead of the person performing a sacrifice with red ochre or vermilion.

bodhi *see* ASHVATTHA

Brahma The creator of the universe and sustainer of the world, according to late-Vedic and subsequent traditions. Brahma is a member of the TRIMURTI, the triad consisting of Brahma, SHIVA and VISHNU. Brahma is the masculine personification of the neuter BRAHMAN of which the essence is reality (*sat*). He represents spiritual power and also equilibrium between two opposite forces, the centrifugal (Shiva) and the centripetal (Vishnu). Originally, he had five heads, but one was cut off by Shiva, so he is represented with four, symbolizing either his omniscience, the four VEDAS, the four YUGAS, or the four CASTES. He carries a KAMANDALU, a vessel with a spout, which is said to represent the earth, the container and sustainer of all things, prayer beads and sometimes a book, said to be the *Vedas*. His VAHANA is the HAMSA (goose). IMAGES of Brahma generally appear alongside those of the subsidiary deities. In renderings of the *trimurti*, either Shiva or Vishnu occupies the central position, but never Brahma. In the whole of India, only two TEMPLES are dedicated to him, Pushkar near Ajmer and Khed Brahma near Idar, on the border between Gujarat and Rajasthan. *See also* BHIKSHATANAMURTI

brahmachari(n) The *brahmacharya*, is the first of the four ASHRAMAS, or stages in the life of a Hindu. A *brahmachari* is a student, whose education begins after the investiture with the sacred thread (UPANAYANA). He is supposed to live in the house of his GURU where he is trained in religious studies, taught how to look after the sacrificial FIRES, where

he practises austerities and strictly observes chastity. This phase lasts for about twelve years.

brahman (neuter) 'All-pervading, self-existent power' (from the root *brih*, 'growth, development'). The supreme entity of the universe, from which all things emanate and to which all return.

Brahmana(s) 'belonging to the BRAHMINS'. A body of literature appended to the VEDAS, composed between around 900 and 600 BCE by the brahmins for their own use. It was intended for their guidance in the use of the hymns and the performance of various rituals. The most important of the *Brahmanas* is the SHATAPATHA BRAHMANA.

Brahmi or **Brahmani** A non-Vedic goddess, later identified with BRAHMA'S SHAKTI. According to some PURANAS, she is the daughter of Brahma and Svayambhuva MANU was born from their union. Brahmi is one of the seven (or eight) MATRIKAS.

brahmin or **brahman** A man belonging to the first of the four CASTES, the sacerdotal class, members of which may be, but are not necessarily, priests. A brahmin is considered chief of all created beings and his person is inviolate. He is entitled to every honour and enjoys many rights and privileges. Traditionally, the chief duty of a brahmin was to study and teach the VEDAS, to perform the various ceremonies, sacrifices and other rituals. Nowadays, however, many brahmins engage in secular occupations.

Brahmo Samaj 'Society of God'. Reform movement founded in 1828 by Ram Mohan Roy (1772–1833) under the name *Brahmo Sabha*. Through it Roy hoped to transform radically the face of Hindu life and Hindu religion. This movement was strongly

The Buddha seated in the lotus position (*padmasana*) on the lion throne (*simhasana*). His right hand is in *abhayamudra*, while his left rests on his lap. Eastern India. Basalt, 11th century.

influenced by the Unitarians, with whom Roy had been associated since 1821. It rejected the CASTE system and the doctrine of reincarnation, no sacrifices or oblations of any kind were permitted and no IMAGES, statues or PAINTINGS were allowed in the hall of worship; only monotheistic services, prayers and hymns were encouraged. The *Brahmo Samaj* survives as a relatively small, but progressive sect, mainly in Bengal.
Brockington, J. L., 1981

Brihashpati 'Lord of prayer'. A Vedic god, the celestial priest. In Vedic lore, Brihashpati is regarded as the divine BRAHMIN who sanctifies the rites of the human brahmins, thus mediating between mankind and the gods. In the course of time, Brihashpati became one of the NAVAGRAHAS, the auspicious planet Jupiter, whose day (Thursday) brings luck. Brihashpati is the teacher of astrology and astronomy, and controls the planets.

Brindavana *see* VRINDAVANA

Buddha 'the enlightened one'. 1. *See* SIDDHARTA GAUTAMA 2. In his ninth incarnation VISHNU is said to have appeared as Buddha, to encourage demons and wicked men to despise the VEDAS, reject the CASTE system, deny the existence of the gods, and thus to effect their own destruction.

Buddhi 'wisdom, divine knowledge'. One of GANESHA's consorts, wisdom personified.

Buddhism, Buddhist Religious movement based on the teachings of SIDDHARTA GAUTAMA (*c.* 568–486 BCE). Some of the doctrines disseminated by him were contrary to basic Hindu beliefs, as Gautama was strongly opposed to sacrifice, religious ceremonies,

religious ritual, the CASTE system among other things. In this sense, Buddhism may be regarded as a reaction against the BRAHMINS and the brahmanical establishment. Buddhism's main preoccupation is, in fact, with moral precepts, rather than with speculations on the soul or man's relationship with God. As such, Buddhism had a profound impact on Hinduism. The respect for ANIMAL life and the notion of non-injury are Buddhist ideas, as are vegetarianism and abstention from intoxicating drinks. The Hindu doctrine of the ASHRAMAS, or stages of life, was inspired by Buddhism. Hindu philosophy was also stimulated by Buddhist thought in the development of a precise system of logical enquiry and intellectual analysis. Even brahmanical religious ideas were reformed by Buddhism. Nor can the importance of Buddhism in Indian cultural history be overemphasized. The first historical records in India were kept by Buddhists and the great universities of Taxila and Nalanda became centres of Buddhist studies, well known in the whole of the East. Most literature in local Indian languages begins with Buddhist works, and the art of the fabulist is of Buddhist origin. Numerous tales that are later found in Greek, Latin and other European languages, derive from the Buddhist tradition.
Conze, E., 1980

Budha The planet Mercury, illegitimate son of SOMA (the moon) and Tara (star), wife of BRIHASHPATI. Budha is the planet of wisdom, speech and the intellect. His day is Wednesday. *See also* NAVAGRAHA(S)

C

Opposite: The moon god Soma or Chandra bearing a conspicuous crescent on the side of his crown. Caption in Telugu. Probably Thanjavur, *c.* 1830. From an album of paintings on European paper watermarked 1820.

calendar Until the European calendar was introduced in colonial times, there was no unified system for measuring time. The traditional Hindu calendar (*panchanga*), now mainly used for ritual and astrological purposes, is based on the lunar month, which is divided into a bright fortnight (*shukla paksha*, 'bright wing'), when the moon is waxing; and into a dark fortnight (*krishna paksha*, 'dark wing') when it is waning. The former is considered auspicious, whereas the latter is believed to be infested by the spirits of the dead. In northern India the month begins with a full moon, and in southern India with a new moon. A lunar month consists of 30 lunar days (*tithi*), or approximately 29½ solar days. A lunar year has 354 to 360 days. Every two or three years, a thirteenth month is added to cancel the difference between the lunar and the solar year.

As well as the solar calendar, the signs of the zodiac (*rasi*, 'scattering', i. e. constellation), were imported from the West, and the names of the zodiac signs and the corresponding months are translations or adaptations from their Greek names. According to the solar calendar, a year is defined as the time it takes the sun to pass through the twelve zodiacal signs. The entry of the sun into each of the twelve houses of the zodiac on the first day of the corresponding solar month, is called *sankranti*, 'entry, incoming'. Particularly important are the *makara sankranti* (winter solstice) and the *mesha sankranti* (vernal equinox). *Makara sankranti* is celebrated with great pomp in southern India, especially in Tamil Nadu, where the festivities last for three days. The sun, rice harvest, cows and other ANIMALS, are all worshipped on this occasion. The solar year is divided into two parts, the 'day of the gods', the period from the winter to the summer solstice (*uttarayana*, 'progress towards north') and the 'night of the gods', from the summer to the

winter solstice (*dakshinayana*, progress towards south). The former period is deemed auspicious, and the latter inauspicious.

The Indian year has six seasons, each divided into periods:
vasanta (spring): *Chaitra* (March–April), *Vaishakha* (April–May);
grishma (hot season): *Jyeshtha* (May–June), *Ashadha* (June–July);
varsha (rainy season): *Shravana* (July–August), *Bhadrapada*, *Bhadon* (August–September);
sharada (autumn): *Ashvina*, *Ashvayuja* (September–October), *Karttika* (October–November);
hemanta (winter): *Margashirsha*, *Aghana* (November–December), *Pausha* (December–January);
shishira (cool season): *Magha* (January–February), *Phalguna* (February–March).

Probably some periods had a five-day week (*pancha-ratra*, 'five nights'), which was replaced by the seven-day week *c.* 200 CE by the Hellenized populations living in north-west India. Following the Graeco-Roman custom, each day is named after its presiding planet: *Ravivara* (Sunday) after RAVI, the sun; *Somavara* (Monday) after SOMA, the moon; *Mangalvara* (Tuesday) from MANGALA, Mars, etc. Days can also be auspicious or inauspicious. *Mangalvara*, for instance, which is possibly derived from the word *mangala*, meaning auspicious, has been given to this inauspicious day, in order to avert misfortune. The most unlucky day of the week, however, is *Shanivara* (Saturday), named after the planet SHANI, Saturn. *See also* JYOTISHA; NAVAGRAHA(S)

castes The term caste is derived from the Portuguese *casta*, 'breed, race, kind', and used to define the various social classes that form Indian society: BRAHMINS, KSHATRIYAS, VAISHYAS, SHUDRAS. Caste

Two southern Indian brahmins in the precincts of the Rajagopalasvami temple at Mannargudi, Thanjavur district, Tamil Nadu.

divisions do not only apply to Hindus, but can also be found among Muslims, Sikhs and Christians. The origin of the various castes is given in the RIGVEDA. The hymn known as the *Purusha-sukta* (Hymn 90, *Mandala* X, v. 12) says, 'The brahmin was his [PURUSHA'S] mouth, the *rajanya* (*kshatriya*) his arms, the *vaishya* his thighs, and the *shudra* his feet.' This passage, which is possibly a later interpolation, was commented upon at length by the learned brahmins, and in due course became the justification for the brahmin class subordinating the remaining ones. This notion was firmly established by the lawgiver MANU. The first three castes, brahmins, *kshatriyas*, *vaishyas*, are known as *dvija*, 'twice-born', because they are born, metaphorically speaking, a second time when invested with the sacred thread (UPANAYANA). The fourth caste, the *shudras*, as well as a sizeable quantity of outcastes (HARIJANS or DALITS), are termed 'once-born', since they are not allowed to undergo the *upanayana*, or any other initiation ceremony, and were prevented from entering TEMPLES and sacred precincts until the Temple Act of 1948.

The existence of the SANSKRIT words for caste, *varna*, 'colour', and *jata*, 'race', has led to the hypothesis that castes were originally determined by skin and hair colour. According to some scholars, ARYAN priests, warriors and traders were the original brahmins, *kshatriyas* and *vaishyas*, the *shudras* were the menial workers and slaves and the various aboriginal tribes were the outcastes. In reality, the caste system was elastic and comprehensive. It is a fact that priests, warriors and other individuals belonging to different backgrounds were assimilated into the various castes. Moreover, distinguished local kings were provided with appropriate genealogical trees and thus formed an integral part of Hindu society. Caste divisions were also based on religious

beliefs and traditions. Even religious groups such as the VIRASHAIVAS, one of the numerous sects that firmly believe in a classless society, form a separate caste within the Hindu setting.

Virtually all castes have myths accounting for their origin; some are associated with landscape features such as hills, pools and MOUNTAINS. Some derive their origin from love affairs of local deities, while others claim descent from a god. Thus, the divine architect VISHVAKARMAN is reputed to be the progenitor of the *Kammalan* cast. A significant number of castes are formed by people in the same trade or profession, as the hereditary transmission of skills from one generation to the next ensured the survival of special techniques or trade secrets. Occasionally, members of the same occupational class living in the same town formed guilds (SHRENI) of craftsmen and tradesmen. A hierarchical order existed among the occupational classes, some occupations being regarded as more prestigious than others, and the division of one caste into sub-castes was not uncommon. The *Kammalan* caste comprises sub-castes, such as goldsmiths, carpenters and stonemasons. Nowadays, there are some three thousand castes and around twenty-five thousand sub-castes which hold rules determining all aspects of the life of their members, birth and death rituals, diet and drinking habits, dress, etc.

Manu, often reputed to be the ideologist of the *chatur-varna* ('four colours' or caste system), was responsible for instituting the rules governing the life of the four main castes. The brahmins, *kshatriyas* and *vaishyas* were allowed to study the VEDAS, to perform Vedic rituals and were expected to lead an exemplary life progressing through the four ASHRAMAS. The *shudras* and the *dalits* were prohibited from studying the Vedas and performing Vedic sacrifices. A strict division existed between

Six-armed Chaitanya uniting in his person Rama and Krishna. The upper arms carry an arrow (Rama), the central ones the flute (Krishna), the lower ones the *kamandalu* and the stick, symbols of the ascetic's life. Kalighat, Calcutta, West Bengal. Watercolour on paper, c. 1885.

the four castes, and social contact, commensality, or MARRIAGE between one caste and another was prohibited. Caste status could be easily lost, by non-observance of religious obligations or caste practices, association with foreigners, journeys abroad – such as Gandhi's journey to Britain – all lead to expulsion from one's caste. However, in the course of history, the system proved to be extremely accommodating. Both Muslim rulers and British authorities had the right to decide on caste matters, and castes that were accorded privileges by the Muslims or British were as influential as those privileged by the laws of Manu. In 1947 the caste system was officially abolished, however it survives not only in India, but also among the Hindu communities overseas. *See also* CHANDALA(S); DALIT(S); HARIJAN(S)

Chaitanya (c. 1485–1533) was the founder of an important VAISHNAVA sect known as Gaudiya Vaishnavism. Born into a BRAHMIN family in Nabadvipa (Bengal), he studied SANSKRIT and other disciplines, and was married at the age of fourteen; a few years later his wife died of a snake bite and he remarried. At the age of twenty-two he visited GAYA, where he met a MADHVA ascetic, who radically changed his outlook on life. He became an ardent worshipper of KRISHNA and two years later he became a SANNYASI and travelled to PURI in Orissa where he spread Vaishnava doctrines, converting a number of people from all walks of life. He journeyed as far afield as the southern tip of India, subsequently visiting DWARKA and the region surrounding MATHURA. Due to Chaitanya's influence, this region containing holy sites, such as Mathura, VRINDAVAN and the Braj country, the backdrop of Krishna's early life, was rescued from a state of poverty and decay. In the eyes of Chaitanya and his followers Vrindavan was, and is, an earthly

paradise. Tradition credits Chaitanya with many wonderful deeds and, on account of his fair complexion, as well as the purity of his soul, he was known among his devotees as *Gouranga*, 'white-limbed', or *Mahaprabhu*, 'great master', and was believed to be an incarnation of VISHNU.

According to Chaitanya's doctrine, Krishna is the origin, support and end of the world, all other deities being manifestations of him, and complete surrender to Krishna is more meritorious than anything else. Krishna is the source of delight (*hladini*) and he experiences delight in the act of sharing it with the devotee. Central to Chaitanya's doctrine is the devotion to RADHA and Krishna, one soul in two bodies, whose love for each other is a constant source of delight. The devotees are encouraged to see themselves as GOPIS and, as such, passionately surrender to Krishna. Although there is nothing necessarily sexual in Chaitanya's conception of God, the suggestive imagery used by him inspired later Vaishnava poets. Emotion and sentiment are fundamental to Chaitanya's doctrine and singing and dancing were fostered as conducive to divine ecstasy. Choral singing (*kirtan*), punctuated by the chanting of the names of Hari Krishna to the accompaniment of cymbals, drums and rhythmic hand-clapping, sometimes escalating to a frenzied pitch, was one of the most popular forms of worship. Chaitanya reputedly organized dramatic performances based on the Krishna legend and night-long recitations of *kathas*, or stories, on the same theme.

Chaitanya spent his later life in PURI, where he died during a fit of epilepsy while bathing in the sea. After his death the sect was organized by his six disciples, whose descendants are the Chaitanya *gosvami*, the builders of the great TEMPLE in Vrindavan. The office eventually became hereditary and the *gosvami* still play an influential role in

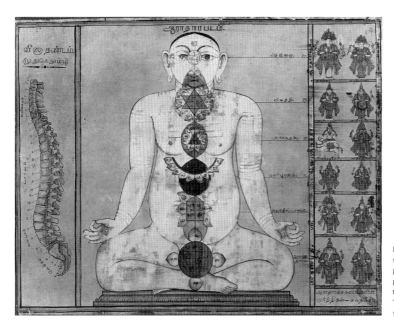

Diagram showing the *chakras* in the subtle body. To the right are the deities presiding over them. To the left their position in relation to the vertebrae in the spine. Southern India, probably Thanjavur. Ink and colour on paper, 19th century.

spiritual and practical matters. Chaitanya left only a brief work, the *Ashtaka*, 'eight couplets', but his influence was nevertheless fundamental in the development of Bengali literature and culture. In the late 19th century Thakura Bhaktisiddhanta (1838–1914) initiated the revival of Gaudiya Vaishnavism. His son Bhaktivinode Thakur (1874–1937) continued his father's work, instituting the Gaudiya Math, which among other activities, included a number of ASHRAMAS dedicated to education and publishing. In 1966 his disciple, Svami A. C. Bhaktivedanta, originally a Calcutta businessman, founded the International Society or Krishna Consciousness (ISKON) in New York, which propagated Chaitanya doctrine throughout the world.

chakra I. 'discus, wheel'. A weapon consisting of a steel ring with a sharp edge. In BUDDHISM and JAINISM, the *chakra* represents the law. In Buddhism it also refers to the first sermon of the BUDDHA at Sarnath, when the 'wheel of law was first set in movement'. In Buddhist and Jaina sculpture a *chakra* on the pedestal defines an image as that of a buddha or a TIRTHANKARA. The *chakra* is one of the attributes of VISHNU, generally held in the upper right hand and symbolizes protection and divine power. In the course of time, Vishnu's *chakra* grew in importance as a cult symbol and became an independent deity, SUDARSHANA. The *chakra* can be depicted with six or eight spokes, representing the directions of space. In the hands of a deity or of a CHAKRAVARTIN it signifies supremacy over the universe. In southern India the *chakra* is depicted with four flames emerging from its rim, which may connect it with its reputed origin as a solar symbol. It is one of the auspicious symbols that are occasionally carved on the soles of deities' feet. Apart from

Vishnu, the *chakra* is connected to other deities including AGHORA, DATTATREYA, DURGA, SKANDA and VARUNA. 2. According to the tenets of the *Kundalini Yoga*, the *chakras* are the six centres of spiritual energy placed along the central channel of the spinal column: *muladhara chakra* (root-*chakra*) at the base of the spine, *svadhisthana* (self-based) in the umbilical region, *manipura* (GEM site) at the base of the stomach, *anahata* (new) at the centre of the chest, *vishuddha* (pure) in the throat, *ajnakhya* (understanding) between the eyebrows. The seventh *chakra*, *sahasrara padma* (thousand-petalled lotus) is placed just above the skull. These *chakras* are the seat of various faculties and divinities. *See also* KUNDALINI

Chakrapurusha 'Wheel-man'. The personification of VISHNU'S CHAKRA. *See also* AYUDHAPURUSHA; SHASTRADEVATA

chakravartin 'Universal ruler'. The term applies both to temporal and to spiritual kingship, particularly in BUDDHISM and JAINISM. However, in Hinduism the term denotes a powerful ruler, whose dominion extends over the whole earth. Characteristic of the *chakravartin* are the 'seven jewels' (*sapta-ratna*) that he is reputed to own: CHAKRA, queen, chariot, jewel, wealth, horse and ELEPHANT. The list varies, however, to include the prime minister and the son. The *chakravartin* is considered to be the ideal man, possessing the thirty-two major signs of excellence and many more secondary signs. The iconographic treatises dwell at great length on the proportions, cognitive signs (LAKSHANA) and auspicious marks on the body of the *chakravartin*, whose figure is reputed to be the epitome of physical and spiritual perfection. In sculpture and painting no distinction is made between the image of the *chakravartin* and

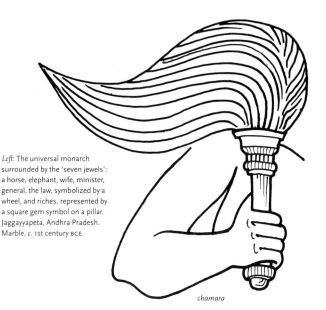

Left: The universal monarch surrounded by the 'seven jewels': a horse, elephant, wife, minister, general, the law, symbolized by a wheel, and riches, represented by a square gem symbol on a pillar. Jaggayyapeta, Andhra Pradesh. Marble, *c.* 1st century BCE.

chamara

that of a Buddha or a Jaina prophet (TIRTHANKARA). *See also* IMAGE; TALAMANA

chamara 'fly-whisk' or 'chowrie', anglicized form of the Hindi *chauri*. A fly-whisk made from the hair of a yak's tail. It is a symbol of royalty and an attribute of many Hindu, BUDDHIST and JAINA sacred images. Female attendants carrying a fly-whisk (*chamaradharinis*) are generally shown flanking a deity. The *chamara* is regarded as an auspicious object.

champaka (*Michelia champaka*). The *champaka* is mainly cultivated for its heavily scented flowers used in the preparations of perfumes. This flower, however, is also used as an ORNAMENT. In southern India women decorate their tresses with a garland of *champaka* flowers, which slowly open up in the course of the day and exude a pleasant perfume. Garlands of the flowers are presented to the deities as offerings and *champaka* trees are frequently found in TEMPLE gardens. The scented oil extracted from the *champaka* blossoms, rubbed on the temples and forehead, is a remedy against vertigo and headache. The bark and fruit of the tree are used in Ayurvedic medicine for a variety of ailments.
Patnaik, N., 1993

Chamunda or **Chamundi** One of the awe-inspiring forms of DURGA, Chamunda belongs to the group of the seven mothers, SAPTAMATRIKAS. The *Markandeya* PURANA narrates how Chamunda emerged as KALI from the forehead of the goddess AMBIKA, who expressly created her to kill the two powerful ASURAS, Chanda and Munda. Once these had been killed, Kali was given the name Chamunda. She is generally represented as a skeletal old woman of darkish complexion, with dishevelled hair and tusks

protruding from her mouth, and whose gaunt frame is at times covered by an ELEPHANT hide. She wears a garland of corpses and, occasionally, children's corpses dangle from her ears. She carries a sword, noose, club and sometimes a bowl made from a skull. A corpse, owl or lion serve as her vehicle and she symbolizes death, destruction and delusion.

chandala(s) Born of a SHUDRA father and a BRAHMIN mother, the *chandalas* were the lowest of the outcastes. Their settlements were outside the towns, near the cremation grounds, where they were generally employed as attendants. They collected, washed and clothed the bodies of the deceased. *Chandalas* were also employed as executioners.

Chanda *see* CHANDI

chandana (*Santalum album*). This small white sandalwood tree (which rarely grows taller than six metres) is found in the wooded Western Ghats. Its oil is used to make perfumes, incense and soaps and its sweet-smelling wood is employed in a number of Hindu rituals. Indian literature is rich in references to *chandana* as a tree and as a cooling perfume. Sacred IMAGES – in particular those representing violent deities – are occasionally smeared with sandalwood paste to 'cool' them down. A forehead mark (TILAKA) of sandalwood paste is often worn by the followers of various deities.
Patnaik, N., 1993

Chandesha or **Chandeshvara** One of the sixty-three SHAIVA NAYANMAR devotees. Chandesha was a BRAHMIN, who, after noticing that the local COWS were neglected by the cowherds, decided to look after them himself. Under his care the herds thrived and Chandesha used some of their milk to lustrate the

Left: The eight-armed skeletal goddess Chamunda, sitting on a corpse seat (*pretasana*). A garland of skulls emphasizes the outline of her bony figure. Her *vahana*, the owl, is perched on the leg of the corpse. Orissa. Sandstone, *c*. 9th century.

Right: Shiva garlands Chandesha. Relief on the Brihadeshvara temple, Gangaikondacholapuram, Tamil Nadu. Granite, first half of the 11th century.

sand LINGA he had fashioned. Eventually, rumours about his misuse of the milk reached his father Datta, who went to confront his son in the fields. The boy was so deep in his devotions that he did not notice his father's presence and the incensed Datta kicked the *linga*. In his anger, Chandesha struck his father's leg with his staff, but through SHIVA's intervention the staff turned into an axe and severed Datta's leg. At this point the god appeared, blessed Chandesha, promised to be a father to him, and healed the repentant Datta's leg.

Chandesha is depicted as a boy with matted locks, standing with his hands in ANJALIMUDRA and holding an axe in the crook of his arm. In southern Indian Shaiva TEMPLES, the shrine of Chandesha is placed to the north of the main sanctuary. Devotees wanting to pay homage to the saint, who is lost in meditation, are supposed to snap their fingers or clap their hands to attract his attention.
Dehejia, V., 1988

Chandi or **Chanda** 'Wrathful'. An aspect assumed by DURGA when killing Mahishasura. Chandi is worshipped in Mysore, Karnataka, as Chamundi, the tutelary goddess of the ruling Wodeyar family and of Mysore city. A local legend claims that Mahishasura was slain here, therefore the town derives its name from him. In the course of the annual *Dasara* FESTIVAL, the goddess's IMAGE is paraded ceremonially on a golden throne carried by an ELEPHANT. In Bengal, the final battle between Chandi and Mahishasura is remembered in the yearly *Durgapuja* celebrations. The goddess is depicted as a young, beautiful woman with twenty arms, seated on a lion.

Chandra or **Chandramas** Name of the moon and the moon god. He appears as a youthful man riding a

three-wheeled chariot drawn by a deer. Occasionally, a crescent is shown behind his head. The association of Chandra with the deer originated in the Vedic tradition, according to which a hunted deer, or a hare, sought the moon's protection. The moon refused, and the ANIMAL kicked him, creating the marks on the moon's surface. There are a number of different myths pertaining to Chandra's origin, beginning from the RIGVEDA, in which the moon is said to have been born from the mind of the cosmic PURUSHA, to the puranic account, in which the moon emerges from the Churning of the Ocean. Eventually, Chandra found a place in astral mythology as SOMA, the king who founded the Lunar dynasty, CHANDRAVAMSHA. From an early date the moon was associated with medicinal plants, which were said to thrive under its light, with AMRITA, rain, sexual energy and semen. According to the AYURVEDA, the moon is believed to have a strong influence on the growth of the embryo and on the amniotic fluid. Although Chandra is generally male, in some esoteric cults, as well as in folk tales from Bihar and Orissa, he is thought of as female. The waxing and waning of the moon is linked with life and death, hence certain times of the months are considered auspicious and others not. According to Kalyanamalla's (1460?–1530) treatise on EROTICS, the *Ananga Ranga*, the phases of the moon also have an influence on lovemaking, since the erogenous zones on a woman's body shift from the right side during the bright half of the month, to the left during the dark half. Among his other names are *Mriganka* 'marked by a deer' and *Shashanka* 'marked by a hare'.
Sivapriyananda, 1990

Chandrashekharamurti 'moon-crested'. Aspect of SHIVA in which he wears a crescent moon either on his crown or in his hair. The crescent moon is

The crescent moon, to the left of the crown of matted hair, identifies the image as Chandrashekhara. In the upper hands are the axe and the leaping antelope. The lower right is in *abhayamudra*. Tamil Nadu. Bronze, *c.* 13th–14th century.

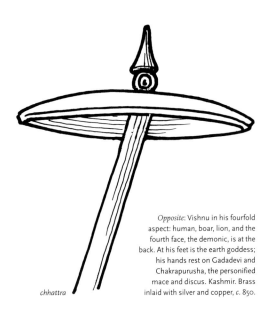

Opposite: Vishnu in his fourfold aspect: human, boar, lion, and the fourth face, the demonic, is at the back. At his feet is the earth goddess; his hands rest on Gadadevi and Chakrapurusha, the personified mace and discus. Kashmir. Brass inlaid with silver and copper, *c.* 850.

chhattra

interpreted as representing time, symbolized in the waxing and waning of the moon, or for others, it recalls the horns of Shiva's bull NANDI. Chandrashekhara is depicted with four arms; in the upper hands he holds an axe and a leaping antelope, while the lower hands are in ABHAYAMUDRA and KATI(HASTA)MUDRA.

Chandravamsha or **Somavamsha** 'Lunar lineage or dynasty'. The descendants of the moon god CHANDRA, who are divided into two main branches: the YADAVAS or descendants of YADU, of which KRISHNA is one of the most distinguished, and the Pauravas, descendants of Puru, ancestor of the KAURAVAS and PANDAVAS.

Chaturmurti or **Chaturvyuha** 'four-fold representation' or 'four kinds of appearance'. A composite aspect of VISHNU with four faces representing a man, a RAKSHASA, a lion, a boar. This iconographic formula can also represent the four manifestations (VYUHA) of Vishnu: VASUDEVA, Pradyumna, Samkarshana or BALARAMA, ANIRUDDHA. The human face, Vasudeva, is at the centre, those to the right and left are of a lion (Samkarshana) and a boar (Aniruddha) and the grimacing *rakshasa* (Pradyumna) is at the back. The figure generally has four arms.

chentu 'horse whip' (Tamil). Term loosely used for various similar-looking objects that are not readily identifiable. The *chentu*, however, which has been described as a crooked stick, is an attribute typical of AIYANAR, of KRISHNA in his aspect as Rajagopala, and occasionally, of SHIVA when shown together with NANDI. The *chentu* is an attribute that only appears in southern Indian, especially Tamilian, IMAGES.

chhattra 'parasol, umbrella'. One of the insignias of royalty and power, the *chhattra* is the emblem of VARUNA, reputed to be the embodiment of kingship. The *chhattra* is also the attribute of various deities, including REVANTA, SURYA and VISHNU in his incarnation as VAMANA.

Chidambaram (South Arcot district, Tamil Nadu). Chidambaram has been one of the most important PILGRIMAGE centres since at least the 9th century. Known to the SHAIVAS simply as *koyil*, the TEMPLE, its ancient name was Tillai after a nearby forest of tillai trees (*Excoecaria agallocha*). Chidambaram is renowned for being the seat of one of the five elemental LINGAS, the ethereal, or invisible *linga*, and more especially, for constituting the centre of the cult of SHIVA in his aspect as 'Lord of the Dance' (NATARAJA).

According to local tradition, some 1,500 years ago, a king from Kashmir afflicted with leprosy visited the shrine, bathed in the tank, and was miraculously cured. As a sign of gratitude, he made donations to the temple and enlarged it. Although Nataraja has played an important role in southern Indian culture since the Pallava dynasty (6th–8th century) his cult gained momentum with the Chola kings (9th–13th century) as he was their family deity. Tradition has it that one of the early Chola kings, Vira, had a vision of Shiva performing the cosmic DANCE near the shrine. He then built the Golden Shrine to honour the deity. The eastern gateway (GOPURA) of the complex commemorates the vision: the 108 dance postures codified in BHARATA's *Natyashastra* are sculpted in high relief on both walls of the passageway. A number of legends are connected with Chidambaram: it is said that Shiva, moved by the devotion of VYAGHRAPADA and PATANJALI, condescended to dance in the *Chit Sabha* – now a

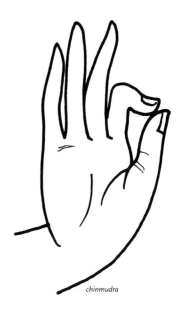

chinmudra

hall at the centre of the sacred complex. Another legend recounts how KALI became the first inhabitant of Tillai. Shiva and Kali entered a dance competition in which the loser was to be banished from Tillai. Shiva defeated the goddess by kicking his right leg high(*urdhva tandava*), a pose that modesty prohibited Kali to assume. She was banished to the northern boundaries of the town, where she is worshipped as Chamundishvari in a temple dedicated to her. Pilgrims visit this shrine at the conclusion of their journey. Later dynasties such as the Vijayanagara (14th–16th century) and the Nayaka (16th–early 18th century) also made substantial donations to the temple and extended it. In its vast precincts the temple houses shrines dedicated to a number of other deities, such as GANESHA, VISHNU, Shivakamasundari, SUBRAHMANYA, and a magnificent tank skirted by elegant colonnades. Chidambaram has been celebrated in the hymns of the three great Tamil saints, APPAR, SUNDARAR and MANIKKAVACHAKAR.

Chhaya 'shadow', personified as a goddess. Samjna, daughter of VISHVAKARMAN was married to SURYA. After the marriage, she discovered that she could not bear her husband's splendour and departed, leaving her shadow Chhaya. Eventually, Chhaya became the mother of the planet SHANI.

chinmudra, vitarkamudra or ***vyakhyanamudra***
'reflection, exposition hand pose'. A gesture in which the tip of the thumb and of the index finger are joined to form a circle, while the palm of the hand faces outwards.

Chitragupta 'Manifold-Secret'. Name of YAMA'S scribe, the god who presides over the dead. He was

born of BRAHMA and his nine sons became the progenitors of various communities of scribes. Chitragupta is depicted carrying a pen and a book in which he records the good and bad deeds of mankind.

Churning of the Ocean (*Samudramanthana*) One of the most important secondary creation myths, narrated in the MAHABHARATA and in some PURANAS. The story differs slightly from text to text. The ocean is seen as the repository of all potentialities. Only by the joint efforts of the gods and the DANAVAS was it possible to churn it, thus retrieving a number of precious objects and divine beings which would benefit mankind. The *Vishnu Purana* notes that this superhuman task only succeeded because VISHNU suggested making peace with the Danavas, and persuaded them to join the gods in this venture. As a reward for their effort, the Danavas would receive their share of AMRITA and thus become immortal. But it was not to be so. Mount MANDARA was chosen as a churning rod, the king of the NAGAS, VASUKI, coiled around it serving as a rope for the gods who held his tail, the Danavas held the head, and Vishnu in the form of a tortoise (KURMA), provided the base for the rod. Both parties took it in turns to pull Vasuki, and from the ocean emerged SURABHI, the COW of plenty, VARUNI, the goddess of wine, followed by the PARIJATA tree, the APSARAS and the moon. The deadly poison (KALAKUTA), which surfaced next, was swallowed by SHIVA at the behest of BRAHMA or, according to another version of the myth, by the *nagas*. The physician of the gods, DHANVANTARI, was the next to emerge carrying the *amrita* vessel, followed by the goddess LAKSHMI seated on a lotus. ANIMALS such as SURYA's seven-headed horse UCHCHAIHSHRAVAS and INDRA's three-headed ELEPHANT AIRAVATA and Vishnu's KAUSTUBHA GEM were also yielded by the

The Cosmic Cow worshipped by a royal figure. On her body are all the deities: the sun and moon are her eyes, various gods, goddesses and sages inhabit her body, the principal mountain ranges are shown on her feet. Nepal. Opaque watercolour on cloth, second half of the 18th century.

ocean. Once the churning operation was over, the gods and the *danavas* sat down to receive their share of *amrita*. The latter, doubting the gods' promise, were on the verge of snatching the vessel, when Vishnu transformed himself into a beautiful girl, MOHINI, who distracted them and recovered the precious vessel. The gods drank their fill of *amrita* and, reinvigorated, resumed their battle against the *danavas* and defeated them. According to the *Vishnu Purana*, the eclipse demon RAHU, managed to taste the *amrita*, before being decapitated by Vishnu.

coconut (*narikela, nalikera*). The coconut is an essential element in Hindu ritual, offered to the gods in TEMPLE and domestic worship. Fishermen offer coconut to the sea to propitiate VARUNA. In wedding ceremonies a coconut, symbol of fertility and of the goddess LAKSHMI, is placed in the opening of a pot, representing the womb. The beginning of a new activity is solemnized by breaking a coconut to ensure the blessings of the gods. Coconuts are also used as a substitute for human heads in rituals, which in the past involved human sacrifice. The coconut is high in proteins, minerals and vitamins and its water, oil, cream and flesh are used in food preparation and Ayurvedic medicine.
Patnaik, N., 1993

cosmology There are a number of theories explaining the origin of the universe. According to the most popular, the universe was created from a cosmic golden egg, HIRANYAGARBHA ('golden womb'), which floated above the waters in the darkness of non-existence. Early Hindu thought identifies it with the Cosmic Soul and later mythology with BRAHMA. Eventually, the egg split into two and heaven, the earth and the twenty-one regions of the cosmos were created. Heaven

emerged from the golden upper half of the shell and the earth from the silver lower half. MOUNTAINS and clouds were created from the inner and outer membranes respectively, the RIVERS and oceans from its veins and fluids. A number of deities joined Brahma in this act of creation. There are, however, other schools of thought, according to which the origin of the world lies in primeval matter (PRAKRITI).

The *brahmanda*, or 'egg of Brahma', contained the whole cosmos and the twenty-one worlds or regions (*loka*). These zones were divided into three main sections: paradise, subterranean regions and hell. These three regions were further subdivided into seven others, thus totalling twenty-one. Their names and descriptions vary considerably according to schools of thought and textual traditions. The *loka*, a generic term applied to the first of the three divisions, houses the paradises (SVARGA) of the various deities, as well as the earth and its atmosphere. *Tala*, 'place', comprises the chthonian regions, such as the kingdom of the NAGAS and the worlds of the ASURAS, DAITYAS, RAKSHASAS and PRETAS. The third division is the NARAKA, or hell, in which the first three sections are reserved for the childless, for those awaiting rebirth and for the evildoers. The torments of hell commence from the fourth section, culminating in the *Kakola*, a bottomless pit for those with no hope of reincarnation.

The cosmic Mount MERU, situated in the region of the various paradises, marks the centre of the universe. The rest of the world lies beneath it, arranged in seven concentric islands (*dvipa*), each forming a continent. The central island is the earth, JAMBUDVIPA ('the island of the rose-apple tree'). It is a flat circle, supported by the head of the serpent SHESHA, who in turn is supported by the tortoise Akupara, whose feet rest on four ELEPHANTS

The relief probably refers to a local legend associated with Govindaputtur village, in which a cow attained salvation by worshipping the *linga* in a local temple. The animal is surrounded by a frame of mythical beasts, culminating in a *kirtimukha*. Tamil Nadu. Granite, *c.* 800.

standing on the shell of the *brahmanda*. Aja-ekapada, whose name means 'one-footed goat', keeps earth and sky apart. The earth is separated from the other continents by an ocean of salt water. Seas of other substances, such as sugar-cane juice, wine, clarified butter, separate each island continent from the next. Finally, a large expanse of fresh water divides the seventh continent from the 'world-no-world', the darkness beyond which stretches the outer surface of the *brahmanda*.

The concept of KALPA, or 'day of Brahma', is another important principle in Indian cosmology. The world undergoes innumerable cycles of creation, fruition and destruction, each of which constitutes a single 'day of Brahma'. At the end of each day, the universe disappears in a conflagration, the 'night of Brahma'. After a period of quiescence, the whole cycle begins again. *See also* GEOGRAPHY

cow Among the various sacred ANIMALS in Hinduism, the cow occupies a prominent position. It stands for fertility, abundance and symbolizes the all-bountiful earth. Archaeological evidence points to the existence of the cult of the bull in the Harappan civilization (*c.* 3000–1700 BCE) and, while worship of the cow was less popular then, it increased markedly during the Vedic period. The cow was reputed to have been created along with BRAHMA, and every part of a cow was believed to be inhabited by a deity. The RIGVEDA expressly prohibited the slaying of milch cows, but this did not preclude the killing of bulls or cows for religious or other purposes. Textual evidence reveals the custom of sacrificing oxen and bulls to the gods and herds of one hundred bulls were apparently offered to INDRA. A share of the flesh was afterwards eaten by the person performing the sacrifice, since meat was then part of the diet. It was only in the early

centuries CE that the worship of the cow became strictly regulated and by the 4th century, killing a cow became a capital offence.

The cow and bull play a major part in Hindu mythology, as KAMADHENU and SURABHI were sacred cows, SHIVA'S bull NANDI has a following in its own right, a substantial part of the KRISHNA legend is associated with cows, cowherds and pastoral life in general, and GOLOKA, 'cow-region', is the name given to Krishna's paradise.

Everything that comes from a cow is considered sacred, including urine and dung. In rural areas, a mixture of dung and water is smeared onto hut floors as an insecticide and disinfectant. Cow dung is regularly collected and used for fuel; cow urine allegedly has medicinal qualities and is drunk after childbirth. Purification can also be achieved by bathing in cow's urine, though according to Hindu rites, the most efficacious method of purification is drinking the *panchagavya* ('the five cows'), a mixture of milk, clarified butter, curds, cow dung and cow urine. Dust raised by cows is also believed to have cleansing properties when collected and sprinkled on the body.

The ram-headed Daksha, standing with hands in *anjalimudra*. Maharashtra or Karnataka. Bronze, 18th–19th century.

daitya(s) 'descendants of DITI' and KASHYAPA. They are mentioned in post-Vedic works and are described as anti-gods or ASURAS. The *daityas* probably represent local tribes who opposed the ARYAN political and cultural influence.

dakhini(s) 'female imp, witch'. A class of semi-divine beings common to Hindu and BUDDHIST traditions. In Hindu myth they are described as eaters of raw flesh and attendants of KALI.

Daksha 'skilled, able'. There are many conflicting versions of Daksha's life. Their unifying theme seems to be his association with sacrificial rites, through which he maintained contact with the gods and thus ensured the stability and permanence of the universe. In epic and puranic literature he is represented as a RISHI, ever present through the various cycles of creation. He had fifty daughters, thirteen were married to KASHYAPA, one, Svaha, to AGNI, another, SATI, to SHIVA, and twenty-seven, identified with the lunar asterisms (*nakshatras*), to CHANDRA. One of the most famous myths celebrated in literature and ART is that of Daksha's sacrifice. Daksha organized a great sacrifice to which he invited everyone except his son-in-law Shiva. Shiva did not resent the snub, but his wife was inconsolable and in her distress, attended the sacrifice only to jump into the FIRE. In order to avenge her death, Shiva created VIRABHADRA, who destroyed the sacrifice and beheaded Daksha. Eventually, Shiva restored Daksha to life and gave him the head of a ram. *See also* BHADRAKALI

dakshina I. 'southern, right'. The auspicious side, in opposition to the inauspicious left (VAMA, which is associated with destruction, famine and death). It is customary to keep one's right side towards venerated persons, such as parents, an elder brother, a teacher and a husband. This rule is also observed in the visual arts, where female figures are generally placed to the left of the male. A TEMPLE or a sacred IMAGE is circumambulated in a clockwise direction. Offerings to the gods are given with the right hand; the left is used only if the offerings are meant for the spirits and other inauspicious beings. Symbols, such as the conch spiralling to the right and the right-handed SVASTIKA, are deemed particularly auspicious.
2. 'gift, donation'. It is customary to make a donation to the priests on completion of a ritual. This is a way of contributing to the upkeep of the BRAHMINS, who, in turn, are responsible for the stability of the cosmic order.

Dakshinamurti 'the south-facing IMAGE (of SHIVA)'. Aspect of Shiva as the supreme ascetic and teacher of knowledge (JNANA DAKSHINAMURTI), music (VINADHARA DAKSHINAMURTI), philosophy (VYAKHYANA DAKSHINAMURTI) and YOGA (YOGA DAKSHINAMURTI). He is the epitome of true knowledge and the symbol of the centripetal force that absorbs all forms and time and, for this reason, he is connected with death. He is the exemplary ascetic lost in contemplation and completely detached from the distractions of life. Images of Dakshinamurti are popular in southern India, where they are invariably found on the south wall of the TEMPLES. The deity is represented seated beneath a tree, surrounded by a number of adoring sages and wild ANIMALS listening to his words with rapt attention. The attributes that Dakshinamurti carries in his hands vary according to the four aspects mentioned above.

dalit(s) 'oppressed'. Name that the untouchables and other groups at the bottom end of the CASTE system

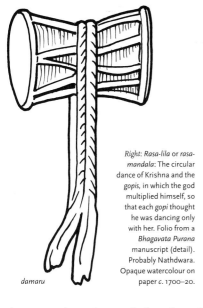

damaru

Right: Rasa-lila or *rasa-mandala*: The circular dance of Krishna and the *gopis*, in which the god multiplied himself, so that each *gopi* thought he was dancing only with her. Folio from a *Bhagavata Purana* manuscript (detail). Probably Nathdwara. Opaque watercolour on paper *c.* 1700–20.

have given themselves. *Dalits* have formed many associations, which strive to achieve a better status for their members. *See also* HARIJAN(S)

damaru Small hourglass-shaped drum carried by many deities, typical of SHIVA in his aspect as NATARAJA. In this context, the *damaru* represents the primeval sound and rhythm from which the universe emerged, and into which it will be reabsorbed. This notion of creation and dissolution is also expressed in the shape of the drum, the triangle pointing upwards represents the male creative principle (LINGA), the one pointing downwards, the female (YONI). Creation begins at the point where the two triangles meet and dissolution will occur when they are separated. *See also* TRIKONA

dana 'act of giving'. A gift or charitable donation.

danamudra 'giving gesture'. Another designation for VARADAMUDRA.

danava(s) 'descendants of DANU', one of the daughters of DITI. The *danavas*, like the DAITYAS, are mentioned in post-Vedic literature as a class of anti-gods or local tribes opposing the progressive influence of ARYAN culture and civilization.

dance According to tradition, dance originated when SHIVA danced the cosmos into being by performing his forceful TANDAVA. As a foil to this masculine dance, his consort PARVATI danced the seductive and feminine LASYA. Some scholars argue that Indian dance originated in the steps that the priests and their assistants enacted during rituals, while the MUDRAS were inspired by their gestures. The first to codify the rules of dance and dramatic performance was BHARATA in his *Natyashastra*. In this work,

Bharata lays down a set of stances, gestures, facial expressions and hand movements, conveying different moods, which are collectively known as *angika*, movements of the body, and form the basis of all classic styles of Indian dance, as well as appearing in the visual ARTS. While dance has always been highly regarded, dancers have been looked upon with suspicion, since in the past, they generally came from the lower strata of society, and dancing girls were classed along with prostitutes. In southern India BHARATA-NATYAM, for instance, was associated with the DEVADASIS (God's servants), who, apart from dancing and singing in the course of rituals, were TEMPLE prostitutes. In the northern part of the country, the bayadères, or nautch girls, were active in the Muslim courts. They specialized in an erotic dance, the *nach* (anglicized in nautch), and their notoriety proved fatal for the dancing profession, which to this day has not yet recovered its prestige. In the early decades of the 20th century, mainly through the efforts of E. Krishna Iyer, Indian dance, especially *Bharata-Natyam*, was partly rehabilitated and began to be known internationally. In the late 20th century, under the impact of the film industry and tourism, Indian dance changed, as *mudras* and expressions were simplified, and great attention paid to costumes, make-up and lighting effects.

There are four main styles of Indian dance: *Bharata-Natyam* (Tamil Nadu), KATHAK (Uttar Pradesh), KATHAKALI (a dance drama from Kerala) and *Manipuri* (Manipur). In recent decades other styles have gained in popularity, first and foremost the *Odissi* and *Chhau* from Orissa, and the *Kuchipudi*, named after a small town in Andhra, where this dance drama originally took place. There are a large number of folk dances performed on special occasions such as MARRIAGES, harvest, rains; one of the most popular is the RASA-LILA, 'play of

passion', a circular dance inspired by the loves of KRISHNA and the GOPIS. Another folk dance is the *Ram-lila*, 'the play of RAMA', which represents the victory of Rama over RAVANA.

danda 'staff, rod', symbol of power and chastisement. In the hands of KALI, it represents destructive power and the rule of force. Although a number of Hindu deities have the *danda* as their attribute, it is typical of YAMA and is occasionally seen as a form of Yama, the personified chastisement. In Hindu statecraft *danda* is one of the four principles of state management.

dandahastamudra or **gajahastamudra** 'hand-staff-gesture'. A gesture in which one arm is held stiffly across the chest.

danta 'tooth, fang, ELEPHANT tusk'. This term indicates either protruding teeth or fangs, typical of awe-inspiring deities, such as BHAIRAVA, BHADRAKALI, CHAMUNDA, etc., as well as DVARAPALAS, ghosts and demonic characters. It refers especially to one of the typical attributes of GANESHA, the broken tusk, which he carries in one hand. There are many different accounts of how he broke it: according to one, the incident happened in the course of a fight with PARASHURAMA. Tradition states that Ganesha used the tusk as a stylus when the sage VYASA dictated the MAHABHARATA to him.

Danu One of the daughters of DAKSHA, who was married to the seer KASHYAPA. From their union the DANAVAS were born.

darbha (*Saccharum cylindricum Linn.*). The most sacred of all GRASSES, *darbha* is said to have originated from the hair of VISHNU. *Darbha* is frequently tied to the TEMPLE flagstaff in southern India.

darshana 'seeing, auspicious sight, point of view'. 1. *Darshana* is the central act of Hindu worship. It refers to the moment in which the eyes of the deity, enshrined in the sanctuary and those of the devotee meet. The expression 'having *darshana*' in modern parlance may also refer to a visit to a GURU or to any influential person. 2. The term *darshana*, in its meaning as 'point of view, theory', is applied to the six systems of orthodox Hindu philosophy: *Sankhya, Yoga, Nyaya, Vaisheshika, Purva Mimamsa* and *Uttara Mimamsa* (or *Vedanta*).
Eck, D., 1985

Dasara, Dussehra or **Dussera** *see* FESTIVALS

Dasharatha '(having) ten chariots'. King of AYODHYA, father of RAMA. One of the major characters of the RAMAYANA.

dashavatara(s) 'ten incarnations'(of VISHNU). *See* AVATARA

Dasyu or **Dasu** 'barbarian'. The term designates the indigenous population of India, who were regarded by the invading ARYANS as barbarians. *Dasyu* may also mean ASURA or anti-god.

Dattatreya 'son of Atri'. 1. The son of Atri and Anasuya, a preceptor of the ASURAS. He was later identified with VISHNU and occasionally mentioned as a separate AVATARA. 2. A composite god, sometimes known as **Hari-Hara-Pitamaha**. Represented as an incarnation of the TRIMURTI (triad) consisting of HARI (Vishnu), HARA (SHIVA) and Pitamaha (BRAHMA), Dattatreya is an attempt to combine three cults in one. He is shown either as these three gods, each with their usual attributes and mounts, or as a three-headed figure – each head

Opposite: Dancers and
musicians. Frieze on the
south staircase of the so-
called Mahanavami Dibba, at
Vijayanagara, Karnataka. Granite,
end of the 14th century.

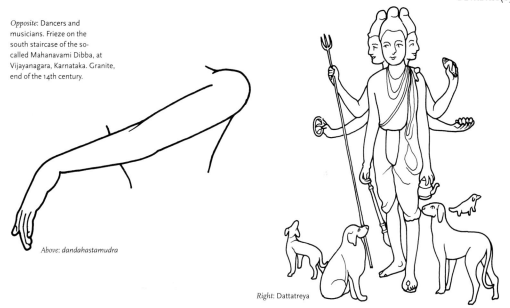

Above: dandahastamudra

Right: Dattatreya

representing one god – accompanied by four DOGS, symbolizing the VEDAS, and occasionally by a bull. The cult of Dattatreya is fairly popular in Karnataka and in Maharashtra, where he is known as Dattoba.

datura, dhattura or **dhatura** (*Datura alba* or *Datura stramonium*). The Indian thorn-apple was probably imported into the country from the West, either from Greece or the region of the Caspian Sea. It grows wild in wastelands all over India. Its fruit contains seeds that have narcotic and toxic properties. Seeds and leaves are used with extreme caution in Ayurvedic medicine to alleviate spasms, coughing fits, etc. The poisonous properties of the *datura* were well known to thieves, who used them to drug their victims, and to murderers, who poisoned their victims. However, crushed *datura* seeds, used externally, were employed as an aphrodisiac. The *datura* flower is prominently displayed in SHIVA's hair in a number of his aspects.
Patnaik, N., 1993

deva 'god, supernatural power'. The word is derived from the root *div*, 'shine', and *dyaus*, 'the bright sky', the abode of SURYA (the sun), AGNI (the fire god) and of the MARUTS (the storm gods). According to the RIGVEDA there are thirty-three gods, presiding over heaven, earth and water. In the early Vedic period there seem to have been only male gods. In the later Vedic period, under the influence of local mother-goddess cults, goddesses, such as USHAS (dawn), SARASVATI (a river-goddess also connected with music, speech and learning) and NIRRITI (the goddess of death and destruction), were included in the Vedic pantheon. To this initial core of deities, renowned heroes, PARASHURAMA, RAMACHANDRA, BALARAMA and KRISHNA, were added and they found a place among the AVATARAS of VISHNU; the same happened with a number of priests, sages and seers.

In early Vedic literature, the *devas* came from heaven and earth; later theories attributed their origin and that of their counterparts (the anti-gods) to the Creator PRAJAPATI. Vedic gods, except Agni, were mortal, though the most important among them were eventually granted immortality. The MAHABHARATA describes the *devas* as forever young; they do not sweat, blink or get dusty; their feet do not touch the ground, they have no shadow and their floral garlands never wilt. In the course of time, the relatively small Vedic pantheon increased to include a substantial number of gods and goddesses, saints and religious teachers. This process still continues, as in the cult of SANTOSHI MATA, a new goddess who became popular in the 1950s. In the last decade of the 20th century, a new god, Andaprabhu, revealed himself in a dream to a person in Chennai (Madras), who initiated a new cult.

devadasi(s) 'God's servant'. The *devadasis* were also known as 'ever-auspicious women', *nityasumangalis*, because, they were married to a deity and could therefore never be widowed. Their presence in private functions and public festivals was indispensable, as their status of *nityasumangalis* attracted luck, fertility and riches. Generally, the *devadasis* were presented to the TEMPLE by their parents, either in fulfilment of a vow, or, if the first child happened to be a girl, in the hope of obtaining a son, or simply to get rid of their daughters, as unmarried daughters were a burden for their families. This custom was officially forbidden by the Devadasi Act of January 1947. The *devadasis* usually started their training before the age of eight and were then married to a deity – or to a *pipal* tree in the temple precincts – in a ceremony that culminated in the tying of the *thali*, a special necklace worn only by married women. They were ritually deflowered by

Two *devadasis*, studio photo. Madras 1920s.

a temple priest, by a privileged person, or by sitting astride a stone LINGA. Their training in dance, music, singing and the subtle arts of seduction continued. They were responsible for keeping the temple premises clean, fanning images with fly-whisks, carrying the ARATI lights, dancing and singing, as well as serving as prostitutes. The temple authorities kept their earnings and their children were unpaid temple attendants; some of them, however, followed their mothers' training in music and dance. There was no disgrace attached to the profession of the *devadasis*; on the contrary, they had more freedom than a married woman could ever achieve, and some of them enjoyed prestigious status. When they grew old, they were dismissed from their duties to fend for themselves.
Kersenboom, S. C., 1984

Devaki Daughter of Devaka, cousin of KAMSA, king of MATHURA. Devaki married Kamsa's minister, VASUDEVA, and usurped the throne after deposing his father UGRASENA. A prediction alerted him to the fact that he was doomed to die by the hand of one of the sons of Devaki and Vasudeva, so he imprisoned the couple and had their first six children killed. By divine intervention, the seventh and eighth child, BALARAMA and KRISHNA, escaped their fate. There are a number of myths explaining this miracle: one account narrates how Balarama's embryo was transplanted into the womb of Vasudeva's second wife, and Kamsa was told that Devaki had suffered a miscarriage. At Krishna's birth, the guards fell into a deep sleep, Vasudeva's chains broke and the doors of the jail opened, allowing him to carry the baby to safety across the YAMUNA river. In due course, Krishna killed Kamsa and restored Ugrasena to the throne. In order to explain the connection between VISHNU, Krishna and Balarama, the *Vishnu* PURANA

states that Vishnu plucked a black and a white hair from his head, which eventually became the dark Krishna and the fair Balarama.

Devasena or **Devasenai** 'divine army'. Name of a goddess who is the personification of the army of the gods. Devasena is the high-caste consort of the general of the gods, KARTTIKEYA. She is generally depicted standing to the left of the god, holding a lotus flower in her right hand, her left arm hanging elegantly by her side.

devata(s) A term applied to the secondary gods and to the spirits. These are divided into village gods (GRAMADEVATAS), diseases, demons, water spirits, tree spirits, etc. Many *devatas* dwell in groups and form the retinue of a major god. Among the various groups are the GANAS of SHIVA, whose leader is GANESHA, the GUHYAKAS, followers of Kubera, the MARUTS or storm gods, who form the entourage of VAYU and INDRA. The benevolent VASUS and VIDYADHARAS belong to Indra's entourage.

devi, **Devi** 'goddess'. A generic designation for any female deity, but, more particularly, for the female energy of SHIVA, MAHADEVI or Great Goddess. Although some *devis* are mentioned in the VEDAS, they are generally seen as wives of the gods, RIVER goddesses or personifications of parts of the Vedic ritual – Ila, for instance, is associated with the specific altar at which prayers and libations were offered. The Vedic goddesses were generally benign. In the post-Vedic period, the generic term *devi* assumed a new meaning, designating the Great Goddess Devi, i.e. Shiva's cosmic energy (SHAKTI), the essence of all things. The concept of Devi developed over a long period of time, in which many local fertility and nature goddesses were absorbed

Devi and the eight mothers in the battle against the *asuras*. In the foreground, the gaunt Kali. From a manuscript of the *Devi Mahatmya*. Kangra. Opaque watercolour on paper, late 18th century.

into the Shaiva tradition to constitute Devi's many facets. Bountiful goddesses, such as Parvati and Gauri, and destructive deities, such as Durga and Kali, merged into her complex personality, but despite their different names and functions, each of them is Devi and she, in turn, represents their totality. For this reason, Devi has many contrasting aspects, on the one hand she is the caring mother, on the other she is sickness and death.

Devi Mahatmya 'glorification of the Great Goddess'. Title of a poem in seven hundred verses, probably composed in the 8th century. It celebrates the victories of Devi over various asuras and is recited daily by her devotees. The *Devi Mahatmya*, also known as *Chandipatha*, is embedded in the *Markandeya* Purana, a 9th–10th century work attributed to the mythical sage Markandeya. Coburn, T. B, 1984

dhama 'abode'. The embodiment of the divine, the location of divine power in a particular place. There are four such sites in India: in the Himalayas the Vaishnava site of Badrinath, connected to the great sages Nara and Narayana; in the far south of Tamil Nadu, Rameswaram, the spot where Rama built the bridge to Lanka with the help of his allies, the vanaras and the Bears; in the west, Dwarka in Gujarat, the capital of Krishna; and Puri in Orissa, on the coast of the Bay of Bengal, sacred to Jagannatha, an aspect of Krishna.

Dhana-Lakshmi 'wealth-Lakshmi'. An aspect of the goddess Lakshmi as bestower of wealth.

dhanus 'bow'. The bow, arrows and breastplate were the typical accoutrements of a warrior and *dhanus* was a symbol of royalty. *Dhanus* and the arrow

(bana) are associated with a number of deities, but are typical of Rama and of the god of love, Kama. Occasionally, bows were personified: Shiva's bow was named Ajagava, 'made of horn', or Pinaka, 'staff'; the two bows of Vishnu were Sharanga, 'made of horn', and Chapa, 'bow'; the bow of Arjuna was Gandiva, 'made of (rhinoceros) horn'. The bow of Kama was made of sugar cane, its string a row of bees, and its arrows five flowers, symbolizing the five senses. Archery was one of the main skills a prince was expected to master. The *Dhanurveda*, a treatise on archery, formed one of the auxiliary branches of learning (Upavedas) appended to the Vedic tradition.

Dhanvantari 'moving in a curve, or arrow moving'. Dhanvantari was the physician of the gods, the first authority on Ayurveda. He is said to have emerged in the course of the Churning of the Ocean, carrying in his hands a bowl containing Amrita, the nectar of immortality.

Dharani 'earth'. Name of the personification of the earth, reputed to be an incarnation of Lakshmi.

***dharma*, Dharma** 'law, custom, moral and religious duty'. 1. The totality of rules that form and uphold law and custom. Treatises, such as the *Dharmasutras* and *Dharmashastras*, regard *dharma* as the cohesive force that holds the community together. At an individual level, *dharma* is the performance of one's duty according to the rules of the caste into which one is born. 2. One of the four aims of life or purusharthas. 3. Name of a mythical sage, believed to be one of the mind-born sons of Brahma. He was married to ten (or thirteen) daughters of Daksha. Their numerous children personify the various moral and religious duties implied in the concept *dharma*. *See also* ethics

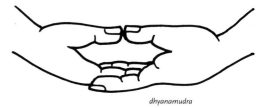

dhyanamudra

Dharmaraja 'king of justice'. An epithet of YAMA. He carries a club, symbolizing time and death, and a noose. Two large fangs protrude from his mouth and his mount is a black buffalo, representing death.

Dhritarashtra 'whose empire is firm'. The blind king of the KAURAVAS, son of VYASA and AMBIKA, one of the major characters in the MAHABHARATA. He married GANDHARI, who bore him one hundred sons, the eldest of which was DURYODHANA. When Dhritarashtra abdicated, his successor Duryodhana led the war against the PANDAVAS.

Dhruva 'firm, fixed, constant'. The Pole star, also known as *grahadhara*, 'pivot of the planets', because it is believed that all planets are bound to it by aerial cords. In VAISHNAVA tradition, Dhruva is believed to be a minor aspect of VISHNU, and is called Dhruva-Narayana. In the MARRIAGE ceremony, Dhruva represents the firmness of character and constancy that a bride is expected to have.

dhruvabhera or *mulavigraha* 'fixed or root IMAGE'. A large icon, permanently kept in a TEMPLE or shrine.

dhvaja 'banner, flag'. The flag on which the emblem or the mount of the deity associated with it, is placed. The *dhvaja* is one of the eight auspicious objects (ASHTAMANGALA). In TEMPLES, a flagstaff (*dhvajastambha*) is placed opposite the entrance to the main shrine, on an axis with the central IMAGE. If it is placed inside the temple, it must pass through the roof, to suggest its infinite height. Generally built of wood, it is encased in sheets of copper or gold and decorated with DARBHA grass. It is an object of great importance and worship. The flag-hoisting ceremony, held on the occasion of special religious FESTIVALS, is celebrated with great solemnity.

dhyana 'meditation'. Mental contemplation, concentrated attention, visualization of an IMAGE.

dhyanamudra 'gesture of meditation', in which the person is seated with both hands resting on his lap, the right hand over the left, with palms turned upwards and extended fingers. It signifies intense concentration focused on a single object of meditation. BUDDHIST and JAINA images are often shown in *dhyanamudra*.

diet A number of items in Indian diet have remained unchanged since ancient times. There is evidence suggesting the cultivation of a number of vegetables and fruit, such as aubergine, pumpkin, COCONUT, banana, lemon and watermelon, and spices, such as turmeric (HARIDRA) ginger, sugar cane, areca nut (BETEL). Small fish were salted and dried. Milk and dairy products were as popular then as they are now. The invading ARYANS, unfamiliar with the local products, brought with them different dietary habits: a love of good food, intoxicating drinks, meat and fish. In the Vedic age, literary evidence shows that buffaloes, bulls and other bovine ANIMALS, including COWS, were slaughtered and that their meat was consumed by everyone, including BRAHMINS. In the epics there are numerous references to contemporary dietary habits. Meat, venison and fowl were regularly served, either curried or roasted. The dietary prescriptions laid down in the 'Laws of MANU' (*Manavadharmashastra*), compiled by authors belonging to different schools of thought, between *c.* 600 BCE and 300 CE, are contradictory. On the one hand there is open condemnation of all persons involved in the slaughter of animals for food, from the slaughterer to the consumer, and on the other hand, for certain occasions, consuming beef is made mandatory, as is drinking liquor.

Sugar cane on sale in rural Tamil Nadu.

Horrible punishments, such as being reborn as an animal twenty-nine times, awaited those who dared infringe this injunction. In the Mauryan period (*c.* 321–181 BCE), the sale of meat was controlled by the official Superintendent of Slaughterhouses. Thousands of animals were slaughtered daily for the kitchens of the emperor Ashoka (*c.* 268–233 BCE), though after his conversion to BUDDHISM the number was limited to one deer and two peacocks.

The authorities writing on Ayurvedic medicine recommended various types of meat, depending on the qualities (GUNAS) believed to be in the food, and on the ailment to be cured. The tonic and aphrodisiac properties of certain meats, such as rhinoceros, were praised by the authors of treatises on EROTICS. Different kinds of flesh were prescribed for the cure of sexual diseases and impotence. In the latter case, a bull's testicles, preferably underdone, were the paramount remedy. Some antinomian religious movements, such as the KAPALIKAS, are renowned for their unorthodox dietary habits, which allegedly included cannibalism and the eating of ordure.

Under the influence of Buddhism and JAINISM, the vegetarian diet common before the Aryan invasion, gained ground. Fa-hien, the Chinese pilgrim who visited India in the early 5th century CE, reports that the upper classes had abandoned eating meat. Despite the dietary habits that vary from region to region, Hindus do not generally eat beef. From the beginning of the common era, the slaughtering and eating of cows has been a major offence. Kashmiri BRAHMINS eat mutton and fish is eaten by the Brahmins in Bengal and Orissa (it is deemed to be 'a vegetable of the sea'). KSHATRIYAS eat all kinds of meat except beef. Southern Indian Brahmins, the strictest of all, eat only vegetables.

The art of cooking was always highly appreciated, though the ancient treatises on *paka-vidya*, 'cooking

knowledge', or *supa-shastra*, 'soup-scripture', have not survived. More recent works, including Mangarasa III's *Supa-shastra*, a Kannada work of the early 16th century, provides an insight into the southern Indian Jaina food tradition. It was not uncommon for heroes and kings to practise the art of cooking, two main examples being BHIMA and NALA. Under Muslim influence, a number of new ways of preparing food were introduced into India. There were also new methods of cooking, as in the use of clay ovens (*tanduri*) or skewers (*kebab*). Among the seasonings were asafoetida (*hing*), cumin (*jiraka*), relishes (*chatni*) and finally the subtle *pilaus*. The European influence on Indian cooking began with the advent of the Portuguese in 1498. Gradually, plants from the New World, such as potatoes, tomatoes, papayas and, above all, chillies, were imported into India and these became so well integrated that Indian food without them is unthinkable.

Further rules govern meal times: the AYURVEDA prescribes one meal in the morning and one in the evening. Food should be prepared by a Brahmin cook, using the appropriate utensils and ingredients; it should never be prepared by a woman during her menses, nor by an individual of a lower class than that of the person who eats it. Furthermore, there are endless details touching on where to eat, ideally facing the East, and sitting on a freshly swept floor smeared with cow dung. There are rules governing the manner of eating, for instance, food should be eaten only with the right hand (with three or more fingers, according to regional custom) and the morsel should be chewed thirty-six times. One should not eat either from wood, porcelain or ceramic plates, since these materials absorb impurities, but from leaves. In orthodox southern Indian houses and public eating places, meals are served on a freshly plucked banana

Dipa-Lakshmi on elephant.
Karnataka. Brass, 18th century.

leaf or on metal crockery. Drinks should be directly poured into the mouth without touching the glass. If an unbaked earthen cup is used, this should be broken immediately when finished with. The rules of commensality are spelled out in even greater detail: among the individuals recommended as eating companions are Vedic scholars and wealthy benefactors, but it is inadvisable to eat in the company of actors, musicians and lepers. As a rule, women eat after the men and a wife is allowed to eat the food left over by her husband, but not the other way round. Couples are not supposed to eat together and the wife is expected to serve her husband and male relatives. Cooked food is easily defiled: the accidental touch of a foot or a garment hem, the presence of a DOG, and in the past, the shadow of a low-CASTE person falling on the food, are enough for it to be discarded. The same applies if anything else accidentally drops into a plate. Leftovers are generally fed to animals and BIRDS. Dining etiquette and the way in which the various items are served are matters that differ according to region, religious group and caste. Further guidlines are given for rinsing the mouth after eating, belching and breaking wind, both of which should happen after the meal, ideally when standing up to rinse the mouth.

Achaya, K. T., 1994
Prakash, O., 1961

Digambara(s) 'sky-clad', i.e. naked. One of the two main sects into which JAINISM is divided: the Digambaras, 'the sky-clad', and the Shvetambaras, 'the white-robed'. The Digambaras are renowned for their extreme asceticism.

diggaja or *dinnaga* 'ELEPHANT of (a quarter) of the sky'. Designates the elephant that accompanies a DIKPALA, a guardian of one of the eight directions.

Since the eight guardians (ASHTADIKPALAS) have other duties to perform, they have as helpers the eight *diggajas* and their female counterparts.

dikpala(s) *see* ASHTADIKPALA(S)

diksha 'consecration, initiation, dedication'. Initiation ritual of which there are many in Hinduism. *Diksha* is a means not only to sanctify the body, eliminating sin in this life, but also to ease the transmigration process (SAMSARA) after death.

dipa 'lamp, light'. Lights play an important part in Hindu rituals. In the course of time they became associated with the goddess LAKSHMI. A special type of lamp, *dipa-lakshmi*, shows the goddess standing and holding a lamp with one wick. Another kind of circular lamp, which was designed to be placed in a niche, is provided with a back piece, on which are shown the images either of Lakshmi or GAJA-LAKSHMI. Lamps with five wicks are used in SHAIVA worship, since five is the number sacred to SHIVA. Another design of lamp, resembling a tree, is called *dipavriksha*, or 'tree of lamps'.

Diti 'limited'. A Vedic goddess, mother of the ASURAS and the sister of ADITI. When INDRA vanquished and killed the *asuras*, Diti resolved to take revenge by producing a child even more powerful than him. Indra, however, divining her plan, entered her womb and with his thunderbolt, the VAJRA, cut the embryo into forty-nine pieces, which eventually became the storm gods (MARUTS).

Divali or *Dipavali* *see* FESTIVALS

divination Divination has been practised in India from time immemorial. Prognostications were

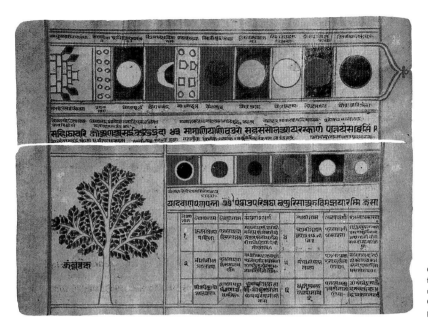

Cosmological charts from an illustrated Jaina manuscript. Gujarat. Opaque watercolour on paper, 16th century.

made in a variety of ways, the most common being the observation of atmospheric phenomena, such as lightning and rain or, during sacrificial ceremonies, the direction of the smoke rising from the altar. Other popular ways of reading the future were to observe the flight and cries of BIRDS, especially the crow and the mynah, or the behaviour and chirping of the gecko. Dreams are one of the most ancient sources of divination, whereas palmistry, one of the favoured divination methods at present, is comparatively recent. However, astrology (JYOTISHA) is by far the most widespread.

Based on the notion that stars, constellations and planets exert a major influence on the lives of individuals, horoscopes are drawn up at birth and are regarded as official documents, not unlike Western birth certificates. They are consulted on occasions such as MARRIAGE, before building a house, going on a journey, concluding important business transactions, etc. It is of paramount importance to know which are the favourable and unfavourable times to start any undertaking. The period between the winter and the summer solstice, *uttarayana*, and the bright half of the month, when the moon waxes, are regarded as favourable. Similarly, the day in which the sun enters a new constellation, especially solstices and equinoxes, and Mondays, Wednesdays, Thursdays and Fridays (except for some hours that can be calculated according to the birth stars of the individual in question), are on the whole good. The same applies to FESTIVAL times, such as *Dasara*, *Divali* and *Nagapanchami*. Decidedly inauspicious are the months between the summer and winter solstices (*dakshinayana*), the dark half of the month when the moon wanes, Sundays, Tuesdays and Saturdays, the four months of the rainy season (*chaturmasa*) and the first day of any month. There is a legend,

according to which AGASTYA set out on a journey to the South on the first day of the month and never returned. A number of additional factors, such as the conjunction of the planets and the lunar mansions, also influence the calculation of auspicious and inauspicious times. There is, however, a minimum period during which the stars can influence either a person or an undertaking, the MUHURTA, which lasts forty-eight minutes. In this period, which can be exactly calculated for each individual, the influence of the stars is at its peak. In the case of a wedding, the crucial rites of the ceremony have to be completed within the *muhurta*, in order to ensure maximum benefit. Conversely, in case of an inauspicious *muhurta*, action must be avoided at all costs within that time. The influence of a planet on the life of an individual lasts a given number of years. Thus the influence of SURYA, the sun (responsible for wealth and success), is of six years; that of CHANDRA, the moon (for mysticism, philosophy, asceticism), is of fifteen years. However, the influence of astral bodies on individuals is determined by their interaction, rather than by a single planet.

Divya Prabhanda *see* NALAYIRA DIVYA PRABHANDAM

Dnyadeo *see* JNANADEVA

dog (*shvan*) In modern India, dogs are considered to be among the most impure ANIMALS, but this was not so in pre-Vedic times. In ancient Indian literature the dog plays a prominent role. The bitch of INDRA, Sarama, is mentioned in the RIGVEDA and its offspring became the watchdogs of YAMA, the lord of the underworld. It is customary in some parts of India to worship them, to prevent them from disrupting the FUNERAL RITES. At the conclusion of

the MAHABHARATA, YUDHISHTHIRA, the last of the
PANDAVAS, refuses to enter heaven (SVARGA) if his
dog cannot accompany him. They both enter and
the dog reveals itself to be none other than Yama,
Yudhisthira's father, who put his son through this
final test. Dogs are associated with a number of
deities: RUDRA, called *Shvapati*, 'Lord of the Dog',
NIRRITI and VIRABHADRA. In some parts of
Maharashtra the dog is revered as the attendant of
SHIVA in his aspect as BHAIRAVA. More importantly,
dogs are said to be the attendants of the god
KHANDOBA, whose epithets include *Shvashva*, 'he
who has a dog as a horse'. Mendicants dress up as
dogs, and are honoured and ceremonially fed at the
yearly festival of the deity. The god DATTATREYA is
shown accompanied by four dogs, symbolizing
the four VEDAS. *See also* ANIMALS

Draupadi One of the main characters of the
MAHABHARATA, the daughter of Drupada, king of
the Panchalas, who had settled in the area around
Bareilly and Farrukhabad in Uttar Pradesh. Her
beauty and accomplishments attracted many suitors
from all over the country, so Drupada decided to
hold a SVAYAMVARA for her to select a husband. The
prospective groom had to undergo a test, which was
to shoot a revolving device in the shape of a fish
(*matsyayantra*) which was mounted on a tall pole.
Some accounts state that the target was to be aimed
at by looking at its reflection in a vat of boiling water,
but there are numerous embellishments on this
theme. Among the contestants were KRISHNA, his
brother BALARAMA and the five PANDAVAS, who were
present incognito. Eventually, ARJUNA, the third of
the Pandava princes came forward, effortlessly
stringed the unwieldy bow and hit the *matsyayantra*.
Both Drupada, who had recognized the five
Pandavas, and Draupadi, who was secretly hoping to

win such a distinguished husband, were overjoyed
and Draupadi threw the floral garland around the
neck of her future husband. The Pandavas then
started deliberating on who should have Draupadi as
wife and, while the matter was still being discussed,
they reached home. When they saw their mother
KUNTI, they reported that they had obtained a great
gift. She replied that they should share it as brothers.
These innocent but fatal words were taken literally
by her sons, and thus Draupadi became the common
wife of the Pandavas. It was decided that she would
stay two days in the house of each husband, during
which time the others were not to disturb her, on
pain of twelve years of exile. Arjuna inadvertently
broke this rule and was forced into exile. He was
doubtless Draupadi's favoured husband and when
he married Krishna's sister Subhadra, she suffered
pangs of jealousy. When YUDHISTHIRA, one of the
Pandavas, lost the game of dice against the
KAURAVAS, sending the five Pandavas into exile, she
went with them. Many adventures befell her during
that period, particularly when at the court of Virata,
Draupadi and her husbands were spending the last
year of exile in disguise. Her five sons died in the
great battle at KURUKSHETRA. At the end of the
Mahabharata story, the Pandavas renounced the
world and she followed them grudgingly, but was
the first to succumb to the hardships of the journey
to the Himalayas.

Passionate and vengeful, uninhibited and proud,
Draupadi is one of the great figures of Hindu legend.
In some parts of India, especially Tamil Nadu, she is
a goddess in her own right, an embodiment of the
Great Goddess. A number of TEMPLES are dedicated
to her and a complex cult has developed around this
intriguing figure. Some of her other names are
Krishna, 'dark' in complexion, Panchali, 'descendant
of the Panchalas', Panchami, 'having five husbands'

Opposite: The disrobing of Draupadi before the
assembled Kauravas and the five Pandavas.
Mahabharata manuscript dated 1669,
Srirangapatna, Karnataka. Opaque
watercolour on paper.

and Sairindhri, 'the maidservant'. The last name
refers to her year in disguise at the court of Virata.
Hiltebeitel, A., 1988

Dravida Name for the population of non-ARYAN
Indians, originally of Mediterranean origin, who
entered India from the west and north-west, at least
a millennium before the Aryans. They spread
through the country, first along the INDUS, then to
the Vindhya MOUNTAINS, and finally to the southern
part of the subcontinent. The proto-Dravidians are
believed to be the originators of the Harappan
civilization (*c.* 3000–1700 BCE) with its remarkable
social and political systems. Their religion had a
deeper impact on Hindu culture than that of the
Aryans. Once established in the south of India, the
Dravidians founded a number of kingdoms, which
had trade contacts with Egypt, Greece and later
Rome. They exported ivory, spices, GEMS, textiles –
especially silk and muslin – and other luxury items.
The main Dravidian languages are Tamil, spoken
mainly in Tamil Nadu, Telugu in Andhra, Kannada
in Karnataka and Malayalam in Kerala.

drinks Although the indigenous people of ancient
Indian drank liquor and offered it to their gods,
the drinks imported by the ARYANS in the second
millennium BCE played a major role in Indian
mythology and literature. One of them is the
intoxicating milky nectar of immortality, AMRITA.
Tradition states that the cosmic sea was made of
amrita and gods and ASURAS churned it searching
for its essence. SOMA is an intoxicating drink, highly
spoken of in the RIGVEDA, which was probably made
from a mushroom with hallucinogenic properties.
The VEDAS mention that the *sura*, made from barley
or rice flour and molasses, was drunk during Vedic
rituals, especially those connected with fertility. *Sura*

then became a synonym for strong drink, frowned
upon by the lawgivers. BRAHMINS and students in
particular were prohibited from drinking liquor;
KSHATRIYAS and VAISHYAS were allowed spirits
provided they were not produced by distillation of
fermented flour. In the ARTHASHASTRA mention is
made of government distilleries and of the
appointment of a Superintendent of Liquor to
control its production and sale.

Indian literature mentions around thirty different
drinks made from a wide variety of ingredients, such
as tree bark, mango juice, flowers, sugar-cane juice
and wine made from grapes imported from
Afghanistan. Attitudes to alcohol are ambivalent: on
the one hand the scriptures condemn drinking, on
the other, the very same texts recommend it for on
certain occasions – drinks should be served to guests
at a house warming party, offered to a bride, when
she arrives at her husband's home, and to women
who dance at weddings. When ill, BUDDHIST monks
were permitted to drink wine; JAINA monks, however,
could not live on premises where wine was stored.
Both the RAMAYANA and MAHABHARATA contain
vivid descriptions of drinking parties, such as the one
for YUDHISHTHIRA'S ASHVAMEDHA, and a drunken
brawl is, eventually, the end of the YADAVAS. There
are numerous references to drinking by both men
and women in the ART and literature of northern and
southern India: in the *Kuttani-Mata* (Lessons of a
Bawd) by Damodara Gupta (8th century), liquor is
said to enhance the charm of a woman, the colour of
her complexion and her amorous disposition.
Achaya, K. T., 1994

drugs From time immemorial various narcotic
substances have been used in India for religious
and other purposes. BHANG (*Cannabis sativa*), a
drink made of *cannabis* leaves, is associated with

Bracket figure: four-armed Durga standing, rather than riding on the lion. Her awesome character is emphasized by her fierce countenance and resolute stance. Kerala. Wood, 18th century.

SHIVA. In some TEMPLES dedicated to him, such as the Lingaraja at Bhubaneshvar in Orissa, the main IMAGE is lustrated with milk, water and a mixture of *bhang*. It is one of the most popular Indian drugs, along with *hashish*, *ganja* and *charas*, which are obtained, respectively, from the stalks and filaments, the leaves and the resin of the *Cannabis indica* plant. In the 14th century, opium was introduced into India, possibly from Persia. An infusion of poppy seeds mixed with other ingredients (*post*, *posta*) was a common method to drug and finally kill a person. There are references to the liberal use of drugs among army personnel: *ganja* was traditionally smoked by the KSHATRIYAS and a number of other drugs were taken by troops, or fed to the ELEPHANTS before an attack. Drugs assisted SADHUS and ascetics, such as the NATHAS, SIDDHAS and followers of Tantric sects, in their search for mystical enlightenment, and were also used as stimulants in occult practices involving sex.

The smoking of fragrant barks and spices is mentioned in post-Vedic literature, though it is difficult to establish exactly when the habit started. Medical treatises describe a number of different types of *dhuma-varti* ('smoke-roll', cigar), which were inhaled for therapeutic purposes. The *Sushruta-Samhita*, a work dating from around 4th century CE, recommends smoking to soothe the nervous system and cure coughs, asthma, headaches and other ailments. Perfumed cigars were generally smoked after meals. Smoking habits completely changed when tobacco was introduced by the Portuguese around 1600. The old style of smoking, taking only three puffs at a time and inhaling the smoke, was abandoned, except for smoking drugs. The *cheroot*, a cigar with open ends, became fashionable, but it was the *huqqa* (hookah, water pipe or hubble-bubble), with its long flexible tube, its *chilam* containing the

finely cut tobacco kneaded with molasses and its charcoal balls, that was most appreciated, both by the British 'nabobs' and by Indians.
Prakash, O., 1961

Durga 'inaccessible'. One of the aspects of DEVI, Durga is a deity in which various village goddesses and supernatural beings connected to forests and MOUNTAINS eventually coalesced. This process of assimilation commenced *c.* 900 BCE, and culminated in Durga becoming the supreme goddess, known by many names, and SHIVA'S SHAKTI. Ambivalent in character, she is both the sustainer and destroyer of men and nature. Early folk religion influenced the formation of Durga and a connection exists with other goddesses, including 'mother goddesses' (UMA, PARVATI), fertility goddesses (ADITI, SARASVATI) and the village goddesses worshipped in southern India today. In the epics and the PURANAS, Durga is described as a female warrior, the destroyer of the ASURAS, the most famous of which is the buffalo demon Mahishasura. In her fierce aspect she is the all-devouring KALI and in her bountiful aspect she is Shakambari, the nourisher of herbs, worshipped in the *navapatrika* or 'nine plants' ceremony, which commemorates her ties with vegetation. Her connection with the mountains is apparent in two of her epithets, Vidhyavasini, 'dweller of the Vindhyas', and PARVATI, 'daughter of the mountain', i.e. the Himalayas. Her village goddess origin is apparent in the ANIMAL sacrifices that take place in a number of TEMPLES, including the famous KALIGHAT temple in Calcutta, where hundreds of goats are slaughtered in her honour on the occasion of the *Durgapuja* in the autumn. Until 1835, when the British Government suppressed human sacrifice, a boy was sacrificed every Friday before her altar. Durga is also known as

Armed with a *trishula*, this Shaiva *dvarapala* guards the entrance to Cave 1. Badami, Karnataka. Sandstone, 6th century.

YOGINI, chief of the *yoginis*, sixty-four goddesses with mystical and magical powers, whom she created to assist her and Shiva.

Durgapuja see FESTIVALS

Duryodhana 'tough fighter'. Eldest among the one hundred sons of the Kaurava king, DHRITARASHTRA. His birth was accompanied by ominous portents, which foreshadowed his tragic and tormented life. As was customary among princes, he was trained in the martial arts, his favourite weapon being the club. In his youth, he developed a bitter rivalry with his cousin BHIMA, also a master of the club, and on one occasion tried to poison and drown him in the Ganges. Bhima survived, but the bitter jealousy came to the fore when the old king Dhritarashtra appointed Duryodhana's cousin YUDHISHTHIRA as heir apparent. Eventually, Duryodhana persuaded the old king to banish his cousins, the PANDAVAS, to the city of Varanavata, where he later tried to kill them in an arson attack. Forewarned, the Pandavas survived unscathed and retired to the forest under the guise of BRAHMINS. The reappearance of the Pandavas at DRAUPADI'S SVAYAMVARA and their growing glory further incensed Duryodhana, who challenged Yudhishthira to a game of dice. Duryodhana won the game with the help of his uncle Shakuni, who had loaded the dice, and as a result, Yudhishthira lost his kingdom, his wealth, his brothers, his wife Draupadi, who was publicly humiliated, and his freedom. A second match, which Yudhishthira undertook in the hope of regaining his fortune, was just as disastrous: the Pandavas were exiled for thirteen years. Once this was over, Duryodhana turned down the Pandavas' proposal to restore half their kingdom and, during the ensuing war, he was slain by his arch-rival Bhima.

Dussehra or *Dussera see* FESTIVALS

Dvaita 'duality'. School of thought founded by MADHVA (12th–13th century), in which God is the supreme cause of the world, yet essentially different from the human soul.

dvapara 1. The second of the four ages of the world. *See* YUGA(S). 2. 'uncertain', the side of the dice marked with two dots.

dvarapala(s) or *dvarapalaka(s)* 'door guardians' placed at the entrance of every TEMPLE, shrine or sacred precinct. Two- or four-handed, they carry in their hands the emblem of the deity enshrined in the sanctuary. Their countenance may be fierce and occasionally fangs protrude from their mouths. Temples dedicated to goddesses have female guardians, the *dvarapalikas*.

dvibhanga 'twofold, bent'. A graceful stance, in which the body is slightly bent sideways.

dvipa 'island'. *See* COSMOLOGY

Dwarka or **Dvarka** 'many-gated'. One of the seven holy cities of India and one of the four DHAMAS. Situated at the north-western tip of the Saurashtra peninsula, overlooking the Arabian Sea, Dwarka is believed to have been the capital of KRISHNA, who settled there with his followers after escaping from the wrath of Jarasandha at MATHURA. On Krishna's death, the whole city, except the temple, disappeared underwater. Thousands of pilgrims visit Dwarka each year, especially on the occasion of Krishna's birthday, *Divali* and *Holi*.

Temple elephant in the Adi Kumbeshvara temple, Kumbakonam, Tamil Nadu. The animal displays on its forehead the syllable *om* in Tamil script.

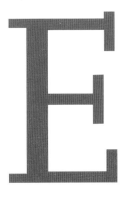

eclipse *see* RAHU

Ekashriga *see* RISHYASHRINGA

elements According to the major schools of Indian thought, the material universe is constituted by five *mahabhutas*, or great elements. These are earth (PRITHVI), water (*apas*), air (VAYU), fire (AGNI) and space or ether (*akasha*).

elephant (*gaja* is the usual term used in the epics and later literature). Symbol of fertility, strength, wisdom and royalty, the elephant is one of the most prominent ANIMALS in BUDDHIST, JAINA and Hindu mythology. Representations of elephants have been found on seals dating from *c.* 3000 to 1700 BCE excavated at Mohenjo Daro and Harappa. By then the elephant had evidently been tamed and was used in times of peace and probably war, although there are no explicit references to the use of elephants in the VEDAS. However, from the reports of the Greek historian Megasthenes (4th–3rd century BCE), it seems that the use of elephants in battle was common.

According to legend, the future BUDDHA descended into the womb of his mother in the shape of a small, six-tusked, white elephant. Each of the mothers of the twenty-four Jaina prophets dreamed of fourteen auspicious objects, among which was an elephant. The elephant-headed GANESHA has been one of the most revered deities of the Hindu pantheon from at least the beginning of the common era. The elephant is also the vehicle (VAHANA) of a number of deities, such as AIYANAR, BALARAMA and, occasionally, SKANDA, and is also one of the seven jewels of the universal ruler (CHAKRAVARTIN). The prototype of all elephants is AIRAVATA, the four-tusked elephant of INDRA, whose name is derived from the word *iravat*, 'possessing moisture', which it draws from the depths of the underworld. It is believed to have emerged from the CHURNING OF THE OCEAN and rain is said to fall when Indra is riding Airavata. According to another account, BRAHMA gathered the two halves of an eggshell that were left after GARUDA had hatched, and recited seven sacred MANTRAS over them. Airavata and a further seven male elephants were born from the half held in the god's right hand, while their female counterparts appeared from that in the left. The eight pairs, all of them white with four tusks, became the DIGGAJAS, the elephants watching over the eight directions of space and supporting the earth. At that time, all elephants had wings and could change their form at will; this explains the connection between elephants and clouds. However, according to legend, some elephants, eager to listen to the words of the sage Dirghatamas, alighted on the branch of a tree, which broke, killing a number of the sage's disciples. He cursed the elephants and they lost their wings and their ability to change shape. The white elephant still maintains the connection with clouds, representing the clouds heavy with rain, which bring water, fertility and abundance. For this reason, it is regarded as particularly auspicious. White elephants are cared for, do not work, and are the exclusive property of rulers. The high esteem in which they are held in Thailand probably has its origin in the worship of Airavata. Richly caparisoned animals with painted eyes, trunks and legs are still used in state or TEMPLE processions, such as the Mysore royal *Dasara* and the Puram FESTIVAL held at Thrissur (Kerala).

The training of elephants remains a special skill. The *mahouts*, or elephant keepers, belong to a specific class whose particular skill lies in capturing,

Krishna and Radha, the lovers par excellence, in an intimate embrace. Orissa. Opaque watercolour on paper, 18th century.

taming and training the animals. Traditionally, a *mahout* was able to choose the best elephants for training them to work, hunt and fight in battle, including breaking down palisades, trampling men and horses, breaking through the gates of a fortress, etc. There are numerous treatises on the training and care of elephants. Among the most renowned are Palakapya's *Hastayurveda*, on how to keep elephants in good health, and Nilakantha's *Matangalila*. Other words for elephant include *hastinmriga*, 'animal with a hand', or *hastin*, 'hand', refer to its trunk. Another common name is *matanga*, 'roaming at will'.

era In ancient India dates were calculated according to the reigning years of the current king. In the 1st century BCE a new method of dating was introduced under the rule of foreigners, the Scythians, Parthians, Kushanas and Bactrians, all of whom had migrated to India between the early centuries BCE and CE, and remained in the north-western parts of the subcontinent. The two most important eras are the Vikrama and Shaka samvat (era). The Vikrama Samvat, commenced in 58 BCE and was reputedly introduced by the Parthian king Vonones on his accession. Imported from Parthia into India, it was first employed by the Malavas, who settled in the region of UJJAIN and became associated with the celebrated king of Ujjain, Vikramaditya. Therefore it was known as Vikrama Samvat. The Shaka era probably commenced on the accession of the Kushana King Kadphises II in 78 CE. It was used in western India long after the decline of Kushana rule, and was eventually adopted throughout the north and the Deccan. Among the most important subsequent Indian eras were the Gupta era, from 320 CE, the date of the foundation of the dynasty by Chandragupta I, the Harsha era, established by

King Harsha of Kanauj in 606 CE, the Kollam (Quilon) era of Kerala, established by the chief of Venad 824–25 CE, when this town became his headquarters, and the Lakshmana era, founded by Lakshmanasena of Bengal in 1119.

erotics Kama, or erotics, is the subject of numerous and detailed treatises (*kamashastras*). In them, love is intended mostly as sensual pleasure in all its facets and has been explored with amazing scientific rigour. The general notion is that intercourse has to be performed for the following reasons: to beget children (taking place between husband and wife), for pleasure (with a courtesan or an experienced woman), to humiliate another man (when committing adultery with his wife) and for occult purposes (in TANTRISM or other antinomian sects). The main concern of the *kamashastras* is the satisfaction of the senses and the methods for achieving this.

The treatises take great pains to classify, with remarkable acumen, the various kinds of *shringara* (sensual love) of men and women, listing their physical and psychical characteristics and preferences at the time of sexual congress. Techniques of seduction are carefully detailed, beginning with the first approaches and courtship and culminating in consummation. Among the various topics considered at length is the choice of a go-between, such as a BRAHMIN, servant, gardener, nurse, widow or nun, for conveying messages and presents and arranging trysts. There were various methods of remunerating the go-between: men received cash and women were sometimes offered remuneration in kind, i.e. sexual favours. The position of the planets, the seasons, the day of the month, the couples' horoscopes, all played a pivotal part in establishing a suitable date for

Opposite: Frieze of erotic scenes on the lower storey of the newly refurbished *gopura* of the Sarangapani temple, Kumbakonam, Tamil Nadu. Concrete and colours, *c*. 2000.

consummation, but, needless to say, there was usually room for compromise: a lover could dispense with all astronomical calculations if his impatience was too great. The meeting place is also discussed in detail (a bedroom in a private house is considered the best option) and helpful hints are offered on décor, ambience, the size of the bed, music, etc. The actual encounter is subject to strict etiquette. Male lovers are instructed on how to talk to women, make them feel at ease, caress them, disrobe them and arouse their passion and on how to make love to them according to their status and degree of experience. These instructions indicate which topics of conversation to employ, the type of love games to play, and how to bring the encounter to a close (lovers are expected not to glance at each other, to use different rooms for their ablutions; however, once bathed and dressed again, they may sit together, eat and drink, and converse pleasantly). If they want to rest, this should take place in separate beds.

Most of the treatises also describe less orthodox practices, such as oral sex, multiple sex, homosexuality, bestiality and flagellation, as well as offering advice on eunuchs and courtesans, remedies for impotence and on more abstruse topics, including the magical properties of semen, YOGA and metaphysics. Kissing is one of the topics discussed in great detail, especially by VATSYAYANA in his KAMASUTRA. Another theme that fascinated the writers was the 'love combat' (*prahanana*), a subtle form of lovemaking, in which advances, retreats, skirmishes, assaults and defences stimulate desire. In the course of the combat, lovers may scratch, bite, pull their partner's hair, punch, etc. Scratches and bites are, in fact, the subject of a thorough classification according to their shape (tiger claws, lotus, crescent moon). Moreover, to heighten passion, a number of cries and ANIMAL

sounds may be uttered in the course of the 'love combat'. Various types of embraces (*alingana*) are given, some of which involve acrobatic skills. Once the discussion of the preliminaries is concluded, the treatises proceed to the actual sexual act, detailing a number of ASANAS (positions) to be assumed, according to the status, age and degree of experience of the partners. The *asanas* are extensively commented upon and, according to Vatsyayana, there are eighty-four basic postures, though he states that there is ample opportunity for improvisation.

Erotic art has its roots in the mythical past. Tradition maintains that it was expounded in 100,000 chapters by PRAJAPATI, the Creator, who discusses the origin of things and the act of creation through sexual union. NANDI, the bull vehicle of SHIVA, had occasion to observe the amorous activities, performed for his benefit, of his lord with his wife PARVATI. This inspired him to condense into 1000 chapters the disquisitions of Prajapati, revealing this science to the sage Shvetaketu, who transmitted it to his successors, reduced to 500 chapters. Later, the teaching of Prajapati and Nandi was further reduced to 300 chapters by Shankha, then to 150 by Babhravya, a sexologist, who lived in Magadha (modern Bihar), and founder of a distinguished sexological school in ancient India. The various branches of this science were the subject of specialized studies undertaken by seven of his contemporaries, though only fragments of these works have survived.

The undisputed authority on erotics in India is Vatsyayana (*c*. 3rd–4th century). His celebrated *Kamasutra* is one of the most famous books on the subject. According to tradition, he was a celibate, who compiled the *Kamasutra* as a reaction against the highly specialized work of the Babrahvya school, to salvage erotics from total oblivion. The work is

filled with valuable details on contemporary life. The central character is the 'man about town' (*nagarika*), the aesthete, whose aim in life was KAMA, the pursuit of pleasure, in its multifarious aspects. Particularly interesting is the discussion on the celebrated sixty-four arts or skills, which form the basis of a refined education, and their importance in enhancing quality of life. Of the numerous commentaries written on the *Kamasutra*, most notable is the *Jaya-mangala*, by the 13th-century author Yashodhara. Another text is Damodaragupta's *Kuttani-mata* (Lessons of a Bawd, end of the 8th century), of which only fragments remain. As the title suggests, the book focuses on the advice an elderly bawd gives to a novice, on the best way to attract lovers and fleece them. The author was the chief minister of Jayapida, king of Kashmir, and his work mirrors the social and religious life of his contemporaries. His text inspired the *Samaya-matrika* (Harlot's Breviary), of another Kashmiri author, Kshemendra (909–1065). Filled with vitriolic wit, the work is a vivid rendering of a courtesan's life. The dates of the next authority on erotics, Koka (or Kokkoka), are vague. It appears that he lived between the 11th and 13th centuries, and that his work, *Rati-rahasya* (Mysteries of Passion), also known as *Koka-shastra*, is based on personal experience. Reflecting the changes in society, it contains a classification of men and women into different categories, a digression on women from different parts of India and their peculiarities, the usual repertoire of technical details on kisses, love marks, different *asanas*, etc., and, in the final parts of the treatise, ways of wooing a wife and women other than one's wife, and the use of love spells and recipes. There followed a number of other authors, writing both in SANSKRIT and in local languages. Among them is Kalyanamalla (*c.* 1460–1530), a Hindu courtier of a Muslim nobleman, Lad Khan, of

the Lodi Dynasty. His work, the *Ananga-ranga* (Theatre of the Love God), dedicated to his patron, is as celebrated as Vatsyayana's *Kamasutra*.
Kokkoka, 1964, Vatsyayana, 1963, 2002

ethics References in SANSKRIT literature to norms of conduct, the final aim of human life, moral philosophy etc., are frequent, though there are few treatises that specifically deal with the subject. It is generally accepted that there are four possible goals in human life (PURUSHARTHAS): ARTHA, wealth, power or possession related to economics and politics; KAMA, sensual enjoyment, mainly connected to erotics; DHARMA, righteousness, dealing with morals, ethics and law; and MOKSHA, final liberation from the cycle of rebirth, achieved through spiritual discipline, religion and meditation. There is neither an exact English equivalent for the term *dharma*, nor a Sanskrit equivalent for ethics. In fact, the meaning of *dharma* is elastic, drawing on the fields of religion, law, social and cosmic order. Leading a life in accordance to the tenets of *dharma*, fulfilled with charitable acts, increases one's individual merit (*punya*), which is crucial for the quality of the next life. The *dharmashastras* (treatises on *dharma*), give a clearer view of the concerns of Hindu ethics, in their discussion of *gunaguna* (virtues and vices), which are embedded in Hindu law. Ethical requirements vary considerably in the texts: some of the UPANISHADS contain a lengthy list, while others, for instance the *Brihadaranyaka Upanishad*, are remarkably brief. The three cardinal virtues are *dama* ('taming', self control), *datta* ('giving', charity) and *daya* ('mercy'). Later texts add more, such as truth, non-injury, continence, duty, compassion, belief *(shraddha)* and devotion (BHAKTI). Other texts prescribe six major virtues (*shatsampat*, six accomplishments), which differ

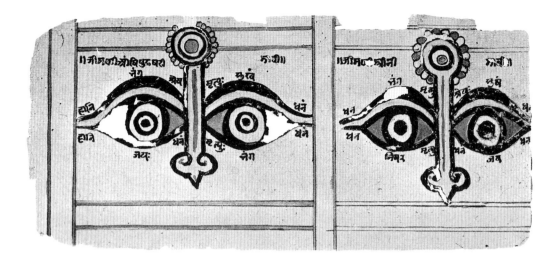

from text to text, but which include, among others, equanimity, patience, continence, compassion, non-violence and indifference. In addition to the major virtues, there are lesser ones, such as restraint, moderation, purity, fearlessness. Bad thoughts and actions, detrimental to the accumulation of merit, are classified as sins (*dosha*, 'flaw, defect'). Over time, the prescriptions ruling the eternal law (*santana-dharma*), contained both in the VEDAS and in the *dharmashastras*, had to be radically altered in the wake of social and political changes. It is accepted that some laws laid down in the ancient texts are no longer relevant.

eyes One of the most striking features of Indian IMAGES is the eyes. Three dimensional images of gods and goddesses are installed in TEMPLES and shrines so that their eyes can meet those of their devotees in the act of DARSHANA. By looking at a sacred image or auspicious object, the viewer receives its beneficent influence. According to Indian belief, the eyes are the last organ to be active, because they only open after birth. From time immemorial this has prompted sculptors and painters to 'open the eyes' of an image when the rest of it is completed. Traditionally, the chief artist, who carves or paints the eyes, is accompanied by an assistant carrying a mirror, which is held in front of the image while its eyes are ceremonially opened. The image's first glance, believed to be too powerful for a human to bear, is received by the mirror. The opening of the eyes is followed by another rite, in which the image is 'enlivened or empowered'. The same ritual, in a simplified form, is used by puppet makers. The moment the eyes are opened, the puppet becomes an extension of the deity it represents. It is also believed that after death a person plunges into darkness again. In Bengal, a

special ceremony called *chaksu-dana* ('eye-bestowal') is performed by *jadu-patua*, or magic painters. A rough portrait of the deceased is prepared and, for a small fee, they paint in the eyes and chant MANTRAS, thus enabling the departed to see once more and find their way in the other world.

A glance of hatred or anger can have fatal consequences. Hindu mythology has a wide repertoire of stories in which the curse and glance of an angered RISHI causes great trouble. Some individuals possess *kudrishti*, evil eye, and children in particular need to be sheltered from its malignant influence. To protect them from danger, talismans, especially tiger claws or *mantras* written on a piece of paper encased in a metal cover, are worn on the body. It is believed that an ugly face will automatically avert evil eye, whereas a beautiful countenance attracts it. Children's eyes are therefore heavily blackened with collyrium, in order to 'disfigure' the face, and, in some parts of India black dots are applied to their faces for the same reason. It is believed that everyone has a third eye, the seat of occult power. Examples in mythology are the third eye of SHIVA, which will eventually consume the universe, and the third eye of DURGA, which created the goddess KALI. The third eye is placed slightly above the eyebrows, where caste or sectarian marks (TILAKA) are generally drawn.

Opposite: Diagram from a
Tantric manuscript, showing the
opening of the third eye in the
ajnakhya chakra, the sixth centre
between the eyebrows which
represents the inner vision.
Rajasthan. Opaque watercolour
on paper, 18th century.

Right: Lakshmi flanked by
Ganesha and Sarasvati,
the three main deities
celebrated at *Navaratri*.
Coloured print, 2001.

festivals To say that every day is a holiday in India is
no exaggeration. Celebratory occasions vary from
state to state, from community to community and
from family to family. A festival (*utsava*) can be
observed by fasting, acts of worship, bathing,
keeping vigils, fairs (*mela*), taking vows (VRATA),
feeding mendicants, as well as by ceremonially
lighting lamps, gambling, or playing games.
Festivals also relate to a wide variety of occasions,
such as the seasons, events in the life of a deity,
important mythological incidents, phases of the
moon, conjunctions of planets, rising and setting
of constellations, solstices and equinoxes, eclipses.
Apart from the celebrations in honour of the major
gods, the minor gods are far from being overlooked.

Some festivals, such as the KUMBHAMELA (festival
of the pot), are celebrated at Allahabad (PRAYAGA)
every twelve years when the sun enters the
constellation of Aries and the planet Jupiter is in
Aquarius. Similarly, every eleven to thirteen years at
the conjunction of the moon with the lunar asterism
called *Maha Nakshatra*, and Jupiter in the
constellation of Leo, the MAHAMAHAM (great *Maha*)
festival takes place at KUMBAKONAM.

Many festivals centre on local TEMPLES, as each
one has its particular feasts: the anniversary of its
foundation or the chariot festival (*Rathotsava*),
when the sumptuously decorated chariots carrying
the metal IMAGES of the temple's main deities are
dragged by the devotees around the streets of the
town. The anniversaries of the betrothal and
wedding ceremonies (*Kalyanotsava*) of the enshrined
god and goddess are lavishly celebrated especially
in southern Indian temples, as in the *Chittirai*
(April–May) festival at MADURAI. On a smaller scale,
the wedding of VIRUPAKSHA, a form of SHIVA, and
PAMPA worshipped at Hampi (Karnataka) is held in
April–May.

Some festivals are named after a deity, such as
the *Ganesh Chaturthi* dedicated to GANESHA, or
Shivaratri to Shiva. Some are named after the month
in which they occur, e.g. *Shravani-purnima*, the full
moon (*purnima*) of the month of July–August
(*Shravana*); others, after the day of the fortnight in
which they occur. The *Vaikuntha Ekadashi* festival,
held in SRIRANGAM on the eleventh day of the bright
half of *Pausha* (December–January) is one of the
most important festivals in honour of VISHNU.

The main festivals observed in India are:
1. *Divali* or *Dipavali* ('row of lamps'), celebrated
throughout India with great pomp, occurs in the
month of *Kartika* (October–November) and lasts for
five days. *Divali* was probably a fertility festival, and
in some parts of India, especially in the south,
farmers worship the fields and bring offerings of
flowers and fruit and light lamps at dunghills. The
first day of *Divali*, is dedicated to the goddesses
LAKSHMI and PARVATI, who are invited to visit the
houses and bring blessings and prosperity, and for
this reason doors and windows are left open.
Businessmen and traders close their accounts, heap
coins on their ledgers and place on them an image
of Lakshmi, the goddess of wealth. The second day is
devoted to gambling, especially with dice. Men and
women play together celebrating the reconciliation
of Shiva and Parvati, who delighted in board games.
The third day, the full moon, is dedicated to the
commemoration of the victory of Vishnu over the
king BALI. This day is also known as *Lakshmi-puja*
(worship of Lakshmi) because the goddess is
worshipped at night after an all-day fast. In Bengal,
the main focus of worship is the goddess KALI. On
the fourth day, the real *Divali*, the lamps – small
earthen bowls filled with oil – are lit and set in rows
inside the houses and on terraces and garden walls
to mark the return of RAMA to AYODHYA after a

Left: Pongal-kolam in rural Tamil Nadu. The drawing executed on the ground, shows the characteristic pots with rice boiling over, flanked by sugar cane. The caption wishes a happy *Pongal* to passers-by.

Opposite: Durgapuja celebrated with great pomp in a Bengali mansion. To the right, an image of the goddess slaying Mahishasura. Calcutta(?). Watercolour on paper by Sevak Ram, *c.* 1807.

fourteen-year exile, and his consecration. The new financial year begins on this day. The fifth and last day of *Divali* is called *Yama-dvitiya* as YAMA dined then with his sister YAMUNA. It is customary for the men of the household to dine either with their sisters or with other female relatives, and they in turn, receive presents. On this day, the clerical CASTE, the *kayasthas*, worship Yama and his scribe CHITRAGUPTA.

2. Ganesh Chaturthi, Ganesha's birthday, occurs on the fourth day (*chaturthi*) of the bright fortnight of *Bhadrapada* (August–September). This festival, popular in Maharashtra, lasts from two to ten days. Clay images of Ganesha are ceremonially set up in private homes and worshipped. At the end of the festivities the images are destroyed by immersion in tanks, pools, RIVERS or in the sea. Especially impressive are the celebrations in Mumbai, when under the pelting monsoon rain, the streets of the city are blocked by the crowds on their way to the beach to entrust the images to the sea.

3. Holi starts about ten days before the full moon of *Phalguna* (February–March), but is celebrated only in the last two or three days culminating on the day of the full moon. Especially popular in northern India, this was once a fertility festival and retains some of its pristine riotous characteristics. Bonfires intended to burn all evil, the erection and worshipping of poles, loud playing of cymbals, horns and drums, use of obscene language and gestures, especially in the presence of women, and numerous swinging rites (*dolayatra*), seemingly part of fertility celebrations, are all facets of *Holi*. The most characteristic feature, however, consists of squirting coloured water or throwing powder at people. *Holi* celebrates the youthful pranks of KRISHNA and, according to some, it is said to commemorate either the death of the demoness Putana, who made and

attempt on Krishna's life, the burning of HOLAKA, daughter of HIRANYAKASHIPU, or the incineration of KAMA by Shiva. The connection of *Holi* with the latter episode is stressed especially in southern India, where women sing the lamentations of RATI over the death of her husband.

4. Janmashtami, Krishna's birthday (*janma*) on the eighth day (*ashtami*) of the dark fortnight of *Bhadrapada* (August–September), is also known as *Gokulashtami*, from GOKULA, where Krishna spent his childhood and adolescent years. The occasion is magnificently celebrated in Mathura and VRINDAVAN, the legendary setting of Krishna's life.

5. Makara Sankranti. A *sankranti* is the entry of the sun into a new zodiacal sign and the beginning of the new solar month; some regard it as a holiday. The entry of the sun into Capricorn (*makara*) on the day of the winter solstice, into Aries (vernal equinox), into Cancer (summer equinox) and into Libra (autumnal equinox) are particularly relevant. The most important of all is the winter solstice, *Makara Sankranti*, marking the beginning of the solar year. On this date, which falls between 12 and 14 January, the sun, according to Hindu astronomical calculations, reaches the southern most point of the ecliptic and starts on its northern course, the auspicious *uttarayana*.

The occurrence is celebrated differently in various parts of the subcontinent; in Tamil Nadu the festival is called *Pongal* and marks the beginning of the Tamil year. *Pongal* literally means 'is it boiling?' and refers to the custom of boiling rice in milk, in new pots bought for the occasion. The date is auspicious for two reasons, as the last month of the year, deemed inauspicious, comes to and end and gives way to the auspicious days of the new month. To protect their families from evil, each morning before dawn the women scour the pavement outside their

front doors and decorate it with intricate geometrical designs, known in Tamil as KOLAM, or more generally as *rangoli*, made from pulverized conches. At the centre of these designs balls of cow dung are occassionally placed and decorated with a citrus or pumpkin flower. At the end of the month, they are all ceremonially disposed of on waste ground. The meaning of this rite has yet to be investigated. The first day, *Bhogi Pongal*, is devoted to the family and immediate relations are entertained. The second day, *Surya Pongal*, is dedicated to SURYA, the sun, and married women, after taking a ceremonial bath and dressed in new clothes, boil milk and rice on an open fire. This day is set apart for visiting friends. The third day, *Madhu Pongal*, also known as cattle *Pongal*, sees cattle driven out of their sheds to the sound of music, to graze and wander for the rest of the day. The festival ends with a procession of sacred images.

6. *Naga-panchami* (the fifth of the NAGAS). Observed on the fifth day of the light half of *Shravana* (July–August), it commemorates the victory of Krishna over the snake KALIYA. The *Naga-panchami* begins with a fast and it is considered auspicious to bathe in rivers, tanks and ponds. Special fairs are held and, most importantly, the images of ANANTA and other *nagas* are worshipped and ceremonially lustrated with water. Milk, water and cooked food are placed before the entrance to the snakes' nests, along with a mirror, comb and cosmetics. On *Naga-panchami* agricultural work is forbidden to prevent a snake being accidentally injured.

7. *Navaratri* (nine nights), a major Hindu festival connected to the autumnal equinox, begins on the first and ends on the tenth day of the bright fortnight of *Ashvina* (September–October). A number of festivals, some having their roots in ancient fertility rites, are celebrated during these ten days. These are centred on two major mythological events, the

goddess DURGA's victory over Mahishasura and Rama's over RAVANA. In northern India Rama has the pride of place, whereas in eastern and southern India, Durga is the focus of the festivities; so much so, that in Bengal, *Navaratri* is known as *Durgapuja*. In Maharashtra and Gujarat both traditions coexist. The celebrations vary from state to state; in some, the first three days are dedicated to the goddess SARASVATI (*Sarasvati-puja*), during which all the sacred books of the household are piled up and the goddess is invited to reside in her image placed on top of them. On the third day she is dismissed after an offering of money. In Tamil Nadu, the first three days of the festival are dedicated to Lakshmi, the next three to Durga, and the last three to Sarasvati. Ancestors are commemorated on *Mahanavami* or the 'great ninth'. *Dasara* (*Dussehra, Dussera*), the tenth and last day, is celebrated differently in the various parts of India. In Bengal, the image of Durga, which has been worshipped for the previous nine days, is taken to the river or ocean and immersed; bulls and buffaloes are then sacrificed in her honour. In those parts of India in which the emphasis of the festival lies on Rama's victory over Ravana, the tenth day is called *Vijaya-dashami*, 'the tenth of victory', so called because it is believed that Rama propitiated the goddess Durga for nine days and offered her oblations on the tenth, before attacking Ravana. For this reason it is a royal as well as a military occasion. Formerly, this date was deemed auspicious to begin a military campaign.

Throughout *Navaratri* episodes from the story of Rama (*Ram-lila*) are enacted, chapters of the RAMAYANA are recited, and on the tenth day the celebrations reach their climax in the ceremonial burning of huge effigies – stuffed with crackers and fireworks – of Ravana, his brother Kumbhakarna and his son Indrajit. The most famous *Dasara*

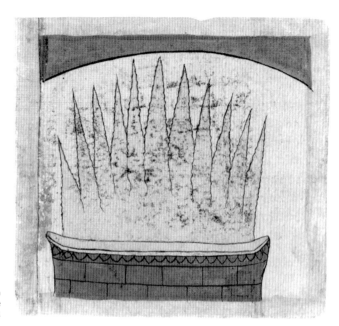

The sacred fire burning on an altar. Rajasthan. Opaque watercolour on paper, 19th century.

celebrations, in which the Maharaja actively participates, are held in and around Mysore palace. One of the great attractions of this particular *Dasara* is the colourful procession in which the goddess Chamundeshvari (a form of Durga), the tutelary goddess of the ruling family, is carried on a golden throne by a sumptuously decorated ELEPHANT.

8. *Rama-navami* (the ninth of Rama) the birthday of Rama, is celebrated on the ninth day of the bright half of *Chaitra* (March–April). The festival, which is especially popular in northern India, lasts nine days. Bathing fairs are held along the banks of the rivers and episodes from the *Ramayana* are recited. In VAISHNAVA temples and Rama shrines a metal image of Rama is given a prominent place to enable the worshippers to pay their respects. Festivals are organized and the image is paraded through the streets of the town on a golden or silver palanquin, or on a ceremonial RATHA (chariot).

9. *Shivaratri* ('Shiva's night') or *Mahashivaratri* ('great night of Shiva') is one of the most important yearly festivals celebrated in the whole country on the first full moon in the month of *Magha* (January–February). The preparations start the day before the night of the new moon, when the devotees take only one meal. Early the next day, they bathe and perform a number of rituals in the temple. The festivities culminate in the night, during which the devotees are supposed to participate in four different PUJAS held on each quarter of the night. In the course of these rituals, selections from the RIGVEDA, YAJURVEDA, SAMAVEDA and ATHARVAVEDA are chanted, while the LINGA is worshipped with flowers, clusters of TULASI leaves and libations. A number of myths relate to this celebration, but the basic significance of this festival emphasizes the fact that as day must come after night, so death is followed by birth, total dissolution by creation. Thus,

it serves as a reminder to enjoy life and success in moderation, and not to be overwhelmed in times of failure and despondency.

10. *Shravani-purnima* is celebrated on the full moon in the month of *Shravana* (July–August) at the height of the monsoon season. COCONUTS are thrown into the sea and rivers, in order to propitiate VARUNA. The day also commemorates Rama's passage to LANKA. The sacred thread worn by the three upper castes are renewed, new sacred threads are presented to deities, and the popular custom of *raksha-bandhan* is observed, whereby women tie coloured threads on the wrists of their brothers or other male relatives. In some parts of the country, serpents are worshipped as on *Naga-panchami*.

11. *Tripuri-purnima*, celebrated on the full moon of *Karttika* (October–November), is one of the great SHAIVA festivals, second only to *Shivaratri*, commemorating the victory of the goddess Kali over the demon Tripura, and Shiva's destruction of the demon's three aerial cities. It is said that the MATSYA AVATARA of Vishnu occurred on this date. This festival is also known as *Karttika-purnima*.
Jagdisha Ayyar, P. V., 1921

fire As well as being one of the ELEMENTS (*bhuta*) constituting the universe, and identified with the god AGNI, fire plays a crucial role in ritual as the mediator between men and the gods. Its numerous aspects, each with its own function are painstakingly enumerated in the sacred texts. The three most important of these include the *garhapatya* ('lord of the household'), or domestic fire, which should be placed towards the west or south-west. It passes from father to son, thus establishing a continuity between the generations. The *garhapatya* is inaugurated when a newly married couple set up their own home and it is the duty of the householder

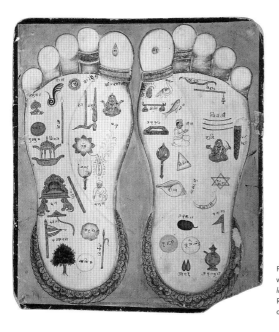

Footprints of Vishnu, adorned with the forty-six auspicious *lakshanas*, or characteristic signs. Rajasthan. Opaque watercolour on paper, 18th century.

to maintain it. Its flame is used in birth, MARRIAGE and death rituals, as well as in exorcisms and incantations to avert illness and other calamities. The second aspect, the *ahavaniya* ('eastern fire'), is the first to be lit and to receive oblations. It is generally used for offerings to the gods. Lastly, comes the *dakshinagni* ('southern fire'), which receives the monthly oblations to the ancestors and is also known as the 'flesh-eating fire', as it is used to light the funeral pyre. This fire is dedicated to the malevolent forces who dwell in the south, the region of death and destruction.

five daily sacrifices *mahayajna* ('great sacrifice') or *pancha-maha-*YAJNA. Five great sacrifices are mandatory for every 'twice-born' Hindu. The name derives from the five types of creatures worshipped and the five ELEMENTS constituting the universe, said to be represented in the ritual.

DEVA-*yajna* ('worship of the *devas*') is an offering to the gods, of GHEE (clarified butter) and other substances, such as milk, curds, sticks anointed with *ghee*, which are poured or placed in the domestic fire.

BRAHMA-*yajna* ('worship of Brahma') is an act of homage towards the sages. It consists in the studying, reciting and meditating on the VEDAS.

PITRI-*yajna* ('worship of the ancestors'), during which rice balls (*pinda*) and water offerings are made to the ancestors.

BHUTA-*yajna* ('worship of the spirits') consists of a ritual that takes place generally in the afternoon, in which benevolent and malevolent spirits alike receive oblations. Since the term *bhuta* means 'existing, living', some perform this ritual by feeding stray ANIMALS and BIRDS.

NARA-*yajna* ('worship of man') is performed by giving shelter and food to mendicants, gifts to the needy and hospitality to guests.

The five elements are revealed by the matter used in worship, as the deities reside in the ether, men on earth; air in the recitation of *mantras*, fire in the sacrificial flames and water in the libations.

foot (*pada*). According to Hindu beliefs, contact of the foot with the earth is of vital importance, as the energies of the earth are channelled through the great toe and the heel into the body. During a number of rituals, the participants are barefoot, to absorb the forces emanating from the earth. The *pada-mudra* ('foot mark'), was reputed to share characteristics of the person to whom it belonged. A number of incantations and magic rituals focused on footprints, one of the most common being to pronounce spells on a girl's footprint to win her love. On another level, footprints of gods, goddesses and saints have become objects of veneration. In early BUDDHISM and Buddhist art, the footprints of the BUDDHA symbolized his presence. In the visual ARTS a deity's footprints are adorned with the appropriate auspicious symbols, a lotus, umbrella or fly-whisk for example. The most frequently represented are RAMA's footprints, those of SITA, VISHNU and, occasionally, the claws of GARUDA. Slabs supposedly representing the feet of some unidentified holy personage are worshipped in remote areas of Karnataka and possibly elsewhere. *See also* PADUKA

funeral rites Although the law books and other texts, especially the *Garuda* PURANA, contain a substantial amount of information on the *antyeshti* or 'final' sacrament in Hindu life, there is a lack of consistency both in theory and in practice. A fourfold division of these ceremonies exists: rituals to be performed before death, those accompanying the disposal of the body, those to help the transition of the soul from the status of ghost (PRETA) to that of ancestor (PITRI), and finally, those in honour of the *pitri*. The rites differ according to the CASTE, community and status of the deceased.

Prior to the second millennium BCE bodies were either exposed to the elements and to the BIRDS, or buried in the earth, at sea, in a RIVER, or occasionally, in a cave or an urn. Cremation then became the usual method of disposing of bodies, with the exception of infants, YOGIS, SADHUS and a few others. It became popular due to the notion that the soul cannot enter a new body until its former one has totally disappeared.

Procedures for cremation vary from place to place. Generally the body is dressed in new clothes, adorned with jewels and is arranged lying on a stretcher or in a sitting position. In southern India in particular, the stretcher is adorned with a profusion of flowers, roses, jasmine and marigolds, which almost cover the corpse completely. The stretcher is then either carried on the shoulders of the relatives, or on a cart pulled by a bullock to the cremation ground (SHMASHANA), which is generally near a river, if not on the river bank itself. There a pyre is set up, on which the corpse is laid facing southwards, the jewels removed, and the chief mourner, generally the eldest son, walks around the pyre three times keeping the body to his left, pouring water onto the pyre from a clay vessel. He either breaks the vessel on the head of the deceased, or is given a mallet to crack its skull. He then sets the pyre alight with a torch lit with the flame of a sacred FIRE. When the body has been consumed, the mourners return home, the youngest leading the procession, followed by the others in order of age. On reaching home the mourners bathe, purify themselves, offer water libations and kindle the fire, while reciting the appropriate MANTRAS. One or two days after the funeral, the chief mourner returns to the burning ground, sprinkles the ashes with water, and collects them along with the unburnt bones in an urn. These may be either buried or entrusted to a river, the most preferable being the Ganges (GANGA), at particularly sacred places, such as HARDWAR (or Haridvara), PRAYAGA (Allahabad) or VARANASI. In southern India, the ashes are immersed in the KAVERI, at Srirangapattana or SRIRANGAM, or at Kanyakumari, where the Arabian sea, the Bay of Bengal and the Indian Ocean merge. A number of rituals accompany this ceremony.

The next phase of the ritual, the *preta-karma*, aims at providing a body for the *preta* or spirit. If this is overlooked, the spirit will never join the world of the ancestors, but will join the BHUTAS, goblin and ghost followers of SHIVA; this part of the funeral rites is deemed inauspicious. It lasts for eleven days, at the end of which the *preta*, along with his father and grandfather, join the ancestors and are worshipped in the SHRADDHA ceremonies.

If a person dies in war, in another country or disappears at sea, the rituals can be performed in the absence of a corpse. If someone who is presumed dead and has undergone the funeral rites, suddenly returns, they are reckoned as dead, until a 'resurrection' ceremony is performed. This involves a new 'birth', in which the person passes between his mother's or any other woman's legs, is washed, dressed in nappies and fed on milk. The other SAMSKARAS (sacraments) marking the various stages of a Hindu's life then take place in rapid succession, at the end of which he is fully readmitted to the world of the living.

Gaja-Lakshmi hanging lamp, Padmanabhapuram Palace, Padmanabhapuram, Tamil Nadu. Kerala. Bronze, 18th century.

gada 'mace, club'. One of the favoured weapons of ancient Indian warriors and mythical heroes, such as Bhima and Duryodhana, and one of the main attributes of Vishnu and Hanuman, the *gada* could be variously shaped and made of wood or iron. The divine craftsman Vishvakarman fashioned a *gada* from bones of the demon Gada, killed by Vishnu, and presented it to him. The club is personified as the beautiful goddess Kaumodaki who carries a fly-whisk. Occasionally, the top of the mace is shown protruding from her coiffure. *See also* Ayudhapurusha

gaja *see* Elephant

gajahastamudra *see* Dandahastamudra

Gaja-Lakshmi 'Lakshmi with the elephants'. Designation of an image of Lakshmi seated on a lotus with an elephant (*gaja*) on either side. The animals pour water over the goddess either from their trunk or from a vessel held in the trunk. This mother, goddess and fertility motif is common to Hindu and Buddhist iconography. It appears on a 3rd-century BCE coin from Kausambi and, in early Indian art, one or two elephants depicted alongside a woman symbolize the birth of the Buddha. Gaja-Lakshmi has four arms and sits in padmasana. In her upper pair of hands she carries a lotus; the lower hands are generally in abhaya- and varadamudra.

Gajasuramurti or **Gajasurasamharamurti** An awesome aspect of Shiva as the destroyer of Gajasura (elephant-asura). Gajasura was created by the magic spells of the sages of the pine forest (*darukavana*) who wanted to kill Shiva. Instead, Shiva killed the *asura*. In this form, Shiva is shown vigorously dancing on the elephant's head, holding

the flayed skin of the animal behind him. In his hands are a number of weapons, as well as the appurtenances of an ascetic, symbolizing on the one hand the involvment in action characteristic of a warrior, and on the other the detachment of the ascetic.

Gajendramoksha 'deliverance of the king of the elephants'. *See* Karivarada

gana(s) 'troop, multitude'. Class of semi-divine beings, attendants of Shiva and whose lord is Ganesha. They are usually depicted as lively, pot-bellied dwarfs dancing and playing musical instruments. In spite of their grotesque appearance they are remarkably elegant.

Ganapati 'Lord of the ganas'. Epithet of Ganesha.

Ganapatya(s) 'followers of Ganapati'. A cult that probably originated in the early centuries of the common era and which regards Ganesha as the supreme deity. One text dating from *c.* 10th century, the *Shankaravijaya* by Anandagiri, describes the doctrines of six groups of Ganapatyas, each having particular iconographic and ritual traditions and following the teaching of a different acharya. Courtright, P. B., 1985

gandabherunda 'having terrible cheeks'. A fabulous double-headed bird, said to devour elephants, was, and still is, the emblem of a number of royal families, including the present-day Wodeyars of Mysore.

Gandhari One of the great figures of the Mahabharata, the daughter of Subala, king of Gandhara, and the wife of the blind king

Ganesha carrying in his upper hands his broken tusk, and the bowl of *laddus* in which he plunges his trunk. In the lower right are prayer beads, the left rests on the mace. His *vahana*, the mouse, is carved on the pedestal. Central India. Sandstone, 13th century.

DHRITARASHTRA. In sympathy with the plight of her husband, Gandhari blindfolded her eyes. In exchange for her kindness and hospitality she was offered a boon from the sage Krishna Dvaipayana VYASA, who was to be the mythical 'author' of the *Mahabharata*. She requested to be the mother of a hundred sons and, in time, became pregnant; but after two years no child had been born so she struck her womb violently and gave birth to a lump of flesh. Vyasa sprinkled some water on it and divided it into 101 small fragments, which he stored in a hundred jars of GHEE. Two years later, DURYODHANA emerged from one of the jars. The portents accompanying his birth were so awesome that Dhritarashtra was requested, in vain, to abandon him. A month later his ninety-nine brothers came forth. Gandhari, however, also wanted a daughter, so Vyasa placed the last portion of flesh that had been left aside in yet another jar of *ghee* and Gandhari's daughter Duhshala was born. After the death of her sons in the great battle at KURUKSHETRA, Gandhari began to curse her nephews, the PANDAVAS, but was restrained by Vyasa. She nevertheless cursed their ally KRISHNA to lose his sons, ministers, friends and relatives and to be killed. Eventually, Gandhari accompanied Dhritarashtra and KUNTI, the mother of the Pandavas, and retired to the forest to spend the rest of their lives there, but they all perished shortly afterwards in a forest fire.

gandharva(s)*, *gandharvi(s) A class of semi-divine beings, whose collective name has been interpreted as 'fragrances'. They have an ambivalent nature, possessing, on the one hand, extraordinary healing powers, and on the other, the capacity to cause madness; it was thought advisable, therefore, to propitiate them with offerings and prayers. According to the RIGVEDA, the *gandharvas* lived in the sky as the physicians of the gods. They had human upper bodies with the face of a BIRD and the hind quarters of an ass or a horse. Later literary sources describe them as handsome young men and beautiful women. In ART they are depicted gracefully flying through the sky with billowing scarves, carrying musical instruments, garlands of flowers or flower petals, which they scatter on special occasions on gods or heroes. They are the musicians and dancers of the gods, and mix freely with humans, with whom they often have passionate affairs; however, these radiant beings can be dangerous and are reputed to haunt remote forest glades and pools. They are common to BUDDHIST, JAINA and Hindu tradition. *Gandharva* MARRIAGE, or marriage by mutual consent, is one of the many legitimate types of marriage.

Ganesha 'Lord of the hosts, or GANAS'. Ganesha, the ELEPHANT-headed god, one of the most popular Indian deities, is the god of wisdom, bestower of favours, giver of success in all undertakings and the one who overcomes obstacles – hence his name Vighneshvara, 'lord of obstacles'. He is worshipped before all religious ceremonies and new undertakings, and is invoked at the beginning of books. Said to be son of SHIVA and PARVATI, or of Parvati alone, Ganesha was originally a folk deity, similar to the YAKSHAS and the NAGAS, and was said to take possession of human beings if not duly propitiated. His aspect, half-human and half-elephant, betrays his animistic origins, and various legends account for his striking appearance. In one, his mother Parvati, proud of her offspring, asked SHANI (Saturn) to look at him, forgetful of the effects of Shani's glance. Shani obliged and the child's head was burnt to ashes. BRAHMA suggested that Parvati replace the head with the first she could find, which

The Ganga, accompanied by two female attendants, one of whom carries an umbrella, and a *dvarapala* leaning on his staff, stands on the foliated tail of a *makara*. The goddess carries a pot. Detail of a door jamb, central India. Sandstone, 10th century.

was an elephant's. Another legend narrates how Parvati created a beautiful youth from the dust of her body, then went to her bath and told her son to guard the door. Shiva, incensed at the sight of the young man who prevented him from entering, decapitated the youth in his anger, and the severed head was eventually replaced by an elephant's. The god is shown with a plump physique denoting well-being and wealth, generally with four arms, and with two or three EYES. His colour is red, his huge ears are shaped like winnowing-fans, suggesting the deity's power of discernment. There are no images of Ganesha pre-dating the 5th century.

Among the attributes the deity carries are: a RUDRAKSHA chaplet, emblematic of SHAIVA mendicants, a broken tusk, a noose, a goad and, occasionally, a lotus flower. He is often shown plunging his trunk into a bowl filled with sweetmeats (LADDUS) of which he is very fond, and sometimes a serpent is shown circling his waist. His VAHANA is the mouse or bandicoot. Ganesha is the chief of the *ganas*, the attendants of Shiva, and his wives are RIDDHI ('abundance, prosperity') and SIDDHI ('success, good luck'). Today he is regarded as the embodiment of success, prosperity and peace. Few, if any, TEMPLES are dedicated solely to him, and the once flourishing cult of the GANAPATYAS has declined, but Ganesha is revered by the majority of Hindus, whether Shaivas or VAISHNAVAS. His other names include Gajanana ('elephant-faced'), Heramba ('glutton'), Pillaiyar ('youth') in southern India, and Vinayaka ('leader').
Courtright, P. B., 1986

Ganesh Chaturthi *see* FESTIVALS

Ganga 'Swift-goer'. In India Ganga is both the name of the RIVER Ganges and the personification of the river as a goddess. The river flows from a glacier, *c.* 4600 metres above sea level, over Gangotri, a holy place, which probably derives its name from *Ganga-avatarapuri*, i.e. the place of the descent of the Ganga. Practically all Indian rivers are revered as deities, however the goddess Ganga has special status. The SARASVATI and the INDUS were the only two great rivers of India known to the early ARYANS, and the river Ganga is mentioned only briefly in the RIGVEDA hymns to rivers. However, when the Aryans extended their occupation to the Gangetic plain, Ganga became the most important of the river goddesses and a whole mythology was created around her. A celestial Ganga, the Akashaganga, indentified with the Milky Way, was said to flow across the sky; it was also known as Mandakini, 'gently flowing', and was reputed to have issued from VISHNU's left foot, hence the goddesses other name Vishnupadi. It was BHAGIRATHA, a royal ascetic who, by performing extreme austerities (TAPAS), obtained the descent of the Akashaganga to earth to purify the ashes of his progenitors, incinerated by the wrath of the sage Kapila. When Bhagiratha worshipped SHIVA and Ganga, the latter violently rushed down and would have swamped the whole earth, had Shiva not caught her in his matted hair and broken her fall. Hence, Shiva is known as Gangadhara, the 'supporter of the Ganga'. However, once caught in Shiva's matted locks, Ganga was unable to find her way to earth and Bhagiratha began to propitiate Shiva once more. Eventually, Shiva relented, and Ganga descended to earth, flowed out to sea and to PATALA, and purified the ashes of Bhagiratha's progenitors, receiving the epithet Bhagirathi. According to some legends, Ganga is the sister of PARVATI, and the second wife of Shiva, the one who has a cooling, soothing effect on the god. In some TEMPLES a water jar (*galantika*) with a tiny hole

Shiva as Gangadhara receives the goddess Ganga on an extended strand of his hair. Relief in the Pallava cave at Tiruchirappalli, Tamil Nadu. Granite, 7th century.

is placed above the LINGA. The dripping water is said to symbolize the Ganga, Shiva's 'liquid SHAKTI'. It is said that Parvati is jealous of Ganga as she nestles in her husband's hair.

The MAHABHARATA relates the story of King Shantanu, who fell in love with Ganga. She married him on condition that he never questioned what she was doing; if he broke this condition she would disappear forever. They lived happily for a time and had seven sons, the VASUS, who were thrown into the river at birth by their mother. Eventually, when the eighth was born, Ganga was on the verge of drowning him when Shantanu lost his self-control and remonstrated with her. She then revealed her true nature and told him that she had been chosen by the gods to be the mother of the eight vasus, cursed to be born in human form, and that by throwing them into the river she freed them from the curse. She reminded her husband of the broken agreement. However, before leaving the earth forever, she bore him a ninth child, Shantanava, who was to be famous as BHISHMA.

The water of the Ganges has many properties: it is a medicine for all ailments, bathing in it cleanses from every sin, and most importantly of all, it ensures that the soul of a person whose ashes or bones are entrusted to her waters will be released from rebirth. Committing SUICIDE by drowning in the Ganges is a sure way to attain bliss. Ganga is depicted along with the other great river goddess, the YAMUNA, on the door jambs of temples or sacred precincts, as a beautiful woman standing on a MAKARA sprouting foliage and creepers. It is believed that the presence of these two goddesses is sufficient to cleanse the entering devotee. Ganga appears as a mermaid among the locks of Shiva in his form as NATARAJA. Her other names include Devabhuti ('born from the gods'), Hara-shekhara ('Shiva's

crest'), Tripathga ('flowing in three strands', i.e. through heaven, earth and the nether world).

Gangadharamurti 'form supporting GANGA'. Aspect of SHIVA in the act of receiving the Ganga on his head. Occasionally, the four-armed god embraces PARVATI with his lower left arm, while with his right he gently lifts her chin. The upper right hand is extended above his head and holds a thick strand of dreadlocks on which the tiny figure of Ganga alights. In the upper left hand the gods carries a leaping antelope (*mriga*).

garbhagriha 'womb-house'. The term refers to the innermost sanctuary of a TEMPLE in which the main deity is enshrined. It is the meeting point of the divine and the human sphere and of the horizontal and vertical axis of the temple, sometimes identified as worldly and spiritual life respectively. It has no windows and only a dim light penetrates through the door. It is generally square, but not invariably.

Garuda 'the Devourer'. A mythical BIRD, VAHANA of VISHNU, symbolizing the wind, the all-consuming rays of the sun and the esoteric teachings of the VEDAS. Garuda is the son of the seer KASHYAPA and of VINATA. He originated from a huge egg and has the torso and limbs of a man, but the talons, wings and beak of an eagle. An ancient rivalry between his mother and her sister KADRU, the mother of the NAGAS, accounts for Garuda's aversion for the *nagas*. When Vinata was enslaved by Kadru, the latter promised her freedom on condition that Garuda stole the AMRITA. Garuda flew to INDRA's heaven and defeated the two huge snakes, guardians of the *amrita*, whose merest glance was deadly, by blowing dust into their EYES, and with the pot of nectar in his beak he rose into the sky. Vishnu was so impressed

Left: Garbhagriha of the 13th-century Ramappa temple, at Palampet, Andhra Pradesh. The *linga* is covered by a sheath of brass in the shape of a coiled cobra, whose extended hood shelters the *linga*. The image is continuously lustrated by drops of water falling from a water pot hanging from the ceiling.

Right: Garuda kneeling with hands in ANJALIMUDRA. His snake-shaped locks, armlets, anklets and his crown indicate his being the arch-enemy of the snakes. Eastern India. Basalt, 11th–12th century.

that he granted Garuda a boon. Garuda requested to become Vishnu's *vahana*, and to achieve immortality without tasting the *amrita*. This was granted. In the meantime, Indra had discovered the theft and hastened to recover the *amrita*. He hit Garuda with his thunderbolt (VAJRA), but Garuda only lost a single feather, and was otherwise unscathed. Eventually, he and Indra made a pact: the pot of nectar would be returned to Indra, if he granted Garuda permission to feed on *nagas*. Indra agreed and Garuda handed the pot of nectar to the *nagas*, suggesting that they cover it with spiky DARBHA grass while taking a purificatory bath. While they were gone, Indra snatched the pot and returned to *devaloka*, the sphere of the gods; when the *nagas* came back, failing to find the pot, they licked the *darbha*, which caused their tongues to bifurcate. And thus Garuda's mother was freed from bondage. From this myth, Garuda is known as the natural enemy of the snakes. It is said that he was the first to teach mankind how to cure snake poison, and that concentrating one's mind on him averts snakes from one's path.

He is also connected to emeralds, as narrated in the *Garuda* PURANA. When Indra killed the ASURA Vala, VASUKI, the king of the *nagas*, took the bile from the corpse, but was confronted by Garuda before he could escape. Vasuki dropped the bile and Garuda carried it away into the sky, but it fell from his beak and on reaching the earth solidified into veins of emerald. From this came the belief that touching emeralds neutralizes the effect of poison.

Garuda is variously depicted: generally he has the upper body of an eagle, and a human lower body. His face is recognizable by its long beak. He may have two or four arms and his earrings, anklets, armlets, bracelets and girdle consist of snakes. In his hands he carries the emblems of Vishnu or the pot containing *amrita*; occasionally, when Vishnu rides

on his back, two of his hands support the deity's feet. Frequently he is shown with only two hands folded in ANJALIMUDRA. His other names include: Amritaharana ('stealer of the nectar'), Gaganeshvara ('lord of the sky'), Nagantaka ('destroyer of serpents'), Shalmalin ('taloned'), Suparna ('having beautiful wings') and Vainateya ('son of Vinata').

Garuda Purana see PURANA(S)

garudadhvaja or ***garudastambha*** A flagstaff (*dhvaja*) or column (*stambha*) bearing an image of GARUDA, placed at the entrance of VAISHNAVA TEMPLES.

Gauri 'brilliant, golden, yellow'. The name of a benevolent goddess, consort of SHIVA or VARUNA. Connected with the rains, she is reputed to be the source of the world and the embodiment of motherhood. She is depicted as a two- or four-armed woman of fair complexion, carrying in her upper hands prayer beads and a water pot, while the lower hands are in ABHAYA- and VARADAMUDRA. She may also carry a mirror, a fish, a lotus, a trident and a floral wreath. Her mount is the *godhika* (iguana). Occasionally she is shown riding either a lion, a wolf, a pig or a goose.

Gaya A town in Bihar, sacred to Hindus (especially VAISHNAVAS) and BUDDHISTS alike. It is one of the seven sacred Hindu cities, an important place of PILGRIMAGE, where, according to legend, the ASURA Gaya sacrificed himself for the good of all mankind. Offerings for the dead ancestors (PITRIS) are made at the foot of a sacred BANYAN tree, the *akshyavata* ('immortal banyan'), thus Gaya is known as Pitritirtha, i.e. 'sacred place of the *pitris*'. Near Gaya lies Bodh Gaya, the spot where BUDDHA is said to have reached enlightenment under the ASHVATTHA tree.

Left: The five-headed goddess Gayatri enshrined in a niche. Parapet above a subsidiary shrine in the Thyagaraja temple complex, Tiruvarur, Thanjavur district, Tamil Nadu. Concrete and colours, end of the 20th century.

Gayatri or **Savitri** A poetic metre consisting of twenty-four syllables. A substantial number of verses in the RIGVEDA are written in this metre and the most sacred among them is generally known as Gayatri, or Savitri, which is addressed to the Sun (SAVITAR). This verse or MANTRA, should be repeated morning and evening by every man of the first three CASTES, i.e. 'twice-born'. Women and members of the lower classes are forbidden to utter it. Gradually, it became identified with a goddess, the wife of BRAHMA, and the mother of the four personified VEDAS. She is rarely represented, but some of her images depict her with five heads.

gems The SANSKRIT term for gems is *ratna*, 'bestowed' (by the gods to mankind). A number of gems emerged from the depth of the Milky Ocean when the gods and the ASURAS churned it in search of AMRITA. Among them were VISHNU'S KAUSTUBHA, which he wears on his chest, and the earrings that he gave to ADITI. A fair share of gems went to the NAGAS, acknowledging the pivotal part played by the serpent VASUKI in the churning process. According to legend, the streets of the *naga* capital, Bhogavati, are paved with gems. The expanded hood of the serpent SHESHA is called *Mani-dvipa*, 'jewel island'. The *chintamani*, or 'thought-jewel', which grants every desire, has pride of place in the centre of the hood and is surrounded by innumerable gems of different colours. Fragments of *chintamani* adorn the hood of the less important *naga* kings. There are a number of other mythical stones: the *divya-ratna* ('divine gem'), which also has the power to grant every wish, the *surya-kanta* ('sun-beloved'), supposedly created by the condensed rays of the sun, the *chandra-kanta* ('moon-beloved'), containing the rays of the moon, and others, all with magical properties. KUBERA is the god who presides over

jewels and precious metals. He possesses nine NIDHIS, or treasures, later personified by his nine attendants. Similarly, there were nine main varieties of gems, the NAVARATNA.

Some families own a family gem which, handed down from generation to generation, is rarely handled or worn, and should never be seen by an outsider or sold, though it may be donated to a TEMPLE to adorn a deity. Gems are worn only by the owner and it is believed that a personal gem can predict good or bad times by changing colour. They are also reputed to cure diseases and to ward off evil influences when worn as amulets, or crushed to powder and drunk. Their intrinsic properties, whether good or bad, are said to be increased by the appearance of marks or blemishes on the stone. These defects (*doshas*) should be carefully examined before a gem is selected for personal use. In bright gems, such as diamonds, the main defects are a scratch, which is reputed to attract poison and expose the potential wearer to the danger of snake or scorpion bites, a slit, which means that the wearer is likely to lose a friend or a relative, and, most inauspicious of all, a crack, which according to commentators on the science of gems (*ratna-pariksha*), could 'dethrone even Indra'. Equally inauspicious are the marks appearing on dark stones, especially rubies.

Indian diamonds extracted from the mines around Golconda (Hyderabad) are renowned for their size and brilliance. The most famous diamond is the Koh-i-Nur, 'the mountain of light', which has been associated with a number of royal houses. It is said that it was first in the possession of an ancient king who passed it to the ARYANS; eventually it was taken in 1304 by Ala-ud-din, Sultan of Delhi, when he sacked Mandu. After passing through the hands of the Mughals, it was owned by Ahmad Shah

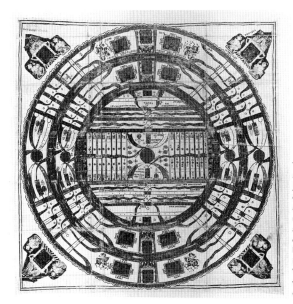

The world of the mortals: at the centre is Jambudvipa, the continent where India and Mount Meru, represented by a circle, are sited. Two other continents, separated by seas, encircle the innermost one. Western India. Opaque watercolour on cotton, c. 1400.

Durrani and finally by Ranjit Singh. When the British annexed Panjab in 1849, all the state jewels that were kept in Lahore were confiscated and in 1850 the Koh-i-Nur passed to Queen Victoria to become one of the crown jewels. It now forms part of the crown that was made in 1936 on order of George VI for his wife Queen Elizabeth.

There are several other stories relating to diamonds, such as the the Orloff diamond, which originally formed the EYE of a Hindu god; it came into the hands of Prince Orloff, who presented to Catherine II of Russia. A number of tales also centre on the curse attached to certain diamonds, the most notorious being the Hope diamond from southern India, of which the owners all died tragically. In 1957 it was donated to the Smithsonian Institution by Harry Winston, a New York jeweler.

geography Traditional Indian geography developed under the influence of mythology. According to Indian COSMOLOGY, the earth (JAMBUDVIPA), the innermost of seven concentric continents, is divided into various regions (*varsha*) of which the centre is Ilavrita, named after its celestial prototype. Around it are a number of regions, the southernmost being BHARATA, or India. The name Bharata (Bharata-*varsha* or Bharata-*khanda*) originates from the mythical Bharata, and its territory comprised the whole of the northern part of the subcontinent. It was divided into three *kranta*, steps or regions, all starting from the Vindhya Range: Vishnu-kranta, from the Vindhyas to Chittagong, including Bengal; Ratha-kranta, from the Vindhyas to Tibet (Mahachina), including Nepal; and Ashva-kranta, from the Vindhyas to the Great Ocean, corresponding to the region of the Deccan.

Northern India was known by different names: Aryavarta or Aryadesha, 'land (*desha*) of the ARYAS',

the term used by MANU and others to designate the Indo-Gangetic plain; Brahmarishi-desha, the area of KURUKSHETRA, roughly between Delhi and Meerut, the home of many of the tribes mentioned in the MAHABHARATA; and Brahmavarta, the territory between the Ganges and the Jumna. It was later extended to the south-east and south-west to include PRAYAGA (Allahabad) and Jaipur. Eventually, Bengal and southern India were included in what is deemed to be the sacred area of Bharata, and so India was known as Asetu-Himachala (from the Setu, or RAMA's bridge, extending from RAMESWARAM towards Sri Lanka and to the Himalayas).

Another way of indicating the position of the various localities was by using the image of a tortoise (KURMA). This tortoise distribution (*kurma-vibhaga*) occurs in the *Markandeya* PURANA. The animal's head lay over Bengal, its right forefoot on Kalinga (Orissa), its left one on Magadha (Bihar), its belly over northern and central India, its right hind foot on Saurashtra, its left on Rajasthan, and its tail pointing to the north-west. There were some variations within this system to include regions such as Assam and Afghanistan, Tibet and Sri Lanka; the head of the tortoise, however, was always oriented towards the east.

The terms 'India' and 'Hindu' are both foreign. They derive from Sindhu, an ancient Indo-European word meaning 'RIVER', the western limit of the early Aryan settlements being the river today known as the Indus. The Persian pronounced the word as *Hindhu*, and consequently, the inhabitants of Hindhu were the Hindus. The Greeks dropped the aspirate and the name was changed to Indos. Eventually both Greeks and Romans employed the name India to indicate the northern part of the subcontinent. The terms Hind and Hindustan, both Persian, came into use at the end of the first millennium CE.

Left: This 17.5-metre granite monolithic sculpture of Gommateshvara, carved in 981 CE, stands on the summit of Vindhyagiri Hill, Sravana Belgola, Karnataka. The deep concentration and immobility of the sage are stressed by the creepers winding around his legs and the anthills at his feet.

Right: The south *gopura*, completed in 1987, of the Ranganatha temple complex at Srirangam.

ghanta 'bell'. One of the many objects used in the course of worship (PUJA). It is an attribute of a number of deities, but first and foremost of DURGA. The sound of her *ghanta* terrifies the enemies of her devotees, which is why it is also counted among her twelve weapons.

ghat(s) 'steps'. The steps leading to a RIVER or tank used for ritual purposes. Burning *ghats* refers to the part of the embankment near a river that is usually reserved for cremation and FUNERAL RITES.

ghee (Hindi) or **ghrita** 'clarified butter'. Used in religious offerings, such as HOMA, it is ceremonially poured into the flame with special oblation spoons, to the accompaniment of the appropriate MANTRAS. Because of its fat content, *ghee* is the epitome of abundance and fertility and is said to be conducive to longevity and good health; it also averts the inauspicious influences of the planets.

Gitagovinda 'Song of the Cowherd'. See JAYADEVA

Godavari or **Godaveri** A RIVER beginning in Trimbak, the seat of one of the JYOTIRLINGAS (*lingas* of light) in the Western Ghats, near Nasik in Maharashtra, and ending in the Bay of Bengal. It was once divided into seven branches, but now only comprises four. Its alternative name, Goda, refers to a legend, according to which the sage Gautama revived a COW, which he had inadvertently killed, by sprinkling on it the water from the Godavari. Later the sage revealed the sacredness of the Godavari, the 'GANGA of the Deccan', to RAMA. Childless couples are advised to bathe in its waters to obtain offspring.

Gokarna 'cow-ear'. A SHAIVA place of PILGRIMAGE located in the northern part of Karnataka, on the Arabian Sea. According to the local legend, YAMA propitiated SHIVA here and became one of the ASHTADIKPALAS, as well as lord of the PITRIS.

Goloka 'world of COWS, place of the cows'. The paradise of KRISHNA on Mount MERU; also the abode of the wish-fulfilling cow SURABHI.

Gokula 'COW house or station'. The pastoral region near MATHURA where KRISHNA spent his childhood and adolescence among the cowherds.

Gommateshvara or **Gommata** A Jaina saint, son of Rishabhanatha, whom the DIGAMBARA sect regards as a prophet. He is represented standing, entwined by creepers and surrounded by ANTHILLS. He is also know as Bahubali, 'strong armed'. *See also* JAINISM

gopa, gopi 'cowherd, cowherdess'. KRISHNA spent his childhood and youth among them. Especially important are the *gopis*, who left their homes, husbands and children to join him on the banks of the YAMUNA river to dance the *rasa*, a circular DANCE, and to flirt with him. Each *gopi* thought she was alone with Krishna, but the *Bhagavata* PURANA states that Krishna multiplied himself and danced with them all. This episode symbolizes the relationship between deity and devotee.

Gopala 'cow-herd'. An epithet of KRISHNA, when he lived among the herdsmen in VRINDAVAN.

gopura(s) Tall, multi-storeyed brick towers erected over the gateways of southern Indian TEMPLES. They are adorned with a wild profusion of vividly coloured stucco images depicting scenes drawn from the PURANAS and the local legends, *mahatmyas*. Famous are the *gopuras* of the MINAKSHI temple at MADURAI.

Krishna as Govardhanadhara, surrounded by herdsmen, their families and cows, lifts Mount Govardhana. Details such as trees, animals, birds and the two snakes hanging down from the mountain are vividly rendered. Halebid, Karnataka. Soapstone, 12th–13th century.

Gorakhnath or **Goraksha** A YOGI and the most famous of the NATHAS who lived in the north-west of India between the 9th and the 12th centuries. A vast mythology developed around him and his followers, because of their unorthodox practices, such as necrophilia and bestiality. The cult, which flourished after the 12th century, includes many elements drawn from SHAIVISM, TANTRISM and, occasionally, from BUDDHISM, as well as a number of magical and alchemical practices. Gorakhnath is believed to be the founder of the order of the Gorakhnathis or Kanphata ('split-ear') *yogis*, so called because the ear cartilage of the novice was split during the initiation ceremony for the insertion of a huge earring. The *Goraksha-shataka* (Hundred Verses of Goraksha), a treatise on *hatha* YOGA, and a number of verses in Panjabi are attributed to him. His followers wrote a number of works on magic, alchemy and occultism. Gorakhnath himself was credited with possessing magical powers that enabled him to revive the dead and make a BANYAN tree grow from seed to maturity within a few hours.
Briggs, G. W., 1973

gotra 'lineage, clan'. The smallest subdivision in a CASTE. MARRIAGES within the same *gotra* are severely restricted or forbidden.

Govardhana 'the increaser of cattle'. Name of a hill in VRINDAVAN connected with a myth that indicates the transition from the cult of the Vedic INDRA to that of VISHNU-KRISHNA. Indra, the most important god of Vedic religion was losing his hold over the inhabitants of the area near the Govardhana hill, who refused to make offerings to him and instead had become followers of Krishna. In order to demonstrate his power, Indra summoned the rain clouds and flooded the area for seven days and seven nights, to drown both men and cattle. But Krishna effortlessly lifted up the Govardhana for ANIMALS and people to shelter beneath it. Indra accepted his defeat, and after paying homage to Krishna, returned to his abode.

Govardhanadhara 'upholder of GOVARDHANA'. Epithet of KRISHNA.

Govinda 'obtainer of cattle'. Epithet of KRISHNA.

graha(s) 'seizer'. The term denotes a particular category of demons who possess their victims. They are responsible for a number of illnesses, mainly insanity. There are different types of *grahas*, each of which have to be propitiated at a particular time and place and by different means. Later, the term *graha* was associated with the nine planets (NAVAGRAHAS) which influence or 'seize' the life of mankind to exert a positive, but also negative influence. They haunt lonely places – lakes, streams, hilltops, solitary trees – and are particularly dangerous to travellers and to those who live in deserted houses.

grahahoma 'oblation [to] the GRAHAS'.
See NAVAGRAHA(S)

gramadevata(s) 'village gods'. They are intimately connected with the village life, on the one hand presiding over the fertility of the fields and ANIMALS and the well-being of the community, and on the other, expressing their wrath by drought, floods and epidemics. Occasionally, they possess a person and make their wishes known through them.
    The majority of *gramadevatas* are goddesses who have a number of features in common with UMA, and bear the title of Amba, AMBIKA, Amma, Ma, Mata and Thakurani, i.e. 'mother' or 'lady'. Frequently

Concrete figures of village deities and guardians. Thanjavur district, Tamil Nadu.

associated with a pot or water jar, both symbols of the womb, they are connected with the fertility cult, and their shrines are located in fairly remote areas near trees. The *gramadevatas* can be represented by a pot or by stone slabs on bearing the rough figure of a multi-armed woman or, more frequently, by crude IMAGES of the female genitals (YONI). Animals – goats, sheep and occasionally, buffaloes – are sacrificed to the *gramadevatas* and the blood of the victims is sprinkled on the devotees, on the lintels and doorposts of the houses and cowsheds and on the boundary stones. *Gramadevatas* are worshipped in various forms throughout the subcontinent by roughly seventy per cent of its rural population.

Among the most important *gramadevatas* are Ellamma or YELLAMMA, who is sometimes said to be the guardian of the Dravidian south against the ARYAN north. There are a number of goddesses associated with illness, e.g. MARIAMMAN, 'the mother of death', goddess of smallpox, whose TEMPLE at Samayapuram, a short distance from Tiruchirappalli, attracts throngs of pilgrims. In western, eastern and central India, the counterpart of Mariamman is SHITALA, 'the cool one', whose name refers to the shiver caused by high fever in her victims. Her worshippers were against the smallpox eradication campaign, because they felt that it robbed the goddess of her privileges. A number of *gramadevatas* are associated with fertility: KOTAVI ('nude'), Tippamma of Srirangapatna in Karnataka, whose worship was accompanied by obscene rites, and Huligamma, a goddess worshipped mainly by eunuchs in northern Karnataka and the Deccan. Other goddesses, such as MANASA of Bengal and Mudama of southern India, are connected with snakes; in Karnataka, Huliamma ('the lady of the tigers') is associated with tigers. The quarrelsome *sapta kannigai*, or seven virgins, sometimes

called seven sisters (obviously a folk version of the SAPTAMATRIKAS), are revered throughout the southern part of the subcontinent as the guardian deities of tanks (reservoirs and wells) and their stone images are placed on tank bunds (embankments). To protect the community from floods, they are said to assume the shape of children who run through the village summoning the inhabitants to protect the embankment when the water rises. However, since they argue among themselves and have fits of temper, they are also believed to damage the tanks by stamping their feet. They are said to roam at night and whoever meets them dies shortly afterwards. Only a restricted number of male deities are among the *gramadevatas*. These include AIYANAR and his most favoured companions Karuppan, 'the black one', and Madurai Viran, 'the hero of Madurai', a historic personality who lived in the 17th century. He was in the service of the Nayak of Madurai, whose daughter fell in love with him. After their death, both Madurai-Viran and his wife were deified.

Gramadevatas are also worshipped by fishermen, in the case of the goddess MINAKSHI ('with fish-shaped eyes'), the tutelary goddess of MADURAI. The town of Mumbai (formerly Bombay) derives its name from the tutelary goddess Mahamba, also called Momba or Mumba, whose worship was popular in that part of western India from the earliest times. Whitehead, H., 1921

grasses (*yavasa*) A number of species of grass were considered sacred and used in ritual. They were arranged around the altar (VEDI), where the offerings were placed and where the invoked deity was invited to sit. Rushes covered the seats occupied by the priests and the *yajamana*, the patron of the sacrifice. It was customary to hold a tuft of grass for the duration of the ceremony and, at the end, to wipe the ritual vessels with it. On certain occasions, the wife of the *yajamana* was supposed to dress in garments of KUSHA grass.

The most renowned of the sacred grasses is the DARBHA which emerged at the time of the CHURNING OF THE OCEAN. It was originally the hair growing on the back of VISHNU's turtle, which came off with the rubbing of the churning pole placed on its carapace. *Darbha* grass has always been associated with the rites performed for the PITRIS. An annual FESTIVAL, the *Darbha-ashtami*, is celebrated in its honour on the eighth day of the light half of *Bhadrapada* (August–September) and an offering of *darbha* on this occasion is said to bestow immortality on ten generations of ancestors. In the course of certain ceremonies, a ring (*pavitram*), made up of three, five or more stalks of *darbha* grass plaited together, is worn as an amulet on the ring finger of the right hand. The *durva* (*Panicum dactylon*) a variety of five-bladed millet grass is also used in ceremonies. A girdle made out of the fibres of the *munja* (*Saccharum munja*), a type of rush, is worn by participants in the UPANAYANA ceremony.

grihastha 'householder'. The second of the four ASHRAMAS. The duties of the householder include all ethical and religious obligations, such as procreation, performing the daily rituals and looking after the extended family.

Grihya-Sutras Collections of texts containing the prescriptions for domestic rituals.

guhyaka(s) 'hidden, secret'. A class of minor gods or goblins, attendants of KUBERA, the god of riches. Like the YAKSHAS they live concealed in caves on Mount KAILASA. They are composite beings (half-horse or half-bird) who guard Kubera's treasures. They assume demonic forms in battle and those who die a heroic death are said to dwell among the *guhyakas*.

guna 'cord or string, attribute, quality'. According to the SAMKHYA system of philosophy there are three *gunas* – *sattva* (purity), *rajas* (energy) and *tamas* (inertia) – which are forces of nature or matter (PRAKRITI), and belong to the theory of creation and evolution.

guru 'the weighty one, or the dispeller of darkness'. A teacher or spiritual guide, especially one who gives the DIKSHA (initiation) to a disciple. The guru is believed to be the spiritual father of his pupil and thus, the pupil regards the guru's wife as his mother, and the guru's daughter as his sister. A guru's function is to give spiritual advice, whereas the priest's is to perform or conduct religious rites.

H

hala

hala 'plough'. Characteristic attribute of BALARAMA, hence his epithet Haladhara. It is also an attribute of other deities, e.g. SHANMUKHA, TRIVIKRAMA and of VISHVARUPA. The *hala*, a symbol of agriculture, may also have been used as a weapon.

halahala *see* KALAKUTA

hamsa 'goose' (*Anser indicus*). The most important of the Indian BIRDS. Revered by Hindus, BUDDHISTS and Jains, it plays a prominent role in mythology, folklore, literature and religion. *Hamsa* has often been translated as 'swan', but it is nevertheless a bar-headed goose that breeds in the lakes of Central Asia and migrates to India during the winter. In Vedic times it was connected with the sun and represented virility. The UPANISHADS saw it as symbol of purity, detachment, divine knowledge, cosmic breath (PRANA) and the highest spiritual accomplishment, because it transcends limitations: it swims in the water, walks on earth and flies in the sky. Moreover, for those who penetrate the secret concealed in its name, it epitomizes the whole philosophy of the *Upanishads*. Inverted, the word *hamsa* becomes *sa-ham* ('this [am] I'), which expresses the essential oneness of the human and the divine. In PRANAYAMA (breath control), the inhalation is said to sound like *ham*, the exhalation as *sa*; *hamsa* is thus the sound of the living *prana* ('vital breath'). As a result of all these associations, the title of *paramahamsa*, or 'supreme swan', is given to those who have reached the highest degree of emancipation. The *hamsa* is the VAHANA of BRAHMA, hence his epithet Hamsavahana.
Vogel, J. Ph., 1962

Hanuman or **Hanumat** 'heavy-jawed'. Son of the APSARA Anjana (hence his name ANJANEYA) and of the wind god VAYU, Hanuman is one of the most popular gods of India. Many stories are told about him and his extraordinarily long tail and superhuman powers, which were attributed to his celibacy and gave him the ability to change shape at will. He is the protector of towns and villages, wrestlers and acrobats, and is famous for being an exemplary devotee and for possessing an in-depth knowledge of grammar and all other sciences. His major claim to fame arises from the pivotal role he played in the RAMAYANA. While searching for the abducted SITA, RAMA and LAKSHMANA arrived at Kishkindha, the kingdom of the VANARAS (monkeys) and met Hanuman, who volunteered to go to LANKA, where Sita was held captive by RAVANA. Using Mount Mahendra as a springboard, he jumped across the sea, but while leaping met two redoubtable adversaries who tried to hamper his progress: Surasa, the mother of the NAGAS, and Simhika, the daughter of DITI. He defeated them both and transforming himself into a cat, entered Ravana's palace. Resuming his original form, he wandered around the gardens and eventually found Sita in the ASHOKA-grove. He made himself known to her, and handed her Rama's signet ring as a mark of recognition, telling her that now that he knew where she was, he would return with her husband to free her. To assess the strength of Ravana's troop before returning to Rama, he wreaked havoc in Ravana's gardens, where he was spotted by the guards and taken captive by Ravana's son Indrajit. Dragged into the presence of Ravana, he sat on his coiled tail and each time Ravana raised his own throne, he lengthened his tail to be higher than the king. Ravana wanted to kill him, but Indrajit prevented him, instead ordering Hanuman's tail to be wrapped in an oil-soaked cloth and set on fire. But Hanuman survived the ordeal unscathed and

Right: Hanuman in his heroic aspect; the right arm is lifted, ready to strike, holding a tree in the left, he strides on the supine body of a warrior. Krishna dancing, Vishnu's conch and discus and five-hooded Ananta embellish the rim of the plaque. Probably Karnataka. Bronze, 18th–19th century.

hamsa

even set Lanka on fire on his way back to Rama. On reaching the ocean, he extinguished his tail in its water and, once in Rama's presence, gave him a detailed report on the expedition.

During the war between Rama and Ravana, many heroes died, Lakshmana among them. Rama then sent Hanuman to the Himalayas to fetch the 'reviving, animating' herb, the *sanjivini*, to restore them to life. On his way, Hanuman met with the ASURA Kalanemi, who had been instructed by Ravana to kill him. Once there, Hanuman was unable to decide on the correct herb, so he uprooted the whole MOUNTAIN and took it to the battlefield for the physician to select the required herbs. At the end of the war, Hanuman followed Rama to AYODHYA, where he was rewarded with everlasting youth and longevity. He is the greatest among Rama's devotees and is believed to spend his time singing hymns in praise of his lord.

Hanuman makes a brief appearance in the MAHABHARATA. As Vayu's son, he was half-brother to BHIMA, who was unaware of Hanuman's existence. One day, while roaming on the Gandhamadana hill in search of a special flower for DRAUPADI, Bhima found his path blocked by an old monkey which he tried to force out of the way. A clash ensued in which Hanuman won the fight, but was impressed by Bhima's prowess; eventually they discovered that they were both sons of Vayu.

Hanuman is depicted as a strong human being with a monkey's face and protruding fangs. He carries a club and, especially in southern India, an uprooted tree, and is shown trampling a supine figure, probably a demon. In his aspect as a devotee of Rama, he kneels at his feet with the clappers and the VINA in his hands. His colour is generally red. His other names are Maruti and Anili (both patronymics), Anjaneya (his metronymic),

Lankadahi ('burner of Lanka') and Yogachara ('master of Yoga').

Hara 'destroyer, seizer'. Epithet of SHIVA. Hara symbolizes death, the inevitable process of decay of both the universe and the individual.

Hardwar or **Haridvara** 'HARI'S (VISHNU'S) gate'. One of the seven sacred cities of the Hindus, which is situated at the foot of the Siwalik hills where the Ganges flows from the MOUNTAINS. The town, once known as Kapila in honour of the Vedic seer who had performed austerities (TAPAS) there, was destroyed in 1399 by Timur. It was given its present name after it was rebuilt. A stone bearing a footprint of Vishnu (*Hari-ke-pairi*) is the focus of devotion and a nearby TEMPLE stands on the spot where DAKSHA'S sacrifice and SATI'S suicide reputedly took place. Hardwar is one of the places where the ashes of the dead are entrusted to the Ganges and where SHRADDHA ceremonies in honour of the PITRIS are performed. On the first day of *Vaishakha* (April–May), the day commemorating the descent of the GANGA to earth, there is an annual ceremony in which pilgrims from all over India participate; at the auspicious moment, all plunge into the RIVER. A KUMBHAMELA is celebrated every six years and every twelve years the same festival occurs on a larger scale. A PILGRIMAGE route leading to GANGOTRI, KEDARNATH and BADRINATH starts from Hardwar. Nearby is Rishikesh, or Hrishikesha, 'lord of the bristling hair', i.e. Vishnu, where RAMA expiated the sin of killing RAVANA.

harem (Arabic: *haram* 'sacred'. In India the word commonly used is *zenana*, a Persian word meaning 'women's quarters'). It is not clear whether the women of ancient India were secluded or not. Some

Ladies in the garden of a palace. Page from an illuminated manuscript of the Ramayna. Mysore. Opaque watercolour on paper, first half of the 19th century.

scholars postulate that in areas such as southern and eastern India, where the patriarchal system was not particularly strong, women enjoyed greater freedom than those in the north and west. On the evidence of Vedic and Epic literature, other authorities go further and maintain that harems were unknown in ancient India and that women enjoyed great freedom. This seemed to change by about the 1st century BCE for the women of the upper classes. Evidence from the Epics, ARTHASHASTRA, poems and other literary works, seems to support the view that royal wives and daughters did not mix freely in society. However, they did not live in seclusion, but took part in religious ceremonies and other occasions, such as the SVAYAMVARA ('bride's choice'), weddings and FESTIVALS. The SANSKRIT words *antahpura* ('inner city, area') and *avarodha* ('enclosure') indicate the women's quarters, which were normally situated in a private part of the house or palace. The doors to these quarters were guarded by female guards, old men or eunuchs. No one was allowed to enter the premises, apart from the master of the house, female relations and servants. The occasional seller of bangles, trinkets or flowers could speak to the women through a screen. Some idea of the life in the *antahpura* can be gleaned from BUDDHIST and JAINA literature, as well as from the *Arthashastra*. The king's visits were scheduled for the late afternoon, when he would spend some time talking to the women to find out their needs. Later, a maid would tell the king which queen he was expected to call on. The chief queen was first in the hierarchical order, followed by the three lesser ones; four was the maximum number of queens a king was permitted to have. The king was obliged to see his wives once a month, but he could spend the rest of the time with his concubines. At the king's death, the harem was inherited by the new king.

Various authors on *niti* (politics) warn readers about the harem. Inmates were not to be trusted, because some were sent by enemy princes, scheming nobles or courtiers with a grudge against the king, and were potentially dangerous. Among them were spies and poison-maidens (beautiful young girls fed from earliest childhood on flesh of poisonous snakes, insects and toxic plants and whose embrace was lethal). Moreover, some girls could smuggle in disguised intruders to make an attempt on the king's life.

In India, the custom of veiling and secluding women was confined to a limited section of the higher classes. Indeed, the use of the veil covering the head and part of the face by Hindu women, especially in the north of the country, was a result of the Islamic conquest. The custom was adopted as a method of protection during the period of Islamic supremacy and still survives in rural areas. The veil was called *parda* (anglicized: 'purdah'), the Persian word for curtain, in particular the curtain or screen that separated the womens' rooms from the rest of the house. Generally speaking, in spite of all these imposed limitations, Hindu women were never obliged to observe the *parda* way of life.

Hari 'yellow-green'. The colour of rice shoots, one of VISHNU's names. In Vedic literature Hari indicates, among other things, the fire (AGNI), the sun (Vishnu) and the lightning (INDRA).

harichandana The sandal tree, one of the PANCHAVRIKSHA, or five trees of paradise.

haridra (Hindi: **haldi**; *Curcuma longa*, turmeric). From a very early period turmeric was used instead of saffron and other yellow dyes. Its colour was deemed auspicious and consequently was believed

This composite image depicts Hari Vishnu, the dark-hued, with a peacock feather on his head, holding a conch and mace; and Hara Shiva, light-complexioned, three-eyed, dressed in a tiger skin, carrying a *vina*. Caption in Tamil. Kalighat, Calcutta, West Bengal. Watercolour on paper, *c.* 1880.

to have protective powers. It figures prominently in MARRIAGE rituals and in all other Hindu functions. It is believed that the positive connotations attached to reds and yellows derive from sun worship and there are also erotic associations, as the body of the bride is smeared with turmeric. Clothes that have been dyed, or stained with turmeric become auspicious. A special ritual, in which only women participate, is performed in Gujarat and, with some variations, in other parts of India: an expectant mother sits on a low stool placed in the centre of a red square, while her friends sing the appropriate songs and her husband's sister smears her forehead with turmeric and rice. In southern India, on auspicious occasions such as a betrothal, a visit to *sumangalis* (women whose husbands are alive) or pregnant women, a root of turmeric is brought as a present. It is also customary on special occasions to sprinkle sacred IMAGES with turmeric powder and it is liberally used whenever good luck is required, as it is believed to keeps demons at bay. The god GANESHA, in his aspect as Haridraganapati ('turmeric Ganesha') receives offerings of the plant.

The antiseptic and aromatic properties of the root of the turmeric plant have been known from time immemorial. The inner part of its tubers is bright yellow and, when ground, is used both as a culinary spice and as a cosmetic. It is customary to have an oil massage before bathing, and the oily film is then removed by rubbing a paste composed of chickpea flour (*besan*) and turmeric onto the skin, a process which allows the skin to retain its natural moisture. Turmeric paste also has a beneficent influence on skin disorders, such as ulcers and blemishes. Its powder stimulates the gastric juices, and it is commonly used in both northern and southern Indian cooking.

Jagdisa Ayyar, P. V., 1989

Hari-hara 'HARI and HARA' in a single figure. A composite image in which the right half depicts Hara (SHIVA) and the left Hari (VISHNU). Both deities carry their usual attributes. The IMAGE demonstrates the synthesis between the SHAIVA and VAISHNAVA cults. In philosophical terms, the union of the centrifugal Shiva and the centripetal Vishnu indicates opposite aspects of reality, which is an uninterrupted process of creation and destruction. The cult of Hari-hara had a following in the Deccan from the 6th century, as demonstrated by one of the earliest sculpted images at Badami (Cave I), and was patronized by the Vijayanagara kings (1336–1565).

Hari-hara-Pitamaha *see* DATTATREYA

Hariharaputra 'son of Hari and Hara'. S*ee* AYYAPPAN

harijan(s) 'child of HARI, child of God'. A name created by Gandhi to designate the untouchables, now called DALITS.

Harivamsha 'the lineage, or genealogy of HARI'. This work in three chapters (*parvan*) appended to the MAHABHARATA, is believed to be the earliest of the PURANAS. The first contains an account of the creation and the genealogy of the YADAVAS, interspersed with mythological narratives. The second describes the life of KRISHNA and his affairs with the GOPIS. The last deals with prophecies about the present age (KALI YUGA) and other matters unconnected with the title of the work.

hasta(s) 'hand' or *mudra(s)* 'seal, sign, token'. Hands as a protective sign have been part of Indian beliefs since time immemorial. In rural areas hand impressions, mainly of the right hand steeped in red dye, are a common sight on houses, cowsheds and

The horse-headed Hayagriva carries in the upper hands a conch and prayer beads. The lower right is in *vyakhyanamudra*, and the left carries a book symbolizing the *Vedas*. Maharashtra or Karnataka. Bronze, *c.* 17th century.

ANIMALS, especially COWS. The terms in ritual and ART denote particular positions of the arms and hands, which are invested with meaning. There are sixty-four *mudras* in dance and in art, and 108 in TANTRISM.

Hastinapura Founded by Hastin, this city to the north-east of Delhi was the capital of the KAURAVAS.

Hayagriva 'horse-necked or horse-headed'. There are two different traditions. One refers to Hayagriva as the DAITYA who stole the VEDAS from BRAHMA, and was killed by VISHNU in his MATSYA AVATARA. The other celebrates Hayagriva as divine, the retriever, protector and promulgator of the *Vedas*. Eventually, he became the eighteenth *avatara* of Vishnu. He is depicted with a horse's head and may have four or eight hands. His attributes are the VAISHNAVA conch, discus, club and lotus. In his eight-armed form, four of his hands are placed on the four *Vedas*, which are depicted in human form.

Himavat 'snow-clad'. The personification of the Himalaya MOUNTAINS, the father of PARVATI and GANGA.

hingu (hindi: *hing*) 'devil's dung' (*Asafoetida*). The resinous, strongly scented and flavoured exudate of an annual plant which has medicinal properties. In India it is used as a spice, especially in food preparation in southern India, Gujarat, Kashmir and Bengal. It is used as a substitute for onion by southern Indian BRAHMINS, who believe that onions have aphrodisiac properties.

Hiranyagarbha 'golden womb'. The cosmic golden egg from which the universe originated. According to one of the many Vedic cosmogonic myths, the egg

floated on the waters of the ocean of non-existence for one year, then broke into two halves, which formed heaven and earth. BRAHMA was born from it.

Hiranyakashipu 'golden-robed'. A DAITYA king who ruled over the whole earth and the personification of ignorance. He was so obsessed by his hatred for VISHNU that he could think of nothing else. The situation was exacerbated by the fact that his son Prahlada remained devoted to Vishnu, despite being tortured by his father. Eventually, Hiranyakashipu asked his son to reveal Vishnu's whereabouts, and Prahlada answered that Vishnu was everywhere, even in the nearby pillar. Hiranyakashipu kicked the pillar which burst open, and Vishnu in his man-lion form (NARASIMHA) jumped out and disembowelled him.

Hiranyaksha 'golden-eyed'. A DAITYA, brother of HIRANYAKASHIPU, who threw the Earth into the Ocean, from which she was rescued by VISHNU in his form as VARAHA, or boar. Like his brother Hiranyakashipu, Hiranyaksha symbolizes ignorance, which is annihilated by divine wisdom.

Holaka or **Holika** An ogress, who had to be placated annually by child sacrifices. Eventually it was the turn of a indigent widow to offer her only son. A holy man advised her to gather together all the children of the town to throw filth and shout abuse at Holaka when she entered the town. This they did, Holaka died of shame, and the children were saved. During *Holi*, a straw puppet chased by children and finally burnt in a bonfire is said to represent her. *See also* FESTIVALS

homa An oblation to the gods celebrated by pouring GHEE into the fire.

horse *see* ASHVA

Horse and subsidiary figures at a shrine of Aiyanar. Thanjavur district, Tamil Nadu. 20th century.

hot and cold The temperature inherent in everything is a basic concept of Ayurvedic medicine. The various types of food, drugs and diseases are classified according to their degree of heat or cold, and are treated by giving the patient the opposite diet and drugs, for example hot food and medicines for cold diseases. This treatment is said to have been derived from Greek medicine, hence its name *Yunani*, 'Ionian', although it was not introduced into India until the 14th century. Heat is the property of air and FIRE, residing in the heart, blood and liver. Hot temperaments tire easily, feel heat and thirst, and hot diseases include measles, scarlet fever, smallpox and whooping cough. Examples of hot fruits and vegetables are apples, figs, dates, nuts, all types of cabbage, leeks, onion, garlic, olives, carrots and potatoes. Tea, chocolate, spirits and some meats (mutton, lamb, pigeon, liver), as well as honey, butter, cream and eggs are also classed as hot.

Cold is the property of earth and water. In the human body, hair, bone and phlegm are the cool components. Typical ailments of cold temperaments are catarrh, weak digestion and feeling the cold. Among cold ailments are rheumatism, pneumonia, diarrhoea and malaria. Cold foods consist of citrus fruits, peaches, pears, prunes, cherries, spinach, marrow, cucumber, lettuce and tomatoes, coffee, wine, beer, beef, veal, fish, brain, milk curds, buttermilk and cottage cheese. Later, two more categories of diseases were added: 'dry', associated with fire and earth, and 'moist', relating to water and air. These, however, along with other sub-classifications such as 'hot and moist', 'hot and dry', were never widely accepted.

humours The theory of the *tri-dosha*, 'three humours', forms the basis of the Ayurvedic system of medicine. This theory is linked to the three GUNAS, or 'inherent qualities', and the constituents of the body. The *doshas* are the factors that enable the body to function properly by regulating the correct balance of the three humours: *pitta* (bile or gall), originating in the liver, *vayu* (wind), originating in the heart and *kapha* (phlegm), originating in the lungs. Their qualities are respectively: purity (*sattva*), energy (*rajas*) and inertia (*tamas*). The word *dosha* signifies defect or default. A balanced proportion of these three elements ensures well-being, while an imbalance produces illness.

Below: Shiva Dakshinamurti and sages.
Dome of a subsidiary shrine, Thyagarajasvami
temple, Tiruvarur, Tamil Nadu. Concrete and
colours, late 20th century.

images Images and image worship have always
played a prominent part in Hindu ritual. The
worship of the phallus and other images was
prevalent among the pre-ARYANS, but there are
conflicting opinions concerning the Aryans' attitude
towards images and their worship. The likeliest
hypothesis is that the early Aryans did not have
image worship, but gradually adopted it. Later
literature refers to image worship, which seems to
have been well established by the time of the Epics.
BUDDHA, in his teachings, forbids the making and
worshipping of images; indeed, for some time after
his death he was only represented by symbols, such
as an empty throne, footprints, the wheel of the law
and a tree. The origin of the Buddha image is still the
subject of animated scholarly discussions. BUDDHIST
art historians maintain that the flourishing of
Buddha images during the 2nd and 3rd centuries CE
signalled the beginning of the iconic representation
of the Buddha. However, textual and archaeological
evidence indicates that an image-making tradition
existed well before the 2nd century BCE. That an ever
increasing number of images were installed both in
TEMPLES and domestic shrines, is documented in the
works of PANINI (5th century BCE) and PATANJALI
(2nd century BCE). Both authors mention the
pratikirti ('likeness'), an image representing a deity
that BRAHMINS took from house to house when
collecting alms in exchange for the deity's blessing.

There is a wide spectrum of images, some
anthropomorphic (e.g. VISHNU), some half-human
and half-animal (e.g. GARUDA), and some merely
symbols (e.g. the BODHI-tree, which refers to
Buddha's enlightenment). Further representations
of the divine are the YANTRAS (tools) used mainly in
Shaktism and TANTRISM, which represent deities in
purely geometrical forms. Other images may denote
the divine in its unmanifested form (e.g. the LINGA),

or partially manifest (the MUKHALINGA, or *linga* with
faces). Quantities of clay images are still made on
special occasions, especially for FESTIVALS, and
immediately after the festive period, when they are
immersed in water and destroyed.

Images are made out of carefully selected
materials, as each kind of stone or metal has a
particular property and when appropriately used
radiates beneficent influence on the place where it
is installed. If wood is chosen, it must come from an
appropriate tree growing in an auspicious place. In
some cases, the tree bears specific marks on its
trunk, such as the CHAKRA (discus) or SHANKHA
(conch), which render it particularly suitable for
VAISHNAVA images.

A set of rules, laid down in the SHASTRAS, details
the proportions, the number of heads and arms, the
attributes, the stance and the VAHANA of each image.
The sculptor starts working (on an auspicious day)
by visualizing the image, often with the help of a
dhyana-shloka (meditative couplet), which describes
the image. He begins work only when he sees the
image in his mind, complete in all its details.
The finished piece is installed in the temple at an
appropriate moment fixed by an astrologer, and its
EYES opened in the course of an elaborate ceremony.
Placed on a specially prepared foundation
(*pratishtha*) in the GARBHAGRIHA of the temple, it is
consecrated during a ceremony (PRANAPRATISHTHA,
'life-implacing'), in which the MURTI, or material
form, is enlivened by MANTRAS and the sprinkling
of holy water. At this point, the deity is believed to
take residence in the form (*vigraha*) of the image,
which then becomes its reflection (*pratima*), and is
ready to be worshipped. The image is treated as an
honoured guest, either permanently occupying the
material of which it is made, or descending into it
whenever invoked by the appropriate *mantras* and

Right: The thousand-eyed Indra guardian of the east, with two *vajras* in the upper hands and an elephant goad in the lower right, sits on Airavata. Caption in Telugu. Probably Thanjavur, *c*. 1830. From an album of paintings on European paper 1820.

prayers. It is honoured by other services (*upacharas*) until finally dismissed.

Almost all religious reformers have criticized image worship, but in vain. Some employ images to assist contemplation of universal truths mediated by the shape, colour and attributes of the icon. Others maintain that since the One God encompasses everything, image worship has no bearing whatsoever on divine unity. Finally, there are those who believe that the image is an aspect of the deity.

Indra The chief of the Indo-ARYAN gods, to whom many hymns of the RIGVEDA are dedicated. His complex personality defies clear-cut definition. The *Rigveda*, the ATHARVAVEDA, the BRAHMANAS and other early texts refer to him as *puru-rupavat*, 'having many forms'. According to the *Rigveda*, Indra's chief characteristics are power and strength. His VAJRA (thunderbolt) destroys enemies, such as VRITRA, the drought demon, whom he pierced with his spear, thus releasing the waters. His virility is compared to that of the stallion or the bull. He is the giver of cattle and of material goods in general. His vigour is sustained by libations of SOMA and various other oblations, which restore and increase his power, enabling him to improve mankind's material welfare. However, his position, as that of all other gods who symbolized natural forces, changed over time. As the hero of many battles he became the embodiment of the power of the warrior class, the KSHATRIYAS, and his ELEPHANT AIRAVATA the prototype of the state elephant.

His origin is shrouded in mystery. According to the *Rigveda*, his mother was ADITI; another passage in the same text, however, describes how Indra and AGNI originated from the mouth of the Cosmic PURUSHA. According to later accounts, he was born of the mythical seer KASHYAPA and Aditi. Finally, the

Avyakta UPANISHAD states that he originated from all the gods, rendering him the most powerful of them all. He resides in AMARAVATI among the APSARAS and the GANDHARVAS, who entertain him with dance and music. A number of early legends relate his violent conflicts with the ASURAS, DAITYAS and DANAVAS, who prevented him from allowing rain and dew to fall on the earth. These spirits, along with obscure forces, such as Vritra, represent natural phenomena, as well as various non-Aryan people who resisted the Aryan invasion. Later legends dwell on his partiality for abundant libations of *soma* and sensual pleasures, and on his shrewdness in drawing human beings into temptation. For instance, ascetics who accumulate too much spiritual power with their austerities and could therefore threaten Indra's position among the gods, are regularly distracted by the *apsaras*, who disturb their meditation with their singing and dancing. Among the many women that Indra seduced were Shachi (also known as INDRANI), the beautiful daughter of the *daitya* Puloman, who eventually became his wife, and AHALYA, the wife of the RISHI Gautama. He fathered a number of sons, among whom were ARJUNA and the monkey king VALI, who was eventually killed by RAMA.

The emergence of new cults relegated the Vedic Indra to a minor role: he lost his divine aura and became a secondary deity, appearing frequently in myths, in which, helpless and not particularly cunning, he suffers defeats at the hand of deities such as VISHNU, SHIVA, KRISHNA, and his power is threatened by *rishis* such as Durvasas and AGASTYA. He became one of the ASHTADIKPALAS, the regent of the east, and in BUDDHISM and JAINISM he appears as a minor deity. He is described as having four arms, with a golden or red complexion, riding on a chariot drawn by two tawny horses. Among his

Left: Ishana, guardian of the north-east, seated on the bull Nandi. In his upper hands he carries the *damaru* and the antelope; in the lower left a staff. Caption in Telugu. Probably Thanjavur, *c.* 1830. From an album of paintings on European paper watermarked 1820.

Opposite: The Jagannatha triad: the dark Jagannath, the fair Balabhadra and at the centre, their sister Subhadra. The huge heads with staring eyes rest on stump-like bodies, and their short arms issue from the ears. Puri, Orissa. Opaque watercolour on cloth, late 19th century.

weapons are the *vajra* (thunderbolt), the lance and a quiver of arrows; his bow is the rainbow. Occasionally, he is armed with an elephant hook and the *Indra-jala*, a net of illusions into which he draws his enemies. MARUTS, VIDYADHARAS and VASUS are his attendants. Apart from Airavata, the other animals associated with him are the white horse UCHCHAIHSHRAVAS, which emerged along with Airavata and other objects from the CHURNING OF THE OCEAN, and the DOG Sarama. His names include Mahendra ('Great Indra'), Marutvan ('lord of the *maruts*'), Meghavahana ('having clouds as a vehicle'), Puramdara ('Destroyer of cities'), Sahasraksha ('thousand-eyed'), Shakra ('mighty') and Vritrahan ('slayer of Vritra').

Indrani The wife of Indra, daughter of the DAITYA Puloman. She was chosen as a wife by INDRA because of her beauty and voluptuousness. She is one of the SAPTAMATRIKAS or seven mother goddesses.

Indraprastha 'INDRA's place'. The capital of the PANDAVAS, believed to be today's Old Delhi.

Indus One of the seven sacred RIVERS of India, now in Pakistan, from which 'India' and 'Hindu' are derived.

Iravata *see* AIRAVATA

Ishana 'ruler, master'. An epithet of SHIVA as regent of the north-east. Ishana is depicted with four hands and riding on a bull. Shiva has five divine aspects, symbolized by his five faces, the fifth being Ishana, the ineffable face which looks towards the sky. On each of the five faces are three EYES. When represented as a separate deity, Ishana can have two, four or ten arms. He accordingly carries different attributes.

ishtadevata 'chosen deity'. A 'personal god' chosen by the worshipper, to whom a devotee owes his main allegiance, and who assists him in his spiritual quest towards the impersonal BRAHMAN.

Ishvara 'lord'. The personification of the Absolute. Epithet of SHIVA.

itihasa '*iti-ha-asa*: so it was'. A story or legend. The term refers to the body of literature consisting of the two Epics, legends and tales. Although this material is not regarded as divine revelation, it is extremely important as a source of religious teaching to which everyone, immaterial of sex and CASTE, has access.

Iyenar *see* AIYANAR

Jagadamba, Jagadambi or **Jaganmata** 'Mother of the world'. Epithet of DEVI.

Jagannatha 'Lord of the world'. A form of KRISHNA worshipped mainly in Bengal and Orissa. The chief centre of this cult is the huge Jagannatha TEMPLE at PURI ('the Town') in the state of Orissa, on the coast of the Bay of Bengal. Three wooden statues depicting Jagannatha, his brother Balabhadra (BALARAMA) and his sister Subhadra are enshrined in its main sanctuary. The IMAGES are renewed every twelve years, the old ones buried in the temple precincts. The origins of Jagannatha are shrouded in mystery. According to some scholars Jagannatha was a deity of the Savaras and other local tribes.

The images of Jagannatha and his family are striking, huge heads resting on stumps, with disproportionately short arms issuing from the ears. Jagannatha is black with large round EYES, Subhadra is yellow, Balabhadra is white, the last two having almond-shaped eyes. The extraordinary appearance of the Jagannatha triad is explained by various myths. The most popular states that when Krishna was killed by the hunter Jaras, his body was left to decompose beneath a tree. King Indradyumna, instructed by VISHNU to fashion an image of Jagannatha in which to enshrine the bones, approached the divine craftsman VISHVAKARMA, who consented to undertake the work on condition that nobody disturbed him until the job was completed. Unable to contain his curiosity, the king interrupted the craftsman after fifteen days and the incensed Vishvakarma left, leaving the image looking like a stump. Eventually, BRAHMA endowed it with eyes and a soul, celebrated its consecration, during which the king sacrificed a hundred horses.

Every year, the RATHA-*yatra* (chariot FESTIVAL) takes place in the bright half of *Ashadha* (June–July).

Borne on huge chariots, Jagannatha, Subhadra and Balarama are taken out of town for an eight-day vacation. The tallest and bulkiest of the three chariots, measuring *c.* 15 metres in height and 11.5 metres in width, is the sixteen-wheel chariot of Jagannatha, which is drawn by 4,200 professional pullers. The English word 'juggernaut' is derived from this cumbersome conveyance. People throng the streets hoping to touch the chariots. Formerly, some were inadvertently crushed to death by the wheels, while others threw themselves beneath them, hoping to attain bliss, a practice stopped by the British authorities. The chariots are dismantled every year, the timber sold as relics, and an exact replica is built the following year.
Eschmann, A., H. Kulke, G. C. Tripathi, 1978

Jainism, Jaina Jainism is a one of the oldest surviving Indian philosophical systems. It was probably first articulated by Parshvanatha, who lived around the 8th century BCE, and later systematized by Mahavira (599?–526? BCE). At present, there are around three million Jainas in India, living in cities in Gujarat, Rajasthan, Maharashtra, Madhya Pradesh and Karnataka.

The main concern of Jainism has been to show how the soul can escape the perpetual cycle of death and rebirth. Jainas maintain that the tenets of their faith have always existed and are periodically repeated by a series of twenty-four omniscient teachers, the TIRTHANKARAS ('ford makers'), also called *jinas* ('conquerors'), whose perfection is the result of having conquered their desires through severe asceticism. Although endowed with superhuman characteristics, the *tirthankaras* are human and were born into human families.

The preoccupation with escaping from the cycle of death and rebirth slowly gained ground in the later

In accordance with Jaina iconography, this *tirthankara* is shown naked, standing upright; the narrow waist is emphasized by the breadth of his shoulders. Other typical features are the closely cropped curly hair, elongated ear lobes and the three folds on the neck. Karnataka. Bronze, 11th–12th century.

Vedic period. There were heterodox groups known as *shramanas* ('strivers'), who opposed the Brahmanical system with its stress on sacrifice, CASTE, etc., and rejected the authority of the VEDAS and the BRAHMANAS, firmly believing that spiritual progress could be achieved only by one's own efforts. Of the many groups of *shramanas*, two survive to the present day, BUDDHISM and Jainism. For Jainism the only way to reach MOKSHA is to embrace the way of asceticism. As all actions, even meritorious ones, cause KARMA for the individual soul, the best way to avoid the accumulation of *karma*, is to undertake severe austerities. In this, Jainism is much more rigorous than Buddhism: BUDDHA himself experienced the path of harsh asceticism, but opted out, preferring the 'middle way' in which both asceticism and the senses held a place – stressing, however, the pivotal importance of meditation as a means of attaining liberation.

The traditional belief in the eternal existence of Jainism notwithstanding, Mahavira ('great hero') is generally believed to be its historical founder. He was born in Kundagrama and lived and preached in the lower Gangetic plain and died nearby at Papa. There is some problem regarding the dates of his life: traditionally he is reputed to have lived in the 6th century, but modern scholarship inclines to date him a century later. The traditional account of his life, elaborated upon by later poets, centres on five main events: conception, birth, renunciation, gaining supreme knowledge and liberation. According to the Shvetambara ('white-clad') Jaina tradition, the future Mahavira was conceived in the womb of a BRAHMIN lady. As *tirthankaras* are usually born into KSHATRIYA families, INDRA caused the embryo to be transferred to the womb of Queen Trishala, wife of King Siddharta. The gods attended his birth and, because there had been an extraordinary increase of wealth in

the kingdom during Trishala's pregnancy, the child was called Vardhamana ('increaser'). Vardhamana led the usual life of young men of his age and status: he married, had a daughter and, at the age of thirty, after his parents' death, he decided to renounce the world. Leaving the town he pulled out his hair in five handfuls as an act of initiation and afterwards led the life of a wandering ascetic, bearing with equanimity its harshness, for which he received the name Mahavira. Eventually, twelve years, six months and fifteen days after his resolve to embrace ascetic life, he attained *kevala-jnana* (knowledge of the true nature of reality) and became the twenty-fourth and last *tirthankara* of the present age. He then wandered and preached until he died aged seventy-two, thus attaining *moksha*. With little variation, this narrative provides the blueprint for the account of the life of the *tirthankaras*, from Adinatha, also called Rishabhanatha, the mythical first *tirthankara*, to Mahavira.

Soon after Mahavira's death dissent arose among the Jains and the group split into at least four different sects. In the 3rd century BCE, during the reign of Chandragupta Maurya, a famine ravaged the northern part of the subcontinent and the head of the Jains, Bhadrabahu (active *c.* 290 BCE), led a migration as far as Shravana Belgola in the present-day Karnataka state. It is said that Chandragupta became a Jain monk and accompanied Bhadrabahu. The latter died by voluntary starvation and his example was followed twelve years later by Chandragupta; however there is no evidence to support this. Around 280 BCE, the emigrants returned north and found that the monks who remained there had ceased to observe the rule of nudity and other basic Jaina tenets. A council was held at Pataliputra (Patna) to discuss the view of the various groups and to collate the Jaina scriptures.

The 24th Jaina prophet Mahavira seated on a throne. Coloured print, 2001.

Eventually, in 80 CE the question of nudity caused the final split between the two sects. The Shvetambara, who had remained in the north during the famine were the most popular and their discipline was less arduous than that of the DIGAMBARA ('sky-clad'). Moreover, they admitted women into the monastic order as, according to their doctrine, women could attain salvation and were permitted to use clothed IMAGES in worship. The council of Valabhi of *c*. 455 CE finally fixed their canonical rules. The Digambaras continued in their strict observance of the original Jaina tenets and even today, the holiest among them observe the rules of nudity, and women are still prevented from attaining sainthood. The majority of the *Digambaras* are settled in southern India. They have no canonical books, because, according to them, the original canon containing Mahavira's teachings is lost. Both Shvetambara and Digambara are split into sub-sects.

From its original base in the Gangetic plain, Jainism spread to central India and southern India. It had a tremendous influence on economy, history and culture across the subcontinent. The situation changed dramatically in the 11th and 12th centuries, when Jainas were persecuted first by the brahmins and in the following century by the Muslims.

The most important of Jain vows is the pledge to non-violence (*ahimsa*). This is followed by monks and laymen alike. Monks and nuns often wear a mask, in order to avoid inhaling insects, and carry a broom with which they sweep the ground free from insects, for *ahimsa* extends to refusing to molest any living creature. Jains refrain from eating meat, eggs, fish, honey (which involves the killing the bees) and any root vegetable (this would result in killing the plant). The water they use is thoroughly filtered to avoid killing organisms. Philanthropy is an extension of the principle of non-violence: hostels for pilgrims, orphans and widows and hospitals, veterinary clinics, etc., have been and still are sponsored by Jains.

Although Jainism started as an atheistic movement, with no creator figure or other deities, in the course of time – and no doubt under the influence of Hinduism – a Jaina pantheon evolved: the numerous spheres of the Jaina heaven are populated by saints (*tirthankaras*) and a number of Hindu gods have also found a place there. In their worship Shvetambaras use a profusion of flowers, fruits and sandalwood paste to decorate the numerous images in their temples. In the course of its long history, Jainism came to accept the difference between castes, but there is little social or ritual discrimination among them. The principle of *ahimsa* had a determinant influence on Jaina life, for Jains are prohibited to engage in agriculture, animal husbandry, forestry and their activities are therefore restricted to sedentary jobs, such as moneylending, banking and trading. Today, a substantial number of the largest firms producing machinery, textiles, paper and cement, are owned by Jains. They have been great patrons of the ARTS, in particular of TEMPLES such as those at Dilvara, Mount Abu (11th century) and Ranakpur (1439). Their remarkable literary output is preserved in exquisitely illustrated manuscripts on palm leaves and paper, which are jealously guarded in their libraries.
Dundas, P., 1992

Jamadagni A famous sage who, according to the MAHABHARATA, possessed a profound knowledge of the VEDAS and the SHASTRAS. Deciding to marry, he chose RENUKA, the beautiful daughter of King Renu; the king consented, fearing the great power of the RISHI. Jamadagni returned to the forest with his wife and they had five sons, including PARASHURAMA.

jata(s)

Right: The vulture Jatayu intercepts with his beak the progress of Ravana abducting Sita to Lanka in his flying chariot. Kalighat, Calcutta, West Bengal. Watercolour on paper, *c*. 1880.

Renuka often went to a stream near the hermitage to bathe and make pots from the RIVER clay. The power of her virtue was such that she was able to bake them by merely uttering a MANTRA.One day, however, walking to the river, she saw a GANDHARVA making love to his wife, which filled her mind with amorous thoughts and prevented her from fashioning her pots. Divining her thoughts and her loss of purity, Jamadagni ordered his sons to kill their sinful mother. Four of them refused and were cursed by their father to become idiots; Parashurama, the youngest, obeyed and decapitated her with his axe. Once Jamadagni's wrath was pacified, Parashurama asked him to restore his mother to life and his four brothers to their original state, and Jamadagni readily complied. A number of other stories deal with the theft of Jamadagni's wish-fulfilling COW KAMADHENU, with Jamadagni's death at the hands of King Kartavirya's sons, and with Parashurama's subsequent revenge.

Jambavan or **Jambavat** The king of the Bears, probably an aboriginal tribe, and an ally of RAMA in the battle of LANKA.

Jambudvipa 'the island of the rose-apple tree'. According to traditional Indian COSMOLOGY, Jambudvipa is located in the middle of seven insular continents, each one divided from the next by one of the seven seas of salt water, sugar-cane juice, wine, GHEE, curds, milk and fresh water. A huge *jambu* tree grows on the mythical Mount MERU at the centre of Jambudvipa, which is identified with India.

jambuvriksha '*jambu* tree' (*Eugenia jambolana*). One of the wish-granting trees (*kalpavriksha*) with branches touching the sky.

Janaka A king of proverbial wisdom and righteousness who ruled at Mithila, the capital of the kingdom of Videha (corresponding today to the region of Tirhut in northern Bihar). Janaka fought for the right of pious KSHATRIYAS to perform sacrifices without brahminical intervention. It is believed that his liberal outlook paved the way for the success of JAINISM and BUDDHISM among his descendants. He is most famous, however, as the father of SITA. Having no issue, Janaka offered a sacrifice for this purpose and, while ploughing the ground in preparation for the ceremony, found his daughter in the furrow, born of the Earth (hence the name Sita, meaning 'furrow'). Janaka possessed a huge bow which once belonged to SHIVA, and which no one could string. When Sita grew up, Janaka organized a SVAYAMVARA ('bride's choice'), ceremony for her, the condition for the MARRIAGE being that her future husband would bend Shiva's bow. RAMA, not only bent, but broke the bow, and thus won Sita's hand.

Janamejaya A mythical king, son of PARIKSHIT and great grandson of ARJUNA. In reparation for killing a BRAHMIN, VAISHAMPAYANA recited the entire MAHABHARATA to Janamejaya. According to the legend, when Parikshit died of a snakebite, Janamejaya avenged his father's death by sacrificing all the snakes, until the RISHI Astika intervened to save the last one, Takshaka. It is possible that the myth conceals some historical fact and that Parikshit was killed by the Naga, a hostile tribe, due to the possible confusion between the name of the tribe and the word for snake (*naga*).

Jangama 'moving, movable'. A VIRASHAIVA itinerant priest. The *jangamas* are held in great veneration by the Virashaivas and exercise an important influence

Leaf from a *Gitagovinda* manuscript. At the start of the *Gitagovinda*, Jayadeva celebrates all the incarnations of Vishnu, which are very finely drawn on the back wall of the chamber. Artist Manaku; Guler, Panjab Hills. Opaque watercolour on paper, *c.* 1730.

on the sect. Some *jangamas* are celibate and lead the life of a recluse, others marry and have families.

Janmashthami *see* FESTIVALS

japa 'repeating, whispering'. The repetition of a MANTRA or a prayer while meditating.

jata(s) 'matted hair, dreadlocks'. A sign of mourning and of indifference towards worldly matters. SHIVA's hair is gathered in a *jatamukuta* (a crown of matted hair) or, when his locks swirl around in the frenzy of his dance, they form a *jatabhara*. In iconography, ascetics, seers and devotees are depicted with *jatas*.

Jatayu or **Jatayus** One of the chiefs of the Vultures. A mythical bird, the eldest son of GARUDA by Shyeni (falcon). Jatayu was DASHARATHA's friend and a helper of RAMA. He witnessed the abduction of SITA and fought against RAVANA, wounding him and destroying his aerial chariot, but Ravana dealt him a fatal blow and he fell to earth. Rama and LAKSHMANA, while searching for Sita, chanced on the spot where Jatayu was dying and he told them of Sita's abduction. Rama and Lakshmana performed his FUNERAL RITES and his soul ascended to heaven on a fiery chariot.

jati 'birth'. Social status based on the family into which one is born and determining one's position in the family and in the CASTE. Although *jati* cannot be altered, exceptions were made and a KSHATRIYA or even a SHUDRA, after performing great austerities, could be admitted to the BRAHMINS.

Jayadeva (*c.* 1100). A court poet of King Lakshmanasena and one of the greatest SANSKRIT poets. Born in Kindavila, Bengal, Jayadeva reformed the KRISHNA cult and influenced a number of VAISHNAVA sects. The traditional account of his life describes him as a wandering SANNYASI, until he met Padmavati, the daughter of a BRAHMIN. Jayadeva persuaded Padmavati's father to let him marry her and settled down. It is believed that his most famous work, the *Gitagovinda*, ('Song of the Cowherd') was composed during this period. The poem is a drama with three characters – Krishna, RADHA and the *sakhi*, Radha's confidante – consisting of monologues, interspersed with lyric passages describing the mood of the lovers and eulogies of Krishna. The vivid and frank depiction of the amorous sports of Radha and Krishna have attracted much criticism, and attempts have been made to explain them as metaphors of the highest religious experience, the union of the human soul with the divine. The plot is simple. It opens with a short passage that briefly narrates Krishna's seduction by the older and more experienced Radha. Some time after the first encounter, Radha and the *sakhi* discover Krishna flirting with the GOPIS, and Radha retreats alone to reminisce sadly on her lovemaking with Krishna and, eventually, falls into a kind of stupor. Meanwhile, Krishna, alone and brooding over the past, regrets his dalliance with the *gopis* and goes to Radha to beg forgiveness. After mediation by the *sakhi*, Radha relents and the couple enter the bridal chamber. The *Gitagovinda* continues to have an enormous impact on ritual, literature and the ARTS. It is sung as part of the daily ritual in the JAGANNATHA temple at PURI.
Stoler Miller, B., 1978

jnana 'knowledge, knowing'. Initially *jnana* seems to have indicated the specific knowledge needed for work such as agriculture and carpentry. It later came to refer to the magical or spiritual knowledge that

Shiva sits on a diminutive Kailasa, surrounded by four sages. In his upper hands are a snake and a flame, the lower right is in *vyakhyanamudra* and in the left is a bundle of *kusha* grass. With his right foot Shiva crushes ignorance, personified by Apasmara. Tamil Nadu. Bronze, 15th century.

was required by the priest. This spiritual knowledge involved psychic powers and the use of MANTRAS and became the sole domain of the priestly class, which had the privilege of communicating with the divine through sacrifice.

Jnana Dakshinamurti 'knowledge DAKSHINAMURTI'. A form of SHIVA, symbolizing supreme knowledge. In this form, Shiva is the supreme GURU, the embodiment of transcendent consciousness. He is generally shown with four arms, seated, with the right foot placed on the APASMARA (ignorance personified) and surrounded by sages and, occasionally, wild ANIMALS. In his upper hands he carries a snake and a flame; the lower right is in *vyakhyanamudra*, and the left holds a bundle of KUSHA grass.

Jnanadeva, Jnaneshvara or **Dnyadeo** (1275–96) A poet saint from Maharashtra, author of VAISHNAVA hymns in honour of VITHOBA and Rukmini, who are forms of KRISHNA and RADHA, worshipped at PANDHARPUR, Maharashtra. He is renowned for a commented paraphrase of the BHAGAVADGITA, known as the *Jnaneshvari* and written in Old Marathi, one of the most popular and revered books in Maharashtra. According to the traditional account, Jnanadeva ended his life the age of twenty-two, at Alandi on the Krishna RIVER, now one of the important PILGRIMAGE sites of Maharashtra. Visitors flock there, especially on the anniversary of the saint's death in November.

jnanamudra 'gesture of knowledge'. The tips of the thumb and index fingers touch, roughly forming a circle, and the hand is held against the heart. *Jnanamudra* is characteristic of JNANA DAKSHINAMURTI, the ALVARS and others.

Jnanasambandar *see* SAMBANDAR

Jumna *see* YAMUNA

Jvalamukhi or **Jwalamukhi** 'mouth of fire'. One of the SHAKTA PITHAS, or seats of the goddess, traditionally associated with parts of the dismembered body of SATI. Jvalamukhi, a volcanic site in Himachal Pradesh, is the place where the tongue of the goddess fell.

Jyeshtha(devi), 'the eldest, chief, best', or **Alakshmi**. An ancient southern Indian goddess, the oldest sister of LAKSHMI, but endowed with the opposite qualities and characteristics. Her worship has spread throughout India. She is often identified with the smallpox goddess SHITALA. In some texts Jyeshtha is depicted as the personification of old age, with a sagging belly and breasts. She rides on an ass, a crow decorates her banner and her weapon is a broom.

jyotirlinga 'LINGA of light'. SHIVA assumed the form of an effulgent *linga*, without beginning or end, to force BRAHMA and VISHNU to accept his supremacy. There are twelve *jyotirlingas* worshipped as radiant symbols of Shiva in various parts of India. Among the most important ones are the Mahakala of UJJAIN, the Kedarnatha from KEDARNATH in the Himalayas and the Omkareshvara, located on an island in the NARMADA river.

jyotisha 'astronomy'. The term *jyotisha* encompasses both astronomy and astrology. It is counted among the six *Vedangas*, limbs of the VEDAS or auxiliary sciences. Though the Vedic sage Bhrigu was believed to have been the first to refine *jyotisha* and to compile astrological charts of every person born or to be born in this world, it seems probable that the

jnanamudra

first rudiments of *jyotisha* were imported from Mesopotamia and from Persia. From the 3rd century India became strongly influenced by Greek sources. The first methodical discussion of the subject takes place in the *Siddhantas*, the earliest treatises on astronomy, in which a number of Greek authorities are mentioned. A major work on *jyotisha* is the *Panchasiddhantika* by Varahamihira (505–587), who gives a digest of the five most influential astronomical works of his time. In all these works, the influence of the Greek school of Alexandria is clear as terms as well as theories are directly borrowed from Latin and Greek. In the 8th century, the contact with the Arab world lent impetus to astronomical studies, from which both nations greatly profited. However, the main concern of Hindu astronomers remained astrology and the casting of horoscopes. The astronomical knowledge of Central Asian Islamic universities was brought to India by the Mughals, and had a strong impact on Indian scholarship. The astronomer king, Jai Singh II (1699–1744), the founder of Jaipur, built five observatories, or *jantra* (YANTRA), in Delhi, as well as in VARANASI, MATHURA (no longer extant), UJJAIN and Udaipur. The instruments, huge masonry structures, are built following the Central Asian models of Ulugh Beg at Samarqand.

Ka 'who?'. SANSKRIT interrogative pronoun used to refer to the ineffable source of the universe. Oblations to *Ka* are offered in silence, because everything undefined or unnamed belongs to him. Later *Ka* was identified with PRAJAPATI.

Kabir (1440?–1518?) Wandering poet saint born in VARANASI to Muslim parents. One of the most revered names in India, venerated by Hindus and Muslims alike, he has been styled 'Father of Hindi poetry' and his total contempt for the contemporary religious establishment earned him the title of 'Indian Luther'. A weaver by trade, Kabir eventually became a disciple of the Hindu reformer RAMANANDA. Under his influence he absorbed some Hindu thoughts, although his doctrine showed influences of southern Indian Christianity. He sought to bring together Hindus and Muslims, and preached that Allah, VISHNU, RAMA, KRISHNA, etc., were different names for the one Supreme Deity. Against both the worship of IMAGES and the theological subtleties of the *mullahs*, he was critical of the VEDAS and the PURANAS, as well as parts of the Koran. He accepted KARMA and rebirth, and maintained that the only way to attain salvation was through BHAKTI (love of God). His writings, in a colloquial form of Hindi, enjoyed mass popularity. His verses, critical of theologians, renouncers, religious ceremonies and image worship, are collected in a number of short maxims (*sakhis*) still in common use, and in his doctrinal poems, the *Ramaini*. His thought and his writings influenced his contemporary, Guru Nanak, founder of SIKHISM, and were introduced into the sacred book of the Sikhs, the *Adi Granth*. Persecuted for his rebellious and reformist ideas, Kabir wandered all over northern India expounding his doctrine and eventually ended his life in Maghar (Uttar Pradesh).

Left: Shiva sits on top of Mount Kailasa, whose peaks are inhabited by ascetics. At the foot of the mountain, Narada, and the three-legged Bhringi. Caption in Telugu. Probably Thanjavur *c.* 1830. From an album of paintings on European paper watermarked 1820.

Opposite: Markandeya embraces the *linga* from which Shiva emerges, as Kalarimurti. The *linga* has a face and a conspicuous *tripundra* mark. Caption in Telugu. Probably Thanjavur, *c.* 1830. From an album of paintings on European paper watermarked 1820.

Far right: The goddess Kali with dishevelled hair, protruding tongue, in a skirt of hands and with a garland of skulls, tramples on Shiva. The upper right hand is in *abhayamudra*, the left brandishes a chopper, the lower right is in *varadamudra*, the left carries a severed head. Coloured print, *c.* 1950.

His disciples, the Kabir-*panthis*, are mostly found in Uttar Pradesh.
Vaudeville, Ch., 1974

kadamba (*Ipomoea aquatica Forsk.*). A tree sacred to KRISHNA and to SHIVA. Its yellow flowers, which open only after dark and emit a rich fragrance, are used for perfume oil. A mild spirit can be distilled from the petals and it is favoured by worshippers of DEVI. The fruit of the *kadamba* is the size of an orange, its juice a remedy against gastric disorders and its thirst-quenching properties effective against fever.
Patnaik, N., 1993

Kadru 'reddish-brown'. One of the daughters of DAKSHA and a wife of KASHYAPA. There are a number of legends about Kadru and it is difficult to gain a coherent picture of her life. According to the *Vishnu* PURANA, the seer Kashyapa promised both his wives, Kadru and VINATA, as many children as they wanted. Kadru asked for a thousand, but Vinata only desired two, which had to be superior to Kadru's thousand. Eventually, they were born as eggs. The serpents hatched from Kadru's eggs and among them were SHESHA and VASUKI. Vinata grew impatient as her eggs gave no sign of hatching. Finally, she opened one of them to find a deformed child, ARUNA, who became SURYA's charioteer. In the second was a handsome youth with unformed feet who, in some myths, is identified with GARUDA. Kadru managed by trickery to enslave Vinata and subjected her to endless indignities, from which she was eventually freed by Garuda, who slew the thousand sons of Kadru and became the enemy of the serpents. The principal theme of the Kadru myth revolves around the serpents (NAGAS). It has been suggested that the name *Naga* may refer to a non-ARYAN tribe opposed to the Aryan culture.

Kaikeyi 'of Kaikeya'. The youngest and the most beautiful of the three queens of DASHARATHA, king of Kosala. She was the mother of RAMA's brother BHARATA. According to legend, when Dasharatha married her, he promised her two favours, which she did not claim until much later, when Rama was about to be installed as a heir apparent. Incited by her hunchback servant MANTHARA, she demanded that her own son, Bharata, be the successor to the throne, and that Rama and SITA be exiled in the forest for fourteen years. This was granted, and initiated a series of momentous events narrated in the RAMAYANA.

Kailasa or **Kailasha** 'crystalline, icy'. Name of a MOUNTAIN range in the Himalayas, but traditionally the name of a single peak, formed like a LINGA, sited to the south of Mount MERU. Kailasa is generally regarded as the abode of SHIVA and KUBERA and the centre of the universe. The GANGA rises from the roots of a huge jujube tree which is said to grow there.

Kaitabha According to a cosmogonic myth, Kaitabha and his companion MADHU originated from VISHNU's ear while he was sleeping on the waters of the primeval ocean. Kaithaba – variously regarded as an ASURA, a DAITYA or a DANAVA – and Madhu planned to kill BRAHMA (seated in the lotus sprouting from Vishnu's navel) and destroy the new world that was on the point of being created. Brahma, however, saw them and invoked the goddess Mahamaya or YOGANIDRA, the personification of Vishnu's sleep, at which point Vishnu awoke and killed the two conspirators. According to another myth, Vishnu in his form as HAYAGRIVA, killed them and retrieved the VEDAS they had stolen and concealed on the seabed.

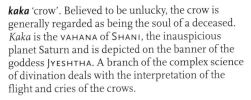

kaka 'crow'. Believed to be unlucky, the crow is generally regarded as being the soul of a deceased. *Kaka* is the VAHANA of SHANI, the inauspicious planet Saturn and is depicted on the banner of the goddess JYESHTHA. A branch of the complex science of divination deals with the interpretation of the flight and cries of the crows.

Kala 'time'. A word derived from *kal* (calculate, enumerate), one of the terms used for time, fate and destiny. It also means 'black' and refers to Kala's function as destroyer, although it is his SHAKTI, KALI, who is the actual destroyer of all creatures. Kala is depicted with fierce bloodshot EYES and carries a noose to capture his victims. Kala is the name of both SHIVA and YAMA.

Kala-Bhairava 'Black, death or time Bhairava'. DAKSHINAMURTI in his aspect as god of death.

Kalaharamurti or **Kalantakamurti** Aspect of SHIVA as conqueror of time and death. *See also* KALARIMURTI

Kalahasti This celebrated SHAIVA PILGRIMAGE centre in Andhra Pradesh, east of Tirupati, is connected with a number of legends, including one in which an ELEPHANT, a snake and a spider gained salvation by worshipping SHIVA. Enshrined in the Kalahastishvara TEMPLE is one of the five elemental LINGAS in southern India, the *Vayu-linga* or 'wind, air linga'. Kalahasti is also connected with KANNAPPA, one of the Shaiva saints and the hunter who plucked out his eyes as an offering to Shiva.

kalakuta or *halahala* 'black (death) substance'. At the time of the CHURNING OF THE OCEAN, the *kalakuta* poison emerged. SHIVA swallowed it and held it in his throat, saving the world from its deadly effect.

It burnt his throat which became blue, hence his epithet Nilakantha, 'blue-throated'.

Kalamukhas 'black-faced'. A sect of the PASHUPATA cult, popular in southern India between the 9th and the 14th centuries, so called because its members wore a black streak on their foreheads. They worshipped KALI and SHIVA in his form as MAHAKALA, the Great Destroyer, or as BHAIRAVA. The contribution of the Kalamukhas to education was substantial. Their main centres were at Balligave and Kuppatur in Karnataka and at Srishailam in Andhra Pradesh. The Kalamukhas seemed to have vanished in the 15th century, when they were absorbed by the VIRASHAIVAS.

Kalantakamurti *see* KALAHARAMURTI

Kalarimurti Aspect of SHIVA as conqueror of KALA or YAMA, the personifications of time and death. This aspect, also called *Markandeyanugraha*, '(form of Shiva) bestowing grace upon MARKANDEYA', refers to a mythical event, in which Markandeya, a youthful devotee of Shiva, was doomed to die on his sixteenth birthday. When the fateful day came, filled with terror at the sight of Yama's hordes he clutched the LINGA. Shiva appeared, kicked Yama in the chest and freed Markandeya from death.

kalasha 'ewer, pitcher, water pot'. One of the most important symbols of Indian culture. In ancient times the *kalasha* symbolized the universe; BRAHMA, for instance carries a *kalasha* in his hand, representing the earth as the container and nourisher of all things. *See also* KUMBHA

kali 1. Name of one of the pieces in the game of dice, *kali* is marked with a single dot, the losing die.

The icon of the goddess Kali in the Kalighat temple. The painting emphasizes her three eyes, extended tongue, dishevelled hair and garland of severed heads. In her hands are the usual attributes. Caption in English. Kalighat, Calcutta, West Bengal. Watercolour on paper, c. 1860.

Krishna dances on the head of the serpent Kaliya. To the left, one of the snake's wives in *anjalimudra*, asks for mercy. Relief on the wall of the Kedareshvara temple, Halebid, Karnataka. Soapstone, 12th–13th century.

2. Name of the fourth YUGA, the 'dark' age. According to the PURANAS, it commenced at the death of KRISHNA and will end when VISHNU appears as KALKI. In the course of this age, civilization, moral and spiritual values will gradually deteriorate and mankind will be plunged into confusion.

Kali or **Kali Ma** (Tamil: **Kali Amman**) Name of one of the most famous goddesses of the Indian pantheon, the all-powerful SHAKTI of SHIVA, the personification of both creative and destructive power of time. Generally depicted as a dark-skinned, naked, gaunt, two- or four-armed old woman devouring all beings, her darkness hints at the dissolution of all individuality in the timeless night, which can also be filled with the potentialities of new life. Her nakedness symbolizes the stripping away of the illusions in which life is entangled. In her hands she may hold a noose, a sword, a club topped by a skull, symbols of her destructive powers, and a severed head, a reminder of the transience of life. Her upper and lower right hand, may be in ABHAYA- and VARADAMUDRA respectively, thus reassuring her devotees and bestowing on them the gift of pure perception, which will lead them to liberation. Sometimes she is shown wearing a garland of skulls or heads and a skirt of chopped arms. She is depicted dancing in the cremation ground, accompanied by a posse of ghouls and jackals. Much of Kali's notoriety in the West derives from the THAGS, who strangled their victims in her name, and from the human sacrifices that were offered to her. Nowadays, goats are used instead. The worship of Kali is particularly widespread in Bengal, where the KALIGHAT TEMPLE, the main centre of her worship, is located.

Kalighat or **Kalighata** 'GHAT of KALI'. Suburb of Calcutta, site of the most sacred of the Kali TEMPLES.

According to legend, after the death of his wife SATI, SHIVA wandered in distress with her body, threatening to destroy the world. VISHNU intervened and with his CHAKRA cut Sati's body into fifty-one pieces, which fell onto the earth, thus creating the *Shakti-pithas* (seats of the goddess) where her spiritual force dwells. Tradition states that her skull fell at Kalighat. This name was also given to a striking school of painting which flourished in and around Calcutta between c. 1830 and c. 1930. Jain, J., 1999

Kaliya Name of a five-headed NAGA, who was said to live in a whirlpool of the river YAMUNA, polluting the neighbourhood with his poison. KRISHNA, a mere child, jumped into the river and fought Kaliya and the other serpents living there. On the verge of being defeated, BALARAMA reminded him of his divine nature and Krishna regained strength, defeated the *nagas* and celebrated his victory by dancing on the hood of Kaliya until he begged for mercy. Eventually, Kaliya and his followers settled near the sea. One of the most frequent representations of Krishna is as Kaliyadamana ('tamer of Kaliya'), in which he is a young child dancing on the hood of a snake.

Kalki or **Kalkin** 'having a white horse'. The tenth incarnation of VISHNU, which will mark the end of the KALI YUGA, when a new era will begin in which righteousness, law and order will prevail. Kalkin is described either as a warrior brandishing a blazing sword riding a white horse, or as a gigantic creature with a horse's head, or simply as a white horse.

kalpa A day and a night of BRAHMA, or one thousand *mahayugas*, the duration of the world, which translated into human years amounts to 4.32 billion years.

Left: The future and tenth incarnation of Vishnu, Kalki is shown here as a horse-headed warrior. Caption in Telugu. Probably Thanjavur, *c.* 1830. From an album of paintings on European paper watermarked 1820.

Right: Kama, armed with a sugar-cane bow, rides on his *vahana*, in this case a *hamsa*. Pilaster of the 17th-century *kalyana-mandapa* (marriage hall) of the Varadaraja temple, Kanchipuram, Tamil Nadu. Granite.

kalpadruma 'tree of a world period'. Wishing tree, granting riches and fame, sacred to INDRANI.

Kalpasutra Body of literature related to ritual. In JAINISM, the *Kalpasutra*, apart from stating the rules for monastic ritual, is the main source for the biographies of MAHAVIRA and the twenty-three TIRTHANKARAS who preceded him.

Kama, kama I. The god of love. The name derives from *kam*, 'longing for, wish or desire'. The origins of Kama are variously given. In the RIGVEDA Kama is, among other things, 'the longing for happiness and fulfilment of desires'; in the ATHARVAVEDA *kama* was the primeval stir or impulse at the beginning of creation. In the PURANAS Kama appears as the youthful god of love, hero of many stories. One of the most renowned myths is the *Kamadahana* ('the burning of Kama') by SHIVA. The power of the gods was threatened by an ASURA who could only be killed by a son of Shiva, so, at the gods' behest, Kama shot an arrow at the meditating god to awaken him from his trance and direct his attention towards PARVATI. Shiva, resenting the disruption, glanced at him, reducing him to a heap of ashes. One of Kama's wives, RATI, the personification of sensual delight, pleaded with Shiva to restore her husband to life. Shiva consented to restore him only as a mental image of true love rather than physical desire. Since this incident Kama is known as Ananga (bodiless).

Generally riding on a parrot, occasionally on a cuckoo or a swan, Kama is depicted armed with a bow made of sugar cane (*ikshukodanda*) bearing a string formed by a row of buzzing bees, five flower-tipped arrows, symbolizing the five senses, and on his banner the MAKARA, an aquatic monster. His second wife is Priti, the embodiment of affection, his daughter is Trishna (or Trisha), 'thirst', a metaphor

for desire. His attendant is VASANTA, the Spring, the season of the renewal of all forms of life. Kama's other names include: Kamadeva ('god of love'), Kandarpa ('satisfier'), Madana ('seducer of the mind'), Mara ('destroyer'), Manmatha ('agitator') and Smara ('rememberer').
2. *kama* or sensual enjoyment is one of the four aims of life (PURUSHARTHA).

Kamadhenu 'wish(-fulfilling) COW'. The mythical cow of plenty who could grant her owner any wish. As the daughter of DAKSHA and the wife of the seer KASHYAPA, Kamadhenu emerged from the sea at the CHURNING OF THE OCEAN. She symbolizes abundance, bountiful nature and continuity of life.

Kamakhya 'wanton-eyed'. A form of DURGA worshipped particularly in the ancient region of Kamarupa, roughly corresponding to Assam. The Kamakhya TEMPLE is situated on Kamagiri, a hill near Guhavati, which is said to have been the backdrop to the ecstatic lovemaking of SHIVA and SATI. When Sati died and was dismembered, her genitals are said to have fallen onto Kamagiri and a temple was built on the hallowed site. There is no IMAGE representing the goddess, but a cleft in the rock, which is kept moist by a natural spring, symbolizes her YONI. When the temple was dedicated in 1565 it is said that 140 men voluntarily offered their heads in her honour, and human sacrifices continued until 1832. The victims, from the *bhogi* class, once accepted for sacrifice, were deemed sacred and were given everything they desired, until they were decapitated at the annual festival in honour of the goddess. Human victims are now replaced by goats.

Kamakshi 'having EYES filled with desire'. An aspect of SHIVA'S SHAKTI worshipped as the Supreme

Left: Kamakshi of Kanchi seated on a throne. In the foreground are a number of ritual implements. Coloured print, 1980s.

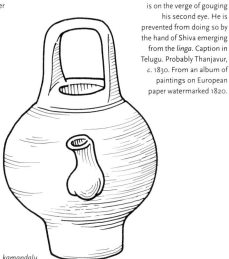

Opposite: One of the sixty-three *nayanmars*, Kannappa is on the verge of gouging his second eye. He is prevented from doing so by the hand of Shiva emerging from the *linga*. Caption in Telugu. Probably Thanjavur, *c*. 1830. From an album of paintings on European paper watermarked 1820.

kamandalu

Goddess in the Kamakshi TEMPLE at KANCHIPURAM. The main icon shows the goddess in her benign form, seated on a throne, carrying a noose, an elephant hook, a sugar-cane bow and arrows of flowers. The ritual, however, focuses on the *Shrichakra* YANTRA, placed in front of her IMAGE. The *yantra* is said to have been installed by the 9th-century philosopher SHANKARA. The present-day *yantra* dates from the 16th century.
Hudson, D., 1993

kamandalu 'vessel, water jar', especially the spouted water jar of the ascetics. Generally it denotes asceticism. However, when the *kamandalu* contains AMRITA, it is connected with immortality. It is an attribute of a number of deities, such as BRAHMA, SARASVATI, SHIVA, VARUNA and the RIVER goddess GANGA.

Kamashastra 'treatise on love'. Body of literature concerned with the art, science and technique of EROTICS.

Kamasutra *see* EROTICS, VATSYAYANA

Kamsa The tyrannical king of MATHURA, putative son of UGRASENA and his queen. In reality, he was the son of the ASURA Drumalika, who fell in love with the queen, assumed the shape of Ugrasena and united with her. Eventually Kamsa usurped the throne and imprisoned his father. VISHNU assumed the form of KRISHNA to avenge this crime.

Kanchipuram One of the seven holy cities of India, sited sixty kilometres south-west of Chennai (Madras), Kanchipuram (anglicized in Conjeeveram) was the capital of the Pallava dynasty from the 6th to the 8th century. Its importance as a religious, cultural

and commercial centre still remains and it has been associated with practically all the religious movements in southern India. According to the 7th-century Chinese pilgrim Hsuen-Tsang, who visited the town in 640 CE, Kanchipuram was one of the great seats of BUDDHIST learning. It boasted a substantial number of Hindu TEMPLES and a sizeable JAINA population.

The religious monuments are distributed across three distinct zones: to the north stands SHIVA Kanchi, associated with the temples of Shiva and KAMAKSHI, one of the centres of SHAKTI worship. Shiva is worshipped in the main sanctuary of the Ekambareshvara temple under the form of the earth LINGA. To the south-east lies VISHNU Kanchi, dominated by the VARADARAJA temple, one of the three most important VAISHNAVA shrines in southern India. To the extreme west, across the Vegavati river, is Jaina Kanchi and its Jaina shrines.

Kankalamurti 'form with a skeleton'. One of the awesome forms of SHIVA, who killed the doorkeeper of VISHNU, Vishvaksena, because he refused him access to his master. Shiva is shown as a mendicant, walking, occasionally accompanied by a deer and a GANA, carrying either a trident or a long staff on which hangs Vishvaksena's skeleton. This representation is very similar to BHIKSHATANAMURTI.

Kannappa 'he who gave his EYES'. One of the sixty-three NAYANMARS, a hunter by CASTE, who offered his eyes to SHIVA. His real name was Tinnappa. One day, as he worshipped, Shiva tested his devotion by making it appear that blood was oozing from the eye of the LINGA. Believing the eye had been damaged, the hunter removed one of his own to replaced the injured eye. He then noticed that the *linga*'s other

Right: Karaikkal Ammeiyar portrayed sitting playing the cymbals and singing the god's praises. The small fangs at the corners of her mouth hint at her fierce nature. Tamil Nadu. Bronze, 16th century.

eye was affected, so he decided to pluck out his second eye. As this would have blinded him and prevented him locating the Lord's eye, he placed his foot on the *linga* at the exact spot of the seemingly injured eye. Pleased with his devotion, Shiva manifested himself, restored the hunter's eyesight and named him Kannappa. Kannappa is worshipped particularly at KALAHASTI, near Tirupati in Andhra Pradesh, where his image is placed near the linga and PUJA is offered to him prior to Shiva.

Kanphata *yogis* 'split-ear *yogis*'. *See* GORAKHNATH

Kanya Kumari 'virgin goddess'. An aspect of DURGA worshipped at Kanyakumari, formerly Cape Comorin, on the southernmost tip of India, at the confluence of the Bay of Bengal, the Arabian Sea and the Indian Ocean. One of the myths connected with her, narrates how the god of Suchindram, a nearby town, had decided to marry the goddess. The gods were displeased at this resolve, as on marriage she would lose her power (*shakti*) and would therefore be unable to overcome demons (ASURA). So they confided in NARADA, who solved the problem with a stratagem. While the god of Suchindram was on his way to the ceremony, Narada imitated the crow of a cock. Thinking he had missed the auspicious hour, the god retraced his steps. Eventually, the virgin goddess was able to kill the *asura* Bana and re-establish peace and prosperity in the land. Her TEMPLE on the seashore is one of the most important PILGRIMAGE places in India.

kapala 'skull cup'. Made out of the upper half of a human skull. It is a common attribute of a number of awesome forms of SHIVA, such as BHIKSHATANA or KANKALAMURTI, as well as of KALI and DURGA. The *kapala* is used in some types of Tantric worship.

Kapalika(s) 'skull carrier'. A southern Indian offshoot of the PASHUPATA sect (one of the oldest SHAIVA sects), notorious for its antinomianism and lax attitude towards CASTE distinctions. The Kapalikas, devotees of BHAIRAVA, eventually became associated with the KALAMUKHAS. The epigraphic information on both sects is fragmentary, and later 12th- or 13th-century accounts are prejudiced against them.

Karaikkal Ammeiyar 'the lady or mother from Karaikkal'. One of the great figures of early Tamil literature and one of the few female saints to be included among the NAYANMARS. Karaikkal Ammeiyar, whose real name was Punitavati, probably lived in the 6th century. She was born in Karaikkal and from childhood was a great devotee of SHIVA. The account of her life in Sekkilar's PERIYA PURANAM states that she was married to a merchant who, awed by her sanctity, decided to move to another town where he remarried and had a daughter. Pleased to see him settled again, Karaikkal Ammeiyar asked Shiva to become a skeletal figure, like the goblins who danced around him on cremation grounds. She then ascended Mount KAILASA on her hands, because she did not want to defile the holy ground with her feet. Shiva freed her from the chain of death and rebirth, and she requested the favour of remaining at his feet and singing his praises during his cosmic dance. She took up residence at Alangadu in Tamil Nadu, remaining there for the rest of her life. She signed her forceful poems, often filled with gruesome images, as Karaikkal *pey* (the goblin from Karaikkal), and is depicted as a seated skeletal figure, with dishevelled hair, distended breasts and protruding fangs, playing the cymbals and singing.
Karavelane, 1956

The peacock *vahana* of the youthful Karttikeya, is emphasized in this print. The god carries in the right hand his typical weapon, the spear, while the left rests around the peacock's neck. A cobra rears beneath the bird's talons. Tamil Nadu. Colour print on paper, mid-1970s.

karandamakuta or ***karandamukuta*** 'basket crown'. Small crown shaped like an inverted bowl, generally worn by consort goddesses and minor deities.

Karivarada 'conferring a grace on the ELEPHANT'. An epithet of VISHNU. It refers to the episode in which Vishnu rescued the king of the elephants, Gajendra, from the fangs of a crocodile. This incident is also referred to as *Gajendramoksha*, 'deliverance of Gajendra'.

karma(n) 'action, ritual act, sacrifice'. Originally the meaning was neutral, referring to the practice of rituals and other religious observances. Later, it was identified with DHARMA and associated with the good or bad intentions behind an action which eventually influence the performer's future life in a positive or negative way.

Karna 'ear'. One of the principal characters in the MAHABHARATA and the great rival of ARJUNA. Karna was the son of SURYA, the Sun god, and of KUNTI who, to conceal her premarital affair, abandoned her child at birth on the shore of the YAMUNA, where he was adopted by a lowly childless family. He became an exceptionally skilled archer, though his humble origins prevented him from participating in DRAUPADI'S svayamvara. When Arjuna won Draupadi's hand, Karna joined the KAURAVAS and was made king of Anga by DURYODHANA, who gained a powerful ally against the PANDAVAS. According to the *Mahabharata*, Karna was born wearing a resplendent cuirass and earrings (hence his name), but later he decided to exchange the cuirass for an irresistible javelin offered by INDRA, with fatal consequences. On the last day of the Great Battle, Karna's chariot became stuck in the mire, the javelin was useless and without his cuirass he was at the mercy of Arjuna. In vain Karna pleaded for time to release the wheels of his chariot; KRISHNA, who was driving Arjuna's chariot, reminded him of Karna's lack of mercy in similar situations and Arjuna killed him. Kunti was filled with remorse for not having previously disclosed the true identity of Karna to her sons, though, she did so after his death. His other names are Adhirathi or Suta ('charioteer'), from his foster-father's profession, Champadhipa ('king of Champa') and Kanina ('bastard').

Karttikeya 'associated with the KRITTIKAS (Pleiades)'. God of war and ruler of the planet Mars. Generally thought of as the son of SHIVA and PARVATI, Karttikeya's origins are differently accounted for. One tradition states that he was born without a mother, from his father who spilled his seed into the sacrificial fire, where it was concealed by AGNI and then transplanted into Parvati's womb. Another tradition maintains that Karttikeya was son of Agni and Svaha. Other accounts claim that Parvati entrusted her unborn son to Agni, who accidentally dropped him in the GANGA, causing him to be called the son of Agni and Ganga. The child, with his six heads and twelve arms, was brought up by the six Krittikas (hence his name).

The PURANAS state that Karttikeya was born in order to kill the mighty ASURA Taraka, who harassed the whole universe. Taraka had obtained the gift of immortality from BRAHMA, on condition that only a son of Shiva could kill him. At that time, however, Shiva had just lost his wife SATI and was engaged in meditation. So the gods resolved to send KAMA, with RATI and Vasanta, the god of Spring, to inspire Shiva with erotic thoughts, and so lead to the birth of a son. Kama was successful in awakening Shiva from his trance as the goddess PARVATI was passing and Shiva's seed spilled onto her, or according to other

kashyadanda

Right: Shankaracharya seated with the *kashyadanda* resting on his right shoulder. His forehead and body are decorated with the three horizontal marks (*tripundra*) and garlands of *rudrakshas*, typical of the followers of Shiva. 20th century.

sources, fell into the sacrificial flame. Subsequently, Karttikeya was born, becoming the leader of the divine armies and killing a number of *asuras*. He is shown riding or standing near his peacock, a symbol of immortality, carrying various weapons, such as a club, battleaxe and chisel, and his typical weapon, the spear. On his banner is emblazoned a cock, a symbol of the sun. Although he appears as a young unmarried god in a number of myths, he is wedded to DEVASENA, and in southern India has a second wife, VALLI. On account of his youthful appearance, Karttikeya is also known as Kumara, the boy around whom the Kaumara cult evolved. Known in Tamil Nadu as SUBRAHMANYA or MURUGAN, Karttikeya is one of the most prominent deities of southern India and has his own cult and mythology. Occasionally, Karttikeya is associated with the SAPTAMATRIKAS, replacing either GANESHA or VIRABHADRA as their guardian and protector. His other names include Guha ('the mysterious'), Shaktidhara ('wielder of the spear'), Senapati ('foremost among generals'), Shanmukha ('six-faced') and Skanda ('attacker').

kashayadanda A staff carried by the ascetics, with a red-brown cloth (*kashaya*) tied to it.

Kashi 'the shiny one'. *See* VARANASI

Kashyapa 'tortoise'. Name of a mythical RISHI whose origins are difficult to trace and around whom a number of conflicting myths have been woven. His name is frequently mentioned in the ATHARVAVEDA and he is believed to be self-generated. He is connected with SURYA and is identified with the sun, whose slow motion through the sky is compared to the progress of the tortoise. According to legend, PRAJAPATI assumed the form of a tortoise and created all living beings. A pun on the word 'tortoise'

prompted another myth maintaining that Kashyapa is the progenitor of all creatures. The MAHABHARATA and the PURANAS describe him as a prolific sage: he was married to thirteen of DAKSHA's daughters, among whom was ADITI, the mother of the twelve ADITYAS. He begot a number of varied creatures, such as the NAGAS, birds, and the DAITYAS and DANAVAS by DITI and Danu. In later legends, his role as creator is replaced by that of a *rishi* or a spiritual adviser, whose descendants are called Kashyapas.

Kathak 'story'. A graceful, yet flamboyant, dance style, characterized by intricate footwork and rapid whirling movements, *Kathak* originated in the northern part of India between the 15th and 16th centuries. Its themes are drawn occasionally from the epics, but more frequently from the various episodes of the KRISHNA story, especially his amorous exploits. *Kathak* used to be a solo dance, but this rule is now not always observed. This style flourished during the Mughal period and gradually became the favoured style of the *nautch*-girls, many of whom were employed by Mughal rulers and noblemen as dancers, singers and musicians. Because of its associations with the *nautch*-girls and their often rather crudely suggestive performances, this graceful style of dancing fell into disrepute. Recently *Kathak* has been revived and a number of dedicated artists seek to restore it to its pristine state.

Kathakali 'story play'. Dance drama of coastal Kerala, possibly originating in village pantomimes. In due course, it received courtly patronage and evolved into an extremely sophisticated form of dramatic art. Traditionally, the performances take place in the open air, without stage props or other appurtenances, except oil lamps, and commencing at sunset, they last until dawn. The orchestra generally consists of two

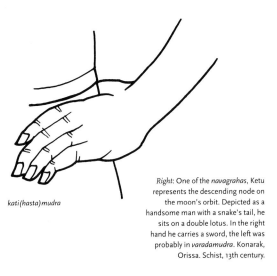

kati(hasta)mudra

Right: One of the *navagrahas*, Ketu represents the descending node on the moon's orbit. Depicted as a handsome man with a snake's tail, he sits on a double lotus. In the right hand he carries a sword, the left was probably in *varadamudra*. Konarak, Orissa. Schist, 13th century.

drummers, a cymbal player and string instruments. The actors do not speak and singers are entrusted with the dialogue. *Kathakali* is a masculine style of dance, involving great speed, agility and vigour. Characters are played by an all-male cast in which boys take on female roles, and colourful costumes, tall, round headgear encrusted with mirrors and elaborate make-up are typical of *Kathakali*. The gestures and stances are highly stylized and years of practice enable actors to control every muscle of the body, including those of the EYES, eyebrows, cheeks, lips and neck, which are used to convey the appropriate mood. The subject of each drama is generally drawn from the epics and the PURANAS. The standard repertoire consists of around a hundred plays, some written in a mixture of SANSKRIT and Malayalam by the ruling princes of Kerala.
Bharata Iyer, K., 1955

kati(hasta)mudra or *katyavalambita(hasta)* A stance or MUDRA in which one arm hangs by the body while the other hand is placed on the loin. This posture indicates ease.

Kaumodaki Name of the mace given either by VARUNA or AGNI to VISHNU. Kaumodaki is an insignia of sovereignty, symbolizing the power of knowledge and all-destroying time, and thus also associated with KALI. She is generally represented as a female, but occasionally as a male. *See also* GADA

Kaurava(s) '(descendants) of Kuru'. The patronymic refers generally to the sons of DHRITARASHTRA, the rivals of the PANDAVAS, whose exploits are narrated in the MAHABHARATA. Following the custom of levirate (*niyoga*), the sage VYASA fathered two sons by the widows of his half-brother Vichitravirya. PANDU was the son of Ambalika, and Dhritarashtra of

AMBIKA, the latter born blind because his mother could not bear to look at the emaciated sage, and closed her eyes while he was embracing her. Dhritarashtra married GANDHARI, who eventually became the mother of one hundred sons, among whom were DURYODHANA and Duhshasana. Ascending the throne after his brother Pandu's death, Dhritarashtra took the five Pandava princes into his care, treating them as his own children. The king and Gandhari died in a forest fire shortly after the great battle at Kurukshetra.

kaustubha A magical GEM that emerged from the waters at the time of the CHURNING OF THE OCEAN and is worn on the chest by VISHNU and KRISHNA.

kavacham see RAKSHA

kavati (Tamil: *kavadi*) A wooden staff, often with intricately adorned ends, surmounted by an arch made of bamboo and covered with cloth, which is carried on the shoulders by the devotees of MURUGAN during PILGRIMAGES and processions.

Kaveri (anglicized Cauvery). Known as the GANGA of the south, the Kaveri flows for approximately 785 kilometres from its source at Talakaveri in Kodagu (formerly Coorg) to Pumpuhar on the Bay of Bengal. Along its course are a number of holy sites, the most important of which is the Ranganatha TEMPLE on SRIRANGAM island. There are a number of myths related to the origin of the Kaveri; the popular story at Talakaveri narrates how the sage Kavera performed penance on a MOUNTAIN nearby to propitiate BRAHMA. The god gifted him with a daughter, Lopamudra, who manifested herself as the Kaveri. Eventually, the sage AGASTYA married Lopamudra and placed the RIVER in his water pot.

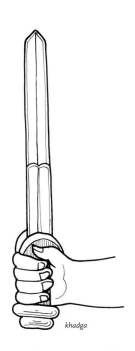

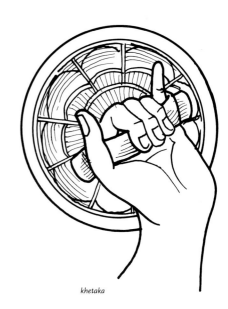

khadga   *khatvanga*   *khetaka*

One day, a crow tipped over the pot and the Kaveri flowed out of it. A similar story is narrated in Tamil Nadu and, through Agastya, an important figure in the myths pertaining to the origin of Tamil civilization, the Kaveri became a symbol of Tamil language, literature and culture. The link with the pot is equally relevant, because it hints at the river's function of sustainer and giver of life.
Michell, G. (ed.), 1999

Kedarnath A famous but remote SHAIVA PILGRIMAGE place in Uttar Pradesh and the location of one of the JYOTIRLINGAS. The site in the Himalayas is accessible only at the peak of the summer. The focus of worship centres around an ice *linga*.

Keshava 'long-haired'. Epithet of KRISHNA.

ketaki (*Pandanus odoratissimus*). A flower that should not be offered to SHIVA. While BRAHMA was flying through the sky in search for the top of the fiery LINGA, he saw a *ketaki* petal which had fallen from Shiva's hair, drifting through the air. He brought it to Shiva pretending that he had reached the top of the *linga*. *See also* LINGODBHAVAMURTI

Ketu 'brightness (?)'. One of the NAVAGRAHAS, the twin brother of RAHU. Both of them are considered inauspicious. Ketu personifies the descending node of the moon. There are different ways of representing Ketu. He can be depicted as a man with the body of a snake, carrying a sword in one hand with the other in VARAMUDRA. In southern India he is shown as a snake-headed man riding a chariot drawn by horses, a vulture or a frog.

khadga '(long) sword, sacrificial knife'. Typical of the warrior class, the *khadga* symbolizes not only

physical, but also spiritual power, as it destroys the veil of ignorance. It is the attribute of a number of deities, including CHAMUNDA, DURGA, KARTTIKEYA and YAMA.

Khandoba or **Khanderao** A local deity of the Deccan, whose worship is popular in Maharashtra, parts of Andhra and Karnataka since the 9th or 10th century and who is known by a variety of names. In Maharashtra his most common name is Khandoba, while in Karnataka it is Mailara or Mallaiah. One of his consorts, Mhalsa (Malavva in southern India) is sometimes referred to as BHAIRAVI. Khandoba appears to have developed from a folk deity into a complex combination of SHIVA, BHAIRAVA and, according to some scholars, SURYA. He is worshipped either as a LINGA or as an IMAGE showing him riding on NANDI or on a horse, with one or both of his wives. His attributes are the same as those carried by Bhairava, a sword, TRISHULA, DAMARU and skull cup and, like Bhairava, he is accompanied by a DOG. Khandoba originally had a dog's head, and this ANIMAL still plays an important role in his cult. The attendants of the TEMPLE at Gudguddapur, the main site of Khandoba worship, are believed to be the descendants of his dogs; at the yearly festival they bark and imitate canine behaviour.

khatvanga A club or a staff, sometimes a shin bone, surmounted by a skull. Attribute of various deities, especially of awe-inspiring ones, such as AGHORA and CHAMUNDA.

khetaka A shield, either round, oval or square, with a handle on the reverse. Typical attribute of a number of deities, such as AMBIKA, BHAIRAVA, CHAMUNDA and MAHISHASURAMARDINI.

kinnara

Below: Kirttimukha on the front porch of the Parashurameshvara temple. Bhubaneshvar, Orissa. Sandstone, 8th century.

kinnara(s), kinnari(s) 'what (kind of a) man?'. Descendants of the ancient seer Pulastya, the *kinnaras* are semi-divine beings, characterized by human bodies and horses' heads, or human faces and BIRDS' bodies with magnificent foliated tails. *Kinnaras* and GANDHARVAS are the heavenly musicians at KUBERA's court. They were possibly folk gods, later absorbed into the post-Vedic pantheon. They frequently appear as decorative motifs on TEMPLE pillars.

kirata(s) Originally the designation for hunters and gatherers living on the MOUNTAINS of north-eastern India, and later extended to encompass any such hill folk. In SHAIVA mythology, SHIVA assumed the form of a *kirata*, Kiratamurti, to test ARJUNA. A fight ensued between the two over a boar which both claimed to have killed. When Arjuna saw that, despite his prowess, his arms were useless, he realized the true identity of his adversary, fell on his knees and worshipped him. Shiva then bestowed on him the powerful *pashupata* weapon. This episode, of which the earliest version survives in the *Vanaparvan* (Book of the Forest) in the MAHABHARATA, was retold and developed by the 6th-century SANSKRIT author, Bharavi in his poem entitled *Kiratarjuniyam*.

kiritamakuta, kiritamukuta or **kirita** 'diadem, crest, jeweled crown'. A conical crown displaying either a jewel or an elaborate design on the front, surmounted by a central pointed piece. Typical of VAISHNAVA deities, VISHNU, KRISHNA, LAKSHMI.

kirttimukha 'face of glory'. Name given to the grimacing face of a lion or YALI face depicted above the doorways of sacred precincts and on the aureole (*prabhamandala*) behind divine IMAGES. Its redoutable aspect is supposed to avert malignant influences and to protect the devotees. This motif is used also in jewelry, e.g. on girdle clasps. The *kirtimukha* is generally flanked by a lush foliage motif.

Kodai *see* ANDAL

kolam (Tamil) 'floor designs'. Complex geometrical designs drawn every day before sunrise in front of the main entrance of the house. These drawings, known under various names in different parts of India, are executed with rice flour or pulverized quartz. This art, almost exclusively practised by women, is probably a vestige of the ancient Sun worship and the *kolam* is a solar symbol to attract auspiciousness into the house. The classic pattern of the *kolam* is geometric, but more recent developments display a tendency towards figural patterns which range from age-revered motifs, such as the pot, to Mickey Mouse. Moreover, while *kolams* were generally white, contemporary ones are executed in vibrant colours. During FESTIVALS such as *Pongal*, the streets of towns and villages are covered with a magnificent *kolam* displays.

Kotavi 'naked woman'. Name of a malevolent southern Indian goddess, later identified with DURGA. Mother of the ASURA Bana, Kotavi was the tutelary goddess of the DAITYAS.

Krishna 'dark blue or black'. Name of one of the most celebrated gods of the Hindu pantheon. Although the eighth incarnation of VISHNU, Krishna is worshipped as a god in his own right. His 'official' biography is narrated in the MAHABHARATA, the HARIVAMSHA and the BHAGAVATA PURANA. He is supposed to have recited the BHAGAVADGITA, his own philosophical doctrine, to ARJUNA on the battlefield of KURUKSHETRA. Tradition narrates that

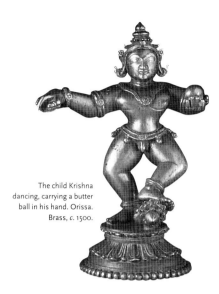

The child Krishna dancing, carrying a butter ball in his hand. Orissa. Brass, *c.* 1500.

Below: Traditional *kolam* made with pulverized conch shell, drawn on the ground. Thanjavur district, Tamil Nadu 1996.

Vishnu incarnated as Krishna in order to free the earth from the tyranny of KAMSA, king of MATHURA. Kamsa, however, had been warned that one of the sons of his cousin DEVAKI would kill him, so he imprisoned her and her husband VASUDEVA and ordered all their children to be killed. Six children were dead when the seventh, the fair-skinned BALARAMA, conceived from a white hair of Vishnu, was miraculously transferred from Devaki's womb to that of Vasudeva's youngest wife, Rohini. The eighth child, the dark-skinned Krishna, conceived from a black hair of Vishnu, was born at midnight in the dark half of the month of *Bhadrapada* (August–September), during the monsoon. At the time of his birth the guards were in a deep slumber and the chains fell from Vasudeva's hands and feet, enabling him to carry the child to the other side of the YAMUNA to his foster-parents, the cowherd NANDA and his wife YASHODA. When Kamsa discovered the disappearance of the child, he ordered all children to be massacred, but Krishna was miraculously saved. He was brought up among the cowherds (GOPAS) and milkmaids (GOPIS) in GOKULA and had an adventurous childhood. A series of demons, sent by Kamsa to destroy him, were killed by Krishna. Among them were the ogress Putana, who wanted to nurse Krishna at her poison-smeared breasts, but Krishna sucked the life out of her. His boyish pranks were numerous; one of his favourite pastimes was raiding the dairies of the *gopis* looking for curds and butter. His parents and his friends were dimly aware of his divine nature, but every now and then they were granted glimpses of it. One day, his foster-mother rebuked him for having eaten some earth. He denied it and so she forced him to open his mouth; to her amazement she saw in it the whole universe and for a brief moment she perceived Krishna's true nature. The

most celebrated part of Krishna's life among the cowherds are his amorous exploits with the *gopis*, headed by his beloved RADHA, the wife of Ayana.

His youth in VRINDAVAN is a mixture of erotic and heroic feats: he taught the cowherds to worship the GOVARDHANA hill instead of paying homage to INDRA. When the incensed god tried to drown the settlement, Krishna outwitted him by plucking the Govardhana and holding it up on his little finger like an umbrella, beneath which the cowherds and their ANIMALS sheltered. A further batch of ogres and fabulous creatures, sent by Kamsa to destroy Krishna, failed. Eventually, Kamsa decided to organize a sports competition in Mathura and sent for Krishna and Balarama. On their way to the games they were confronted again with Kamsa's demonic emissaries, but nevertheless reached the arena where they were faced by fearsome adversaries, such as the giant wrestler Chanura, the boxer Mushtika and many more, including the mad elephant Kuvalayapida. Finally, Kamsa himself entered the arena and Krishna slew him and dragged him by the hair to the Yamuna, then reinstalled Kamsa's father UGRASENA.

For some time Krishna and Balarama lived in Mathura; they met their real parents and underwent a series of ceremonies to purify themselves of the taint of having lived among the herdsmen. They were then invested with the sacred thread, instructed in the sixty-four arts and in various martial skills. After a series of more or less successful attacks on Mathura, Kamsa's powerful father-in-law Jarasandha decided to join forces with other kings. Under pressure from his adversaries, Krishna abandoned the city, shifting his capital to DWARKA on the Arabian Sea. His life continued at the previous rapid pace: he fought against numerous *asuras*, DAITYAS and others, married 16,108 girls, among them RUKMINI and Satyabhama, and ruled Dwarka.

Krishna armed with an elephant tusk grabs Kamsa by the hair and drags him from his throne. The royal insignias, crown and parasol, lie in the foreground. Behind Krishna is Balarama. Folio from a *Bhagavata Purana* manuscript. Basohli, Panjab Hills. Opaque watercolour on paper, *c.* 1725.

His life then became inextricably linked to the vicissitudes of the PANDAVAS, related to him through their mother KUNTI, the sister of Vasudeva. In this phase of his life, Krishna appears in the guise of wise counsellor, a role that he mastered to perfection. He was present at DRAUPADI'S SVAYAMVARA, where he first met the Pandavas, to whom he became close, giving his sister Subhadra to ARJUNA in marriage.

Krishna attended YUDHISHTHIRA's royal consecration and closely followed the Pandavas' rise to power and subsequent loss of their kingdom at a fateful game of dice. When they returned from their exile, they demanded the return their kingdom from DURYODHANA. Sensing, however, that the KAURAVAS would not comply, both parties prepared for the imminent war and sought out Krishna. Krishna gave them a choice: one of them could have his huge army, the other could have himself alone, unarmed and non-combatant. Arjuna decided to have Krishna and Duryodhana Krishna's army. But before the battle, Krishna headed an embassy of peace to the Kaurava court. This failed and war was declared. On the battlefield Krishna recited to Arjuna the *Bhagavadgita* and manifested himself to him in his 'universal form' (VISHVARUPA). After eighteen days' carnage, Krishna and the Pandavas travelled to HASTINAPURA to pay their respects to DHRITARASHTRA and GANDHARI. Gandhari cursed Krishna, foretelling the end of his kinsmen, the YADAVAS, and his own death in the wilderness. Many years later, during a PILGRIMAGE to Prabhasa on the west coast of India, the Yadavas fought each other in a drunken brawl, of which the only survivors were Krishna, Balarama and Krishna's charioteer. Krishna then moved towards the forest where Balarama was lying beneath a tree. He saw a serpent issuing from his mouth and moving towards the ocean, for Balarama was none other but an aspect of Vishnu's serpent SHESHA, now returning to the sea. Krishna then dismissed his charioteer and settled beneath a tree resting one foot upon his knee. His foot was mistaken for a deer by a hunter, Jaras, who shot an arrow at it. He begged Krishna's forgiveness as soon as he realized his mistake and Krishna consoled him, and died shortly afterwards. That day the ocean engulfed Dwarka and the KALI YUGA commenced. Krishna's other names include Balaji ('boy'), Dwarkanatha ('lord of Dwarka'), Madanagopala ('passionate cowherd'), Mohan ('delighting'), Murali ('flute player') and Shyam ('black').

Krishna Dvaipayana *see* VYASA

krita 'perfected, accomplished'. 1. The side of the dice marked with four dots, the winning dice. 2. Name of the first of the four YUGAS (ages of the world), also called *Satya-yuga*, the 'age of truth', corresponding to the Western notion of a golden age.

Krittika(s) The constellation of the Pleiades, believed to consist of six stars personifying the six wives of the RISHIS. The Krittikas, associated with AGNI, were the nurses of KARTTIKEYA; deemed to be inauspicious, they are sometimes represented by a flame or a sword.

kshatriya(s) A member of the warrior CASTE. The term *kshatriya*, derived from the word *kshatra* ('supremacy, power, dominion'), has a much wider meaning than 'warrior', as it also denotes the members of the royal household, the nobles and their families. There was a close connection between the interdependent BRAHMINS and *kshatriyas*. The priest of the royal household, the PUROHITA, was responsible for ensuring smooth relations between

Opposite: Kubera, guardian of the north, armed with a sword rides on a horse. Caption in Telugu. Probably Thanjavur, *c*. 1830. From an album of paintings on European paper watermarked 1820.

BRAHMINS and *kshatriyas*. Traditionally, the main duty of a *kshatriya* was to protect the people with his weapon, the others were to study, to sacrifice and to bestow gifts.

kshetrapala 'lord of the field (or region)'. In southern India this is the generic name applied to a tutelary deity of a region or field (*kshetra*) whose TEMPLE is generally in the north-eastern corner of a settlement. *Kshetrapalas*, as guardians of SHAIVA temples, are worshipped prior to each rite to ensure its efficacy. They are represented as nude, three-eyed, awesome figures, with dishevelled hair, brandishing a number of weapons and accompanied by DOGS. They are often identified with BHAIRAVA.

Kubera or **Kuvera** Originally Kubera was an earth spirit of ancient Indian folklore, eventually assimilated into the BUDDHIST, JAINA and Hindu pantheons. In the latter, he is the head of the hosts of YAKSHAS, RAKSHASAS and other mysterious spirits who guard his treasures. Regarded as the lord of wealth and riches, hence his name of Dhanapati ('lord of riches'), he is associated with virility and generative power; his name is invoked at weddings. He is said to dwell on Mount KAILASA in a palace surrounded by magnificent gardens. A number of myths account for his origin both in the epics and the PURANAS. His half-brother RAVANA defeated him and usurped his throne. When he abducted SITA, Kubera became RAMA's ally, hence he is worshipped by VAISHNAVAS, although he is generally regarded as one of the deities of SHIVA's entourage. He is one of the ASHTADIKPALAS, the guardian of the north, and is shown riding either a horse, an ELEPHANT or a man. Generally pot-bellied, he may carry a club, a pomegranate, a water jar and a money bag, or sometimes a mongoose vomiting coins or jewels.

kukkuta 'cock'. Symbol of the rising sun, the cock is associated with AIYANAR and KARTTIKEYA. It is emblazoned on their banners and occasionally carried by Karttikeya.

kuladevata(s) 'family god(s)'. These gods are normally worshipped by a family (*kula*) on special occasions, although connected more to the house or locality than to the family itself. It is customary for family members who have settled elsewhere to return periodically to their 'ancestral home' and worship their *kuladevatas*. The *kuladevatas* may be symbolized by a KUMBHA placed in the new home.

Kulashekhara One of the ALVARS, about whose life little is known, except that he was a remarkable poet. He probably lived in the 8th century, a king of Kerala and author of ten exquisite poems in Tamil, the *Tirumal Perumoli*, in honour of VISHNU, and also of the *Mukundamala*, a SANSKRIT poem in forty verses, singing the praises of Vishnu. He is reputed to be the incarnation of Vishnu's KAUSTUBHA jewel. Dehejia, V., 1988

Kumara 'boy, youth'. Epithet of KARTTIKEYA.

Kumbakonam A vibrant and affluent commercial town in the Thanjavur district of Tamil Nadu, on the south bank of the KAVERI, hailed as the KASHI of the south, celebrated for its TEMPLES, learning and the great MAHAMAHAM festival which takes place every eleven to twelve years. Kumbakonam was an important centre from the 7th century onwards, first under the Cholas, whose supremacy lasted from the 9th until the 13th century, then under the Vijayanagara and Nayaka dynasties and, finally, under the Marathas, whose power ceased in the early 19th century.

Devotional print produced on the occasion of the 1989 *Kumbhamela* at Prayaga (Allahabad). At the centre are the confluence of the Ganges, Yamuna and Sarasvati, and a plan of the city. Various deities and icons decorate the edges.

kumbha 'pot, pitcher, jar'. The *kumbha* symbolizes the womb, the generative power, identified with the mother goddesses. In Indian mythology there are a number of personages, e.g. AGASTYA, who are born from a pot and it is also seen as the receptacle of all forms of life. Pots filled with water and variously decorated with intricate string patterns, flowers and leaves, played a prominent part in the ancient rituals, and this custom still survives. KULADEVATAS, and the Divine in general, are symbolized by pots, the containers of life, sustenance and fertility.

Kumbhakarna 'pot-eared'. A RAKSHASA, brother of RAVANA. BRAHMA had blessed him – some say cursed him for tyrannizing the gods and mankind – to sleep for six months at a time, to awake for only one day in order to sate his prodigious appetite, then go back to sleep. When RAMA besieged LANKA, Ravana resolved to wake up Kumbhakarna, a seriously difficult task. Eventually, he joined his brother, wreaked havoc among Rama's allies, but finally was decapitated by the Rama's arrow.

Kumbhamela 'pot FESTIVAL'. Probably the largest gathering of Hindu ascetics and holy men of all sects, which takes place at regular three-year interval at PRAYAGA (Allahabad), HARDWAR, NASIK and UJJAIN. The most important of these occurs at Prayaga every twelve years, when the sun enters Aries and Jupiter is in Aquarius. The latest *Kumbhamela* took place in January 2001. The *mela* (festival) has its origin in remote antiquity; pots filled with various kinds of grain were brought to certain places along the RIVER banks, dipped into the water and then sown with other seeds to ensure a plentiful harvest. There is a mythical reason why these four cities have been selected for the *Kumbhamela* celebrations. While the CHURNING OF THE OCEAN

was in progress, the pot containing the nectar of immortality (AMRITA) emerged and the ASURAS immediately grabbed it and ran off. However, four drops of *amrita* fell at four different places, making them fitting sites at which to celebrate the *Kumbhamela*. The first evidence for this festival dates from the 7th century, when Emperor Harsha of Kanauj (606–648) invited the Chinese pilgrim Hsuen-Tsang to visit the festival. A PILGRIMAGE to the *Kumbhamela* is regarded as extremely meritorious. Millions gather on the river banks to bathe, offer prayers and bestow gifts on the holy men. A dip in the river at that auspicious time is thought to cleanse all the sins of the last eighty-eight generations and to purify and save the bathers. Unfortunately, the *Kumbhamelas* were also notorious the occasional spread of plague and cholera and for crimes and disorders, especially when the crowds gathered to touch the procession of naked holy men in the hope of achieving salvation.

kumkum (Hindi: **kesar**; *Crocus sativus*). The stamens of this plant are the source of saffron, which is either used dried, in filaments or powdered. Such large quantities of crocus flowers are required for even the smallest amount of saffron that it is restricted to the wealthy. Saffron was the most valuable cosmetic, spice and dye in Asia and Europe. Ayurvedic medicine prescribes it for its antiallergenic and tonic properties. It was used as a cosmetic and was thought to be an aphrodisiac and a remedy against depression and melancholy.
Patnaik, N., 1993

kundala 'earring'. ORNAMENTS were worn as talismans to protect various parts of the person from evil influences. The shape, size and materials used indicated the status of the wearer.

Vishnu as *kurma*. In the upper pair of hands are discus and conch, the lower are in *abhaya*- and *varadamudra*. Caption in Telugu. Probably Thanjavur *c*.1830. From an album of paintings on European paper watermarked 1820.

Kundalini 'coiled'. Aspect of SHIVA'S SHAKTI, embodying the latent energy lying at the base of the spine (*muladharachakra*). Kundalini is visualized as a female snake coiled eight times, which, through complex yogic techniques, can be awakened and raised from the *muladharachakra* to the highest of the CHAKRAS, the *sahsasrara*, at the top of the skull. This feat enables the adept to have a vision of DEVI and to attain MOKSHA or liberation. Kundalini represents the supreme female energy (*paramashakti*), the origin of the universe, without which there is no life.

Kunti or **Pritha** One of the main characters in the MAHABHARATA, Pritha was the daughter of Shura, a king of the YADAVA lineage. Shura had promised his first-born daughter to his childless cousin, Kuntibhoja, hence Pritha became known as Kunti. The young girl grew up at the court of Kuntibhoja, helping him to entertain his numerous visitors, including the notoriously difficult RISHI Durvasas. The sage was so taken by her that he bestowed upon her a MANTRA, by which she could summon any god she wished and would beget a child by him. Kunti summoned SURYA and shortly afterwards discovered she was pregnant. To avoid any scandal, she abandoned the newborn child on the banks of the river YAMUNA, where a charioteer, Adhiratha, and his wife adopted him and called him Vasusena. He was subsequently named KARNA and became the arch-rival of ARJUNA. Later, Kunti married PANDU and she never disclosed to her sons the true identity of Karna until after she heard that Arjuna had killed his half-brother in battle. This embittered the victory of the Pandavas. Finally, Kunti accompanied the king DHRITARASHTRA and his wife GANDHARI, the sole survivors of the KAURAVAS, to a retreat in the forest, where later they died in a fire.

kurma 'tortoise'. 1. The *Shatapatha Brahmana* gives the following account of the origin and symbolism of the tortoise. PRAJAPATI, the creator, opened the egg-shaped cosmos and the tortoise emerged from the juice flowing from the squeezed shells. Its carapace represents the earth, its upper shell the sky and its body the atmosphere. It is said to symbolize the creation process and is associated with Prajapati, who, having transformed himself into a tortoise, generated all forms of life. 2. *Kurma* AVATARA: VISHNU assumed the form of a *kurma* in his second incarnation to support Mount Mandara, which was used as the churning stick at the time of the CHURNING OF THE OCEAN. The tortoise became a symbol of stability as the earth is believed to rest on the head of VISHNU's serpent who in turn is supported by Akupara, a tortoise; in traditional GEOGRAPHY, India is represented as a giant tortoise facing eastwards. The *kurma* is the vehicle of a number of gods, including the RIVER goddess YAMUNA, the planet RAHU and ANANTA.

Kurukshetra 'land of the Kurus'. A vast expanse of land in the Delhi region, supposed to have been the scene of the Great War between the KAURAVAS and the PANDAVAS. On a metaphorical plane, the battle of Kurukshetra signifies the struggle between right and wrong; symbolically, Kurukshetra represents the human body in which the battle between the mind and the senses is fought and liberation won or lost. Nowadays, Kurukshetra, along with GAYA and PRAYAGA (Allahabad), is one of the three PILGRIMAGE sites visited by Hindus in honour of their ancestors.

Kusha, *kusha* 1. One of the twin sons of RAMA and SITA; the other was LAVA. 2. (*Poa cynosoroides Retz.*). Sacred grass with long pointed stalks used in certain forms of worship. Attribute of BRAHMA.

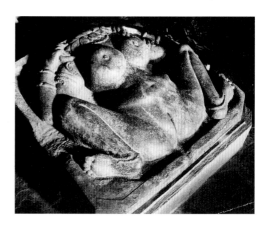

Lajja Gauri. Her link to fertility is symbolized by the displayed pubic region, as well as by the lotus blossom at the place of a head. Black basalt, c. 8th century.

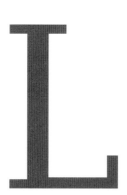

laddu or *ladduka* A small ball-shaped sweet made from pulses or flour, sugar and spices, and fried. GANESHA's trunk is often seen nuzzling the *laddus* heaped in a bowl held in one of his hands.
See also MODAKA

Lajja Gauri A fertility folk goddess, euphemistically called *lajja* ('modesty') Gauri. She has been worshipped in the Deccan, a region prone to droughts and famine, since ancient times. The earliest surviving depictions from the 3rd century, show her naked, her fertility aspect emphasized by the display of her genital region, as well as by the blossoming lotus replacing her head. Such figures continued to be made until recent times. She is invoked for progeny and abundant crops.

lakshana 1. 'Mark, sign, characteristic, symbol, attribute'. In iconography the *lakshanas* are the typical attributes of a deity. 2. In the treatises on physiognomy, the *lakshanas* are the marks of the body that may be auspicious or inauspicious. For instance, crescent-shaped eyebrows indicate wealth, while those irregularly shaped can denote penury.

Lakshmana 'endowed with auspicious marks'. Son of DASHARATHA and Sumitra, half-brother of RAMA. Regarded as the epitome of the loyal brother, according to some he is the incarnation of ANANTA. *See also* RAMAYANA

Lakshmi 'mark, sign' Originally a personification of the earth and a fertility goddess, Lakshmi was worshipped under several aspects. She was later associated with VISHNU and identified with his consort SHRI, the goddess of beauty, prosperity, luck and wealth. Because of her connection with wealth,

Lakshmi is often linked with KUBERA. Her main attribute is the lotus, hence her epithet Padma or Kamala (meaning 'lotus'), and she is also called Jaladhija ('water-born'), because she emerged from the waters at the CHURNING OF THE OCEAN. She accompanies Vishnu in each one of his AVATARAS, as the consort of RAMA she appears as SITA, and as RUKMINI in Vishnu's KRISHNA aspect. Lakshmi is popular with Hindus, BUDDHISTS and Jains and her IMAGE is carved on door lintels to protect and bless the inhabitants of a house. Other names include Chanchala or Lola ('fickle'), Dharani ('earth') and Loka-mata ('world mother'). *See also* GAJA-LAKSHMI; FESTIVALS

Lakulisha 'lord with the club'. Reputed to be either the founder or the first teacher of the PASHUPATA doctrine, Lakulisha lived in Kayarohana (today's Karvan in the Kathiawar peninsula) in the early 2nd century. He is the author of the *Pashupatasutra* and regarded by some as the twenty-eighth incarnation of SHIVA. Often found in eastern India, Gujarat and the Kathiawar peninsula, his IMAGE depicts him as a naked, ithyphallic YOGI, carrying prayer beads, a club, a skull cup and a trident, occasionally accompanied by ANIMALS.

lalatatilakam see URDHVATANDAVA

Lalita 'lovely, charming'. Aspect of the goddess PARVATI, the personification of playfulness as the source of creation. She is one of the ten MAHAVIDYAS. *See also* LILA

lalitasana A posture denoting relaxation. One leg is placed on the throne or seat (PITHA), the other hangs down, sometimes resting on a lotus or supported by an attendant.

Below: Rama and Sita in the hut, watch Lakshmana cutting off Shurpanakha's nose. On the top right Shurpanakha, reverting to her demonic form, flies to Lanka. Folio from a *Ramayana* series by Pandit Seu; Guler, Panjab Hills. Opaque watercolour on paper, *c.* 1720.

Right: Lakshmi, the goddess of prosperity, as usually depicted in popular colour prints in West Bengal. *c.* 1980s.

Lanka Name used in the RAMAYANA for the island of Ceylon and its capital. According to one of the many accounts of the origin of this island, it was once the summit of Mount MERU, blown into the sea by the wind god VAYU, thus becoming an island. Lanka, is mainly known as the seat of RAVANA and his RAKSHASAS. According to the *Ramayana*, the capital of Lanka was beautifully built on a forested hill, protected by strong walls and encircled by a moat. Although the *Ramayana* is a work of fiction, its description of the island and of its buildings agrees with BUDDHIST literature, which states that Lanka was cultured and highly civilized, a fact that has long been forgotten, especially in northern India, where Ravana and his followers have a doubtful reputation.

lasya 'dancing'. A type of sensuous, languorous DANCE performed by PARVATI, the counterpart of SHIVA's masculine TANDAVA.

Lava Son of RAMA and twin brother of KUSHA. The sage VALMIKI taught the RAMAYANA to Lava who, together with Kusha, wandered around the country reciting the epic.

lila 'whim, divine play or game'. Often translated as 'sport', *lila* is applied to spontaneous acts of creation or destruction, emanation and reabsorption by the gods, continually repeated throughout the cyclic time. This notion of unrestrained, unpremeditated action is exemplified by the account of KRISHNA's life, therefore Krishna is also known as *lila-purushottama*, the 'supreme player'. Shiva's many manifestations, especially the sixty-four that took place at MADURAI, are also referred to as *lila*. This spontaneous, ever creative power is personified by the goddess LALITA, the embodiment of the universe.

lime *see* NIMBU

linga or *lingam* 'emblem, gender, mark, sex, symbol', any characteristic sign. The *linga* is the most complex and comprehensive symbol associated with SHIVA. A number of figurines depicting generative symbols, particularly the phallus, the epitome of cosmic energy, have been discovered among the remains of the Harappan civilization (*c.* 3000–1700 BCE). These representations seem to be the prototypes for the later *linga*, Shiva's *mulavigraha* ('fundamental form'). Shiva, as the Absolute, is necessarily without qualification, therefore he can only be perceived through his creation. The *linga* symbolizes Shiva, the energy supporting all existence and the beginning and the end of every cosmic process. The *linga* expresses the unmanifested nature, while the female generative organ, YONI, expresses the manifested nature.

In SHAIVA TEMPLES the main IMAGE is invariably a *linga*, placed at the centre of the GARBHAGRIHA, or sanctuary. This can be a *svayambhu*, or 'self-generated' one, i.e. not man-made, such as the ice *linga* worshipped at KEDARNATH, or an egg-shaped stone, the BANALINGA, the shape of which recalls that of the Cosmic Egg. The *linga* can also be a *manushalinga*, a man-made *linga*, fashioned according to precise rules and which determines the dimensions of the temple housing it. *Manushalingas* can be made of the most diverse material, from the perishable, such as sand, flour, cooked rice, used only once, to precious metals and stones. They are generally constituted by an unadorned shaft with a rounded top and are inserted into the PITHA, which represents the *yoni*. This union symbolizes the supreme creative energy. *Manushalingas* are occasionally provided with faces (MUKHALINGA, 'face-*linga*') which may vary from one to five, placed

Left: Silver-covered *linga*, with flower decoration in the shrine at the source of the Kaveri, at Talakaveri, Karnataka, in the Western Ghats on the border with Kerala.

Right: Lingodbhavamurti. Vishnu, as a boar, is shown at the bottom left, and Brahma as a gander is at the top right. Tamil Nadu. Granulite, early 12th century.

on the four sides of the shaft, and the fifth on the top (*panchamukhalinga*). Among the most important *lingas* are the five elemental *lingas*, representing the ELEMENTS constituting the universe. These five are the earth *linga* worshipped at KANCHIPURAM, the water *linga* at Tiruvanaikkaval on SRIRANGAM island, the fire *linga* at TIRUVANNAMALAI, the air *linga* at KALAHASTI and the ether *linga* at CHIDAMBARAM. The twelve JYOTIRLINGAS, the effulgent *lingas* of light, are scattered throughout the subcontinent.

Linga Purana *see* PURANA(S)

Lingayat(s) *see* VIRASHAIVA(S)

Lingodbhavamurti A representation of SHIVA as he emerges from the blazing LINGA to crush the pride of BRAHMA and VISHNU, a popular IMAGE in southern Indian TEMPLES, generally carved on the western wall of the shrine. Brahma and Vishnu were arguing over who was the greatest of them both, when Shiva appeared in a blazing pillar of light which had no beginning or end. Brahma then assumed the form of a HAMSA (goose) and flew towards the sky, hoping to discover the top of the pillar, while Vishnu, as a boar, dived into the ocean looking for its base. Brahma failed in his attempt, but seeing a KETAKI flower falling to earth, he caught it and claimed to have reached the top. He was punished by Shiva, who cursed him to be no longer worshipped in temples, and severed the head that had uttered falsehood. Finally, the two gods acknowledged Shiva's supremacy and worshipped the blazing *linga*. Shiva is shown as a four-armed figure sculpted into the *linga* from the knees upwards, thereby suggesting that no one can measure his height. The deity carries his usual attributes which include an axe and leaping antelope, and his hands are generally in ABHAYA- and VARADAMUDRA.

loka 'world, region or sphere' (of a deity). *See* COSMOLOGY

lokapala(s) 'guardians or protectors of the world'. *See* ASHTADIKPALAS

lolahastamudra 'moving, or restless hand pose'. A hand pose frequently found in southern Indian sculptures, in which the arm and the hand hang loosely, and the hand, at a right angle to the wrist, suggests the oscillating movement of walking. Another definition of the term is: hanging down 'like the tail of the COW', where the arm hangs by the side of the body. This MUDRA is typical of female figures when not holding an attribute.

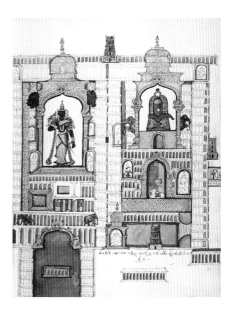

View of the shrines of Minakshi and Sundareshvara at Madurai. Caption in Telugu. Probably Thanjavur, *c.* 1830. From an album of paintings on European paper watermarked 1820.

Madana 'Seducer of the mind', another name of KAMA.

madhu, **Madhu** 1. 'honey, sweetness, inebriating'. Wild honey played an important part in Indian life. It was reputed to be the essence of all vegetal life, a remedy against disease, a tonic for mind and body, the source of long life, and it was used by warriors as an invigorating drink. For this reason it is customary to allow a newborn infant to lick some honey.
2. Name of a DANAVA, symbolizing darkness, defeated by VISHNU/KRISHNA, hence his epithet of Madhusudhana, 'slayer of Madhu'. *See also* KAITABHA

Madhva or **Madhvacharya** (13th century), also known as Anandatirtha. A VAISHNAVA BRAHMIN born in Udupi, Karnataka, who was the author of several works, including the *Sarvadarshanasamgraha*, a compendium of philosophical systems. Extremely critical of the teachings of the ADVAITA, or monistic philosophy, he founded the DVAITA, a dualistic system, which emphasizes the essential difference between the first cause (BRAHMAN) and the human soul (ATMAN). Everything, although originating from God's will, has its own individuality. Only through divine grace is it possible to attain release (MOKSHA). This is achieved through active devotion and worship of the deity in the form of an IMAGE. The famous image of Krishna, venerated by crowds of pilgrims in the Krishna TEMPLE in Udupi, was installed by Madhva. His philosophy reveals features, such as eternal damnation, which were inspired by his contact with the Syrian Christians of Malabar. Madhva is said to be an AVATARA of VAYU, the wind god who, in his philosophy, reveals some similarity with the Holy Ghost.

Madurai 'sweet, sweetness'. The most renowned of the temple cities of Tamil Nadu and one of the oldest

cities of India, Madurai is the cradle of Dravidian culture and of the Tamil language. Tradition maintains that the city was the seat of the famed *Tamil Sangam*, a literary academy of poets, which had definitive control over Tamil literature. It is said that the works to be tested by the academy were thrown into the Golden Lily tank, opposite the shrine of the goddess MINAKSHI, and only those of literary merit floated. Located in a picturesque spot on the Vaigai RIVER, a number of myths account for the foundation and early history of the TEMPLE city. Among the numerous mythological events reputed to have occurred at this hallowed place are the story of Minakshi, the tutelary goddess of the town and the sixty-four LILAS ('playful manifestations') of SHIVA. The town is renowned for its magnificent Minakshi-Sundareshvara temple, where soaring GOPURAS encrusted with thousands of vibrantly painted stucco sculptures dominate its skyline. The core of the present-day city lies the old city built around the Minakshi temple, a lively place of worship visited daily by some twenty thousand devotees. The main yearly event is the twelve-day *Chittirai* FESTIVAL, taking place during April–May (*Chittirai*). It celebrates the MARRIAGE of Minakshi to Shiva in his aspect as Sundareshvara ('handsome bridegroom') and her coronation as queen of the town.

Although early Indian sources are shrouded in myth, information on the town is provided in Greek literature. The Greek historian Megasthenes (4th–3rd century BCE) records Madurai being ruled by a Pandyan princess. Ptolemy (2nd century CE), commenting on the brisk trading relations between 'Modura', the Greeks and the Romans, calls it 'the Mediterranean emporium of the south'. It was the capital of the Pandya rulers from the 1st to the 13th century CE. After being sacked by the armies of the Sultan of Delhi, the city was captured in the

Battle scene from a
Mahabharata manuscript.
Srirangapatna, Karnataka.
Opaque watercolour
on paper, 1669.

14th century by the forces of the expanding
Vijayanagara empire. In the mid-16th century the
power passed to the Nayakas, originally Vijayanagara
governors. During Tirumala Nayakas reign (1623–59)
ARTS, culture and an unprecedented building activity
flourished. The Nayaka rule ended in 1736 and
by 1801 the British were controlling Madurai.

Mahabharata 'the great Bharata'. One of the two
great SANSKRIT epics of India, the other being the
RAMAYANA. Possibly the world's longest poem, the
Mahabharata has 110,000 couplets, in eighteen
sections (*parvans*), plus an additional nineteenth
section, the HARIVAMSHA. Mythology, ethics,
theology, didactic passages, folk tales, philosophic
teachings – the most important of which is the
BHAGAVADGITA – were gradually incorporated into
the main poem, which describes the rivalry and
strife between two related families for the conquest
of Upper India, referred to in the poem as BHARATA.
According to legend, the author or compiler of the
poem was the sage VYASA, who was helped in this
massive task by some of his disciples. Vyasa
eventually dictated the work to the god GANESHA.
The text was recited to JANAMEJAYA, great-grandson
of ARJUNA, by one of Vyasa's disciples,
Vaishampayana, during the intervals in a lengthy
religious ceremony. A vast number of poets, editors,
representatives of different schools of thought have
tampered with the original text, so that the beliefs
and doctrines appearing in the work are often
contradictory. KRISHNA emerged as one of the main
characters of the poem and its chief deity, sometime
between the 2nd century BCE and the 2nd century CE.
It is assumed that, although the date of composition
and the identity of the author are unknown, the
poem in its present form was probably compiled
between the 4th century BCE and the 4th century CE.

The first book, *Adiparvan* (Book of the
Beginnings), contains the genealogies of the
KAURAVAS and the PANDAVAS, their rivalries and
DRAUPADI'S svayamvara. The second, *Sabhaparvan*
(Book of the Assembly), narrates of the fateful game
of dice and defeat of the Pandavas. The third,
Vanaparvan (Book of the Forest), describes the life
of the Pandavas in the forest, containing some of the
poem's most famous episodes, such as the story of
NALA and Damayanti, the meeting of Arjuna with
the KIRATA and an outline of the RAMAYANA. The
fourth, *Virataparvan* (Book of Virata), recounts the
life of the Pandavas at the court of Virata. The fifth,
the *Udyogaparvan* (Book of Efforts), deals with the
preparation for the great battle. The sixth, seventh,
eighth and ninth books are named after the
distinguished Kaurava leaders: BHISHMA, Drona,
KARNA and Shalya, who die in the battle. The
Bhishmaparvan contains the *Bhagavadgita*. The tenth
book, *Sauptikaparvan*, narrates the night attack by
the three surviving Kauravas on the Pandava camp.
The eleventh, *Striparvan* (Book of Women),
describes the lamentations of GANDHARI and the
other women over the death of their relatives.
Gandhari curses Krishna to die an ignoble death and
his followers to be exterminated. The following two,
Shantiparvan (Book of Peace and
Anushasanaparvan (Book of Precepts), contain ethic
and moral teachings, as well as YUDHISHTHIRA'S
consecration. In the fourteenth,
Ashvamedhikaparvan (Book of the ASHVAMEDHA),
Yudhisthira performs the horse sacrifice. The
fifteenth book, *Ashramavasikaparvan* (Book of the
ASHRAM), describes the life of DHRITARASHTRA,
Gandhari and KUNTI in the hermitage and their
death in a forest fire. The sixteenth, *Mausalaparvan*
(Book of the Clubs), narrates the death of Krishna,
BALARAMA, their followers, the YADAVAS, and the

The supreme form of Shiva. Although only three faces have been shown, some scholars have contended that a fourth, at the rear, and a fifth, facing upwards are implied. The three faces are said to represent Aghora, Shiva and Uma. Cave temple, Elephanta. Basalt, *c.* 550.

disappearance of DWARKA into the sea. In the seventeenth, *Mahaprasthanikaparvan* (Book of the Great Sojourn), the Pandavas renounce their kingdom and journey to the Himalayas towards Mount MERU, the heavenly residence of INDRA. In the eighteenth, *Svargarohanaparvan* (Book of the Ascent to Heaven), Yudhisthitra, his brothers and Draupadi ascend into heaven. The nineteenth book, *Harivamsha*, was added at a later point in time. There are two recensions of the *Mahabharata*, northern and southern, which, in turn, can be subdivided into other versions. A great number of discrepancies and variations exist in these two recensions and, as yet, there is no recognized standard text of the poem. This work continues to be an inexhaustible source of inspiration in the ARTS and literature. Many of its episodes are retold and interpreted in religious discourses.

Mahabhashya 'Great Commentary'. *See* PATANJALI

Mahadeva or **Maheshvara** 'great god'. An epithet of SHIVA. To help Shiva destroy the three aerial cities of the ASURAS, BRAHMA and VISHNU gave him a portion of their powers. He symbolizes the continuity of creation, ever recreating what it destroys. According to some, Mahadeva is the transcendent Absolute. He is generally represented with three faces: the central face is the auspicious SAUMYA, the one to the right, the awesome AGHORAMURTI, and to the left, SHAKTI.

Mahadevi or **Maheshvari** 'great goddess'. The supreme goddess of the SHAKTAS, Mahadevi is an epithet of PARVATI, the SHAKTI of MAHADEVA, who has a benign and destructive aspect and embodies the totality of SHIVA's cosmic energy. Symbolized by the LINGA combined with the YONI, their union created the universe.

Mahakala 'great time'. Name of a destructive aspect of SHIVA, in which he devours time and creation, dissolving every kind of life in the ocean of non-existence; from this the new creation emerges and it will eventually return to it. The female counterpart of Mahakala is MAHAKALI, symbolizing the inexorable passing of time. Occasionally, Mahakala is accompanied by KALA and MRITYU, time and death personified. Mahakala is depicted with a black complexion, carrying the same attributes as Shiva in his four hands. His vehicle is a lion and among his emblems are a tiger skin, staff, club, KAPALA, KHATVANGA, necklace of skulls and axe.

Mahakali 'great KALI'. Awesome aspect of PARVATI, symbolizing the power of time represented as a goddess, with a black complexion, four or eight arms, flame-like hair harbouring a snake, round, bulging EYES and small fangs protruding from her mouth. A garland of skulls encircles her neck and her headdress displays one or more skulls. Among her attributes are a trident, goad, club, KAMANDALU, discus, skull cup, sword, shield, noose, conch, VAJRA and pestle. One of her hands is in ABHAYAMUDRA, to reassure her devotees.

Mahamaham (Tamil: **Makamakam**) The greatest FESTIVAL celebrated in KUMBAKONAM every eleven to twelve years, at the conjunction of the moon with the lunar asterism *Maha Nakshatra*, and also when Jupiter is in the constellation of Leo at the full moon of the Tamil month of *Thai* (February–March). Crowds of pilgrims flock to Kumbakonam to wade through the shallow waters of the *Makamakam* tank and sprinkle themselves with water from the several springs that feed it, as it is believed that this cleanses from every sin. The festival lasts nine days; on this occasion the metal IMAGES of the deities of the main

Opposite: Tile depicting a *makara*: its lush, foliated tail symbolizes the *makara's* connection with water, fertility and love. Central India. Sandstone, *c.* 6th century.

Left: Four-armed Durga transfixing with the trident and a spear the *asura* Mahisha, emerging from the carcass of the buffalo. Above the head of the goddess are a *kirttimukha* mask, flanked by groups of flying *gandharvas*. Orissa. Schist, 13th century.

TEMPLES are paraded on palanquins or on chariots through the town. The latest festival took place from 9 to 18 February 1992.

Mahamaya 'great delusion'. *See* YOGANIDRA

mahapralaya 'total dissolution' of the universe, which occurs at the end of each KALPA. Everything is then reabsorbed into VISHNU for a period of quiescence called *maharatri* ('great night'), before the reappearance of a new BRAHMA and the rebirth of the unliberated beings. MAHAKALI presides over the *mahapralaya*.

maharishi(s) 'the great seers'. Collective name referring to the seven great RISHIS, the *saptarishis*, mentioned in the RIGVEDA. In the PURANAS they are often identified with the seven stars of the Great Bear.

mahatmya 'celebration, glorification'. *See* STHALAPURANA

mahavidya(s) 'great (supreme) knowledge'. Ten Tantric goddesses embodying *mahavidya*, divine knowledge and magical power. They are parts of KALI and reflect the various facets of her personality. Seven of them represent the creative forces and the other three destructive forces that operate in the processes of expansion and absorption of the universe.

Mahavira 'great hero'. *See* JAINISM

Maheshvara 'great lord'. *See* MAHADEVA

Maheshvari 'great lady'. *See* MAHADEVI

mahisha, **Mahisha** 'buffalo' 1. YAMA's vehicle. 2. Name of an ASURA who through his immense power

established himself in heaven. The gods were wandering aimlessly on earth when they were advised by VISHNU and SHIVA to concentrate their powers. These took the shape of a flame from which DURGA emerged. Each of the gods endowed her with some of their own weapons. Thus, armed and riding on a lion she attacked Mahisha who continued changing shape, until finally he transformed himself into a buffalo, and she slew him. He then tried to escape from the carcass, but the goddess decapitated him with her sword, hence her name MAHISHASURAMARDINI, 'the slayer of the *asura* Mahisha'. The gods then returned to heaven.

mahishi 'she-buffalo'. Term designating the chief queen. During the ASHVAMEDHA ceremony, the chief queen had sexual intercourse with the sacrificial horse.

Mahishasuramardini or **Mahishamardini** 'the slayer of the (*asura*) MAHISHA'. Form of DURGA. *See* MAHISHA

maithuna 'couple'. *See* MITHUNA

makara A mythical aquatic monster, usually identified with a crocodile, although often shown with an ELEPHANT's trunk, a fishtail or a foliated tail. The term is occasionally translated as dolphin. The *makara* symbolizes water, the source of all existence and fertility, and is the conveyance of GANGA and VARUNA, as well as being the emblem of KAMA, or Makaradhvaja, 'having a *makara* (on the) flag'. In astronomy *makara* is the sign of Capricorn. The *makara* motif, one of the most enduring in Indian ART, is found depicted on the crossbars of the early gateways (TORANAS) of BUDDHIST monuments, such as the Great Stupa at Sanchi (beginning of the 1st century), on the backs of thrones and as an ear

Right: The snake goddess Manasa sits on a double lotus throne beneath the expanded seven hoods of a snake. In the left hand she holds a snake, in the right a cup. A number of *nagas*, ascetics and a donor couple, surround the goddess. Eastern India. Basalt, 12th century.

ORNAMENT (*makarakundala*). Its form was often found in gargoyles and waterspouts. This auspicious symbol also appears in sculpture as the *prabhavali*, or aureole of an IMAGE, which issues from the mouth of a *makara*.

Makara Sankranti *see* FESTIVAL

makuta *see* MUKUTA

mala 'garland, necklace, prayer beads, wreath'. Garlands are said to be auspicious and are therefore included among the ASHTAMANGALAS; a number of deities wear garlands and many decorative patterns are based on the garland motif. The GANDHARVAS, VIDYADHARAS and YAKSHAS are shown carrying garlands and VISHNU wears either the *Vaijayantimala* ('the garland which forecasts victory') made of five rows of GEMS, or the *Vanamala* ('the flower of the forest garland') consisting of five rows of flowers. VAISHNAVAS wear the *tulsimala* made of TULSI seeds. SHIVA wears either a garland of skulls representing the MAHAPRALAYA, or the AKSHAMALA or RUDRAKSHA-*mala*, the garland made from berries of the forest, likewise his followers. As prayer beads, the *mala* represents cyclical time and is depicted in the hands of BRAHMA, a number of other deities, and ascetics.

Mallanaga or **Vatsyayana** Author of the *Kamasutra*. *See* EROTICS

manas 'mind, intellect, understanding, organ of cognition'.

Manasa 'spiritual'. A folk goddess, the leader of the snakes, worshipped mainly in Bengal, parts of Bihar, Orissa and Assam as a goddess of fertility, connected to MARRIAGE rites. The cult probably originated among the jungle tribes, but Manasa was eventually absorbed into the brahminical pantheon. The first evidence of her cult appears in poems composed in her honour early in the 14th century where there is a conscious effort to associate her with SHIVA's entourage. Thus, in a sequel to the story of Shiva swallowing the poison that emerged from the CHURNING OF THE OCEAN, Manasa, removes it from his throat (hence her epithet Vishahari, 'remover of poison') and divides it among snakes, scorpions and other insects, so becoming Vishadhari, 'giver of poison'. She is able to assume any form and perform miracles. One of the most famous stories, hinting at a rivalry between the cult of Shiva and that of Manasa, relates how a merchant, a staunch SHAIVA devotee, refused to worship Manasa, but was persuaded by his daughter-in-law to change his attitude after the goddess revived his son who had died from a snakebite. Various myths account for her origin: she is believed to be either the daughter of KASHYAPA, and sister of ANANTA, or to have been born from Shiva's semen, which fell into a lotus flower and reached down to PATALA, the section of the nether world inhabited by the snakes, and was transformed into a beautiful girl by the mother of the snake VASUKI.
Maity, P. K., 1966

Manasara Title of a treatise on ARCHITECTURE in seventy chapters, dating to the 7th century and noted for its similarities with the work of the Roman architect Vitruvius (1st century BCE).

manavantara 'period of Manu'. *See* MANU

mandala 'circle, circular magical diagram' 1. Magic circle delimiting a sacred area. *Mandalas* are

complex diagrams comprising a circular border which encloses geometrical figures, such as squares and triangles. At its centre is drawn the deity, the emblem or the mystical syllable representing it. These diagrams help to concentrate one's thoughts on the object of meditation. They can be drawn on any support or traced on the ground. A Hindu temple is intended to represent a *mandala* in stone. 2. A section or chapter of a work.

mandapa Porch or pillared hall in a TEMPLE. The word can also designate a special pavilion into which the IMAGE is brought on special occasions, e.g. *kalyana-mandapa*, 'wedding pavilion', *natya-mandapa*, 'dance pavilion'.

Mandara, *mandara* 'slow'. The mountain that served as the churning stick during the CHURNING OF THE OCEAN, and which is supported by VISHNU in his tortoise (KURMA) incarnation. 2. A coral tree (*Erythrina indica*); its vibrant red flowers bloom before the leaves appear. *See also* PANCHAVRIKSHA

Mangala, *mangala* 'auspicious' 1. Another name of BHAUMA, the planet Mars, with whom KARTTIKEYA, the general of the divine armies, is identified. The name Mangala is probably a euphemism, since the planet is associated with war and blood. Its colour is red, hence his Tamil name *Cevvay* 'the red one'. He rides on a golden chariot drawn either by eight red horses, a lion or a goat. His attributes are a club, spear and trident. *See also* NAVAGRAHA 2. *Mangala* denotes anything auspicious. *See* ASHTAMANGALA

Manikkavachakar 'he whose utterances are rubies'. One of the 'four reverend ones' among the SHAIVA NAYANMARS, Manikkavachakar lived in the 9th century. An unusually talented youth, born of

BRAHMIN parents, he followed in the footsteps of his father, becoming a minister at the court of the Pandya king of MADURAI. According to legend, he was sent by the king with a large sum of money to buy horses. On his way he met a Shaiva GURU who was none other than SHIVA in disguise. Forgetting his mission, he built a Shiva TEMPLE embezzling the king's money. The incensed Pandya imprisoned him, but after a series of miraculous events, Manikkavachakar was freed to follow his vocation. The saint devoted the rest of his life wandering from temple to temple singing the praises of Shiva and spent his last days at CHIDAMBARAM, where he composed many hymns. He is said to have disappeared in the sanctuary of NATARAJA and to commemorate this a set of his works is placed near IMAGES of Nataraja. One of his major works is the *Tiruvachakam* (Sacred Utterances), a collection of hymns in praise of Shiva. The saint is depicted standing, carrying a book in his left hand and with his right hand in VYAKHYANAMUDRA, the gesture of explanation.
Dehejia, V., 1988

Manmatha 'Churner or Agitator (of the mind)'. Epithet of KAMA.

Manthara The hunchback servant who persuaded KAIKEYI, the youngest wife of DASHARATHA, to turn against RAMA. *See also* RAMAYANA

mantra 'magic formula, mystical syllable(s)'. There is no adequate translation of the term *mantra*, which could be defined as the power of words or of sounds when grouped together in a verse or formula. In the VEDAS *mantras* were generally verses used to invoke gods, to avert natural calamities, to overcome difficulties and to receive long life. Occasionally, short utterances with no specific meaning, but

Opposite: Parankusha *mandapa*, at the end of the chariot street leading to the Vitthala temple. Vijayanagara, Karnataka. Granite, first half of the 16th century.

Right: One of the four most important sixty-three *nayanmars* is Manikkavachakar, depicted here standing, carrying in the left a palm-leaf manuscript, probably of his poems, and with the right in *chinmudra*. The simplicity of his attire contrasts with the elaborate hairstyle. Southern India. Bronze, *c*. 1500.

believed to have profound symbolical power, were spoken before or after the verses. *Mantras* consist either of a syllable (BIJA), a word, or a group of words, which are either chanted, recited or meditated upon by the worshipper according to specific rules to ensure success in communicating with the appropriate deity. *Mantras* are transmitted from GURU to pupil in the course of DIKSHA, or initiation.

Manu from SANKSRIT *man*, 'to think' I. The first man and progenitor of mankind, who, in the absence of a wife, ensured propagation by means of one of his ribs, a myth probably influenced by the Bible. This myth was elaborated upon and eventually the original Manu of the RIGVEDA became one of fourteen. This is based on the Puranic notion of a succession of creations, or of a single one divided into fourteen immensurable spans of time called *manavantaras*, each commencing after the dissolution of the previous, and each ushered in by a new Manu as progenitor. The Manu of the current era is the seventh, Vaivasvata Manu, son of Vivasvat, the Sun. 2. The reputed compiler or author of the MANU-SMRITI.

Manu-smriti, Manavadharmashastra or **Manu-samhita** 'The Code or Institutes of Manu' authored by the mythical MANU Svayambhuva ('the self-born Manu'), the first of the fourteen Manu. He probably belonged to a KSHATRIYA community and his work is a compilation of the laws and norms that regulated the life and activities of the individual and the community during almost the whole first millennium BCE. Although this work is traditionally dated to remote antiquity, historic references mentioning YAVANAS, Greeks, SHAKAS, Scythians, Pahlavas and Persians, set the lower date limit for its compilation to 100–300 CE. The *Manu-smriti*

constitutes the first systematization of Hindu law and the first of the *Dharmashastra(s)* or brahminical treatises on law. It is regarded as the most relevant work after the VEDAS and the *Shrautasutras* (commentaries on ritual practices). The Code lays down the social, ethical and moral tenets that should rule the life of the people, and the guidelines for the performance of rituals and ceremonies. All Hindus should abide by Manu's law. The work, consisting of twelve books, begins with an account of the beginning of the world; books II to VI detail the four stages of life and give specific instructions on the duties of the BRAHMACHARI (celibate student), the GRIHASHTHA (householder), the VANAPRASHTHA (forest dweller) and the SANNYASI (renouncer). Book V discusses the rules regarding women, their conduct, dietary habits, etc. Books VII, VIII and IX respectively discuss the sources of law, kingly duties and general rules on politics, civil and criminal law, debts, ownership, domestic law, rules governing women, husbands and MARRIAGE, children and parents, inheritance, deaths and funerals. Book X gives an account of the origins of CASTES, their development, rules for each one of them and their occupations. Book XI centres on morality, good and evil, sins and their atonement, sacrifices and gifts. The consequences of good and bad actions, the path to MOKSHA (final emancipation) and the doctrine of SAMSARA (transmigration) are discussed in book XII. The *Manu-smriti* seems to have been compiled to grant divine sanction to the caste system, emphasizing the supremacy of the BRAHMINS, and is contested by the lower classes who regard it as the tool of their oppression.
Bühler, G., 1969

Mara 'killing, death; destroyer; tempter'. Death, mainly associated with pestilence. An epithet of

The goddess Mariamman, whose head is surrounded by flames, sits on a sumptous throne. In her upper hands she carries the *damaru* and a snake; in the lower, a sword and a skull cup. At her feet are trays with offerings and standing lamps. Tamil Nadu. Colour print, early 1970s.

KAMA, the god of love, ensnaring all beings in the realm of the senses, thus binding them to the cycle of death and rebirth.

marga 'way or path'. Derived from *mriga* 'tracking, searching, following a way'; the meaning of the word was extended to the sphere of ethics and morality, signifying the appropriate way (of conduct). There are four means of attaining perfection: through knowledge (JNANA), acts (KARMA), devotion (BHAKTI) and YOGA (mental and physical discipline).

Mariamman 'the lady of *mari*' (pestilence, death). Goddess of smallpox and one of the most important goddesses worshipped in every village of Tamil Nadu. She is not worshipped with the *sapta kannigai* (seven sisters) because she is reputed to be superior to them and more fearsome. Her emblems are a DAMARU encircled by a snake, a skull cup, noose, sword, trident and parrot. *See also* GRAMADEVATA(S)
Whitehead, H., 1921

marjara 'cat'. The vehicle of the goddess SHASHTHI.

Marjaranyaya 'school of the cat'.
See SHRIVAISHNAVISM

Markandeya A sage and devotee of VISHNU, who, when the earth was about to be engulfed by water, begged Vishnu to rescue him. The god appeared in the form of a child floating on a leaf from a VATA tree, told the sage that he was Time and Death and requested him to enter his mouth. Markandeya obeyed and found that the whole world, the gods and the sages were all contained within Vishnu. Emerging, he saw Vishnu, still as the child floating on the leaf. In his youth, Markandeya was rescued from YAMA's hordes by SHIVA. *See* KALARIMURTI

Markandeya Purana see PURANA(S)

marriage (SANSKRIT: *Vivaha*). One of the most important SAMSKARAS in the life of a Hindu and the only one permitted to SHUDRAS and lower classes. According to the MANU-SMRITI, marriage is indissoluble, and the divorce and remarriage of widows are forbidden. Nowadays, however, widows are allowed to remarry and the 1955 Hindu Marriage Act permitted divorce. The paramount purpose of marriage is to produce sons, as only sons can perform the various domestic and funerary rites, as well as to perpetuate the family. The ideal age of the partners was thirteen for the girl and sixteen for the boy. This age limit was lowered and it became mandatory for a father to have his daughter married before puberty, which led to the notorious child-marriage custom. Generally, marriages are arranged by the families after consulting an astrologer who examines the horoscopes to assess the compatibility of bride and groom. The first meeting of the prospective partners takes place at the girl's house, when the couple formally agrees to the union and when the matters regarding dowry and other financial arrangements are finally settled. At this point the astrologer sets the auspicious time for the wedding ceremony. Most weddings are celebrated between the end of December and March, when the sun is on its northern course.

There were eight different types of marriage, some of them are now obsolete: the *paishacha*, named after the PISHACHAS, where the girl was drugged and abducted. Although frowned upon, this type of marriage was legal. The *rakshasa*, named after the RAKSHASAS, occured when a girl was a spoil of war and was carried away by her captor. The KSHATRIYAS were allowed this form of marriage, which did not entail the consent of the families concerned. The

The marriage of Virupaksha and
Pampambika, a local form of Parvati.
Detail from a painting on the ceiling of
the Virupaksha temple, Hampi,
Karnataka. Late 18th or early
19th century.

marriage of KRISHNA and RUKMINI and of ARJUNA
and Subhadra are cases in point. The *gandharva*,
derived from the GANDHARVAS, is realized when the
partners are in love with each other and consummate
their marriage without undergoing rituals; if
sanctified by the appropriate ceremonies, this was
considered to be the best type of marriage. An
instance of this is the marriage between ANIRUDDHA
and Usha. The custom of SVAYAMVARA ('bride's
choice') was sometimes classed as a form of the
gandharva marriage. Named after the ASURAS, the
asura involved the prospective groom paying money
to the bride herself and not to her father. The
prajapatya, derived from PRAJAPATI and the *arsha*
(RISHI-like), are obsolete forms of marriage on which
little information exists. In the *daiva* ('divine') the
father gave his daughter with all her ORNAMENTS to a
priest as a gift or sacrificial fee. Finally, the *brahmya*
('BRAHMIN-like'), in which the father gave his
daughter with all her ornaments and a suitable dowry
to a brahmin. Nowadays, this type of marriage forms
the basis of the traditional Hindu wedding with pre-
nuptial agreements between the families, a suitable
dowry and appropriate religious ceremonies. There
are numerous examples of *brahmya* weddings in
literature, e.g. SHIVA and PARVATI.

The marriage rite itself varies from community to
community, but some features are pan-Indian. At
the beginning of the celebrations, a short SHRADDHA
ceremony in honour of the ancestors is performed
separately by the fathers of the couple. The place
where the marriage is celebrated is prepared by
smearing the floor with cow dung mixed with water
and decorated with auspicious patterns. The altar for
the sacred FIRE is made ready and all the ritual
implements are set up in the required order. On the
wedding day, the bride has to undergo a variety of
ablutions and other rites, among which is the

dusting of the body with turmeric (HARIDRA), which
is said to generate desire. She is assisted preferably
by married women who have given birth to a son.
The bridegroom also undergoes a series of ritual
baths and dusting with turmeric and, once ready, he
is preceded by a band of musicians and accompanied
by male friends and relatives to the bride's house.
There he is welcomed by his future father-in-law
and the series of ritual acts begin. The first is called
arghya 'respectfulness', i.e. hospitality. The father of
the bride receives the groom and his party with
due honour and respect by sprinkling him with
perfumed water and offering him a drink of honey
and curds. Then follows the formal gift of the bride
to the groom or *kanyadana*, 'giving the virgin'. This
second stage is solemnized in various ways, one of
the most current is to slip new bangles on the girl's
wrist. The third phase of the ceremony is the
presentation of the eight auspicious gifts
(*mangalashta*), among which are COCONUTS, rice and
seeds. In southern India the *tali*, a small golden
jewel on a chain, is tied around the bride's neck to
solemnize the marriage. In some parts of India, for
instance among the Bengali VAISHNAVAS, the climax
of the ceremony is reached with exchange of bead
necklaces (*kanthibadala*). The groom formally
accepts the bride by grasping her hand (*pani-
grahana*) over the sacred fire. At this point of the
ceremony the edge of the bride's *sari* and of the
groom's *dhoti* are tied together and the bride is
enjoined to be steadfast, faithful and obedient to
her husband. Holding hands, bride and groom offer
libations to the sacred fire, and the bride is led in a
clockwise direction around it (*agni-pradakshina*).
Finally, bride and groom take the seven steps
(*saptapadi*) before the fire. These are symbolic of the
seven blessings for which they pray: food, strength,
wealth, happiness, progeny, cattle, devotion. Once

The rescuing of humanity from the floods is suggested in this carving by the shrine which Vishnu, in his form as Matsya, carries on his back. He is surrounded by a multitude of ascetics, *nagas* and other figures. Central India. Sandstone, 9th century.

the seventh step is taken, the marriage is irrevocable. There are a number of additional rituals, such as the *garbhadana* ('impregnation') to ensure progeny, which can be performed at any time during the wedding ceremony.

Martanda '(born from a) lifeless egg'. One of the ADITYAS, an aspect of the sun god. His mother ADITI cast him away to die after his birth, but then brought him back again. This is a metaphor for the daily rising and setting of the sun.

maruts or **marutagana** Vedic storm gods whose number varies between 21 and 180, depending on the myths narrating their origin. According to some, they are the sons of DITI who requested her husband KASHYAPA to give her a son fit to destroy INDRA. Kashyapa agreed, but imposed some conditions. Diti, however, forgot to comply with one of these conditions and Indra, with his VAJRA, carved the embryo into seven parts. The wounded embryo cried and Indra in his anger cut each of the seven parts into three more. In another story, the *maruts* are the offspring of RUDRA and the earth goddess, who, on that occasion, had assumed the form of a bull and a cow respectively. The *maruts* are depicted as brilliant, shining like lightning, carrying golden weapons and dressed in golden garments.

Mathura One of the seven holy cities, sacred to BUDDHISTS and Hindus. The town on the Jumna (YAMUNA) is mainly associated with King Kamsa and the birth of KRISHNA, and its surroundings are linked with the youthful exploits of the god. However, due to its geographical position at the junction of three great trade routes, from Gandhara in the north, the coast of the Arabian sea in the west and Pataliputra (Patna) in the east, Mathura

established itself as an important commercial and cultural centre. Its history is connected with a number of prestigious dynasties, among which were the mythical YADAVAS, the Kushanas (1st–3rd century) and the Guptas (4th–6th century). The importance of this cultural and artistic centre in the development of Indian civilization and its expansion overseas, especially under the Guptas, can hardly be stressed enough.

matrika(s) or **matri(s)** 'mother', more specifically 'divine mother'. The term refers also to a class of goddesses, originating in the remote past and linked to the forces of nature. They are generally seven in number (SAPTAMATRIKAS), eight (*ashtamatrikas*) or more, up to sixty-four. In the Vedic period they were connected with earth, water, fertility and the sun god, who was the power activating their potential fertility. Later, the *matrikas* were identified with the SHAKTIS, or energies of the gods. They are of the same appearance and possess the same attributes as their male counterparts. They are depicted sitting in a row, occasionally with a child near them or on their lap, with VIRABHADRA and GANESHA, or KARTTIKEYA as their guardians. It has been suggested that the term *matrika* may be a euphemism to denote a class of fierce YOGINIS.

Matsya *avatara* 'fish incarnation'. The first incarnation of VISHNU visualized either as a great fish or as half-man and half-fish, carrying in his four arms Vishnu's emblems. Matsya symbolizes existence emerging from the waters of non-existence. Tradition narrates that at the end of the last era when the world was engulfed by waters, one ASURA snatched the VEDAS from BRAHMA's hands and disappeared into the depths of the sea. Eventually Matsya helped MANU to recover them.

On a backdrop of a soaring *gopura*, the goddess Minakshi is depicted standing on a lotus at the centre of the Golden Lily tank in her temple at Madurai. In her right she carries the sceptre. A general view of the temple in its urban context is in the foreground. Tamil Nadu. Colour print, early 1970s.

Matsya Purana see PURANA(S)

matsyayugma 'pair of fishes'. An ASHTAMANGALA, symbol of fertility, prosperity and happiness.

Matsyendranatha Believed to be the founder of the esoteric sect of NATHA YOGIS, Matsyendranatha lived between the 9th and 10th centuries. He was one of the eighty-four great SIDDHAS and became the patron deity of Nepal. He was also reputed to have been the GURU of GORAKHNATH, with whom he founded the *hatha yoga* system. Both are associated with the KANPHATA YOGIS.

maya, **Maya** I. 'Illusion, magic, phenomenal reality, creative power'. All manifestations are regarded as transitory and conjured up by magic. The individual is under the illusion of being in control of the situation, but everything is determined by *maya*, the flux in which everything is created, dissolved and recreated. 2. The name of DEVI – Mayadevi or Mahamaya – in her dynamic aspect as SHAKTI, source of the universe and creative power.

mayura 'peacock'. A sacred BIRD, symbol of immortality, which is believed to have been created from the feathers of GARUDA. The peacock is often depicted as killing a snake, the symbol of cyclic time. It is associated with a number of deities, such as Kaumari and SARASVATI, and serves as the vehicle of KARTTIKEYA. Bundles of peacock feathers (*mayurapichchha*) are an attribute of numerous deities, e.g. KRISHNA, as well as being used for dusting sacred IMAGES and implements.

Meru or **Sumeru** The mythical golden MOUNTAIN, the centre of the universe, is located in the Himalayas and is believed to be the abode of the gods. The celestial GANGA falls on its summit before flowing to earth in four streams, each directed towards the four cardinal points.

Minakshi 'fish-eyed'. The tutelary goddess of MADURAI and consort of Sundareshvara ('the handsome bridegroom'), a form of SHIVA. The epithet 'fish-eyed' may also mean 'with EYES filled with love', the fish being an emblem of KAMA. The myth of Minakshi's birth and MARRIAGE to Sundareshvara is recorded in the STHALAPURANA of the TEMPLE at MADURAI. The king of Madurai was childless, but eventually, after having performed numerous sacrifices, a three-breasted girl was born. The king was perplexed, but a celestial voice reassured him, telling him to raise his daughter as a son, and that the third breast would disappear the moment she met her husband. When the king died, the girl succeeded him, and she embarked on a victorious campaign of conquests, and after having conquered the world, she moved towards Mount KAILASA. The divine armies of Shiva began to lose ground, so Shiva decided to enter the fray. As soon as Minakshi saw Shiva, her third breast disappeared and she was overcome with shyness and modesty. One of her attendants remembered the prophecy uttered by the divine voice at her birth and told her that Shiva was her future bridegroom. So she took him to Madurai, where they married. The myth emphatically states that Minakshi is the local goddess who eventually attracted Shiva to Madurai, which is her own kingdom. It is significant that she discovers her husband in battle, a theme common to many Tamil myths, in which a violent, bloodthirsty goddess is transformed into a gentle wife. The marriage of Minakshi and Sundareshvara is celebrated every year with great pomp during the twelve-day *Chittirai* (April–May) FESTIVAL.

Mithuna beneath a flowering tree. Pillar
bracket in the porch of Cave 3. Badami,
Karnataka. Sandstone, 578 CE.

Mirabai (1450?–1547?) A mystic and poetess, whose
life history has generated a great number of myths.
Reputed to be a Rajput princess from Chitorgarh,
who was given in marriage to a prince of Udaipur,
she was a great devotee of KRISHNA to whom she was
secretly wed. Consequently, she neglected her wifely
duties towards her mortal husband. As if this had not
been enough to incur the displeasure of her husband
and in-laws, she became the disciple of RAIDAS, a
low-CASTE saint. She was then persecuted by her
husband and his family, but this did not affect her
single-mindedness. She was fully absorbed in the
worship of Krishna Giridhari (GOVARDHANADHARA)
and composed a number of hymns in his honour.
Eventually, the god appeared to her and told her to
leave her husband and follow him to VRINDAVAN.
There she spent the rest of her life worshipping the
image of Krishna. It is said that her religious fervour
was such that the IMAGE came to life, the earth
opened and both disappeared. Her works written in
Braj, a dialect of Western Hindi, continue to be sung
especially in Rajasthan and Gujarat.
Pandey, S. M. and N. Zide, 1964

mithuna or **maithuna** 'couple, the act of pairing'.
Depictions of embracing figures on doorways and
walls of sacred precincts are considered auspicious
symbols of creation. Their union represents
cosmogonic ideas, such as heaven and earth, LINGA
and YONI, the union of PURUSHA and PRAKRITI. In
the ARTS, these concepts were illustrated by divine
couples such as SHIVA and PARVATI, VISHNU and
LAKSHMI, or others. Sexual imagery is also used in
the UPANISHADS, to explain that the delight of the
knowledge of BRAHMAN is mirrored in that of sexual
union. In another instance, the loss of individuality
experienced in sexual union is compared with that of
the individual mortal self united with the Universal

Self. In some temples associated with Tantric cults,
the sexual imagery becomes more explicit. The
partners complement each other and united they
transcend their individuality.

Mitra 'friend, companion'. One of the ADITYAS and
associate of VARUNA. He is the guardian of the law,
of contracts and of friendships. He is represented as
two- or four-armed, carrying lotuses, the SOMA plant
and a trident. He rides on a horse-drawn chariot,
accompanied by his attendants Danda and Pingala.
Mitra is the equivalent of the Iranian sun god
Mithra, whose cult became very popular in the
Roman empire at the beginning of the common era.

mlechchha(s) 'foreigner'. The term designates
mainly non-Hindus, such as Muslims, Christians
and others, regarded as impure by the Hindus.

modaka 'sweetmeat'. A rice cake or a round sweet,
attribute of GANESHA. The term is also used for
fruits, such as mangoes and sugar cane, carried by
deities, indicating the fertility of the earth and
plentiful crop.

Mohini 'the enchantress'. When the AMRITA emerged
from the CHURNING OF THE OCEAN, VISHNU
assumed the form of a beautiful woman to divert the
attention of the ASURAS and deprive them from their
share of nectar. In another story, Vishnu transformed
himself into MOHINI, the personification of lust, to
test the steadfastness of the RISHIS dwelling in the
Pine Tree forest (*darukavana*) who were proud of
their chastity. SHIVA fell in love with Mohini and
from their union AYYAPPAN was born.

moksha or **mukti** 'liberation, perfection'. Liberation
from the endless chain of death and rebirth.

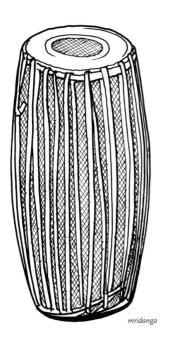

mridanga

moon *see* CHANDRA

mountains A number of mountains and mountain ranges are revered, because of the deities dwelling on their peaks, the sages living in their caves, or because they provided a backdrop for mythological events. The mountains were once endowed with wings, but since their endless circling upset the stability of the earth, INDRA severed their wings and set them at appropriate places to stabilize the world. Hence they are known as immoveable (*achala*). According to the PURANAS, there are seven variously identified main mountain ranges, known as *kula parvata* or 'family ranges'. The most celebrated are the Himalayas, 'the abode of snow', which play a conspicuous role in Indian culture. A number of myths involving gods, semi-divine beings and RISHIS are set against the backdrop of the Himalayas. The Vindhyas, dividing the northern and the southern part of the subcontinent, are said to have been mightier than the Himalayas, but they bowed respectfully before the sage AGASTYA, thus losing their height. The Sahya or Sahyadri (Western Ghats) are notorious for being the abode of demons and malevolent spirits. When most of the earth was submerged by the flood waters, they were the last to be engulfed, so they became known as Sahya, 'enduring'. At the request of PARASHURAMA, who wanted some land for the BRAHMINS, the sea god VARUNA retreated and a narrow strip of land emerged. Parashurama pinched it with his fingers creating the Malaya hills of Malabar, stretching from the Nilgiris to KANYAKUMARI. Mahendra, or 'great Indra', form the Eastern Ghats, which were once ruled by kings who opposed the gods, and who were eventually routed by them. This range is also associated with Parashurama.

There are other ranges, as well as innumerable hills and peaks, which are renowned for their sanctity and celebrated in local STHALAPURANAS. The most famous single peak is the KAILASA, the abode of SHIVA, which stands above the Manasarovara lake, where the wild geese migrate in the breeding season and at the beginning of the monsoon. The right hand of SATI is said to have fallen there. Other famous hills include PALANI, near Dindigul (Tamil Nadu), sacred to KARTTIKEYA, TIRUMALAI ('holy hill') near Tirupati, renowned for the VENKATESHVARA temple, and Arbuda ('serpent'), popularly known as Abu, in the Aravalli range in western Rajasthan. The sage VASISHTHA is reputed to have lived there. It is here that, according to tradition, the RAJPUTS emerged from the fire pit; it is also considered a sacred place by the Jains and is where the 11th-century Solanki rulers built the famous temples at Dilvara. A short distance from Dilvara lies Achalgadh, the seat of many temples, one of which contains a toe of Shiva. Another sacred JAINA mountain is Girnar in Junagadh, associated with the 22nd TIRTHANKARA, Neminatha. The Solanki rulers constructed a number of temples here also. Situated near Palitana in Kathiawad is yet another hill, Shatrunjaya, originally a BUDDHIST place of PILGRIMAGE, but now linked with the first Jaina *tirthankara*, Rishabhanatha. On this hill stand over 860 temples and 11,000 IMAGES, dating from 960 CE onwards. Since the hill is only for gods, pilgrims must bring their own food and at sunset all must climb down the hill, to leave the gods undisturbed.

mridanga(m) Barrel-shaped drum.

mriga 'antelope, gazelle, deer' In Harappan civilization (*c.* 3000–1700 BCE), the antelope, a symbol of all living beings, is associated with SHIVA. He is often depicted holding a leaping antelope in the upper left hand, the animal symbolizing his

lordship over nature. The antelope is also associated with the wind god VAYU and the goddess Shanti, personifying peace; a white antelope draws the chariot of the moon god CHANDRA.

Mrityu 'death, personification of death'. In the Vedic period death was seen as a repetition of life on earth: the body was restored and one could experience all the pleasures of mortal life. Despite this, death was dreaded, as testified by the numerous MANTRAS, spells and incantations aimed at averting it, at retarding physical decay and avoiding illnesses. Once, even the gods had to die, but PRAJAPATI became immortal through his austerities and told the other gods how to attain immortality. As far as mankind was concerned, one could become immortal only after death. According to Puranic accounts, Mrityu is the son either of BRAHMA or Bhaya (fear), and MAYA (illusion).

Mudama *see* NAGA, NAGAKAL(S)

mudra(s) 'seal, sign, token' or **hasta(s)** 'hand'. Hands as a protective sign have been part of Indian beliefs since time immemorial. In rural areas hand impressions, mainly of the right hand steeped in red dye, are a common sight on houses, cowsheds and ANIMALS, especially cows. The terms in ritual and ART denote positions of the arms and hands, which are invested with meaning. There are sixty-four *mudras* in DANCE and in art and 108 in TANTRISM.

muhurta The thirtieth part of a day, i.e. 48 minutes. *See also* CALENDAR

mukhalinga 'LINGA with a face'. Each face represents an aspect of SHIVA. The number of faces carved on the *linga* determines its purpose. Thus, the one-faced

linga should be set up in villages, the two-faced one on hills, the ones with three and four faces should be placed in temples with three or four doors respectively, and the five-faced *linga* on a hill or MOUNTAIN.

mukti *see* MOKSHA

mukuta or **makuta** 'crown'. *See also* JATA; KARANDAMAKUTA; KIRITAMUKUTA

mulavigraha 'fundamental, root IMAGE', i.e. the LINGA.

muni 'sage, seer'. An ascetic, especially one who has taken a vow of silence.

munja *see* GRASSES

murti 'form, likeness, statue'. IMAGES depicting the different aspects of the deities.

Murugan, Murukan (Tamil: 'young man') or **Subrahmanya**. Name of a divine youth around whom a number of myths have been woven. He is a god dwelling in forested hills and was worshipped with flowers and orgiastic dances. Later identified with KARTTIKEYA, Murugan is one of the main deities of Tamil Nadu. In the winter months crowds of devotees visit six TEMPLES, scattered throughout Tamil Nadu, connected with seminal events in the life of the god. *See also* PALANI

musha or **mushaka** 'rat, mouse'. GANESHA'S conveyance, often represented seated at the feet of his lord, guarding the bowl of LADDUS. The mouse symbolizes the ability to overcome obstacles, as it gnaws its way through or sneaks around them.

Far left: This type of icon is termed both *chaturmukha* or *panchamukha linga* (four- or five-faced *linga*). Above the four visible faces is Shiva's fifth and quintessential face, symbolically present on top of the *linga*. Eastern India. Black chloritic schist, *c.* 800.

Opposite: Murugan, carrying spear and staff, stands atop the Shivagiri hill at Palani. Caption in Telugu. Probably Thanjavur, *c.*1830. From an album of paintings on European paper watermarked 1820.

Below: The mouse or bandicoot, Ganesha's *vahana*, eating some of his lord's *laddus*. Khajuraho, Madhya Pradesh. Sandstone, 11th century.

mushala or *musala* 'pestle'. A wooden pestle, or a pestle-shaped club, the typical weapon of BALARAMA. The *mushala* symbolizes agriculture and is the attribute of a number of gods, such as GANESHA and MAHAKALI.

mushtimudra 'clenched hand, fist (hand pose)'. A *mudra* denoting strength.

Muyalaka(n) Tamil name of APASMARA.

nabha or *nabhi* 'navel, centre'. In cosmogony *nabha* designates a central point, e.g. the mythical Mount MERU, the 'navel of the earth', the meeting point of heaven and earth, the life-giving source. BRAHMA emerges from the lotus sprouting from VISHNU's navel, seat of universal energy. Often a lotus rhyzome, symbolizing the vital breath (PRANA) and the force of nature, is depicted sprouting from the navel of the YAKSHAS. In SHAIVISM, the *nabha* is the focus of meditation.

nada 'sound, resonance, vibration'. In TANTRISM the term indicates the primordial sound or tone vibration initiating the process of creation.

nadi 'river'. 1. *See* RIVERS 2. In TANTRISM, the term refers to the fine vessels of the body through which the psychic energy (SHAKTI) circulates.

naga, nagi or *nagini* 'snake, serpent', especially cobra. 1. The term denotes a category of semi-divine beings, half-human and half-snake, reputed to be the guardians of precious minerals, GEMS and other riches stored beneath the earth. They dwell in splendid subterranean or sub-aquatic abodes, or in inaccessible MOUNTAIN caves. The *nagas* are shown as handsome, richly clad and bejeweled men and women with a snake's lower body. Their heads are crowned by three, five, or seven fully expanded cobra hoods. Renowned for their wisdom, superhuman powers, skill and beauty as well as for their quick temper, they play a major role in folklore and in many BUDDHIST, JAINA and Hindu legends. Moreover, the *nagas* are associated with religious personalities and deities. In a number of IMAGES, such as that of the twenty-third Jaina prophet Parshvanatha, and occasionally, the BUDDHA and VISHNU, they are shown standing, sitting, or

Left: A seven-hooded *nagaraja* and wife sit on a throne, flanked by an attendant carrying a staff. Sculpture at the entrance of Cave 19, Ajanta, Maharashtra. Late 5th century.

Right: Five-hooded *naga* carved on to a slab. Andhra Pradesh(?). Steatite, *c.* 17th century.

reclining, sheltered by the hoods of a *naga*, while cobras adorn SHIVA's body. Traditionally the *nagas* are associated with fertility, water (especially of reservoirs and RIVERS) and tree worship and, even today, many pools and groves are believed to be inhabited by them. Because of their capacity to slough their skin and renew themselves, the snakes symbolize immortality and the eternity of cyclic time.

In Hindu mythology, the *nagas* are stated as being the descendants of KASHYAPA and KADRU and are regarded as the chief enemies of GARUDA. Among the important *nagas* are ANANTA (the king of the *nagas*), KALIYA, the snake goddesses MANASA and Mudama, and VASUKI, who played a pivotal role in the CHURNING OF THE OCEAN. *Nagas* play a prominent role in folk religion; they protect their devotees and are implacable towards their enemies. In southern India, especially on the west coast, many houses have a snake shrine or a snake grove in a corner of the garden, where offerings, especially of milk, are made to the snakes. In this region snakes were considered part of the property and expressly mentioned in the sale contract. In Karnataka if a snake, especially a cobra, is killed accidentally, a coin is put in its mouth, libations of milk and saffron are poured over it and the body is cremated in the course of a solemn ceremony. 2. Naga: Name of a people and their country, Nagaland, sited in eastern Assam on the border with Myanmar.
Vogel, J. P. 1962

nagakal(s) 'snake stones'. Votive stone slabs bearing the IMAGE of NAGAS. Women desiring offspring set *nagakals* beneath PIPAL and NIM trees in the vicinity of a river or a well. This custom is popular in southern India, particularly in Karnataka. The image carved on the stone represents a *naga*, a *nagini*, the snake goddess Mudama carrying in her arms two small snakes, or a *naga* and a *nagini* intertwined. Before being erected, the carved stones are immersed in a pool for half a year, in order to absorb the life-giving forces of the water. The stones are then decorated with flowers, daubed with vermilion powder and offerings are placed before them.
G. Ravindran Nair, 1993

nagakundala 'NAGA(-shaped) earring'. *See* ORNAMENTS

nagaloka 'the world of the NAGAS'. One of the divisions of the nether world, of which the capital is the wonderful Bhogavati, the seat of the king of the snakes ANANTA.

Nagapanchami 'the fifth of the *nagas*'. *See* FESTIVALS

nagavalaya 'NAGA(-shaped) bracelet'. *See* ORNAMENTS

nagi, nagini *see* NAGA

Naigamesha A ram- or antelope-headed demon, supposed to injure or seize children. Naigamesha appears in JAINA and Hindu mythology and is connected with procreation. He is also known as Harinaigameshi(n).

nakshatra(s) 'star, constellation, lunar mansion'. The *nakshatras* represent the twenty-seven or twenty-eight divisions of the lunar month. Each day the moon enters a different mansion and its position is crucial for the calculation of horoscopes and other astrological forecasts. All have special properties: some are propitious for MARRIAGE, others for setting off on travels or to begin some undertaking. Generally, *nakshatras* associated with the waxing moon are auspicious, while the others are deemed

Left: The goat-headed deity with two children perched on his shoulder: his right hand is in *abhayamudra* and the left clutches that of a small boy. Originally two more children may have been near his feet. Uttar Pradesh. Mottled red sandstone, 2nd century.

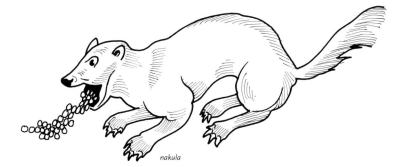

nakula

to be inauspicious. They are reputed to be the daughters of DAKSHA and wives of CHANDRA, the moon.

Nakula, *nakula* 'mongoose'. 1. Name of one of the PANDAVA princes, famous for his skill in handling horses, the twin brother of SAHADEVA. The two princes were sons of Madri by the ASHVINS. 2. The mongoose, the natural enemy of snakes and mice. According to tradition the mongoose is thought to be the receptacle of all riches and it is often depicted vomiting jewels and precious stones. This association with gems links it to KUBERA, the guardian of the north and the god of wealth, as well as to SHRI and the YAKSHAS.

Nala The king of the Nishadas who, with his wife Damayanti, is the protagonist of one of the most famous stories in the *Vanaparvan* (Book of the Forest) of the MAHABHARATA. The romantic story of their love, of Nala's passion for gambling, which eventually caused him to lose his kingdom and to be exiled along with his wife, of their wandering in the wilderness and, finally, of the triumph of their love, has been the inspiration for numerous poetic and dramatic works.

Nalayira Divya Prabhandam ('four thousand holy hymns'), also known as the 'Tamil *Veda*'. Title of the collection of hymns composed by the twelve ALVARS, compiled by Nathamuni between the 9th and the 10th centuries. This work marks the beginning of the 'canonization' of the twelve VAISHNAVA poet saints, whose verses are still sung today.

namam 'mark'. Term designating the mark drawn on the forehead with coloured earth. sandalwood or ash. *See also* TRIPUNDRA; URDHVAPUNDRA

naman 'name'. Names are believed to be the essence of a person and to influence the character of the bearer, so great care is taken in selecting the appropriate one. The name-giving ceremony takes place on the tenth or twelfth day after birth. The choice of names, either drawn from mythology, local deities, place names and others, varies according to regions and communities. Many names derive from holy places, occupations or status. Generally, boys are named after a god (e.g. Vinayaka) or a hero (e.g. Abhimanyu) and girls after goddesses (e.g. Ambika), flowers (e.g. Champaka) or GEMS (e.g. Ratna). Some parents name their children according to the NAKSHATRA under which they are born. A boy has generally two names, but the most important name is the 'secret name', whispered in his ear by his GURU in the course of the initiation ceremony. The secret name has ritual significance and is reputed to be the sole part of the person that does not end with death.

A change of status, such as entering religious life, entails a change of name. A number of flattering epithets may be added, especially in the case of rulers, e.g. the emperor Ashoka (*c.* 268–233 BCE) whose title was 'Piyadasi', 'beloved of the gods'. Deities have strings of names such as the 1000 names of VISHNU, the 1008 names of SHIVA, the 40 names of HANUMAN, which are regularly recited in order to acquire merit.

namaskaramudra 'gesture of salutation'. Similar to ANJALIMUDRA, except for the hands which are held against the forehead instead of against the chest.

Namdev or **Namadeva** (1270?–1350?) One of the most influential poet saints of Maharashtra, born in PANDHARPUR, an important VAISHNAVA PILGRIMAGE place. His father was a tailor and Namdev followed in his footsteps. Tradition reports that in his youth

Below: The humped bull of Shiva, garlanded and decorated with bells is depicted crouching, the legs neatly tucked beneath him. Such an image was originally placed opposite a Shaiva shrine. Southern India. Granite, 16th century.

Namdev led a dissolute life and eventually came under the influence of JNANADEVA, who inspired him to change his lifestyle and worship VITHOBA (VISHNU) the main deity of Pandharpur. From then on, Namdev devoted the rest of his life to the worship of Vithoba. His family, consisting of twelve members and a servant, were all poets and it is said that through their joint efforts Namdev was able to fulfil his vow of composing a billion hymns (*abhangas*) in honour of the deity. A number of them are still sung in the course of worship at Pandharpur. With his compositions, both in Marathi and Hindi, he is one of the earliest personalities of the Vaishnava revival.

Nammalvar 'our ALVAR'. The greatest of the Tamil poet saints, who probably lived in the 9th century. He was a SHUDRA and is also known as Maran, Satagopa or Parankusha, born in a small town of the Tirunelveli district (Tamil Nadu), now called Alvar Tirunagari in his honour. According to the traditional account of his life, when he refused to eat he was abandoned by his parents before an IMAGE of VISHNU in a temple. He then walked to a tamarind tree nearby and sat beneath it, never uttering a word for thirty-five years. Eventually, Madhura-kavi *alvar* spotted him and posed him a difficult question. Only then, it is said, did Nammalvar break his long silence, accepted Madhura-kavi as a disciple, and commenced singing his rapturous hymns in praise of Vishnu. Among his most celebrated works are *Tiruvaimozhi*, *Tiruviruttam* and *Periya-Tiruvandadi*. The mythical tamarind tree is now an object of worship in the extensive Adinatha temple. The saint, easily recognizable by his topknot tied at the side of the head, is generally portrayed seated with his hands either in DHYANA- or VYAKHYANAMUDRA.
Ramanujan, A. K., 1981

Nanda 'joy, delight'. Name of a cowherd, KRISHNA'S foster-father.

Nandi or **Nandin** 'rejoicing, gladdening'. Name of SHIVA'S conveyance, the white bull, son of KASHYAPA and of SURABHI. Nandi was probably a folk deity later incorporated into the brahmanic lore. However, although the bull appears in Vedic literature, there is no evidence of a direct connection between an early bull cult and Nandi. Nandi symbolizes on the one hand moral and religious duty (DHARMA), and on the other, virility, fertility and strength. It has been suggested that the bull was originally a theriomorphic aspect of Shiva. Apart from being Shiva's vehicle, Nandi, in his form as Nandikeshvara, depicted as a human with a bull's head, is believed to be one of the great masters of music and dancing. In southern India his recumbent IMAGE is placed either opposite the main sanctuary or in the hall leading to it, facing the LINGA.

Nandini 'the happy one'. A mythical COW that yields all kinds of good things. Her milk is said to have magical rejuvenating properties and she is said to be either the daughter or the mother of SURABHI, the 'cow of plenty' owned by the sage VASISHTHA.

nara 'man'. In the VEDAS, *nara* designates man. However, in the post-Vedic tradition, the name Nara refers to the first man, the progenitor of mankind or a kind of creator.

Narada 'giver of advice'(?) One of the seven great sages (SAPTARISHI), Narada son of KASHYAPA, is reputed to be the author of a number of works, including the *Naradiya Dharma Shastra*, a treatise on law and ethics, some hymns of the RIGVEDA, as well as a work on musical theory. He is the inventor of the

Opposite: Nara and Narayana performing austerities in the wilderness, suggested by tree canopies, deer and lion. The flying figure at the centre is Urvashi, the *apsara*, who emerged from Narayana's thigh. Dashavatara temple, Deogarh, Madhya Pradesh. Sandstone, early 6th century.

Right: Twelve-armed Narasimha disemboweling Hiranyakashipu. The triumphant god holds the *daitya*'s entrails in two of his hands. On the left, Prahlada in *anjalimudra*. In the sky deities and their consorts and *gandharvas* strew flowers. Caption in Telugu. Probably Thanjavur, *c.* 1830. From an album of paintings on European paper watermarked 1820.

VINA (lute) and the chief of the GANDHARVAS. He is generally depicted with long matted hair, carrying a *vina* on his shoulder.

naraka 'hell'. There are various hells, of which the number differs from text to text, from six in the MARKANDEYA PURANA to twenty-eight in the AGNI *Purana*. The hells, each divided into 144 sections, rise one above the other. According to Hindu thought, the sinners sojourn in hell for a limited period, after which they are reborn as higher or lower beings according to their merits.

Narasimha 'man-lion'. The fourth incarnation of VISHNU, depicted as a human with a lion's head. Narasimha, whose origin lies in the ancient cult of the man-lion, symbolizes divine strength and valour and is worshipped particularly by warriors and kings. According to the myth, Vishnu assumed the form of Narasimha in order to protect his devotee Prahlada from the persecutions of his father, the DAITYA king HIRANYAKASHIPU. BRAHMA had promised the king that he would not meet death at the hands of men, beasts, gods or demons and that he would not die inside or outside the house, by day or by night, nor by any weapon. In his extreme arrogance, Hiranyakashipu forbade the worship of Vishnu in his kingdom, but Prahlada defied his father's orders. Finally, provoked by the king's mockery of his son, asking him whether the deity resided in a pillar of the verandah, Vishnu as Narasimha burst out of the pillar, grabbed Hiranyakashipu and killed him at dusk by disemboweling him with his claws.

Narasimhi One of the seven or eight mothers (MATRIKAS), depicted as a handsome woman with a lion's face. She is the SHAKTI of NARASIMHA.

Narayana 'the refuge of man' or 'moving on the waters'. This term refers to VISHNU reclining on the snake ANANTA, floating on the primeval waters after the dissolution of the universe at the end of a cycle (MAHAPRALAYA). From Narayana's navel sprouts a thousand-petalled golden lotus, symbol of creation, on which BRAHMA is seated. The god, Ananta and the waters are seen as a threefold manifestation of the vital energy animating all forms of life.

narikela or *nalikera* see COCONUT

Narmada One of the seven holy RIVERS of India and the name of the goddess identified with it. The Narmada, second only to the Ganges in holiness, flows from the Amarakantaka Hill in the Eastern Vindhyas to the Arabian Sea. In its bed are found LINGA-shaped pebbles, which add to the river's sanctity. It is believed that the purificatory power of this river is such, that one's sins are wiped away by the mere sight of it. In order to accrue their merit, some devotees walk from the Arabian Sea to the sources of the river and return along the opposite bank, a journey that can take up to two years.

Nasik (Nasik district, Maharashtra). Located 130 kilometres north-east of Mumbai, near Trimbak, the source of the GODAVARI, Nasik is one of the holy cities of the Hindus. Its religious importance derives not only from the Godavari, but also from its connection with the RAMAYANA story, in which RAMA, SITA and LAKSHMANA spent part of their exile in this area. This town, once an important trading centre, at the crossroads of the great trading routes from central India to the western coast, was known to Persians, Greeks and Romans, and is referred to by the Greek astronomer and geographer Ptolemy (2nd century CE) as Nasika. A KUMBHAMELA is held at

Shiva as Nataraja performing the *anandatandava*, the dance of bliss, the seventh, and most auspicious of his dances, said to taken place at Chidambaram. Thanjavur district. Bronze, 11th–12th century.

Nasik every twelve years. The town is one of the chief centres where registers of the genealogies of high-CASTE Hindu families are kept. The record books containing such information are kept by a special class of priests, the *pandas*, and updated by the heads of the families who periodically visit the town.

Nataraja, Natesha, Nateshvara or **Nriteshvara** 'Lord or King of the DANCE'. Aspect of SHIVA as the Cosmic Dancer. Nataraja dances the universe into being, sustains it with his rhythm, and eventually dances it into annihilation. Nataraja's energy is manifested in the following five activities or *panchakriya*: creation (*shrishti*), preservation of creation (*stithi*), destruction or reabsorption (*samhara*), veiling reality, illusion (*tirobhava*) and grace (*anugraha*). In depictions of Nataraja the *panchakriya* are expressed in the position of the hands and feet of the IMAGE. In his upper right hand Shiva holds a DAMARU, out of which emerges the universe through its rhythmic beat, while from his upper left hand leaps a flame, symbolizing the dissolution of all creation. The open palm of the lower right hand is in ABHAYAMUDRA, while the lower left is extended across the chest and points to the raised left foot. The raised foot signifies the bestowing of grace and a refuge for the devotee. The right foot is firmly planted on a dwarfish creature, the APASMARA, symbol of ignorance and delusion (*maya*). Shiva is surrounded by a halo of flames (*prabhamandala*), symbolizing the vital force of nature emanating from his energy. Conversely, the flames may also denote the god's destructive force.

natha(s) *see* GORAKHNATH

Nathdwara or **Nathdvara** 'Gate of the Lord'. Holy town near Udaipur (Rajasthan), the principal seat of the cult of Shri Nathji and of the VALLABHA sect.

navadurga(s) 'nine DURGAS'. Group of nine goddesses representing different aspects of Durga. Eight are placed at the eight points of the compass, the ninth in the centre. In Bengal, the nine aspects of Durga are symbolized by the *navapatrikas*, or 'nine plants', worshipped in a festival celebrated in autumn, representing the link between the goddesses and the vegetation.

navagraha(s) 'nine planets'. Traditionally the nine planets are the sun (SURYA), the moon (SOMA), Mercury (BUDHA), Venus (SHUKRA), Mars (MANGALA or BHAUMA), Jupiter (BRIHASHPATI), Saturn (SHANI), RAHU and KETU. The *navagrahas* influence the life of the individual and great care is taken to propitiate them, especially in critical or dangerous times. Shani, Rahu and Ketu are particularly inauspicious, and are believed to cause diseases. In southern Indian SHAIVA TEMPLES, the *navagrahas* are worshipped as minor gods. They are placed on a special square altar, no two of them being made to face each other. Surya, as the chief of them, occupies the central space, while the remaining eight are placed at the eight cardinal points. In northern Indian temples the IMAGES of the nine planets are generally located on the door lintel, in order to protect both building and visitors from evil influences. *Grahahoma* are offerings of cooked food, grain and milk products to the *navagrahas*. Each planet has its own fare, such as sweet rice for Surya, rice, sugar and GHEE for Soma and mutton for Rahu.

navaratna 'nine GEMS'. The nine gems representing the nine planets (NAVAGRAHAS) are often worn as a talisman against the evil eye. Generally they are set in a ring or a pendant; a pearl represents the moon, ruby the sun, topaz Jupiter, diamond Venus, emerald Mercury, coral Mars, sapphire Saturn, cat's eye or

Budha	Soma	Brihashpati
Shukra	Ravi	Shani
Rahu	Mangala	Ketu

Diagram showing the placement and symbols of the *navagrahas*.

moonstone the waxing moon (RAHU), and sardonyx the waning moon (KETU).

Navaratri *see* FESTIVALS

nayanmar(s) 'leader'. The SHAIVA counterpart of the ALVARS are the sixty-three *nayanmars* who lived and flourished in southern India from *c.* 6th to the 9th centuries. They belonged to all walks of life, the hunter KANNAPPA and the outcaste Nanda being as much entitled to sanctity as the BRAHMINS among the *nayanmars*. Their lives are described in the PERIYA PURANAM, compiled in the 12th century by Sekkilar. The devotional poems of the *nayanmars*, which caused a great upsurge of Shaivism, are divided into eleven collections, all written in Tamil. These, together with the *Periya Puranam*, form the Tamil Shaiva canon. The four 'most reverend ones' among them are APPAR, MANIKKAVACHAKAR, SAMBANDAR and SUNDARAR.

nidhi 'treasure'. KUBERA, the god of wealth, is said to have eight or (nine) treasures or *nidhis*. These represent the different aspects of material wealth and prosperity. Of these, Shankhanidhi and Padmanidhi are the most popular and are frequently represented in personified form as the attendants of Kubera.

Nidra 'sleep'. A goddess, the personification of sleep. At the end of each cycle of creation, Nidra enters the body of VISHNU as he sleeps on the primeval waters. At the command of BRAHMA, Nidra leaves Vishnu so that, once awake, he may create a new world. *See also* YOGANIDRA

Nilakantha 'having a blue throat'. Epithet of SHIVA. *See* KALAKUTA

nilotpala (*Nymphaea cyanea*). The blue water lily or night lotus which opens at night. It is an attribute of a number of deities, such as CHANDRA and GANESHA.

nim (Hindi) or **nimba** (SANSKRIT). The neem-tree (*Azadirachta indica*) is a sacred tree, with medicinal and magical properties. Bunches of *nim* leaves are tied above the door lintels of houses in the case of birth or death, as well as for protection against evil spirits. In some parts of India mourners chew the leaves on returning from the funeral to cleanse themselves before re-entering the house. In rural India a *nim* twig is still used as a toothbrush and to massage the gums. A custom exists in southern India of marrying a *nim* tree to an ASHVATTHA, by training the trees in such a way that the trunks become closely intertwined. Snake stones (NAGAKAL) are usually placed at the foot of these trees to ensure the community's prosperity and fertility.

nimbu (Hindi) or **nimbuka** (SANSKRIT) 'lime'. The lime is used in Ayurvedic medicine as an antidote to poison, as an effective way to counteract dehydration and to fight coughs and colds. It is widely employed as a cosmetic, a hair conditioner and a skin tonic. In southern India garlands of limes are offered to potentially violent deities, such as DURGA, KALI and MARIAMMAN, to 'cool down' their tempers. The lime is also a symbol of fertility and plays an important part in MARRIAGE ceremonies, in which the bride and the groom each hold a lime during the ceremony. A lime and two chillies are hung on door lintels every new- and full-moon days as protection against evil influences.

Nirriti 'misery, decay, dissolution'. One of the ASHTADIKPALAS, the regent of the south-west.

The guardian of the south-west, Nirriti riding on the shoulders of a human being. Caption in Telugu. Thanjavur, c. 1830. From an album of paintings on European paper watermarked 1820.

Originally Nirriti was a Vedic goddess, personifying misfortune, calamity and death. Later, she was regarded as a male (Nirrita or Nairrita) of dark complexion, with protruding fangs and knitted brows. His vehicle may be an ass, a lion, a DOG or a man. In his hand he carries a spear or javelin, a staff, a sword and a shield.

nirvana 'extinction'. A term indicating in Indian mysticism the transcending of all desires, the severing of the fetters of illusion (MAYA), thus interrupting the cycle of rebirths.

Nriteshvara *see* NATARAJA

Nrittamurti or **Nrityamurti** 'dancing form'. The term applies to any dancing aspect of a deity, particularly to SHIVA as the lord of music and DANCE.

nupura 'anklet'. A type of anklet with small bells which produce a pleasant sound when the wearer moves.

nyagrodha *see* BANYAN

nyasa 'placing, putting down'. A ceremony in which parts of an IMAGE or of the body are assigned to different deities by the uttering of appropriate MANTRAS.

om, omkara or **AUM** *Om* is both the most sacred and the source or seed (BIJA) of all MANTRAS. Its symbolism is variously explained: generally, *om* is believed to be the eternal root of creation and, consequently, of dissolution. An auspicious sound associated with the primeval vibration, the cause of creation, *om* is uttered at the commencement of any ritual. Past, present and future are encompassed in the three letters A, U, M, which symbolize, among other things, the three GUNAS and the TRIMURTI: A is BRAHMA, U VISHNU and M SHIVA. AUM represents also the All Pervading, transcending space, time and form.

omens A number of involuntary actions, such as sneezing, the cries of various ANIMALS and BIRDS are interpreted as good or evil omens, depending on whether the person experiencing it is a man or a woman and on innumerable other signs, which are believed to indicate the success or failure of an undertaking. Astrological calculations, DIVINATION and the science of interpreting omens play an important role in Indian life. Thus, certain days, such as Mondays and Saturdays, are not recommended for travelling eastwards, Thursdays southwards, Fridays and Saturdays westwards, and Tuesdays and Wednesdays northwards, and Saturday is generally deemed unsuitable for travel. The braying of a donkey is always considered auspicious, whereas the chirping of a lizard can be a good or a bad omen, depending on whether the sound emanates from the left or the right, whether the hearer is a man or a woman and, finally, on the day of the week. The cries of certain birds, such as the cawing of a crow, foretells the arrival of guests. Particular attention is given to the sneezing of a person in determinate circumstances as, for instance, in the course of planning some

om

undertakings, and to certain animals, such as the howling of dogs, a definite sign of calamity.

Of great importance when starting on a trip or on a new undertaking is the sight of certain persons, animals, or objects. Thus, a young girl, a BRAHMIN, a COW, with or without its calf, a mother and child, fruit, flowers, a pot of curds, ELEPHANTS, bulls, rice, sandal paste and corpses, are considered positive omens. To accidentally hear music, the braying of a donkey and the cry of the Brahmani-kite is auspicious, but the actual sight of a donkey or of the kite is inauspicious. Conversely, a jackal can be seen, but its cry is inauspicious. Particular animals and sounds, such as weeping or lamentations heard on the beginning of a journey, are liable to jeopardize the undertaking. Whereas birds such as peacocks and parrots and animals (tigers, buffaloes and jackals) crossing the path from left to right, are good omens. However, if the same birds and animals were to cross the path from right to left, it would be advisable to retrace one's steps. The howling of jackals and the cawing of crows have been the subject of detailed studies, for example the *Shivavidya*, 'jackal science' (*shiva* or *shivalu*, 'auspicious', is a euphemistic name for the ill-omened jackal) and the *Kakarutashastra*, a manual on the cawing and flight of crows.
Jagdisha Ayyar, P. V., 1989

ornaments Like no other country in the world, India can boast millennia of uninterrupted adornment traditions. Jewelry and decoration of the person are believed to have magical and protective properties. The archaeological finds of the Harappan culture (*c.* 3000–1700 BCE) settlements have yielded necklets, rings, amulets, earrings set with precious stones and other ornaments. Gold jewelry was commonly worn, and gold embroidery or borders

adorned the clothes of the wealthy. The Greek scholar Megasthenes, who visited India between the 4th and 3rd centuries BCE, mentions 'robes worked in gold'. Some seven hundred kinds of ornaments are mentioned in SANSKRIT literature, among them are *keshabandha* ('hair band'), a generally thin fillet occasionally encrusted with precious or semi-precious stones. The *chudamani* ('crest jewel') or diadem and the *makuta* or *mukuta* worn by deities and some rulers. There are various types of *makuta*, as for instance the KARANDAMAKUTA worn by goddesses or minor deities, and the KIRITAMAKUTA, used by important deities. The neck was adorned by a *hara*, a necklace of various designs. Men and women generally wore more than one neck ornament, a torque and a necklace consisting of one or multiple strings of beads and pearls, with or without pendants. KUNDALAS are earrings of different shapes were worn by both sexes, and among the most popular, to mention only a few, were the simple round earrings, the leaf-shaped *patrakundalas*, the MAKARA-shaped *makarakundalas*, the serpent-shaped *nagakundalas*, generally worn by GARUDA and the NAGAS, and the lion-shaped *simhakundala*. Sacred IMAGES wear *skandhamala* or *skandhabharana* ('shoulder ornaments'), which roughly resemble epaulettes consisting of various strings of beads or pearls and, occasionally, the *chhannavira*, an ornament of two chain-like elements worn on the shoulders and crossing on the chest. On the upper arms both men and women wore *keyuras* ('armlets') and *valayas*, bracelets of various designs, graced their wrists.

Among the popular designs are the serpent-shaped *nagavalaya*, a typical ornament of Garuda, and the gem-studded *valayakumuda*. Wristbands and bangles of various thicknesses and materials covered the forearms of women. A number of finger

Hanuman running, bearing in his right hand the mountain on which grow the healing herbs, to restore the dead warriors to life. Southern India. Bronze, 18th–19th century.

rings, such as thumb rings, archers' rings and mirror rings were popular. Particularly interesting is the *pavitram* or purification ring. This type of ring, made of DARBHA grass, is worn in rituals and on auspicious occasions. The replica in gold or other metal, in which the design imitates the intricate knot of the grass ring, is worn by men on the ring finger of the right hand and is believed to drive away evil forces. Some rings bear the image of the bull (*vrishabha-mudra*) or other sectarian symbols, while others are set with the NAVARATNA, the nine GEMS symbolizing the planets. Women wore a *kuchabandha*, a breast band, occasionally embellished with jewels and special attention was given to waist ornaments. There are various kinds of girdles (*mekhala*) among them the *kanchidama*, to which small bells are attached by thin chains. A stomach band (UDARABANDHA) of embroidered cloth or light metal was worn by men. The *kathibandha*, or hip band, enhanced with an ornamental clasp, was worn by both sexes. In the case of men, the band, if worn long, fell down in front in elegant pleats. Anklets with tiny bells (NUPURAS) and toe-rings of various designs completed a woman's attire. The first mention of nose decoration in a Sanskrit text occurs *c.* 1250, which leads to suppose that it was probably imported by the Muslims.
Untracht, O., 1997

oshadhi A medicinal plant or herb. According to Indian tradition, the moon is associated with the growth of medicinal plants and is also known as Oshadhigarbha ('producer or generator of herbs'). The ASHVINS, the physicians of the gods, have as attribute the *oshadhipatra*, a bowl containing medicinal herbs. This attribute is also typical of the earth goddess BHUMIDEVI.

Oshadhiparvata 'MOUNTAIN of medicinal herbs'. In one of the most renowned episodes of the RAMAYANA, HANUMAN uproots the mythical Oshadhiparvata and carries it to the battlefield in order to restore the dead heroes to life.

Vase with lotus flowers flanked by geese.
Detail of a pillar of the railing Stupa 2, SW
section pillar 52A. Sanchi, Madhya Pradesh.
Sandstone, *c.* 100 BCE.

P

padma (*Nelumbium speciosum*) 'lotus'. This aquatic plant, filled with associations and symbols, plays an important role in JAINA, BUDDHIST and Hindu thought and iconography. In Hinduism it represents creation, cosmic renewal and purity, as in JAINISM and BUDDHISM, because its flowers grow on long stalks rooted in the mud; it also symbolizes detachment, represented by the drops of water which slide off its leaves. The lotus is said to have originated from VISHNU's navel as a thousand-petalled flower on which BRAHMA sat. In this case, the lotus has been interpreted as the very essence of creation. In ARCHITECTURE, the lotus moulding at the base of a building suggests that its support is a full-blown lotus flower – the earth – floating on the water. The lotus pedestal, on which the majority of sacred IMAGES are depicted either standing or sitting, indicates their unsullied nature. The auspicious nature of the lotus, believed to be a symbol of wealth, both material and spiritual, is reflected in the number of gods and goddesses who it as their attribute: KUBERA, the god of wealth, whose attendant is Padmanidhi ('the lotus treasure'), LAKSHMI, one of whose epithets is Padma, and SURYA.

Padmanabha 'lotus navel'. Epithet of VISHNU from whose navel sprouts the cosmic lotus, ushering the commencement of a new creation.

Padma Purana see PURANA(S)

padmasana 'lotus seat, or posture'. 1. In iconography, a square, oval or circular seat or plinth, adorned with one or two rows of lotus petals. 2. A meditation posture, in which the legs are crossed and the heels touch the upper thigh joints, also known as *yogasana* ('yoga posture').

paduka 'slipper, shoe'. A deity may be symbolized by a pair of sandals. This is the case in numerous temples throughout southern India where the sandals of a deity are the focus of worship. A common practice exists of blessing a devotee by placing on his head a *shatari*, a beautifully crafted jeweled crown, on which the divine footprints or sandals are embossed. A literary allusion to the symbolic significance of the sandals is found in the RAMAYANA episode, when RAMA is in exile and his sandals are placed on AYODHYA's throne by his brother BHARATA, as a sign of his presence.

painting Little can be said of early Indian painting, except that is was a flourishing ART practised by extremely skilled artists, as exemplified by the earliest surviving paintings, the murals in the BUDDHIST caves at Ajanta (Aurangabad district, Maharashtra), which were probably executed between the 3rd and the 7th centuries CE. These early works already reveal the delicacy and fluidity of the line, the love of colour, and a number of conventions that informed later painting.

As testified by the numerous textual references mentioning paintings on walls, wooden boards, palm leaves and cloth, the art of painting was highly appreciated and existed well before the beginning of the CE. Because of the fragility of the materials, as well as other hazards, such as insects, rodents and climatic factors, nothing survives of early Indian painting, except in literary sources. Poems and other works mention the *chitrashala*, painted halls or galleries in the royal residences. Themes in the paintings consisted of human and animal figures, as well as ornamental designs. The walls of private apartments were decorated with murals and there were clear rules governing the choice of suitable themes for either public or private quarters.

The youthful Murugan, with the spear in the left, and the right in *abhayamudra*, towers above Palani town, one of the six holy sites of the Murugan cult. This coloured print, made for tourists, shows the most important features of the place. Tamil Nadu, early 1970s.

The art of painting, supreme among the arts, is considered to be of divine origin. According to the *Chitralakshana* of Nagnajit, dating from the 5th or the 6th century, one of the earliest treatises on the subject, the first painting on earth was executed by a king to restore to life the young son of a BRAHMIN who had met an untimely death. In the treatise BRAHMA teaches the king to paint a portrait of the deceased, imbues the painting with new life, and returns the youth to his father. Brahma then gives the king formal instructions establishing the principle of painting. The text focuses on the image of the CHAKRAVARTIN, the universal ruler. From at least the 11th century, illustrated manuscripts were produced on palm leaf and later on paper. Buddhist manuscripts were created under the patronage of the Pala-Sena dynasty in Bengal; in Gujarat, Jain patrons commissioned copies of the KALPASUTRA and other canonical texts. In the late 12th century, the Muslim conquest brought courtly painting, but it was not until the 16th century that, inspired by the Mughals, local Hindu and Muslim courts set up their own ateliers, and schools flourished in Rajasthan, the Panjab Hills, the Deccan and southern India.

A number of texts on ARCHITECTURE, SCULPTURE and iconography contain sections on painting, but the most perceptive passage on the theory of painting is found in the commentary on the KAMASUTRA, by the 13th-century author Yashodhara. It enumerates the 'six limbs' (*shadanga*) or principal guidelines of painting. These are: classification of forms (*rupa-bheda*); the detailing of the characteristic marks or LAKSHANAS, which distinguish one figure from others of the same category; measure (*pramana*), dealing with the canons of proportions or TALAMANA, used for depicting various categories of images; conveying the emotion (*bhava*) of the represented scene; infusing 'salt' (*lavana-yojanam*),

i.e. beauty, grace, charm into a painting; resemblance (*sadrishya*); and finally, classification or analysis of the colours (*varnika-bhanga*), or appropriate use of the pigments. Some of the definitions of these six categories are obscure and scholarly discussion continues on their interpretation.

Palani One of the six main PILGRIMAGE sites and perhaps the most famous MOUNTAIN abodes of Subrahmanya or MURUGAN. The town lies fifty-seven kilometres west of Dindigul (Tamil Nadu), on the Vyapuri tank with a view over the Palani hills. According to legend, AGASTYA wished to build a dam and instructed the demon Itumban to carry mounds of earth in two baskets tied to a bamboo pole (KAVATI), but Itumban dropped the earth creating the two hills of Palani. To commemorate this event pilgrims carry *kavatis*, filled with offerings, to the temple built on the summit of the mountain. The temple, dedicated to the god in his aspect as Dandayudhapani ('bearer of the staff'), rises above Shivagiri hill and is reached by climbing 659 steps on which holy feet (*padas, see* FOOT) and names of devotees are engraved. The image of the deity is allegedly fashioned out of nine different poisons blended to form a wax-like substance.

Pampa Name of the RIVER Tungabhadra personified as the goddess Pampa, the tutelary deity of Hampi village (Bellary district, Karnataka). This local goddess was absorbed into the brahmanical pantheon between the 11th and the 14th centuries, and is regarded as the spouse of VIRUPAKSHA, a form of SHIVA. Pampa is also considered an aspect of the goddess PARVATI, and is often referred to as Pampambika.

Pancha 'five'. A magical and mystical number, particularly associated with SHIVA.

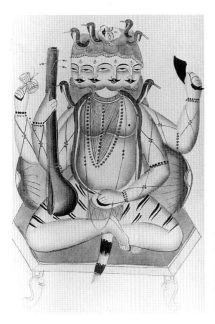

The five faces of Shiva represent his five-fold activities, the five elements and the five directions. Here the artist stresses the musical facet of Shiva's character by showing him with a *vina* and a drum. Kalighat painting, Calcutta, West Bengal. Watercolour on paper, *c.* 1880.

panchakriya 'five activities'. *See* PANCHANANA

Panchanana 'five-faced'. Epithet of SHIVA. The five faces represent the five ELEMENTS constituting the universe: earth, water, fire, wind and ether, and are called respectively Sadyojata, Vamadeva, Aghora, Tatpurusha and Sadashiva (or Ishana). These five faces also indicate the five directions of space: Mahadeva (East), Bhairava (South), Nandivaktra (West), Umavaktra (North). The fifth face, Sadashiva, indicates the zenith. These five faces further symbolize the *panchakriya*, the god's five activities: Sadyojata is associated with creation (*shrishti*), Vamadeva with its maintainance (*stithi*), Aghora with the eternal destruction and renewal (*samhara*), Tatpurusha with the power of delusion (*tirobhava*) and Sadashiva with final emancipation (*moksha*).

Pancharatra A VAISHNAVA sect, of which the name and origin are obscure, but believed to have originated in Kashmir around the 1st century BCE or later. Its teachings were codified, probably *c.* 100 CE, by Sandilya who, in his *Bhaktisutra*, stresses the importance of devotion (BHAKTI) to VISHNU as the supreme deity. The cult is based on a body of texts, the *Pancharatra Agamas*, which were seminal for the development of IMAGE worship. The devotees not only followed the textual tradition, but also emphasized the importance of the visual representation of the various aspects of Vishnu. The Bhagavata-Pancharatra doctrine, believing in the separate reality of God, world and man, was influential in the development of the theology of SHRIVAISHNAVISM. *See also* VYUHA

panchavriksha 'five trees'. The five trees of Indra's paradise: MANDARA, PARIJATA, *samtana*, *kalpavriksha* and HARICHANDANA.

Pandarinatha 'Lord of PANDHARPUR'. *See* VITHOBA

Pandava(s) The putative sons of PANDU, brother of DHRITARASHTRA. The sons of Pandu by KUNTI were YUDHISHTHIRA, BHIMA and ARJUNA; the twins NAKULA and SAHADEVA were by Madri. The story of their rivalry with their cousins, the KAURAVAS, is told in the MAHABHARATA.

Pandharpur The most famous PILGRIMAGE town in Maharashtra, Pandharpur (Sholapur district) is located on the RIVER Bhima. It is crowded with TEMPLES, the most important being dedicated to VITHOBA or Vitthala, a form of VISHNU. In spite of the antiquity of this cult, known since the 13th century, Pandharpur was only developed in the mid-17th century by the Maratha rulers, and in the second half of the 18th century by the Holkar and Shinde families. The main pilgrimage season occurs during June and July when holy IMAGES are carried in palanquins (*palkhi*), from all over Maharashtra to Pandharpur by devotees of the Varkari sect.
Mokashi, D. B., 1987

Pandu 'the pale'. The brother of DHRITARASHTRA was on a hunting expedition, when he killed an antelope that was in the process of mating. The ANIMAL, who was a RISHI in disguise, cursed him to die while having sexual intercourse. Scared of fathering his own children, he requested his wives KUNTI and Madri to have children from various gods. Thus, DHARMA was the father of YUDHISHTHIRA, VAYU of BHIMA, INDRA of ARJUNA and Madri's twins were fathered by the ASHVINS.

Panini The author of the *Ashtadhyayi*, the earliest work on SANSKRIT grammar. Panini's life is shrouded in mystery. He probably lived between

Left: Parashurama, armed with a conspicuous axe, a bow and a quiver filled with arrows slung over the shoulder in compliance with his martial character. Caption in Telugu. Probably Thanjavur, *c*. 1830. From an album of paintings on European paper watermarked 1820.

parashu

the 6th and the 4th centuries BCE. The *Ashtadhyayi* (Eight Chapters) has been celebrated as the most detailed scientific grammar composed before the 19th century.

parashu 'battleaxe'. A popular weapon of the KSHATRIYAS made of bronze or iron, also an attribute of a number of deities: SHIVA's *parashu* symbolizes the severing of all worldly cares, as well as his divine powers. The *parashu* is also an attribute of CHAMUNDA, MAHAKALA and others.

Parashurama 'RAMA with the battleaxe'. According to tradition, Parashurama was a member of the Bhargava clan, a priestly family believed to have descended from the mythical RISHI Bhrigu. The clan settled in Gujarat and, once the Haihayas conquered western India, their king, Kartavirya, nominated the Bhargavas as their priests, endowing them with conspicuous wealth. Eventually, the king's family demanded the restitution of the endowments, but the Bhargavas refused and fled to Kanyakubja (Kanauj). In spite of their brahminical status, which prohibited them from engaging in warfare, they armed themselves and married into important KSHATRIYA families, such as that of the king of Kanyakubja. Parashurama's father, JAMADAGNI, was the son of Satyavati, the daughter of the Kanyakubjan king, and of Richika, one of the Bhargava leaders. Parashurama later avenged the oppression of his family and death of his father by the descendants of Kartavirya. According to the MAHABHARATA, Parashurama is the sixth AVATARA of VISHNU, descended on earth to re-establish the social order disrupted by the arrogance of the *kshatriyas* who tried to claim spiritual leadership for themselves. After twenty-one attempts, Parashurama is said to have exterminated all the

kshatriyas on earth, and gifted their lands to the sage KASHYAPA. Eventually, however, Parashurama was defeated by the seventh incarnation of Vishnu, RAMACHANDRA.

Parashurama is connected with a number legends, suggesting that he played a pivotal role in the opening up of southern India. According to one myth, it was the COW of plenty, KAMADHENU, entrusted by INDRA to Jamadagni, that was the prize coveted by Kartavirya and his followers. They would have been successful, had Parashurama not intervened. Once the battle was over, Parashurama's ambition grew, and VARUNA (the god of law) told him that he could have all the land within a bow shot. But, fearing Parashurama's prowess as an archer, Varuna requested YAMA to transform himself into an ANT and gnaw at the bowstring. Thus, Parashurama's shot only reached Malabar, a region said to have been created from the watersof the ocean. The VAISHNAVA tradition is silent on the gory part of the Pashurama myth, and he is normally referred to as Bhargava Rama, or Jamadagni Rama, to distinguish him from BALARAMA and Ramachandra.

parijata (*Erythrina indica*) 'Indian coral tree'. One of the five trees (PANCHAVRIKSHA) that emerged in the course of the CHURNING OF THE OCEAN, and which grows in INDRA's paradise. Its three-pointed leaves symbolize VISHNU (centre), BRAHMA (right), SHIVA (left). Its flowers are an attribute of VARUNI, the goddess of wine.

Parikshit Posthumous son of ABHIMANYU and UTTARA and grandson of ARJUNA. YUDHISHTHIRA abdicated the throne in his favour. According to the BHAGAVATA PURANA, Parikshit, who had offended an ascetic, was doomed to die within seven days. To

Left: Parvati standing elegantly in the *tribhanga* pose, has her right hand slightly raised, and the left hanging loosely at her side. When in worship, the right hand of this image would have held a flower. Tamil Nadu. Bronze, *c.* 13th–14th century.

pasha

prepare himself for his imminent death, he sat on the banks of the Ganges and was advised to listen to the recitation of the *Bhagavata Purana* to ensure that, at the moment of death, his mind would be focused on VISHNU.

Parvata 'MOUNTAIN'. The father of PARVATI, the Himalaya range personified.

Parvati 'daughter of the MOUNTAIN'. A benign goddess, wife of SHIVA. In the PURANAS, she is identified with various local goddesses, e.g. PAMPA, which were eventually assimilated into the SHAIVA pantheon. When depicted on her own, she is four-armed and generally carries prayer beads, a mirror, bell and citron. If she appears with Shiva, she is two-armed. Her VAHANA is a lion or a tiger. Her other names include Ambika ('the mother'), Gauri ('golden'), Shyama ('dark'). In her fearsome aspect she is called Bhairavi ('awesome'), Durga ('inaccessible'), Kali ('black').

pasha 'noose, snare, fetter'. Weapon used by riders in warfare. Famous is the *pasha* with which INDRA binds VRITRA, the drought demon, releasing the rain; VARUNA gathers evildoers with his noose. The *pasha* is an attribute of various deities, including AGNI, GANESHA, RUDRA and SHIVA.

pashu 'animal, cattle'. A term indicating cattle, goats and other ANIMALS and creatures, in particular the five that were sacrificed in the Vedic age: COWS, horses, sheep, goats and men. The antelope (*mriga*), one of the most conspicuous attributes of SHIVA, symbolizes the animal world and his lordship over it. Metaphorically, the word designates a soul that has been tainted by impurity, and has lost its innate omniscience.

pashupata 1. 'the herdsman's staff'. A magical weapon variously depicted as a kind of trident, bow or VAJRA, with which SHIVA will annihilate the universe. 2. The Pashupata sect is considered to be one of the oldest SHAIVA cults, founded by Shiva himself and later reorganized by LAKULISHA in the 2nd century CE.

Pashupati 'lord of ANIMALS (or men)'. Epithet of SHIVA.

patakahasta or *patakamudra* 'flag or streamer handpose' in which a hand is stretched horizontally from the shoulder. The open palm is held upright, with fingers close together and the thumb slightly bent to touch the base of the forefinger. This MUDRA signifies assurance, power and it is characteristic of various aspects of SHIVA, VAYU and VISHNU as VISHVARUPA.

patala 'nether world'. The collective designation for the seven regions of the nether world. It also refers to the region of the NAGAS, ruled by the serpent VASUKI, which has Bhogavati as its capital.

Patanjali 1. Patanjali, who lived in the 2nd century BCE, was the author of a number of important works, including a grammar, the *Mahabhashya* and possibly the *Charakasamhita*, a treatise on medicine. 2. The author of the first three books of the *Yoga-sutras*. The fourth book was probably added in the 5th century CE. In this work, Patanjali states that he was not the inventor of the YOGA techniques, but the compiler and editor of the doctrines and techniques prevalent among early ascetics. It is not clear whether the grammarian and the author of the *Yoga-sutras* are the same person. 3. A great devotee of SHIVA who, along with VYAGHRAPADA, witnessed the

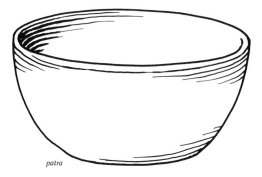

patra

DANCE of Shiva at CHIDAMBARAM. When represented in this aspect, Patanjali has the lower body of a snake and his hands are folded in ANJALIMUDRA.

patra 'almsbowl, cup'. The term may also denote the KAPALA (skull cup).

Periya Puranam (Tamil: The Great Purana) or **Tiruttontarpuranam** (The Purana of the Holy Devotees). Legendary poetic account of the lives of the sixty-three NAYANMARS, compiled in the 12th century by Sekkilar.

According to tradition, the 8th-century poet saint SUNDARAR was inspired by SHIVA to sing the *Tiruttondar-Tokai* (Assembly of the Sacred Slaves). This hymn is the oldest list of the SHAIVA saints in which their names are not in chronological or alphabetical order, nor grouped according to profession or CASTE. However, since it is deemed to have been sung under divine inspiration, the sequence of the names remained unaltered. In the 10th century, the poet saint Nambi Andar Nambi received a royal order to elaborate upon this list. Eventually, in the 12th century, it was arranged and codified by Sekkilar, a minister of the Chola empire, who had the possibility of consulting the records pertaining to the life stories of the Shaiva saints. He made several tours throughout the country and was probably able to collect current traditions and other information. He later retired to CHIDAMBARAM, where he began to compose his work. On completion, it is said that the king came to Chidambaram and listened for a year to Sekkilar's commentary on his *Periya Puranam*, which was then added to the corpus of Shaiva canonical works.
Zvelebil, K. V., 1995

personified weapons *see* AYUDHAPURUSHA

pilgrimage (*yatra*) 'going, travelling'. Visiting holy places, is one of the important religious duties of a Hindu. A pilgrimage is said to please the deity, give inner peace and increase the devotee's spiritual merit or *punya*. India is rich in holy places (TIRTHAS), which are specially revered by SHAIVAS, VAISHNAVAS and SHAKTAS. However, there are no religious distinctions. Hindus will visit shrines dedicated to other deities and offer their homage to non-Hindu holy places, such as the Basilica of Our Lady of Health at Velankanni (Thanjavur district, Tamil Nadu) or the tomb (*dargah*) of Muslim saints, such as that of Sikander Shah at Tirupparankunram near MADURAI.

Tirthas, often set in dramatic surroundings (caves, MOUNTAINS, lakes, streams or forests), are connected with a deity or a mythical event. Thus, Shaiva *tirthas* are those sites at which a LINGA, generally of miraculous origin, is enshrined. Vaishnava *tirthas* are associated either with VISHNU, or his incarnations, as for instance, the shrines at Ahobilam (Kurnool district, Andhra Pradesh), located in a forested area of the Eastern Ghats, are connected with NARASIMHA, or with the characters and episodes of the RAMAYANA. Shaktas will visit those sites where fragments of SATI's body are believed to have fallen to earth, such as KAMAKHYA in Assam.

Among the most important *tirthas* are the seven holy cities: AYODHYA, MATHURA, GAYA, VARANASI, UJJAIN, HARDWAR and DWARKA; the seven sacred RIVERS: GANGA, YAMUNA, SARASVATI, GODAVARI, NARMADA, INDUS and KAVERI; sacred mountains (e.g. KAILASA) and hills (e.g. PALANI); as well as a number of holy lakes, such as the Manasarovara at the base of Mount Kailasa in the Himalayas. A number of STHALAPURANAS or *mahatmyas* narrating the mythical events that occurred in the area, celebrate the connection of a *tirtha* with saints, heroes and gods, contributing both to its fame and

Print of Hampi (Vijayanagara), showing the various sacred places and shrines. At the centre, the images of Virupaksha and Pampambika, the tutelary deities of the place. Immediately below, the temple and the chariot festival. Coloured print, early 1980s.

sanctity. These texts, locally compiled and printed, are available in a number of Indian languages and, occasionally, in English for the guidance and edification of the pilgrims.

A visit to a holy place generally starts with a purifying BATH in a river or a lake. The pilgrims will then worship the main deity and visit all the other TEMPLES at the site, and finally leave a donation for the upkeep of the temples, the feeding of the BRAHMINS, or any other charitable cause. A significant part of the visit consists of the PRADAKSHINA or *parikrama* ('circumambulation'), which may be of the temple, the whole site, or a holy mountain, as for instance, at TIRUVANNAMALAI (North Arcot district, Tamil Nadu). An ambitious pilgrimage is the *mahaparikrama* ('great circumambulation'), in which pilgrims carry a pot of Ganges water from the Himalayas to RAMESWARAM, at the southern tip of India, pour it onto the *linga* enshrined there, and return northwards with sand collected at Rameswaram to deposit in the Ganges.

Sacred sites in southern India are connected by a network of related divinities, which determine the pilgrims' itinerary, as for example, the five elemental *lingas* of Shiva, or the six holy sites connected with the life of SUBRAHMANYA. A pilgrim may decide to perform the journey on foot, rolling on the ground, hopping, kneeling or lying flat, standing up and walking the same distance as the length of his body, then lying flat again. The more laborious the progress the more merit gained. Dying in the course of a pilgrimage ensures salvation. Nowadays, however, although the time spent on pilgrimages has been drastically reduced by the pressures of modern life, pilgrimage is a flourishing industry on account of bus and car transport which is available even to the most remote holy places.

Eck, D. L., 1982

pinaka 'staff'. *See* DHANUS

pinda or *puraka* A ball of rice or flour mixed with other ingredients, varying from community to community, which is offered to the PITRIS. In the course of the FUNERAL RITES, five *pindas* are placed on the corpse. These should serve as nourishment for the deceased, and help in the formation of a new body which his spirit may inhabit.

pipal see ASHVATTHA

pishacha(s) Flesh-eating demons, whose origin is obscure. According to some, they were created by BRAHMA, or were the sons of either Krodha or of DAKSHA's daughter Pishacha. They roam in the darkness, haunting the cremation grounds, along with other demonic beings, such as BHUTAS and VETALAS. *Pishachas* may change their form at will or become invisible and enter the body of those who yawn without covering their mouth. They are said to possess human beings, but can be driven away by appropriate MANTRAS. Anyone who sees the demons is doomed to die within nine months, unless they propitiate them with the appropriate rites. On festive days the *Pishachas* receive their share of offerings, such as defiled or unconsecrated food, liquor, flesh, sesame seeds and black cloth. They are depicted as dark, gaunt, with bulging veins and dishevelled hair. They speak their own language, *Paishachi*, and their name is given to one of the forms of MARRIAGE.

pitha 'seat, throne, pedestal' also 'site, sacred site'.
1. In iconography the word *pitha* refers to the seat or pedestal of the IMAGE, which may be square, hexagonal, octagonal, twelve-sided, sixteen-sided, elliptical, circular, triangular or semicircular, and made of stone or metal. 2. The term *pitha* refers to a

place of religious significance connected with one of the many aspects of DEVI. According to tradition each *pitha* enshrines a fragment of SATI's body. The number of *pithas* may vary from 4 to 108 according to different traditions.

pitri(s) 'ancestors'. In this category are included the progenitors of mankind, as well the ancestors that have undergone the appropriate last rites. They are reputed to be equal in status to the gods and to live either on the moon or in heaven (*pitriloka*), the world of the *pitris*. The world of the ancestors, however, perceived as one of the nether worlds, is situated in the South and identified with *Yamaloka*, the sphere of YAMA.

Plakshadvipa 'island of the *plaksha* tree'. One of the seven continents surrounded by a sea of sugar-cane juice, symbol of abundance. At its centre grows a *plaksha* tree (*Ficus religiosa*) sacred to SHIVA.

Pongal *see* FESTIVALS

pradakshina 'moving to the right'. Circumambulatory motion around a sacred IMAGE, TEMPLE, person, sacred tree or ANIMAL, signifying submission and respect. The circumambulated person or object must always be kept to the right. If it is performed in the opposite direction, it is called *prasavya* and is considered inauspicious.

Prahlada *see* HIRANYAKASHIPU, NARASIMHA

Prajapati 'Lord of Creatures' or 'Lord of Creation, progenitor'. INDRA and other deities are termed Prajapati in the VEDAS; the term later referred to BRAHMA and his ten mind-born sons. These are called *Prajapatis*, *brahmarishis* or *brahmaputras*, and

preside over the secondary process of creation, being the progenitors of the MANUS, the gods, the minor gods, the natural phenomena and animal life.

prakriti 'nature'. The matter or material substance from which the universe is created. According to SAMKHYA philosophy, *prakriti* is nature, of which the infinite potentialities can become actuality only in combination with the spirit, PURUSHA.

pralaya 'dissolution'. The process marking the end of each age, when all forms merge into an undifferentiated mass. After some time, creation starts afresh.

pramana 'measure, proportion'. *See* TALAMANA

prana 'vital breath, life principle'. The principle that separates the animate from the inanimate. *Prana* is identified with the cosmic essence, ATMAN, and with the all-pervading power, BRAHMAN.

pranapratishtha 'endowing with breath'. Ritual by which an IMAGE is consecrated and endowed with the vital breath of the deity it represents.

pranayama 'breath control'. A breathing technique used in YOGA and meditation for cleansing the body and concentrating the mind.

prasada 'grace, divine grace or favour'. Fruit, flowers, food are offered to the deity and blessed by it, and then shared among the devotees as the deity's gift.

Prayaga 'place of sacrifice'. Also known as Allahabad it is one of the seven holy cities of the Hindus, situated at the confluence of the GANGA, the YAMUNA and SARASVATI, hence its epithet Triveni or

Raja Sidh Sen of Mandi seated on a cheetah skin and performing *puja*. His right hand, carrying prayer beads, is concealed in a pouch. Various sacred implements are placed opposite him. Mandi, Panjab Hills. Opaque watercolour on paper, *c.* 1720.

'triple braid'. This town is reputed to be the 'navel of the earth'. The name derives from the legend that Brahma performed the first Ashvamedha here, to celebrate the recovery of the lost Vedas. Prayaga has a long tradition as a place of pilgrimage, hence its epithet *tirtha-raj* or 'king among tirthas'. Each year, in the month of *Magha* (January–February) a great fair or *mahamela* is held here, attracting crowds of pilgrims who bathe at the confluence of the holy rivers, and every twelve years the grand Kumbhamela is held here. This city is one of the three places, along with Gaya and Kurukshetra, that must be visited by the devout Hindu to fulfil his obligations towards the ancestors. At the end of the age, when all creation will dissolve into non-entity, Prayaga will be the sole place to survive.

preta(s) 'deceased'. The intermediate stage a person goes through between death and union with the ancestors. Under the influence of local legends and customs, this definition has been enlarged to accommodate various categories of *pretas*. Although not necessarily malevolent, the *pretas* are said to haunt their former abodes and to trouble children, if not duly propitiated. To avoid a *preta* becoming dangerous, it is necessary to perform the funerary rites correctly, so that the deceased can join the sphere of his ancestors.

pretasana 'corpse seat' 1. A corpse that serves as a seat; typical attribute of the goddess Chamunda. 2. In yoga: a position (asana) of relaxation, in which the person lies on their back with outstretched arms.

Pritha *see* Kunti

Prithvi 'the wide or extended one'. The earth and its personification as a goddess. In the Vedas she is celebrated as the mother of all creatures and the consort of the sky. She is associated with fertility and with Vishnu, originally a solar god.

puja 'worship, homage'. An act of worship in which the deity is invited to descend into its image and is treated as a guest. A *puja* takes many forms according to the religious affiliation of the worshipper, his community and the occasion. It can take place in a temple or at home and may range from a simple offering of fruit, flowers, leaves, occasionally sweets or sugar and water, to an elaborate ceremony involving a number of participants and offerings of various sorts. A *puja* consists of a number of acts or *upacharas*: invitation of a deity (*avahana*), offering a seat (*asana*), greeting (*svagata*), washing the feet (*padya*), rinsing the mouth and hands (*arghya*), offering water for sipping (*achamanya*) or water mixed with honey (*madhuparka*), lustration (*abhisheka*), clothing (*vastra*), perfume (*gandha*), flowers (*pushpa*), incense (*dhupa*), lamps (*dipa*), offering of food (*naivedya* or prasada), prostration (*namaskara*) and the send-off (*visarjana*).

pundra *see* Tilaka

Purana(s) 'stories of old'. A collection of ancient myths concerning the creation of the world, its destruction and re-creation, the genealogies of the gods and the patriarchs, the reigns and periods of the Manus and the history of the Solar and Lunar dynasties. Traditionally, these are the five main topics, or *panchalakshana*, that should be included in a *Purana*, but rarely are. The narratives are interspersed with theological, scientific, ritual, astrological and iconographic information. Written mainly in verse, the text takes the form of a dialogue

Purnaghata filled with foliage and lotus buds, and decorated with beaded bands, is sculpted on a pillar in the Kashinatha temple, Pattadakal, Karnataka. Sandstone, 8th century.

between the main narrator, often a RISHI, and a group of disciples, whose questions anticipate those of the devotees. The *Puranas* were a way of disseminating the principles of religion and ethics among the illiterate, among women and all who were prohibited access to the Vedic lore. It is not clear when the first *Purana* was composed, although some consider the HARIVAMSHA of the early centuries CE to be the first example of this genre. There are eighteen great or principal *Puranas* (*mahapuranas*) and eighteen minor ones (*upapuranas*). Among the most significant are:

Agni Purana (10th century?), originally recited to VASISHTHA by AGNI. A compendium containing, besides some original passages, quotations from other works on ritual worship, cosmology, history, warfare, a section on grammar, one on law and one on medicine.

Bhagavata Purana (9th–10th century?), the most famous of the *Puranas*, also known as *Srimad Bhagavatam*. The most important sections are those books dealing with the life of KRISHNA, i.e. *Bhagavata*. The work is narrated to PARIKSHIT, who is preparing to die. It stresses the need for BHAKTI and interprets the loves of Krishna and the GOPIS as an allegory of spiritual devotion.

Garuda Purana, of which many versions exist; it is debatable whether its original text is still extant. This text deals with FUNERAL RITES, the reconstitution of a new body for the PRETA, the judgment of deeds and misdeeds, and the various stages between death and re-birth. It also deals with the worship of SURYA. It is not clear why this *Purana* is named after GARUDA.

Linga Purana (*c.* 8th century), in which SHIVA explains, among other things, the importance of LINGA worship and the correct rituals to be followed.

Markandeya Purana (*c.* 9th–10th century), a collection of legends and myths with no particular sectarian bias, narrated by the sage MARKANDEYA. However, embedded in this work is the DEVI MAHATMYA (Glorification of the Great Goddess), probably composed before the 8th century.

Matsya Purana (*c.* 12th–13th century?) narrated by VISHNU in his form as MATSYA to MANU. It contains material from the *Vishnu* and *Padma Purana* as well as from the MAHABHARATA.

Padma Purana (*c.* 12th century?), a substantial work narrating the time when the world was a golden lotus (PADMA) and describing creation, the various zones of earth, heaven and the nether world. A section on devotion was added to it.

Shiva Purana (*c.* 7th century?), a variant of the earlier *Vayu Purana*. As the name indicates it is devoted to Shiva and his many aspects, and it is among the oldest of the *Puranas*.

Skanda Purana (*c.* 6th–15th century?), the longest of all *Puranas* recited by SKANDA. The text only exists in distinct parts, for instance the *Hemakuta Khanda*, describing the SHAIVA traditions in the Hemakuta region near Vijayanagara (Karnataka), the *Kashi Khanda* describing those at VARANASI, and the *Utkala Khanda*, an account of practices in Orissa.

Vamana Purana (*c.* 16th century) contains the narrative of Vishnu's incarnation as VAMANA (dwarf). It eulogizes both Shiva and Vishnu.

Vayu Purana (*c.* 5th century?), the most ancient of the *Puranas*, it is devoted to Shiva and contains information concerning GAYA and its sacredness.

Vishnu Purana (*c.* 6th century?), the most important of all *Puranas*, dedicated to Vishnu, celebrated as the beginning and the end of creation. The text deals not only with the five essential subjects, but also with other topics. The core of the work dates probably from the 1st century BCE. The *Vishnudharmottara Purana*, a treatise on the arts (*c.* 7th–10th century), was appended to it.

purnakalasha

Puri 'town'. The eastern of the four DHAMAS, Puri is situated on the Bay of Bengal and was originally an important BUDDHIST site. The name Puri is an abbreviation of Dantapuri, meaning 'town of the tooth', because one of the BUDDHA's teeth was reputedly enshrined there. With the decline of Buddhism between the 9th and 10th centuries, the town became an important VAISHNAVA centre and, by the 15th century, the cult of JAGANNATH was well established there.

purnaghata 'vase of plenty'. An auspicious motif consisting of a vase filled with foliage, flowers and fruit.

purnakalasha 'full vase'. An auspicious motif symbolizing fertility and life-force. Its depiction is similar to that of the PURNAGHATA.

purna avatara 'full or complete AVATARA'. The term refers to an incarnation of VISHNU that covers the whole span of a human life from birth to death, such as RAMA or KRISHNA. All other *avataras* are considered to be only partial manifestations.

purohita 'appointed, placed in front'. Before the advent of the Mauryas (*c.* 321 BCE), the government of a kingdom consisted of the king, who was in charge of the army, and the *purohita*, or royal chaplain, whose function it was to advise the king and protect him with his magical powers. He was the chief officiant in prestigious rites, such as the royal consecration and the ASHVAMEDHA. One of the most distinguished *purohitas* was Kautilya, the reputed author of the ARTHASHASTRA.

purusha 'man, male'. In the *Purusha-sukta* of the RIGVEDA (Hymn 90, *Mandala* X), the *purusha* is depicted as the cosmogonic force encompassing the whole earth. The entire creation emerged from his dismembered body and the *purusha*'s sacrifice became the prototype of all other sacrificial actions. Of particular interest is the origin of the four CASTES: the BRAHMINS emerged from his mouth, the KSHATRIYAS from his arms, the VAISHYAS from his thighs, and the SHUDRAS from his feet. This passage had dramatic consequences for the structure of the caste system. In SAMKHYA philosophy, *purusha* is the passive complement of the active creative principle or PRAKRITI.

purushartha(s) 'the [four] goals of man'. The four aims of life to be striven for or realized: ARTHA (wealth), DHARMA (righteousness), KAMA (sensual enjoyment) and MOKSHA (final liberation).

putra 'son'. This word is explained in popular etymology as saviour (*tra*) from hell (*put*). The chief duty of a son, apart from continuing the line, is to perform the appropriate FUNERAL RITES to ensure that his ancestors reach the world of the PITRIS. Their souls would otherwise be doomed to remain in the hell of those without issue (*Put*). However, in some cases a daughter could be declared a son in order to fulfil the requirements of the last rites.

Radha coyly draws her veil to cover her face, while shyly touching Krishna's foot. Kalighat, Calcutta, West Bengal. Watercolour on paper, c.1860.

Radha 'prosperity, success'. One of the GOPIS of VRINDAVAN who became a central figure of VAISHNAVA theology, wife of Ayanaghosha, the beloved of KRISHNA. Although early literature speaks of a favourite among the *gopis*, her name does not appear until the 11th century. The 12th century saw her emergence as Krishna's favourite *gopi* and the epitome of the beloved in JAYADEVA's *Gitagovinda*. She is occasionally regarded as an incarnation of LAKSHMI and is the focus of devotion in Gaudiya Vaishnavism, or 'Bengal Vaishnavism', founded by CHAITANYA in the 16th century. Radha's selfless devotion to Krishna is regarded as a model for devotees, and she is also seen as the intermediary between man and God. According to other interpretations, Radha's love for Krishna symbolizes the human soul's yearning for God.

raga, *ragini* A musical note or a melody. The term derives from the SANSKRIT verb *ranj-* which means 'colour', red in particular. A *raga* is supposed to tinge the listener's soul with emotion. The six male *ragas* are wedded to five or six *raginis*, and from their union are born the *ragaputras*, 'children of the *ragas*'. Each *raga* or *ragini* is associated with an emotion and should be performed at the appropriate hour of the day or night, season or occasion. One of the greatest creations of Indian miniature PAINTING are the *Ragamala* ('garland of *Ragas*') albums, in which the musical melodies are visualized either as deities or human beings involved in various activities.

Raghava 'descendant of RAGHU'. *See* RAMA

Raghu One of the most famous kings of the Ikshvaku or Solar dynasty, son of Dilipa and great-grandfather of RAMA. Both Raghu and his father appear in the *Raghuvamsha* (Ancestry of Raghu), one of the most famous works by the SANSKRIT poet Kalidasa (5th century) celebrating Rama's ancestry and life.

Rahu 'seizer'. One of the NAVAGRAHAS. Rahu is a DANAVA, responsible for the eclipses of the sun and the moon. At the time of the CHURNING OF THE OCEAN, Rahu appeared disguised as a god and sat among the other deities waiting for his share of AMRITA. He was eventually spotted by SURYA and SOMA (the sun and the moon gods) who informed VISHNU. The latter decapitated Rahu, but, as he had tasted a drop of *amrita*, the head began to circle in the sky, pursuing the sun and the moon in the vain attempt to swallow them, thus causing eclipses. In Indian astronomy Rahu is identified with the ascending node of the moon, while his tail is identified with KETU, the descending node. *Rahu kala* ('Rahu time') is an inauspicious time occurring daily at different hours. It is advisable to avoid new or difficult entreprises during this period.

Raidas or **Ravidas** (15th century). A *chamar*, or leather worker by profession, he became the disciple of RAMANANDA, and later one of the most important exponents of the VAISHNAVA *bhakti* movement. Especially revered in northern India and as far south as Maharashtra, he left a lasting impact on Hindi literature with his impassioned devotional verses. The appeal of his works was such that some of his compositions were incorporated into the *Adi Granth*, the holy book of the SIKHS. Although despised by the BRAHMINS for his humble origins and for his teachings, he had among his thousands of followers a number of high-CASTE disciples, including MIRABAI.

Raja(n) 'king, chief'. The word appears in the RIGVEDA as a title applied to deities such as INDRA,

Left: One of the *navagrahas*, Rahu is responsible for eclipses. He was cut in two by Vishnu's discus, and hence he is shown as a fiercely countenanced half-man. In his hands are two crescents, probably symbolizing sun and moon. Konarak, Orissa. Schist, 13th century.

rajalilasana

AGNI and VARUNA, the archetypes of the terrestrial king. The principal duty of a ruler was to protect his kingdom and its citizens, and to lead the KSHATRIYAS into battle. In return for protection, the citizens maintained him, the warriors and the priests, including the chief priest, the PUROHITA.

rajalilasana 'position of royal ease'. A sitting position in which one foot touches the ground, while the other leg, flexed at the knee, is raised and supports one arm. The body, supported by the other arm leans slightly backwards.

rajas 'energy'. *See* GUNA

rajasuya 'royal consecration'. Originally a simple inauguration ceremony, it slowly grew in complexity, extending over one or two years. It involved a number of different rituals performed at various times of the year under the direction of a PUROHITA. According to some authors, the *rajasuya* contains elements suggesting a re-enactment of cosmic principles, such as death and rebirth, the fertility of the earth and the movements of the sun and the planets. With this ceremony the king acknowledged the superiority of the BRAHMINS, while the KSHATRIYAS and the members of the other CASTES recognized him as their ruler and assured him of their loyalty.
Heesterman, J. C., 1957

Rajput(s) 'king's son(s)'. Collective name designating a large number of KSHATRIYA clans, which settled in Rajputana, now Rajasthan, and were famous for their chivalric behaviour, the prowess of their heroes and their unswerving allegiance to Hindu tradition. Among the various legends surrounding their origin, one maintains that the

Rajputs were created by the gods from the sacrificial fire pit of the sage VASISHTHA on Mount Abu to help the BRAHMINS against the onslaught of the barbarians. Thus, their lineage is known as *Agni-kula* or 'fire family'. However, the Rajputs probably descend from warrior groups that invaded India from the 4th to the 7th centuries. These eventually settled and married into local families creating new clans, replacing those celebrated in the epics. Despite their various origins, Rajput clans claim to be of ARYAN descent, tracing their families back to the Solar and Lunar dynasties. They played a pivotal role in fighting the Muslim invaders, but in the 16th century some of the Rajput families were won over by the Mughals and entered their service, while others persevered in their desperate resistance. The history of the Rajput clans is filled with tales of violence and warfare, of celebration of heroism and martial tradition. Their strict code of honour dictated that, when a fort was about to fall, the men would come into the open and die fighting, while the women would commit *jauhar*, i.e. mass SUICIDE, to avoid being captured alive. In questions of ceremony and purity they were as strict as the most orthodox of Hindus. They took pride in their ART and ARCHITECTURE, as testified by numerous monuments, such as Hindu and Jain TEMPLES, forts, and their superbly decorated palaces. The Rajput tradition of Indian PAINTING is among the finest in India.
Tod, J., 1920

raksha 'protection' or *kavacham* 'cuirass'. Both terms indicate a protective device, such as a talisman or amulet, or a thread worn on the wrist. In TEMPLE jewelry *kavacham* is the metal body cover worn by the sacred IMAGES on particular occasions. In a MANTRA, the term applies to the mystical syllable (BIJA) intended as a source of protection.

Left: Rama carrying a
bow in his left hand
and the typical
crescent-shaped arrow
in the right. A quiver
brimming with arrows
is slung over his
shoulder. Caption in
Telugu. Probably
Thanjavur, *c.* 1830.
From an album
of paintings on
European paper
watermarked 1820.

rakshasa 'demon'. 1. A generic term for malevolent
spirits. The *rakshasas* roam at night, preferably in the
dark half of the month or on the night of the new
moon, assuming many forms at will. They are
especially dangerous to infants and women. While
eating, men must be wary, lest a *rakshasa* enter their
mouth and cause insanity. 2. ARYAN term designating
aboriginal communities whose customs differed
from those of the Aryans. Thus in the RAMAYANA, the
terms *rakshasa* (demon) and *vanara* ('inhabitant of
the forest, monkey'), both unflattering terms,
designate the indigenous communities.

Raktabija or **Raktavija** 'blood-seed'. Name of an
ASURA who fought against the goddess CHAMUNDA.
The goddess wounded him, but each drop of blood
that fell on the ground became a powerful warrior.
Eventually, the goddess defeated him by drinking
the drops before they reached the ground.

Rama 'pleasing, charming(?)'. The three famous
Ramas of Hindu mythology are PARASHURAMA, also
known as Bhargava ('descendant of Bhrigu') or
Jamadagnya ('son of JAMADAGNI'), RAMACHANDRA,
son of DASHARATHA, also called Raghava
('descendant of RAGHU'), and BALARAMA, the elder
brother of KRISHNA. Because of them, the term
Rama is symbolic for the number three.

Ramachandra or **Rama** 'Rama the moon'. This epithet
refers to RAMA's handsome face. Ramachandra, the
seventh incarnation of VISHNU and eldest son of
DASHARATHA, king of AYODHYA, was banished from
Ayodhya through the intrigues of KAIKEYI, the
youngest wife of Dasharatha, who wanted her own
son, BHARATA to be the heir apparent. Accompanied
by his brother LAKSHMANA and his wife SITA, he
retired to the forest and was involved in many

adventures, including Sita's abduction by RAVANA.
After defeating and killing him, Rama rescued Sita
and returned to Ayodhya to be crowned king. Later,
Rama banished Sita from the kingdom, under the
pressure of public opinion which cast doubts on her
chastity. This triggered a series of tragic events
which overshadowed Rama's later years. His career
is narrated in the RAMAYANA. Although an
incarnation of Vishnu, Rama, like Krishna, has
become a deity in his own right. He is the epitome
of the perfect son, brother, husband and king.

Ramananda (14th–15th century). Born in PRAYAGA
(Allahabad), Ramananda was originally a follower of
RAMANUJA, and the fifth leader to succeed the great
philosopher. He eventually retired from that order
to found a new sect, the Shri *sampradaya* (sect), of
which the followers are called Ramanandis. Active in
northern India, especially at VARANASI and Agra,
Ramananda preached in simple Hindi. Although not
criticizing the Hindu pantheon, he made RAMA and
SITA the centre of his devotional movement, as he
taught that Rama alone could liberate mankind from
the cycle of rebirths. He maintained that all were
equal before God and opposed the CASTE system,
admitting into his order people of humble origin and
women. His order was divided into twelve sub-sects,
each headed by one of his main disciples, among
whom were KABIR and RAIDAS. Distinguished
members of his sect were MIRABAI and TULSIDAS.
The headquarters of the Ramanandis are
in AYODHYA.

Ramanuja (died 1137). BRAHMIN philosopher, born
in Sriperumbudur, south-west of Chennai (Madras),
founder of the *vishishtadvaita* (qualified monism)
school of thought and the most prominent of the
SHRIVAISHNAVA acharyas (teachers). According to

Opposite: Ramanuja, with hands in *anjalimudra*, sits in *padmasana* on a lotus pedestal. The typical staff with a cloth or banner is resting on his left shoulder. A prominent Vaishnava *namam* adorns his forehead. Southern India. Copper, 18th–19th century.

Friezes depicting the *Ramayana*. Inner face of the enclosure wall, Ramachandra temple, Vijayanagara Karnataka. Granite, 15th century. Photo taken at the end of the 19th century.

tradition he was a disciple of the famous philosopher Yamunacharya and, after a difficult youth and many unhappy events, he became a SANNYASI. He visited a number of holy places throughout India and finally settled in SRIRANGAM. When the Chola king ordered him to convert to SHAIVISM, Ramanuja fled to Melkote in Karnataka, where he lived for some time and organized a centre of VAISHNAVA learning. On the death of the Chola king, Ramanuja returned to Srirangam for the rest of his life. He wrote several SANSKRIT commentaries on various texts, such as the *Brahmasutras*, the UPANISHADS, and the BHAGAVADGITA, and was profoundly influenced by the work of the ALVARS. Ramanuja taught that in surrendering to God's will, a person can earn God's grace and, eventually, salvation. Later, the Shrivaishnas split into Tengalais (southern school) and Vadagalais (northern school); both recognize Ramanuja as their foremost teacher.

Ramayana 'the career of RAMA'. One of the two great SANSKRIT epic poems, the other being the MAHABHARATA. The *Ramayana* consists of *c.* 96,000 verses in seven books. There are three main recensions of the text: the northern version, which is the oldest, the Bengal and the Bombay. These show marked regional influences, differing on many points and varying in length. The poem has been attributed to a single author, the mythical seer VALMIKI. However, recent scholarship suggests that this text underwent various phases of development and contains numerous interpolations, as well as the addition of the first and the last books. The passages representing Rama as an incarnation of VISHNU are regarded as additions, since they are not consistent with the human traits that characterize Rama in the original core of the poem. The *Ramayana* in its present form consists of disparate elements including romantic stories, myths, legends and vague historical information. The first book, *Balakanda* (Childhood Book), narrates the childhood and adolescence of Rama, his victory over the various demons infesting the jungle and threatening the religious activities of the RISHIS, and his MARRIAGE to the princess SITA. The second book, *Ayodhyakanda* (Book of AYODHYA), is devoted to the intrigues at the court of Ayodhya resulting in the banishment of Rama by his father DASHARATHA. In it, Rama leaves Ayodhya for fourteen years of exile accompanied by his brother LAKSHMANA and Sita. The third book, the *Aranyakanda* (Book of the Forest), describes the wanderings of the exiles, their conversations with the sages dwelling in the forest, and Sita's abduction by RAVANA, the king of LANKA. The fourth book, *Kishkindhakanda* (Book of Kishkindha), introduces some of the main characters of the epic, such as SUGRIVA, the king of the VANARAS (monkeys) and the great hero HANUMAN. Rama and Sugriva join forces and begin their search for Sita. The fifth book, *Sundarakanda* (Beautiful Book), recounts the adventures of Hanuman in Lanka, the building of the Lanka bridge and the arrival of Rama and his allies in Ravana's capital. The sixth book, *Yuddhakanda* (War Book), describes the war between Rama, his allies and Ravana. After numerous episodes of gallantry on both sides Ravana is defeated. Sita is recovered and undergoes the fire ordeal to prove her chastity, after which the couple and their entourage return to Ayodhya, where Rama is consecrated king. The seventh book, *Uttarakanda* (Last Book), contains Rama's life as king of Ayodhya, Sita's banishment, the birth of his twin sons, KUSHA and LAVA, his recognition of them and of the innocence of his wife, their reunion, her death and his ascent into heaven.

There is no unanimity about the date of the *Ramayana*, though the work seems to predate the

View of Rameswaram temple. At the centre, the decorated Rameswaram *linga*, surrounded by various *lingas* and the four Ganesha shrines. Caption in Telugu. Probably Thanjavur, *c.* 1830. From an album of paintings on European paper watermarked 1830.

Mahabharata. Opinions concerning the dating of the core of the poem vary from 500 BCE to 200 CE. This story has inspired countless versions of the *Ramayana* in local languages, each highlighting different points of the narrative and introducing numerous local myths and cultural elements. Among the most important versions of the poem are the Tamil *Iramavataram* (Descent of Rama), by the poet Kamban, who lived between the 9th and the 10th centuries CE, and the 16th-century Hindi *Ramayana* by TULSIDAS. The popularity of the story of Rama throughout the whole of India and South-East Asia, as well as its impact on the literary, visual and dramatic ARTS, cannot be overemphasized.

Rameswaram or **Rameswaram** 'lord of RAMA'. One of the four DHAMAS, Rameswaram is an island situated between India and Sri Lanka and one of the most famous PILGRIMAGE places, due to its association with Rama and SHIVA. Tradition narrates that after having defeated and killed RAVANA, the king of Lanka, Rama wished to purify himself and sent HANUMAN to VARANASI to fetch him a LINGA to worship. Since he was slow in returning, SITA fashioned a sand *linga* that he then worshipped. When Hanuman arrived he regretted what had happened, and Rama requested him to pull out and discard the sand *linga* and set up the one he had brought. Despite Hanuman's efforts he could not shift the *linga*, obviously of divine origin. The second *linga* was installed beside the first, and both were worshipped. The main TEMPLE on the island, dedicated to Shiva, is supposed to have been founded by Rama, however the core of the present temple is attributed to the Pandya period (*c.* 7th–13th century) and was subsequently enlarged. A number of other sacred places are located on the island, among which is Dhanushkoti ('bow notch'), the spot from which

Rama allegedly destroyed the Lanka bridge, to prevent any further invasion of Lanka.

rasa 'sap, juice, mercury, essence, semen, taste, inclination, feeling, emotion'. In Indian theory of aesthetics, *rasa* denotes the emotion experienced through a work of art, mainly drama or poetry.

rasa-lila, *ras-lila* or *rasa-mandala* 'passion play or round of passion'. A circular DANCE around a fixed central point. Famous is the *rasa* dance of KRISHNA and the GOPIS. Krishna was in the centre of the circle and during the dance he multiplied himself so that each *gopi* thought that she was the only one dancing with him. Krishna's devotees interpret this as an allegory of the individual relationship between God and the *bhakta*, which is undiminished by the multitude of souls.

ratha or *ter* (Tamil) 'chariot'. Throughout India, especially in the south, the ceremonial processions of the deities are prominent features of public life. At least once a year any TEMPLE of importance celebrates a chariot FESTIVAL, *rathotsava*. On this occasion the metal IMAGES are placed on huge chariots, sumptuously decorated and pulled in a clockwise direction along the main streets skirting the temple, or follow an established processional route.
Michell, G. (ed.) 1992

Rati 'desire, passion, love'. Personified as one the wives of KAMA.

ratna 'jewel, gem'. *See* GEMS

Ravana 'roaring' or 'causing to cry'. The ten-headed and twenty-armed chief of the RAKSHASAS and the king of LANKA. As a descendant of the sage Pulastya,

Left: The goddess Rati riding on a parrot. Pilaster of the *kalyana-mandapa* (marriage hall) of the Varadaraja temple. Kanchipuram, Tamil Nadu. Granite, 17th century.

Right: The ten-armed and twenty-handed Ravana on the battlefield. The small fangs at the corner of his ten mouths indicate his fearsome character. Caption in Telugu. Probaly Thanjavur, *c.* 1830. From an album of paintings on European paper watermarked 1820.

he was a BRAHMIN, an authority on Vedic ritual. Because of his great austerities, he was granted the gift of invulnerability by BRAHMA, of which he took advantage, rapidly conquering the gods, their realms, and leading them captive to Lanka, where they became his servants. His chief queen and mother of his sons was Mandodari. His unrestrained concupiscence took him from the divine realms to the nether world, running after goddesses, APSARAS and NAGA princesses.

The enemity between RAMA and Ravana has a long history. A legend narrates that when Ravana conquered the whole earth and had all the kings taken captive to Lanka, only one, the king of AYODHYA, refused to submit and was killed by Ravana. Before dying he cursed Ravana to be destoyed by one of his descendants, i.e. Rama. The curse came into effect when Ravana heard of SITA's beauty and abducted her. For once, his behaviour towards her was chivalrous and considerate. When Rama discovered the wherabouts of Sita, he made plans to invade Lanka. During the decisive battle, Rama, who was losing ground, defeated Ravana thanks to a mystical weapon, the *brahmastra*. Ravana was mortally wounded and his army routed. The views on Ravana differ: in the northern part of the country he is seen as a villain, the counterpart of the blameless hero Rama. In the south, he is thought of as a tragic hero, driven to his destruction by fate. Ravana's ten heads are symbolic of his great learning, his twenty arms of his prowess, and he is said to be a giant with a fierce countenance, changing his form at will. Among his other names are Dashanana ('ten-faced') and Dashakantha ('ten-throated').

Ravananugrahamurti 'form showing favour to RAVANA'. A benevolent aspect of SHIVA. The god is shown seated with PARVATI on Mount KAILASA,

beneath which Ravana is imprisoned. The latter is depicted kneeling, vainly attempting to shake the MOUNTAIN. This aspect refers to a famous story, in which Ravana was flying towards Mount Kailasa in his aerial chariot when he was refused permission to proceed by Shiva's attendant, Nandisha. In a fit of rage, Ravana tried to uproot the mountain, but Shiva pressed the mountain back into place with his toe, imprisoning him. For thousands of years, Ravana sung hymns of praise to Shiva until the god finally forgave him and presented him with a divine sword.

ravi 'sun'. *See* SURYA

Ravidas *see* RAIDAS

Renuka Wife of JAMADAGNI and mother of PARASHURAMA.

Revanta 'rich'. Son of SURYA and Samjna, he was born fully armed, brandishing a sword and riding a horse. He is said to be the chief of the *guhyakas*, the spirits of the forest, and he is invoked as protector against the dangers of the forest, such as robbers and forest fires. There is no general consensus on the origin or function of Revanta, but his worship seems to have originated in eastern India.

Riddhi 'prosperity'. One of GANESHA's consorts.

Rigveda 'Veda of praise'. The most ancient and most important of the four VEDAS, the *Rigveda* is a collection (*samhita*) of SANSKRIT hymns in honour of the main ARYAN deities, composed by inspired seers (RISHIS). It consists of some thousand hymns arranged either in ten books (*mandalas*), or into eight sections (*ashtakas* or *khandas*), with an appendix containing further hymns. Opinions differ regarding

Rishyashringa, recognizable by his one-horned-deer head, performs a fire oblation. The spirit of the sacrifice, *yajnapurusha*, emerges from the flames. Carving on a pillar of the *kalyana mandapa* (marriage hall) of the Varadaraja temple, Kanchipuram. Granite, 17th century.

the date of this work; currently the accepted date is between 1500 and 1200 BCE. However, on the basis of astronomical observations contained in the hymns, Indian scholars date the work to between 4000 and 3000 BCE. Mythically speaking, the *Rigveda* is said to have originated from BRAHMA's eastern mouth; according to many Indian thinkers, the *Rigveda* always existed and was arranged in its present form by the mythical editor VYASA. For a considerable amount of time its hymns were transmitted orally from one generation to the next, and it was solely the privilege of the BRAHMINS to study and recite them. Vedic hymns are still chanted in the course of various rites of passage, such as weddings and funerals, and orthodox Hindus firmly believe in the infallibility of the Vedic tenets.

rishabha or *vrishabha* 'bull' I. *see* NANDI 2. Rishabha: name of the first JAINA TIRTHANKARA, also known as Adinatha, 'first lord'.

rishi 'seer, singer of sacred verses, inspired poet'. The term refers generally to a sage. *Rishis* play an important part in Indian mythology, in which they are portrayed as elderly, extremely wise, possessing awesome powers that intimidated gods, humans and the ELEMENTS. A number of them were born in extraordinary circumstances, such as the pot-born AGASTYA. They lived in forests in simple dwellings, the ASHRAMAS, where they were surrounded by their disciples. Many of them were credited as being the authors of Vedic hymns, founders of philosophical schools, poets, as for instance VALMIKI, the reputed author of the RAMAYANA, and VYASA, the 'editor' of the MAHABHARATA. Some of them were notorious for their short temper and frightful curses. Their awesome austerities caused much concern to the gods, who sent the APSARAS to seduce them, and the

sages generally succumbed, thus losing their accumulated powers. There are a number of different categories of *rishis*, of which the most prominent are *brahmarishi*, those born from BRAHMA's mind, the reputed progenitors of mankind, and *saptarishi*, 'the seven *rishis*', the legendary founders of the orthodox BRAHMIN GOTRAS. They are often identified with the seven stars of the Great Bear and their wives with the Pleiades. The *saptarishis* are KASHYAPA, Atri, VASISHTHA, VISHVAMITRA, Gautama, JAMADAGNI and Bharadvaja. *Devarishi* ('divine *rishi*') refers to a sage who has attained an almost divine status, such as MARKANDEYA. The term *rajarishi* ('royal *rishi*') applies to kings who, because of their wisdom and intellectual capacities, were endowed with the title of *rishi*. Among these is King JANAKA.

Rishyashringa 'deer-horned' or **Ekashringa** 'unicorn'. A famous *rishi* whose name derives from his being born of a doe and from the slight protuberance on his forehead. Rishyashringa possessed magical powers that he used when a terrible drought struck the kingdom of Anga. Lompada, the king, decided to give his adopted daughter Shanta in MARRIAGE to Rishyashringa, provided he could end the drought. The marriage took place and shortly afterwards the rains came. Rishyashringa was the chief officiant at the great sacrifice instituted by DASHARATHA, which resulted in the birth of RAMA.

rivers There are thousand of sacred pools, rivers and lakes and, although the names on the list may vary slightly, there are only seven holy rivers in India: the GANGA (Ganges), YAMUNA (Jumna), SARASVATI, GODAVARI, NARMADA, INDUS and KAVERI. The last two may occasionally be replaced by the Tapti and the Kistna. The rivers are the veins in the earth's

While in northern India the rivers Ganga and Yamuna are distinguished by their *vahanas*; in southern India, both are depicted standing on a *makara*, from whose mouth sprouts an elegant creeper. Eastern *gopura*, Vitthala temple, Vijayanagara, Karnataka. Granite, 16th century.

body and, apart from a handful such as the Son, Indus, Brahmaputra, Gogra and Sutlej, are all regarded as female. Their source, the places where their course turns northwards, and their confluence (*sangam*), such as that of the Ganga, Yamuna and Sarasvati at PRAYAGA (Allahabad), are believed to be especially sacred.

Rudra 'roarer, howler'. The Vedic god of storms, occasionally identified with AGNI and INDRA. Rudra was possibly a pre-Vedic deity associated with cattle and other domestic ANIMALS and later with fertility. Revered and feared at the same time, no FIRE oblation was ever offered to Rudra. His offerings were left at crossroads and other inauspicious places. Eventually, Rudra became the fierce aspect of SHIVA.

rudraksha 'Rudra-eyed'. Berries from a shrub (*Elaeocarpus ganitrus*), picked to make *rudrakshamala* (prayer beads) used by the followers of SHIVA. The *rudrakshas* have five divisions, symbolizing the five faces of the god.

Rukmin The eldest son of Bhishmaka, king of Vidarbha. Rukmini, his sister, fell in love with KRISHNA, but Rukmin had other plans for her. She was betrothed to SHISHUPALA, king of the Chedi, but on the eve of their wedding, Krishna abducted her. Rukmin, Shishupala and their armies pursued them, but were defeated in the ensuing battle. Eventually, Krishna married Rukmini, who became his chief queen in DWARKA and the mother of Pradyumna.

rupa 'form, figure, image, symbol'. The term is applied to SCULPTURES or PAINTINGS of deities to distinguish them from rocks, pebbles and natural objects untouched by man, which are referred to as *a-rupa*, i.e. aniconic.

sacrament *see* SAMSKARA(S)

sacred thread *see* YAJNOPAVITA

sacrifice *see* YAJNA

Sadashiva 'eternal, supreme SHIVA'. Represented with five faces and ten arms, this is the highest and most complex form of Shiva revealing his fivefold activities (*panchakriya*): creation, destruction, preservation, illusion and bestowing of grace. *See also* PANCHANANA

Sadhu 'coming, leading straight to the goal'. One who has attained magical powers through rigorous spiritual training. A general term designating SHAIVA ascetics.

Sagara 'poisoned'. Name of a mythical king of AYODHYA, whose sixty thousand sons were incinerated by the wrath of the RISHI Kapila. Their descendant, Bhagiratha, practised awesome austerities to obtain the descent to earth of the heavenly GANGA, to purify their ash and perform the appropriate last rites.

Sagara The personified ocean.

Sahadeva 'together with the gods'. One of the PANDAVA princes, the twin brother of NAKULA.

samadhi 'concentration, absorption, unification'. 1. In YOGA, *samadhi* is regarded as a state of supreme cognition, by which the person and the object of meditation merge. 2. Tomb of a saint or a GURU.

Samaveda 'the VEDA of sacred songs (*saman*)'. A collection of hymns mainly drawn from the RIGVEDA

Left: The Churning of the Ocean: Vishnu, as a tortoise, supports Mount Mandara, the churning stick; the snake Vasuki is the rope, pulled by gods and *asuras;* in the background are the retrieved objects. Vishnu, in his divine aspect, seated on the Mandara, supervises the procedure. Thanjavur. Opaque watercolour on paper, *c.* 1800.

and arranged to melodies. *Samans* were sung by the priest (*udgatar*) and his assistants during sacrifices.

Sambandar, Jnanasambandar or **Tirujnanasambandar** (7th century). One of the four most important NAYANMARS, devotees of SHIVA, and author of a number of hymns. As a three-year-old, the hungry Sambandar was left crying on the steps of a TEMPLE tank, while his father took his ritual bath. According to legend, the goddess PARVATI appeared and gave the child a cup of divine milk, causing him to burst into rapturous song. This episode marked the beginning of his career. He wandered from temple to temple in Tamil Nadu singing the praise of Shiva and Parvati at each shrine. At the age of eight, he met the saint Tirunavukarasar, whom he called APPAR, 'father', and thereafter was known by this name. Among the most important events of his life is the conversion of the JAINA king of MADURAI, Neduraman, to SHAIVISM. At sixteen, Sambandar was married and at the end of the ceremony he sung his last hymn, in which he expressed the wish to merge with Shiva. A great effulgence appeared and engulfed him, his wife, their parents, relatives, friends and sages. He is generally represented as a child with a cup in one hand and the index of the other pointing upwards.
Dehejia, V., 1988

samharamurti(s) 'destructive forms' of SHIVA, e.g. GAJASURAMURTI.

Samkarshana *see* BALARAMA

Samkhya or **Sankhya** One of the six Hindu orthodox systems of thought (DARSHANA) attributed to the sage Kapila (6th century BCE). A dualistic and atheistic system focusing on PURUSHA and PRAKRITI,

or spirit and matter, as the fundamental elements of existence. The *purusha* is manifold, *prakriti* is one and composed of three elementary principles (GUNAS), which are perfectly balanced, until the creative process begins. *Prakriti*, using the three *gunas*, creates the phenomenal world, and the *purusha*, inactive at first, becomes enmeshed in worldly life and cares. When the *purusha* recognizes the limitations of the human situation, he starts the process of liberation from all the entanglements of the world, in the quest for his own pure consciousness. Eventually, the spirit sheds his attachment to the material world and attains perfect freedom.
J. L. Brockington, 1981

samsara 'bondage of birth, death and rebirth, metempsychosis'. The series of rebirths in different situations experienced by the individual soul, according to the laws of KARMA. On a cosmic plane it refers to the ever returning cycles of creation and reabsorption.

samskara(s) 'refinement, cleansing, purification'. Commonly translated as 'sacrament' this term refers to the rituals that mark the various phases of the life of a Hindu. The rules governing them are based on the VEDAS, PURANAS, *Dharmasutras* and others. Almost every *samskara* includes FIRE sacrifices, prayers, oblations, lustrations and a number of other ceremonies. The most important *samskaras* are organized into various groups: those that take place before birth, such as *garbhadana*, or 'impregnation', to ensure the birth of a child, *pumsavana*, celebrated in the third month of pregnancy, for the birth of a boy, and, eventually, *jatakarman* directly associated with childbirth. The second phase of ceremonies is celebrated between the tenth or twelfth day after the

Opposite: Santoshi Mata surrounded by devotees participating in a *homa* or fire oblation. At the centre, an auspicious vase in which are stuck a coconut and mango leaves. Coloured print, *c.* 1995.

Right: The *saptamatrikas* accompanied by only one male figure (left) instead of two: three of them have a child sitting on the lap. Easily recognizable is Varahi, with the boar's head. Unusual is Chamunda's snake headdress (extreme right). Madhya Pradesh. Sandstone, *c.* 10th century.

child's birth and within the first year. Among these are *namakarana*, or 'giving of a name', *surya-darshana* or 'sun showing', the first outing when a child, generally about four months old, is placed in the sun for the first time, *anna-prashana*, the first time the child is given solid food, generally in the sixth month. A special ceremony, *vidyarambha*, is celebrated when a boy begins learning SANSKRIT at the age of five. The UPANAYANA, the sacred thread ceremony at the age of seven or eight, marks his starting school and the *samvartana*, marking the end of his education any time after the age of fifteen. Then follow *vivaha*, or MARRIAGE, and eventually *antyeshti*, or last rites.

Samudramanthana *see* CHURNING OF THE OCEAN

Sanskrit (from *samskrita*: 'perfected, polished, refined, cultivated' in contrast to the dialects, *prakrits*: 'common usage'). An Indo-ARYAN language, possibly the oldest, which was the classical and sacred language of ancient India, and from which the principal languages of northern India evolved. As the name indicates, Sanskrit was a highly articulated language with an extremely rich vocabulary. It developed gradually from Vedic, the language of the VEDAS, to the earliest phase of Sanskrit as codified by PANINI *c.* 400 BCE, the author of the *Ashtadhyayi*, the earliest work on Sanskrit grammar. The second phase is the epic Sanskrit exemplified by the language of the MAHABHARATA and the RAMAYANA. The third phase is the classical and most refined Sanskrit, the richest in literary forms: *kathas* (narratives or stories), dramas, *kavyas* (ornate poetry) and PURANAS. The last phase, termed 'medieval Sanskrit', includes technical literature such as the SHASTRAS (handbooks, treatises).

Sanskrit's syllabic alphabet, called *nagari*, consisting in its final form of forty-eight signs, was introduced in the Gupta era (4th–6th century). It derived, as all other Indo-Aryan scripts, from the 8th- or 7th-century BCE Brahmi script. Sanskrit is still taught and studied not only in India, but in various universities worldwide.
Keith, A. B., 1928

sannyasi(n) 'renouncer'. Designates one who has renounced the world for a life of solitude, engaging in meditation. This stage is the last of the four ASHRAMAS. The appropriate moment to become a *sannyasi* is at the birth of the first grandson. Deemed to be immortal, a *sannyasi*'s death is regarded as a trance-like state (SAMADHI). A *sannyasi* is not cremated, but buried seated cross-legged, as if in meditation. The term is loosely applied to itinerant mendicants, particularly SHAIVA.

Santoshi Mata 'Mother of contentment'. A recent Indian goddess, who emerged during the 1950s or early 1960s, and quickly gained astonishing popularity in northern India. It was probably the large number of booklets about her and the Hindi film-musical *Jay Santoshi Ma*, a box office success for well over five years, that contributed to the spread of her popularity. She belongs to SHIVA's family, being the daughter of GANESHA and his wife RIDDHI. Like all other goddesses, she can be both benevolent and awesome. Her followers are mainly women of the lower middle class.
Brand, M., 1982

saptamatrika(s) 'seven mothers'. Although referred to in the RIGVEDA, their names are unknown until the post-Vedic period. They are: BRAHMANI, MAHESHVARI Kaumari, Vaishnavi, VARAHI, INDRANI

Seated on a double lotus seat, beneath a canopy supported by two *gandharvas*, the goddess Sarasvati, with a lotus flower in each hand, is flanked by two attendants with fly-whisks. Niche in the wall of the Rajarajeshvara temple, Thanjavur, Tamil Nadu. Granite, 11th century.

and Chamundi (or CHAMUNDA). Apart from Chamunda, the remaining six are the SHAKTIS of their respective male counterparts: BRAHMA, SHIVA, KUMARA, VISHNU, VARAHA, INDRA. When painted or sculpted, they appear in this order flanked by VIRABHADRA and GANESHA, their usual guardians, or occasionally, by KARTTIKEYA.

saptarishi 'seven *rishis*'. *See* RISHI

Sarasvati 'the flowing one'. 1. One of the most sacred RIVERS of north-western India and a celebrated goddess, frequently mentioned in the RIGVEDA. Although often identified with the modern Sarasvati, which disappears into the sand at Vinashena near Patiala (Panjab), this identification is controversial. According to the myth, the Sarasvati is believed to flow underground and merge with the GANGA and the YAMUNA at PRAYAGA (Allahabad).
2. The goddess of speech and learning, the inventor of SANSKRIT, patroness of the ARTS and wife of BRAHMA, Sarasvati is equally revered by Hindus, BUDDHIST and Jains. She is regularly worshipped in libraries, schools and educational institutions. Generally represented with four arms, she carries a book, the VINA and a lotus. Her mount is either the HAMSA or the peacock and occasionally, the parrot. Other names include Vach ('speech'), Vagdevi, Vagishvari ('goddess of speech').

Sati, sati 1. Sati, one of the daughters of DAKSHA, wife of SHIVA, who resented her father's offensive behaviour towards her husband and immolated herself in the sacrificial FIRE. According to the generally accepted version of the story, Shiva retrieved her body from the flames and carried it on his head as an act of penance. Fearing that Shiva's power would be greatly increased by this, VISHNU

gradually cut the body into pieces by throwing his discus. The sites on which the parts of Sati's body fell became a *shakti*-PITHA ('seat of SHAKTI') and a centre of PILGRIMAGE. The official number of *shakti-pithas* varies between 4 and 108, however over a thousand places claim this honour.
2. The term, anglicized as 'suttee', derives from the noun *sati*, meaning 'true, good, virtuous' and is applied to those women who, on their husband's death, immolated themselves on his funeral pyre or ascended their own shortly afterwards. Immaterial of whether their self-immolation was inspired by sincere devotion to their husband, or by pressure on the part of relatives, their *sahagamana*, or 'going with' their husband expressed the indissoluble bond between husband and wife, and was believed to increase the merit of the family, as well as to wipe out all its sins. Although the *sati* was regarded as a goddess, she was not worshipped in her own name, but was assimilated into the goddess Sati. This practice, albeit symbolic, was apparently current in Vedic times: the widow lay beside her husband's body on the pyre, but once it was lit, she was led away by a relative. *Sati* ceremonies were observed by a number of foreign travellers, the earliest of which was Strabo at the end of the 1st century BCE. According to him, this custom was prevalent among the KSHATRIYAS. It is not clear however, whether the ceremony was symbolic, as in earlier times, or actual. It seems to have fallen into disuse until it was resumed in the 6th century CE when it was taken up in various parts of the subcontinent, such as Bengal, the Rajput states and other areas. In 1829 *sati* was declared illegal.

satikal '*sati* stone'. Memorial slab erected at the place where a faithful wife committed SATI. The raised arm of the woman, bent at the elbow, with the hand

Left: Shiva, mad with grief, carries the charred body of Sati on his left shoulder. In the background, to the right, Vishnu prepares to cut the body into pieces by throwing his discus. Bengal. Colour print, late 1940s.

Right: A standing couple, probably the deceased and his *sati*, are shown in the lower register. The top portion of the pillar is occupied by the depiction of an arm bent at the elbow, with the extended palm. Northern India. Sandstone, *c*. late 18th century.

in ABHAYAMUDRA and bangles on the wrists (which proudly proclaim her married status), is the essential feature of all *satikals*. On some slabs, however, only the right, bejeweled raised hand of the *sati* is shown as if emerging from a pole or a pillar, thus emphasizing her last blessing before entering the FIRE. Her raised arm continues to bless her devotees.

sattva 'good, pure'. See GUNA

satya 'true, truthful'. See YUGA

Saumya 'auspicious, gentle'. Gracious aspect of a deity, especially of SHIVA.

Savitar 'vivifier, animator'. See SURYA

Savitri I. see GAYATRI 2. The daughter of the Ashvapati king of Madra, whose story is narrated in the MAHABHARATA. When she reached a marriageable age, her father sent her to visit various kingdoms to select a husband. She did not find anybody suitable, until on her way back she met Satyavan, a prince unjustly deprived of his kingdom who was living in the forest. Savitri was warned that the youth's days were numbered, but she nevertheless married him. Savitri soon started a life of penance and when the day of his death arrived, she accompanied him into the forest to collect fruit and wood. Eventually, he fainted and Savitri cradled him in her arms and sat under a BANYAN tree waiting for the coming of YAMA. When the god of the dead appeared to carry away Satyavan's soul, Savitri followed him. All his efforts to prove to her the futility of her appeals were in vain. He offered her many gifts instead of Satyavan's life, but to no avail. In the end, moved by her steadfastness, Yama restored Satyavan to life.

scorpion *see* VRISHCHIKA

sculpture The earliest testimonies of sculpture in the Indian subcontinent are seals and figurines discovered in the ruins of the Harappan sites, dating from *c*. 3000 to 1700 BCE, revealing an extraordinary observation in the rendering of animals and human figures. Apart from some terracotta figurines dating from the pre-Maurya period, little can be said about Indian sculpture until the flourishing of BUDDHIST art, of which the earliest known works date from the 3rd century BCE. The great majority of Indian sculpted IMAGES are rooted in religious tradition, Buddhist, JAINA or Hindu, created by craftsmen who were not only responsible for fashioning sacred images, but also profane works, and were well versed in the techniques of relief carving and modelling in the round. The materials used by the craftsmen (clay, wood, stone or metal) were carefully selected according to the specific properties of the material and the required image; thus clay was used for temporary images which were immersed in water at the end of a festival, and stone for those that were permanently set up in TEMPLES. Moveable images carried in processions were generally made of metal or wood. The most famous example of metal images are the refined and exquisite southern Indian bronzes from the Chola period (9th–13th century).

Different kinds of wood were prescribed for the various categories of divine and semi-divine beings and special attention was given to the auspicious marks of the tree from which the sacred image would eventually be fashioned. Immaterial of the medium, once the work was completed, the EYES of the image were ritually opened and, after a number of other ceremonies, it was endowed with the 'breath of life' (PRANAPRATISHTHA) of the deity it represented, and was thus fit to be worshipped.

shakti

The fashioning of images followed certain well-established canons relating to their proportions (TALAMANA). Each deity was endowed with special cognitive marks (LAKSHANAS), such as a kite's beak and wings for GARUDA, or an ELEPHANT's head for GANESHA. The multiplicity of arms, heads and EYES, as well as the combination of human and animal forms, such as the human and elephant in Ganesha, or male and female in the ARDHANARISHVARA form of Shiva, perhaps the most baffling characteristic of Indian sculpture to the Western viewer, symbolize the superhuman powers of the deity. Equally important were the postures (ASANAS) the bends (*bhangas*), the hand gestures (MUDRAS), the various objects held in the hands, the mount (VAHANA), and the deity's entourage. These conventions, although firmly established, vary through time and according to regional traditions.
Michell, G., 2000

shabda 'sound, word'. The correct utterance of syllables and words has been the subject of profound study, especially by the priests chanting the hymns of the SAMAVEDA, grammarians and philosophers. It is believed that properly uttered sounds have magical and purifying properties.

Shachi 'divine power', the wife of INDRA. *See* INDRANI

Shaiva *see* SHAIVISM

Shaiva Siddhanta 'SHAIVA doctrine'. The Tamil Shaiva Siddhanta originated in the 10th century from the devotional compositions of the NAYANMARS. Their hymns, one of the major literary sources of this system, were arranged into the *Tirumurai*, or 'canon', consisting of twelve books. The other textual authorities on which this system is based are the

VEDAS, the twenty-eight Shaiva AGAMAS, believed to be revealed by SHIVA himself to his devotees, and the fourteen Shaiva SHASTRAS, written by a succession of six teachers, all of non-BRAHMIN origin. Among them was Meykantar, author of the *Shivajnanabodha* (written *c.* 1221), the first systematic exposition of Shaiva Siddhanta's philosophy.
Brockington, J. L., 1981

Shaivism, Shaiva 'relating to SHIVA', 'the cult of Shiva', 'a devotee of Shiva'. The origins of Shaivism are lost in the mists of time, when the beliefs of different ethnic groups coalesced. The name *shiva*, or 'auspicious', a euphemism designating the storm god RUDRA in his aspect as dispenser of rain, appears in the RIGVEDA. In time, Rudra lost his epithet, and Shiva became a deity in his own right. His divine status is proclaimed in the *Shvetashvatara* UPANISHAD, and in the Shaiva AGAMAS. Shaivism not only had to contend with BUDDHIST and JAINA doctrines, but also with its rival cult, VAISHNAVISM. Eventually, the rivalry between the two sects ended, although theological differences still persist.
 There are a number of Shaiva sects of which the most influential were the PASHUPATA and the Pratyabhijna, a Kashmiri sect, of which the tenets were laid down in the 9th century by Vasugupta and later expanded and commented on by distinguished thinkers, including ABHINAVAGUPTA. The Lingayata or VIRASHAIVA was an important sect which emerged from obscurity in the 12th century under the guidance of BASAVA, a Kannada BRAHMIN. Finally, the SHAIVA SIDDHANTA developed between the 10th and the 13th centuries. It has been said that Shaiva philosophy encompasses all facets of Hindu thought.

Shaka(s) A group of nomads and pastoralists, probably originating in the region of the Caspian

A *shalabhanjika* embraces the trunk of a tree. This was originally a bracket from one of the gateways of the *stupa* at Sanchi, Madhya Pradesh. Sandstone, *c.* 1st–early 2nd century.

Sea, known as Sacae or Scythians to the Romans. It is assumed they were Caucasians. Probably in the course of their nomadic existence they intermixed with other peoples and with their neighbours the Parthians. In the second half of the first millennium BCE, the Shakas became politically influential. They not only acted as governors for the Persian kings in the north-western provinces of India, but were also employed by Chandragupta Maurya (*c.* 321–297 BCE) and Ashoka (*c.* 268–233 BCE) for their administrative ability. Under Kanishka, the Kushana emperor (1st century CE), they were still governors, however, by the end of the 2nd century they controlled a number of scattered provinces, such as Kapisha in Afghanistan, UJJAIN in Malwa (now Madhya Pradesh) and Nasik (Maharashtra). The Shaka ERA, commencing in 78 CE, takes its name from them.

Shakta This term designates both a follower of SHAKTI, as well as one important cult focusing on the divine power or energy, i.e. *shakti*. According to Shakta philosophy, the female principle (*shakti*) is the supreme cause of existence. The origins of this belief are to be traced to the RIGVEDA and subsequent works, however, the Shakta cult did not come into its own until *c.* 9th century.This cult is divided into two: the 'Right hand' (*dakshinachara*) and the 'Left hand' (*vamachara*). Although this cult is intimately associated with SHAIVISM, PARVATI is elevated to the status of supreme goddess, as vividly expressed in the Shakta proverb: 'SHIVA without *shakti* is a corpse'.

Shakti, *shakti* I. 'energy, divine power'. The personification of the female dynamic power. The energy of any deity. The concept of an energy, not inherent to the gods, but deriving from another source, is briefly mentioned in Vedic literature.

Although both BRAHMANAS and UPANISHADS are preoccupied with esoteric speculations, they do not elaborate on the subject; it is probable that on another level the cult of local and nature-goddesses was gaining ground. They were later assimilated into SHAIVA mythology, which provided a mythological background for goddesses such as AMBIKA, DURGA, KALI and all the other Shaktis. These, however, although bearing various names, are merely a facet of the supreme great goddess MAHADEVI. The concept of Shakti is not particularly prominent in VAISHNAVISM, although there are eight Shaktis who channel the beneficient energies of VISHNU. One possible explanation for this difference between the two religious systems is that, while Vaishnavism owes its origin to a patriarchal and brahminical society, Shaivism is based on a matriarchal and indigenous tradition. 2. A spear or javelin, one of the most important weapons of a warrior and a typical attribute of SUBRAHMANYA.

Shakuntala The daughter of the APSARA Menaka, and of the RISHI VISHVAMITRA. Shakuntala was the mother of BHARATA, the founder of the first northern Indian empire. The story of her love for king Dushyanta is narrated in the MAHABHARATA and is the subject of one of the most famous dramas by the 5th-century poet Kalidasa.

shalabhanjika 'breaking the branch of a *shala* tree'. A young girl clinging with one arm and one leg to the trunk of a tree, while holding one of its branches with a hand. The term also designatesa tree goddess.

Shalagrama, *shalagrama* I. A VAISHNAVA PILGRIMAGE place on the Gandaki RIVER in Nepal. Its name derives from the *shala* (*Vatica robusta*) trees. 2. Name of a fossilized shell of an extinct species of

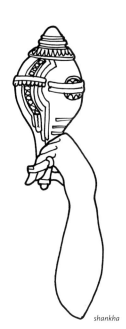

Left: Seated on a lotus pedestal, the planet Shani carries in one hand prayer beads, in the other a flask. Konarak, Orissa. Schist, 13th century.

shankha

mollusc, found both in the Gandaki river and at DWARKA. The black stone either resembles a CHAKRA, or bears small marks or holes reminiscent of VISHNU's discus. The *shalagramas* are sacred to Vishnu and believed to be pervaded with his essence.

shami (*Prosopis spicigera* or *Acacia suma*). A hardwood tree reputed to contain FIRE and therefore used to kindle the sacrificial flame.

Shani 'slow-moving'. One of the NAVAGRAHAS, the inauspicious planet Saturn, generally clad in black garments, whose VAHANA is a crow. Occasionally, he holds a staff in his right hand, while the left is in VARADAMUDRA. Shani is worshipped particularly on Saturdays.

Shankara or **Shankaracharya** 1. 'master Shankara' (788–820). Said to have been born in a Nambudiri BRAHMIN family in Kaladi, Kerala, he is regarded as the founder of the ADVAITA school of Vedanta, according to which the self, ATMAN, and the ultimate reality, BRAHMAN, are identical. During his brief life he wrote an impressive number of philosophical works, including his major commentary on the *Brahmasutras*, a commentary on the BHAGAVADGITA, on several of the UPANISHADS, as well as many independent works. Apart from writing and teaching, he established four important *mathas* or religious centres, at BADARINATHA in the north, PURI in the east, Shringeri in the south and DWARKA in the west. He founded an order of SANNYASINS, now represented by ten groups, of which three are for brahmins only, while the others are open to the remaining social groups. Shankaracharya's followers regard him either as an incarnation of SHIVA, or a person inspired by the god. 2. Shankaracharya is the

title given to the head of any of the four *mathas* established by him.

Brockington, J. L., 1981

shankha, Shankha 'shell' 1. The name generally applies to the conches that were used as ORNAMENTS, amulets, libation vessels and trumpets, once their points were cut. The *shankha*'s sound is said to avert disasters, destroy ignorance and evil influences, and it is therefore heard in the course of rituals. The *shankha*, along with the CHAKRA, is the most typical attribute of VISHNU, symbolizing his power. But it is also associated with other deities, including BALARAMA, INDRA and occasionally, SHIVA, and is also believed to symbolize space. Its origin is discussed in various myths, one of which maintains that it emerged from the CHURNING OF THE OCEAN. As a war trumpet, the *shankha* was used by a number of heroes such as ARJUNA and BHIMA. 2. Name of the ASURA who stole the VEDAS and was killed by Vishnu in his MATSYA avatara.

Shanmukha 'six-headed or six-faced'. *See* KARTTIKEYA

Sharabha or **Sharabheshamurti** A composite form, part-human, part-ANIMAL and part-BIRD, assumed by SHIVA to punish NARASIMHA for disemboweling his great devotee HIRANYAKASHIPU. This myth reflects the rivalry between SHAIVAS and VAISHNAVAS. Sharabha is variously described as having eight legs, two hands, one to three horns, a lion's face, fierce claws, two wings, spikes for hair and an incandescent body.

Shasta 'ruler of the country'. *See* AYYAPPAN

Shashthi(devi) 'the sixth'. The personification in the form of a goddess of the sixth day following the birth

Right: Northern Indian *shikhara*: the central tower element is repeated both at the corners and at the centre of each face. Parshvanatha temple, Khajuraho, Madhya Pradesh. Sandstone, *c.* 975.

of a child, when it is believed that the immediate risk of illness or death for mother and child is over. Shashthi, a goddess of Bengali origin, is worshipped by married women, especially those desiring offspring. She protects children from evil and illness, particularly smallpox. The goddess is depicted carrying a child in her arms and her conveyance is a cat (*marjara*). Shashthi is also called Skandamata and is sometimes thought of as a form of DURGA or identified with LAKSHMI.

shastra 'treatise, manual'. The name indicates a class of works, generally in SANSKRIT, dealing with a particular subject. These take the form of *dharmashastras*, or law treatises, *nitishastras* on politics, *vastushastras* on ARCHITECTURE, *shilpashastras* on iconography, SCULPTURE and PAINTING, and many more. The works of KAUTILYA and VATSYAYANA, the ARTHASHASTRA and the KAMASUTRA are two of the most famous examples of this literary genre. There is practically no human activity that has not been systematized in a *shastra*. The language of these works is rather obscure, which makes their interpretation problematical, but they remain an invaluable source of information.

shastradevata from *shastra*, 'knife, dagger, any cutting instrument'. Personified weapon. *See* AYUDHAPURUSHA

Shatapatha Brahmana 'the BRAHMANA of a hundred paths'. The most extensive and best known of all *Brahmanas*, attached to the White YAJURVEDA. In it are discussed a vast number of religious, ritual and philosophical topics. There are detailed descriptions of the five main sacrificial ceremonies of ancient India, among which are the ASHVAMEDHA and the RAJASUYA. The text lends an insight into the complex relationship between the ruling and priestly classes, and on the role of the PUROHITA as royal adviser.

Shatrughna 'destroyer of foes'. Half-brother of RAMA and twin of LAKSHMANA, Shatrughna was the son of DASHARATHA and SUMITRA.

Shesha 'remainder'. Another name of ANANTA, 'endless', the thousand-headed cosmic serpent. Shesha's head supports the earth, the creatures inhabiting it, and the heavenly spheres. When the universe dissolves at the end of an age, only VISHNU and Shesha remain to restart the process of creation. Shesha represents either the remains of the universe, or, according to another interpretation, the residue after the process of creation has been completed. He is also known as Adishesha, 'the primeval Shesha'.

shikhara 'spire, tower'. The tower rising above the sanctuary. Its slightly curved profile is typical of the northern Indian architectural style.

shilpa 'art, craft'. *See* ARTS

shilpashastra 'craft manual'. Treatise on fine ARTS or crafts compiled at various points in time and attributed to mythical authors. These manuals generally contain sections on the canon of proportions for fashioning IMAGES, the rules of PAINTING and SCULPTURE, and the iconography of the various deities. *See also* SHASTRA

Shishupala 'child protector'. One of the characters of the MAHABHARATA. Shishupala, the ruler of the Chedis, was invited to the royal consecration of YUDHISHTHIRA in which KRISHNA played a major role. Shishupala resented this, and in the course

Eight-armed Shiva elegantly resting his elbow on the hump of Nandi. Sculpture in one of the niches of the sanctuary walls of the Durga temple at Aihole, Karnataka. Sandstone, 8th century.

of the ensuing quarrel he was killed by Krishna. A legend in the VISHNU PURANA suggests that in a previous existence Shishupala was HIRANYAKASHIPU, who was disemboweled by NARASIMHA. Later, Shishupala was believed to be an incarnation of RAVANA. It has been suggested that these legends reflect sectarian rivalries between SHAIVAS and VAISHNAVAS, as Shishupala, Hiranyakashipu and Ravana refuse to recognize Vishnu or one of his aspects as the supreme deity.

Shitala(-Mata) or **Shitaladevi** 'the mother (or goddess) Cold'. Shitala is the goddess of smallpox. The etymology of her name is unclear, though the allusion to cold refers to the shivers caused by high fever, and she belongs to the redoubtable 'seven sisters' all connected with disease. Her shrines are outside villages and she is worshipped especially in Bengal, Orissa, Gujarat and Panjab. The victims of smallpox are not cremated, as it is believed that this would injure the goddess who has entered the patient's body. In southern India she is known as MARIAMMAN; one of the most important TEMPLES dedicated to her is at Samayapura, near Tiruchirappalli. It has been suggested that Shitala is another name of the goddess JYESHTHA; she is occasionally identified with KALI, and is the arch-enemy of SHASHTHI.

Shiva 'auspicious'. The word *shiva* appears in the RIGVEDA as a propitiatory epithet of the storm god RUDRA who, although destructive, was also the rain-giver and thus ensured the growth of crops and the prosperity of the community. Later, the epithet became part of the name Rudra-Shiva and, by the 2nd century BCE, the epithet *shiva* acquired its own identity. Thereafter, Shiva was worshipped as an independent deity. Anthropomorphic

representations of Shiva, either with two or four arms, wielding a TRISHULA (trident) and accompanied by his bull NANDI, appear in the early Kushana coins of the 1st century CE. However by the late Kushana (2nd and early 3rd century) and early Gupta (4th century) periods, the LINGA, as well as the bull and the *trishula* appear in SCULPTURE. The cult of the *linga* existed in Harappan times (c. 3000–1700 BCE), as demonstrated by archaeological finds. Condemned by the ARYANS, the worship of the generative powers, symbolized by *linga*, YONI, and the bull, survived at a rural level and was incorporated into that of Shiva, along other aboriginal cults and folk deities. These ancient local traditions are reflected in the god's epithets, forms and complex mythology. In the light of the Harappan finds it has been suggested that there was a proto-Shiva cult, but this has been refuted by more recent scholarship. Although there a cult of the *linga* undoubtedly existed then, it was unconnected with the early representations of the 2nd century BCE. Immaterial of what popular myths and beliefs might have been, the complex and composite nature of Shiva was gradually accepted because it fitted into the Vedic concept of the multiple aspects of a sole divine power in which all opposites merge.

The baffling personality of Shiva is reflected in his 1008 epithets, as well as in the wealth of imagery inspired by the intricate mythologies woven around him. He is easily recognizable among the Hindu gods, as his body is smeared with ash (VIBHUTI) and he has matted hair (JATA), a symbol of detachment, on which occasionally are shown the crescent moon, symbol of time, and a stream of cascading water representing the GANGA. At times a skull may be shown in the deity's dreadlocks. His face has three EYES, the third placed vertically at the centre of the forehead. They symbolize the sun, the moon and the

The goddess Shri flanked by two elephants. In the upper pair of hands she carries lotuses, while a shower of golden coins falls from her lower hands. In the foreground a capacious bowl filled with coins, stresses her bountiful aspect. Coloured print, 2001.

FIRE of destruction and of supreme wisdom. He wears two types of earrings, a MAKARA-shaped one in his right ear, representing his male nature, and a circular one with a hole in the middle in his left, symbolizing his consort DEVI, who changes her aspects according to Shiva's manifestations. He generally wears white garments, his loins are clad occasionally in tiger skin and on his shoulders the flayed hide of the ELEPHANT demon Gajasura is draped. He bears the sacred thread, and snakes, symbols of worldly attachment, adorn his body. His mount is the white bull NANDI. Among his main attributes are an hourglass-shaped drum (DAMARU), a trident (*trishula*), an axe (PARASHU), a leaping antelope (MRIGA) and prayer beads (*rudrakshamala*). Shiva's depictions are divided into the following categories: the destructive (SAMHARAMURTIS), the beneficient (ANUGRAHAMURTIS), the dancing (NRITTAMURTIS), the musical and philosophical (DAKSHINAMURTIS) and those of a wandering mendicant (BHIKSHATANAMURTI and KANKALAMURTI). Among his other names are Gangadhara ('Bearer of the Ganga'), ISHANA ('the Ruler'), ISHVARA ('the Lord'), MAHADEVA, Maheshvara ('great god'), NATARAJA ('Lord of the Dance'), Shankara ('Auspicious'), Sundareshvara ('the beautiful Bridegroom') and VISHVANATHA ('Lord of the Universe').

Shiva Purana *see* PURANA(S)

shmashana 'burning place, cremation ground'. Occasionally used as a place of meditation for ascetics belonging to extreme Tantric sects. It is believed that the burning grounds are the dwelling places of SHIVA and SHAKTI and their hosts of goblins. For this reason, some Shakta TEMPLES were built near cremation grounds and burial places. Witnessing or assisting at a cremation ritual is encouraged by Hindu orthodox schools, as one is reminded of the transitory nature of life, and the necessity of curbing egotism in order to escape from the bondage of SAMSARA.

shraddha A ceremony that forms part of the last rites and is performed by the son of the deceased. It consists of offerings of *pindas* (small balls or cakes of rice and other ingredients) and water to the deceased, to feed them on their way to the world of the ancestors (*pitriloka*).

Shrauta-sutra(s) 'aphorisms on SHRUTI'. Commentaries composed to elucidate the phases of sacrificial ritual exposed in the BRAHMANAS.

Shravani-purnima *see* FESTIVALS

shreni 'guild'. Their existence is well documented from the 5th century BCE. Guilds covering all kind of activity, except the life-destroying ones, such as hunting and fishing, existed in all major towns. Some guilds became wealthy and acted as bankers and trustees of religious endowments. One of the most famous guilds was that of the ivory carvers of Vidisha (modern Bhilsa, Madhya Pradesh), which, in the 1st century CE sponsored part of the southern gateway of the Great Stupa at Sanchi. Each craft had its own body of legends and traditions, and the trade was transmitted from father to son down the generations. Daughters were excluded because, once married, they could betray the 'secrets of the trade' to their husband's family.

Shri, shri I. 'prosperity, good fortune, luck'. This Vedic term was gradually personified as a shining goddess, Shri or Shridevi, bestowing on gods and

The goddess Shri stands in *tribhanga* on a double lotus pedestal. Her rich attire, apart from the usual jewelry items, includes breast band and shoulder tassels. Her right arm hangs loose, while the thumb and the index of the left hand are joined to hold a flower. Tamil Nadu. Bronze, *c.* 1000.

mankind all good things. Many myths were woven around Shri and provided the link with the post-Vedic goddess of prosperity, LAKSHMI, who emerged from the CHURNING OF THE OCEAN. The association of Shri and Lakshmi and their complex mythology reveals the influence of numerous and diverse traditions. Apart from evoking glory, luck and prosperity, Shri is associated with rice cultivation and fertility. Her epithet *Karishin* meaning 'rich in dung', reveals her connection with agriculture and food. She is generally depicted sitting on a lotus, holding two lotus flowers, or one lotus and the fruit of the BILVA tree. 2. *shri* 'illustrious'. Title of respect used for men and deities, as in the case of DURGA, who is referred to as Shri Durga.

Shri Nathji *see* VALLABHA

Shrivaishnavism, Shrivaishnava One of the most important VAISHNAVA sects, it takes its name from the role that the goddess SHRI plays in its theology. The origins of Shrivaishnavism are rooted in the devotional poetry of the ALVARS, whose works were organized around the 10th century by Nathamuni, regarded as the first of the Shrivaishnava ACHARYAS. His immediate successor Yamunacharya, believed to be his grandson, began to develop Shrivaishnava theology and his work was continued and perfected by the brahmin philosopher RAMANUJA. He emphasized that VISHNU is the sole principle of salvation, yet he saw Shri as the mediatrix between humans and God, whose compassion and grace eventually win forgiveness for the devotee. By the 14th century, Shrivaishnavism had split into two branches, the northern, or Vadagalai, centred on the Sanskritic tradition and based at KANCHIPURAM, one of the holy cities of India. This school is also known as Markatanyaya ('school of the monkey'), which

maintains that, like the young of a monkey clings to his mother for safety, a person striving for God's grace has to actively cooperate. The southern school, or Tengalai, based equally on the Sanskritic and the Tamil tradition, has its principal seat at SRIRANGAM, Tiruchirapalli district. This school is known as the Marjaranyaya ('school of the cat'), because it believes that a person is saved by God's grace, like a cat carries her kitten to safety without its active participation or effort.

shruti 'hearing'. Sacred knowledge revealed to the ancient sages and subsequently orally transmitted, from generation to generation by the BRAHMINS. The term usually refers to the VEDAS and the BRAHMANAS, the UPANISHADS and other works.

shudra(s) The fourth of the traditional CASTES, the *shudras* are said to have originated from the feet of the cosmic PURUSHA. This class consisted originally of prisoners of war and of conquered people, but, as a result of shared professions and social factors, the *shudras* later merged with the VAISHYAS.

shuka 'parrot'. It is generally associated with KAMA, whose chariot is drawn by parrots and occasionally with AGNI and a number of goddesses, including RATI, SARASVATI and MINAKSHI, on whose hand is perched a parrot. Parrots were among the most popular pets and play a considerable role in Indian folklore and tales.

Shukra 'bright, clear'. One of the NAVAGRAHAS. Originally an ancient RISHI, the teacher of the DAITYAS, the personification of the planet Venus and patron deity of male fertility.

shula see TRISHULA

Two scenes are depicted here; to the left Shurpanakha approaches Rama, to the right Lakshmana cuts off her nose and her ears. Maharashtra(?). Opaque watercolour on paper, 19th century.

Shurpanakha 'having fingernails as winnowing fans'. RAVANA's sister who fell in love with RAMA; he rejected her, but suggested she try her luck with LAKSHMANA. Furious because of the latter's rejection, she tried to vent her anger on SITA. But the irate Lakshmana cut off her nose and her ears and, according to southern Indian tradition, her breasts also. Thus mutilated, she returned to Lanka and, to avenge herself, described Sita's beauty to Ravana in the most glowing terms, encouraging him to abduct her. This eventually led to his defeat and death.

shvan see DOG

shvetambara 'white-robed'. *See* JAINISM

siddha(s) 'perfected, liberated'. A category of YOGIS who have mastered the 'eight *siddhis*' or supernatural powers. Their perfection is such, that they are believed to have attained the status of *jivan-mukti* (liberated souls while still living) and will never die. They are reputed to be the ideal GURUS. The *siddhas* were also said to be alchemists, possibly both in a literal and metaphorical sense, because, as with base metals transmuted into gold, their discipline and spiritual achievements refined their spirit to its utmost essence.

Siddharta Gautama, known as 'the Enlightened' i.e. Buddha. Founder of BUDDHISM, he lived in the 6th century BCE. He was the son of Shuddhodana, a distinguished member of the Gautama clan and chieftain of the Shakhyas. Their territory extended from the foot of the MOUNTAINS in south-eastern Nepal to the river Rapti in the Kosala region, now part of modern Uttar Pradesh. Siddharta was born at Kapilavastu, midway between AYODHYA and Basti. His mother died when he was only a week old, and he was brought up by his maternal aunt, the second queen of Shuddhodana. He received an excellent education, as befitted a young man of his status. At the age of nineteen he married his cousin Yashodhara and led a sheltered life, but his sharp mind was quick to discover the miseries of human life. A series of chance encounters with an old man, an invalid and a corpse, led him to realize the impermanence of life and the hopelessness of existence. On a fourth occasion, he met an ascetic with a begging bowl. This moved him to leave his life of luxury, his wife and newly born son, and to become an ascetic, aged twenty-nine. He joined various groups of ascetics, but their teachings did not satisfy him, so he abandoned them and wandered alone until he arrived at GAYA (now Bodhgaya in Bihar). There he sat under a BODHI tree, resolving to stay until he had attained enlightenment. After seven weeks, on the full moon of the month of *Vaishaka* (April–May) – the year is variously dated between 533 and 528 BCE – he had a vision of the endless cycle of birth and death and realized that birth inevitably involves evil, and hence rebirth. He was then thirty-five years old and embarked on a forty-five-year career as a wandering preacher throughout the Gangetic plain. His sermons were in the plain language of the people, and the truths of his doctrine were couched in parables. He soon made a conspicuous number of converts, among the first being Sariputta and Moggallana, two of his former colleagues. Siddharta died at the age of eighty in Kusinagara, now in the Gorakhpur district of Uttar Pradesh. His remains were cremated, divided into ten parts and distributed among the RAJAS who ruled the territories visited by the Buddha in his lifetime. STUPAS mark the places where his remains were buried.

Conze, E., 1980

View of the Hari Mandir, Golden Temple, the holiest shrine of the Sikhs at Amritsar. Here the *Adi Granth* (Original Book) is kept and read. The temple dates from the 18th century and parts of it were added later.

siddhi(s), **Siddhi** 1. 'success, achievement, fulfilment'. Collective designation for the magical powers mastered through yogic exercises and meditation by the SIDDHAS. 2. Name of one of GANESHA's consorts.

Sikhism, Sikh This reformist movement was founded by GURU Nanak (*c.* 1469–1539), son of a village accountant of restricted means, who from his early years showed religious interests. Although he lived like any normal Hindu boy, he started questioning the orthodox tenets of his faith and soon grew critical of the CASTE and priesthood. He married quite young, worked along with his father, but after the birth of his second son, left home and became an itinerant mendicant. According to legend, at the age of thirty-five, while meditating, he heard a voice enjoining him to spread the teachings of the true faith. For the next forty years, Nanak wandered singing religious songs and spreading his doctrine. To his disciples, or *sikhs*, Nanak was the *guru*. Shortly before his death, Nanak appointed one of his disciples, Guru Angad, as his successor. This tradition of guru-ship lasted until Guru Gobind Singh (1666–1708, proclaimed guru in 1675) the tenth in the line of succession, abolished it. Originally, Sikhism was a pacifist religion, but by the time of Guru Gobind Singh it had assumed a militaristic form, and his teaching was far removed from the tolerant message spread by Guru Nanak. From then on, the history of this movement became filled with conflicts. Eventually, the Sikhs founded their own state and ruled over a substantial part of north-western India. On the death of their great leader, Ranjit Singh in 1839, and after two bloody Anglo-Sikh wars, the British annexed the former Sikh territories in 1849.

The bible of the Sikhs is the *Adi Granth* (also known as *Guru Granth*) or the 'original *Granth*', to distinguish it from the later *Granth*. It is a collection of compositions by Guru Nanak also containing writings and aphorisms of various saints, reformers and gurus pre-dating him. These are in various languages such as Old Punjabi, Old Marathi, Old Western Hindi and Persian. The *Adi Granth* is thus a repository of the earliest BHAKTI poetry. The teachings of Sikhism originate mostly from Guru Nanak who, in turn, was greatly inspired by KABIR. The latter gurus only contributed additions. Over time Sikhism underwent a number of doctrinal changes and took on many Hindu features. The teachings of Guru Gobind Singh, collected in a separate *Granth* (the *Dasham* Granth or 'tenth *Granth*'), reflect his militaristic strain and the violent age in which he lived.

There are many groups among the Sikhs with various levels of strictness and different religious traditions. Orthodox Sikhs are distinguished by the 'five *k's*': the topknot (*kesha*) – a true Sikh never cuts his hair – short drawers (*kachha*), the iron bangle (*kara*), the comb (*kanga*) and the short sword (*kirpan*). The honorific *Singh* is usually appended to the name after a formal initiation, but this is no longer strictly the case. Since the 16th century, the most important place in Sikh history and culture is Amritsar (Panjab), celebrated for its Golden Temple, the holiest among the Sikh *gurudvaras* (TEMPLES), where the *Adi Granth* is kept and read.
McLeod, W. H., 1997

simha 'lion'. A symbol of strength, royalty and valour. A ruler, deity or prophet, such as MAHAVIRA or BUDDHA, sits on a lion throne (*simhasana*), i.e. a low stool supported either by lion figures or by legs shaped like lion's feet.

Sita 'furrow' 1. The earth furrow personified and revered as the goddess presiding over agriculture.

Hanuman, concealed in a tree, drops Rama's signet ring in the lap of Sita, held captive in Ravana's *ashoka* grove. Two armed *rakshasis* guard her. Maharashtra(?). Watercolour on paper, *c.* 1800.

The furrow, as receptacle of the seeds, was identified with female genitals. 2. Name of RAMA's wife who emerged from the furrow when her father, King JANAKA, participated in the ritual ploughing of the fields at the beginning of Spring. When she attained marriageable age, King Janaka arranged a SVAYAMVARA for her, inviting all eligible princes to take part. The contest consisted in bending the huge bow that SHIVA had given to the king. Among the numerous contestants was Rama, who won her hand. When Rama was exiled Sita insisted on following him into the forest, but was then abducted by RAVANA and held captive in his palace until she was rescued by Rama and his allies. She proved her faithfulness to Rama by undergoing the FIRE ordeal that left her unscathed. Eventually, Rama was crowned king, but doubts about Sita's chastity were raised again. Rama allowed public opinion to force his hand and Sita was sent to the forest, accompanied by LAKSHMANA who was instructed to kill her. At that time Sita was pregnant and Lakshmana, who did not have the heart to follow his brother's orders, dipped his weapon in the red sap of a tree and returned, announcing that he had fulfilled his brother's request. Sita took refuge in VALMIKI's hermitage, where her twins KUSHA and LAVA were born. They lived there for some fifteen years until, one day, Rama's sacrificial horse roamed into the hermitage. The boys caught it and refused to return it to its rightful owner. A battle ensued in which Kusha and Lava not only routed the royal forces, but wounded Lakshmana, SHATRUGHNA, BHARATA and HANUMAN. Rama resolved to face these two youthful warriors. Eventually, Valmiki revealed their identity and Rama then requested Sita to return with him to AYODHYA. But, remembering the injustices that had been meted out to her, she refused, calling upon her mother the Earth to receive her. The ground opened and she was engulfed by the earth from which she had originally emerged. She is regarded as the epitome of a chaste wife and as an aspect of LAKSHMI.

Her other names include Ayonija ('non-womb-born'), Bhumija ('born from the earth'), Parthivi ('earth-born'), Janaki ('[daughter] of Janaka').

skambha or **stambha** 'prop, support, pillar'. The word is often used in a metaphorical sense to indicate the cosmic pillar connecting heaven and earth. In the ATHARVAVEDA, the *skambha* is conceived of as the scaffolding supporting creation. In Indian ARCHITECTURE there are a number of *stambhas* with various functions, such as the *dhvajastambhas* or flagstaffs, placed opposite the entrance to the main shrine, on an axis with the central IMAGE, the *dipastambhas* or lamp standards, the *kirttistambhas*, erected to commemorate a victory. *Stambhas* may also mark boundaries. Among the most famous *stambhas* are those bearing the edicts of Ashoka (268–233 BCE) engraved on their shafts, and surmounted by an elaborate capital.

Skanda 'the attacker'. *See* KARTTIKEYA

Skanda Purana *see* PURANA(S)

smriti 'that which is remembered, tradition'. Collective designation of those texts that are not 'revealed' (SHRUTI) such as the VEDAS, but nevertheless, have great religious authority. Among these are *Vedangas*, or auxiliary Vedic sciences, the epics, the PURANAS, and numerous ethical and didactic works.

soma, Soma I. A plant, the juice of which has a hallucinogenic effect and was used in special rituals

Below: This typically Tamilian processional image shows Somaskanda: Shiva, baby Skanda and Uma seated together on a plinth. Tamil Nadu. Bronze, *c.* 1100.

View of Sri Ranganatha temple at Srirangam with the seven concentric enclosures of the town, subsidiary shrines and pillared halls. At the centre, the main cult image: Ranganatha. Caption in Telugu. Probably Thanjavur, *c.* 1830. From an album of paintings on European paper watermarked 1820.

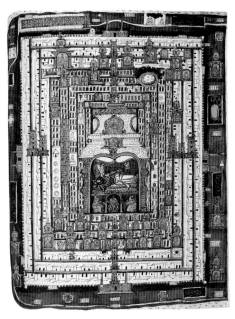

in Vedic times. The preparation of the drink was a ritual in itself: the juice was extracted by crushing the plant and other substances were added, such as milk and water. The identification of the plant is still the subject of heated debate. Later the *soma* was identified with the nectar of immortality, AMRITA, believed to be stored in the moon: its waning was due to its *soma*-reserves being drunk by the gods, and once empty they would fill it up again. 2. Soma is another name of the Moon, in his aspect as god of medicinal herbs: generally shown riding a three-wheeled chariot drawn by antelopes. *See also* CHANDRA

Somaskanda(murti) 'representation [of SHIVA] with Uma and Skanda'. 'Family' group showing the four-armed Shiva and Uma, with the infant Skanda standing, sitting, or dancing between them. This representation originated in the Pallava period (6th–8th century) and is popular in southern India.

Somavamsha *see* CHANDRAVAMSHA

Srirangam (Tiruchirapalli district, Tamil Nadu). This temple, dedicated to Ranganatha, a form of VISHNU reclining on the serpent ANANTA, flanked by his consorts, is today the most important centre for the southern branch (Tengalai) of SHRIVAISHNAVAS. It was the residence of a number of VAISHNAVA ACHARYAS, of whom RAMANUJA, the founder of the Shrivaishnava community, is the most important. The history of the TEMPLE, the origins of which reputedly date to the beginning of the common era, has been recorded in the *Shriranga Mahatmya* and the *Koil Olugu*. This imposing monument is one of the largest and most complete sacred complexes in southern India. It was founded during the Chola period (9th–13th century CE), but received its first substantial additions under the patronage of the

13th-century Pandya and Hoysala dynasties. In the early 14th century the temple was twice sacked by the Muslim invaders. Systematic expansion took place in the 16th and 17th centuries under the Vijayanagara and Nayaka rulers, and the outer gateway on the south, measuring seventy-two metres in height, was completed in 1987. The legend accounting for the situation of the temple on the island in the KAVERI river, associates it with the legendary hero-devotee VIBHISHANA and the Chola rulers, whose original capital was Uraiyur on the south bank of the RIVER, beside Srirangam island. According to this story, Vibhishana, the younger brother of RAVANA who sided with RAMA, accompanied the victorious hero back to AYODHYA for his coronation. Rama rewarded him with a shrine containing the IMAGE of Shri Ranganatha. While returning to LANKA with the shrine, Vibhishana rested on Srirangam island for a while and left the image there while he visited his friend, the Chola king. When he attempted to proceed on his journey he found that the image could not be moved and the deity informed him that he wished to remain there, but would face south, so that Vibhishana could worship him from Lanka.

At a short distance from the Sri Ranganatha temple stands the great Shaiva temple, Tiruvanaikkaval, in which one of the five elemental LINGAS, the water-*linga* (*appu-linga*) is enshrined. Because the *linga* is placed under an old *jambu* (rose-apple) tree the place is a also known as Sri Jambukeshvara.

sruk A large wooden ladle used to pour GHEE into the sacrificial FIRE. The *sruk*, measuring roughly an arm's length, has a round or quadrangular receptacle with a spout.

sruva or ***shruva*** Small wooden sacrificial ladle used to pour GHEE onto the *juhu*, a type of SRUK.

Left: Drum slab depicting a *stupa* resting on a lotus base. It is guarded by an elegant five-hooded *naga*. From the top of the dome emerge a profusion of honorific umbrellas. From the *stupa* at Amaravati, Andhra Pradesh. Marble, 2nd century.

Right: Sudarshana. The sixteen-armed figure, issues from two interpenetrating triangles inscribed into a circle. A crown of flames encircles his head. Caption in Telugu. Probably Thanjavur, 1830. From an album of paintings on European paper watermarked 1820.

stambha 'pillar'. *See* SKAMBHA

sthalapurana or **mahatmya** A *sthalapurana* ('story of the place') is a particular type of literary genre narrating the foundation myth of a temple and the merits gained by worshipping its deities. A *mahatmya* (glorification, eulogization) may be composed both in honour of a site, e.g. *Chidambaramahatmya*, on CHIDAMBARAM, as well as of a deity, such as the DEVI MAHATMYA.

stupa 'crest, top, summit'. The term originally designated the topknot of hair, or top of the head. Later it was used as an architectural term to indicate a hemispherical monument built over the remains of the BUDDHA or of a religious master.
Dallapiccola, A. L. (ed.), 1980

Subrahmanya 'dear to Brahmins, very kind, pious'. One of the main deities of Tamil Nadu. *See* MURUGAN, KARTTIKEYA

suchihasta 'needle hand pose'. A hand pose in which the index finger is extended pointing either upwards or downwards, while the other fingers remain bent. *See* MUDRA(S)

Sudarshana 'beautiful to behold'. Name of VISHNU'S CHAKRA, symbol of infinite power and swiftness of thought and action. As is the case with most of the divine emblems, Sudarshana was also personified (CHAKRAPURUSHA). In southern India, Sudarshana has a cult of its own. He is personified as a youth, with a number of arms ranging from two to sixteen, emerging from a six-pointed star, formed by two inverted triangles, inscribed into a circle rimmed with small flames.
Begley, W., 1973

Sugriva '[having a] beautiful, strong neck'. One of the heroes of the RAMAYANA, Sugriva is the son of SURYA and king of the VANARAS or monkeys. After having lost his power to his brother VALI, Sugriva was reinstated by RAMA.

suicide The attitude towards suicide is ambivalent: on the one hand it is frowned upon, but on the other, it is commended as an act of great merit. A substantial number of inscriptions found in the Deccan celebrate those who took their own life in fulfilment of a vow. There are a number of places that are specified for this purpose, such as Amarakantaka at the source of the NARMADA, where a person can starve to death, drown in the RIVER or leap into a FIRE. In PRAYAGA (Allahabad) it is meritorious to drown at the confluence of the GANGA and the YAMUNA. Two of the most notable examples of suicide by drowning were CHAITANYA who walked in the Bay of Bengal at PURI, and TUKARAM who drowned himself in a river.

Self-immolation by fire was common among YOGIS; Strabo reports that in 20 BCE, a *yogi*, who was part of an Indian embassy visiting Caesar Augustus in Rome, burnt himself to death. In RAJPUT history, *jauhar* (collective suicide by fire) was the last resort of the Rajput women to preserve their honour in the face of defeat. SATI was the mandatory method of suicide for women whose husbands had died. Suicide by starvation was common among Jains, as well as Hindus and numerous inscriptions testify to this custom. Another method of ending one's life was to jump from an elevated spot: particularly famous is the Bhairavjap, a rock near Girnar (Kathiawar). Scenes of self-immolation by disemboweling or decapitating oneself – occasionally with the assistance of a special contraption – are depicted on memorial stones.

One of the four most important among the Shaiva saints or *nayanmars* is Sundarar. This image, based on the set of the sixty-three *nayanmars* worshipped in the Mylapore temple in Chennai, is the work of a contemporary artist, Mohan *sthapati*. Copper alloy, early 1990s.

A less bloody method was to die of exhaustion in the course of a PILGRIMAGE. The first literary reference to this kind of suicide is found in the MAHABHARATA, when the PANDAVAS embarked on their last journey to the Himalayas, to die one after the other. In the past, a number of pilgrims attending the yearly FESTIVAL at Puri, threw themselves under the wheels of JAGANNATHA's chariot in the conviction that they would attain salvation.

There are a number of reasons for committing suicide quoted in the sources: Jains maintained that it was a stepping stone towards spiritual enlightenment, some killed themselves in a religious frenzy, others offered up their life as an act of atonement, others, in fulfilment of a vow or when unable to perform their religious duties.

Sontheimer, G. D., 1982

Sumeru *see* MERU

Sumitra Wife of DASHARATHA, mother of LAKSHMANA and SHATRUGHNA.

Sundarar or **Sundaramurti Nayanmar** One of the four prominent NAYANMARS, of the 8th century. Legend tells of how his MARRIAGE was interrupted by SHIVA, who, in the guise of an old man, appeared and claimed him for a slave. Subsequently, he wandered from TEMPLE to temple until he reached Tiruvarur (Thanjavur district, Tamil Nadu) where he fell in love and married Paravai. It is said that it was there that he recited the *Tiruttondar-Tokai*, a list of the sixty-three *nayanmars*. In the course of his eventful life, he continually wandered singing the praises of Shiva and performing miracles. Eventually, Cheraman Perumal, king of the Chera country, Kerala, hearing of his fame travelled to Tiruvarur to meet him. They became friends and started on a PILGRIMAGE together. After some time, Sundar grew weary of life and asked Shiva to release him from this burden. Shiva then sent a white ELEPHANT to fetch him and Cheraman followed him on his horse. It is said that the saint persuaded Shiva to allow the king to accompany him.

Dehejia, V., 1988

Surabhi 'juicy, well-flavoured'. Name of the wish-fulfilling COW KAMADHENU.

surasundari A heavenly beauty. *Surasundaris* are usually sculpted in various graceful attitudes on the external walls of temples and on the pillars in temple halls.

Surya or **Savitar** The sun god, the first and foremost of the ADITYAS, plays a prominent role in Hindu mythology. His character consists of various strains derived from a number of Vedic and solar deities. He is the centre of creation and is shown standing or sitting, holding in his hands fully blown lotuses (in northern India) or half-opened (in the south), which symbolize his life-giving functions. Surya's chariot has only one wheel, suggesting the annual cycle of seasons, and is drawn by seven horses, or by his seven-headed horse UCHCHAIHSHRAVAS. His charioteer is the legless ARUNA, brother of GARUDA, whose body protects the world from the scorching heat of the sun. Surya's feet are hidden by boots, an element that led some scholars to postulate a non-Indian origin of this figure. He is flanked by Danda and Pingala and by two female attendants, symbolizing two phases of the dawn, whose arrows dispel the darkness. VISHNU has often been associated with Surya. His three steps as TRIVIKRAMA are said to symbolize the positions of the sun at dawn, midday and in the evening. Surya's epithet

Left: A heavenly beauty, surrounded by a creeper. This type of figure is also known as *latasundari*, or creeper beauty. Carving on a pillar in the 17th-century *kalyana-mandapa* (marriage hall) of the Varadaraja temple at Kanchipuram, Tamil Nadu. Granite.

Right: Standing Surya with a lotus flower in each of his hands. At his feet two diminutive attendants, armed with bow and arrows, chase the darkness away. Karnataka, Hoysala period. Soapstone, *c.* 13th century.

Savitar ('vivifier, animator') refers to his light, knowledge and life-giving powers. Surya, as supreme generative force, is worshipped with the famous GAYATRI MANTRA, the most sacred of *mantras* uttered by every BRAHMIN in his daily devotions.

Suryavamsha 'the solar lineage'. A dynasty, of which the founder, Ikshvaku, is said to be descendant of the sun. There were two main branches of this family, the one ruling Mithila, the other AYODHYA. A number of notable kings, among whom RAMA, claim to belong to this family.

sutra 'thread'. A type of literary composition written in a concise, often obscure style, and needing commentary. The word *sutra* may derive from the thread holding together the old manuscripts written on palms. The earliest *sutras* were the *Dharma-* and the GRIHYA-SUTRAS.

svarga 'light of heaven(?)' INDRA's paradise.
See also COSMOLOGY

svastika 'of good fortune; all is well'. Mark connected with solar symbolism. The auspicious right-handed *svastika* symbolizes the northern course of the sun and the awakening of nature in spring and summer. It appears in BUDDHISM, JAINISM and Hinduism. In Hinduism it is associated with VISHNU, originally a solar deity. *Svastikas* are normally painted on houses, carts, animal sheds, etc., to avert the evil eye. The inauspicious, left-handed *svastika* symbolizes the southern course of the sun in autumn and winter and the dying back of life.

Svayambhu 'self-existent, not created'. 1. This term applies to the Upanishadic BRAHMAN, the transcendent, divine source of all existence. Later,

this term was used by both VAISHNAVAS and SHAIVAS to indicate that their chosen god was the most important, the *brahman* or Absolute.
2. *Svayambhu-linga, see* LINGA

svayamvara 'one's [bride's] own choice'.
See MARRIAGE

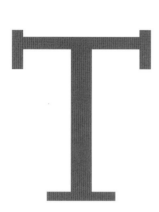

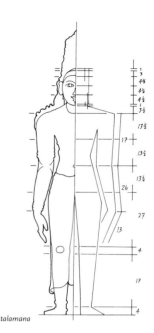

talamana

tabla Set of two small kettle-drums used mainly in northern Indian music.

tala 1. Set of two cymbals. Attributes of various saints such as SAMBANDAR and KARAIKKAL AMMEIYAR. 2. 'Palm of the hand'. Unit of measurement in iconometry. One *tala* contains twelve *angulas*, i.e. the width of twelve fingers. *Talas* and *angulas* have served as units of measurement since Vedic times.

talamana or **pramana** 'measure, proportion'. Canon of proportion according to which the sacred IMAGES are painted or sculpted. The ideal proportions of the main categories of sacred images are painstakingly detailed in the SHILPASHASTRAS. Possibly the earliest information on iconometry is to be found in the *Brihadsamhita*, a 6th-century work by Varahamihira.

talasamsphotitam 'the surface made to burst'. A DANCE of SHIVA, in which a foot stamps violently on the ground, while the other is raised at knee height.

tamas 'darkness, illusion, inertia'. Character trait that a deity assumes when fighting or destroying demons. *See also* GUNA

tambura Stringed instrument played to accompany the voice.

tandava 'leaping, jumping'. A frenzied type of DANCE emblematic of SHIVA's power of creation and destruction. Its gyrations symbolize the eternal cycles of birth, growth, decay and death, of the individual and the universe. The cosmic dance of Shiva takes place at the burning ground in the presence of goblins, imps and other spirits. There are many variations of *tandava*, among which is the *anandatandava* or 'dance of bliss', visually expressed

in the NATARAJA image.
Coomaraswamy, A. K., 1958

Tantra(s) 'thread, warp and woof'. This term refers to both religious and non-religious works, the textual sources (AGAMAS) of TANTRISM, a philosophical school which appeared *c.* 7th century, and influenced all Indian religions: BUDDHIST, Hindu and JAINA. The *Tantras* deal mainly with ritual, magic and mysticism.

Tantrism Although the tradition is ancient, Tantrism emerged *c.* 7th century. It was probably of BUDDHIST origin and later adopted by Hinduism. There are two main currents: the left-handed, or *vamachara*, which stresses the worship of goddesses, and the right-handed, or *dakshinachara*, in which the cult of male deities is paramount. In Hinduism, however, Tantrism is mainly connected with the worship of SHAKTI. Tantrism emphasizes the necessity of involving all facets of human personality in the process of spiritual searching, in order to experience the interrelation of the individual with the cosmic forces, and their place in the universe. Serious and systematic work on Tantrism and TANTRAS developed comparatively late in the 20th century, possibly because of its highly encoded vocabulary inaccessible to the non-adepts, and its juxtaposition of metaphysics with explicit sexual imagery. Some forms of Tantrism are associated with occultism, necrophilia, magic, alchemy and demonology.
Bharati, A., 1965

tapas 'heat, asceticism'. Intense form of meditation, involving both yogic and physiological techniques. It was believed that, by retention of semen, the *tapasvin*, or 'incandescent ascetic', could build up extraordinary reserves of energy, by which he could threaten the power of the gods and finally force

General view from the south of the Kandariya Mahadeva temple at Khajuraho, built in sandstone, and completed in 1030. *See plan of temple overleaf*

them to grant him whatever he wished. In Indian symbolism, the opposite of *tapas*, the heat caused by chastity, is KAMA, the heat caused by sexual desire.

tarjanimudra 'threatening finger'. A hand pose indicating admonition; the index finger points upwards, while the others are closed to form a fist.

Tatpurusha *see* PANCHANANA

temple The temple is not only the dwelling place of a deity, but it is also a TIRTHA, a point at which the worlds of the gods and of men meet. It is thus not surprising that the *vastushastras* (treatises on ARCHITECTURE) are particular in the selection of the site on which the temple is to be built, its layout, proportions, iconographic programme, etc. Each phase of the construction is carefully planned and marked by special rituals. According to the canonic rules of the SHASTRAS, temples should be laid on an east-west axis, so that the first rays of the sun can penetrate into the sanctuary. This rule, however, is not always followed.

The most essential element in a temple is the sanctuary, GARBHAGRIHA ('womb house'), a small, generally square, dark, unadorned room, in which the IMAGE or symbol of the deity is enshrined. It is placed at the intersection of the horizontal and vertical axis of the temple, so that its power radiates both outwards through the walls of the *garbhagriha* and upwards. Above the sanctuary rises the superstructure, a tapering tower or SHIKHARA ('crest, peak'). The summit of the *shikhara* is aligned with the image or symbol of the deity enshrined in the sanctuary, and it is generally crowned by a pot-shaped element, the KALASHA or AMRITAKALASHA, the vessel containing the nectar of immortality, the tip of which marks the point of human and divine

intersection. The interior of the *garbhagriha* is plain, except for the main image, but the door is decorated with a number of frames with auspicious motifs. DVARAPALAS (guardians), the RIVER goddesses GANGA and YAMUNA and their attendants are carved on the door jambs. On its lintel there can be either a small image of the deity to whom the temple is dedicated, or that of the goddess GAJA-LAKSHMI. Usually, a small pillared hall (MANDAPA) was erected opposite the entrance. Later, to this basic design were added closed or open-pillared halls, corridors, subsidiary shrines and, occasionally, an enclosed *pradakshinapatha* (circumambulation path) around the central shrine.

Devotees enter the temple precincts and, after paying homage to the subsidiary shrines containing the images of the *dvarapalas*, or, in the case of a SHAIVA temple, to the images of GANESHA and SUBRAHMANYA, proceed to worship the *dhvajastambha* (flagstaff) and the god's mount enshrined in a separate pavilion placed on an axis with the *garbhagriha*. They then proceed to circumambulate the building in a clockwise direction (PRADAKSHINA), paying homage to the various images enshrined in its niches, and looking at the narrative carvings adorning its walls. Once the *pradakshina* is completed, they enter the temple and progress through a series of pillared halls, from daylight and a wealth of images, to the dim, sparsely decorated interior, until they reach the antechamber of the *garbhagriha*. There, the priest (*pujari*) will take their offerings (generally a COCONUT, bananas, flowers, camphor, incense and sugar crystals) and present them on their behalf to the enshrined sacred symbol or image. In the course of the PUJA, the visitors have the opportunity to have DARSHANA of the deity (when the devotees' EYES meet those of the deity) and offer their prayers. The camphor

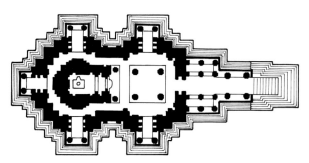

Plan of the Kandariya Mahadeva temple at Khajuraho (*see ill. p. 187*)

flame (ARATI) is lit and the visitors stretch their hands over it and, purified by the the flame, pass them over their eyes and head; the *pujari* then returns the offerings (PRASADA), sanctified by the contact with the image, to the devotees who, in turn, leave a small offering for his services. Afterwards, the visitors sit down for a few moments in one of the many *mandapas* or in the temple gardens, eating the *prasada*.

Southern Indian temples are generally larger than those in the north and have a number of subsidiary halls; moreover, the shrine of the main deity is flanked by the smaller, but equally elaborate shrine of his consort or consorts. Either in the temple precincts, or at a short distance lies the *teppakulam* (temple tank) where, on particular occasions, the richly decorated processional images of the main deity and consort are set on a float, and towed around by night.

The temple is usually provided with a spacious access road, where the decorated VAHANAS bearing the metal images of the deities are carried in procession and, once or twice a year, the RATHA is pulled by the devotees. In some temples the chariot is dragged along the four streets bordering the temple compound. In southern India some temples are self-contained units. SRIRANGAM, for instance, is a miniature town consisting of seven concentric enclosures, built around the central shrine. In each of these are smaller shrines, the houses of the BRAHMINS and other temple employees, schools, shops and other amenities. Each enclosure opens onto the next through four entrances placed at the cardinal points. Above the entrances soar tall GOPURAS, encrusted with a multitude of multicoloured plaster images.

Tengalai *see* SHRIVAISHNAVISM

ter (Tamil) 'chariot'. *See* RATHA

Thag(s) 'robber' (anglicized: 'thug'). A fraternity of robbers and assassins on whose origins there has been much speculation. Their patron deity was Bhavani, 'giver of existence', or KALI, to whom they offered their strangled male victims – women were never offered to the goddess. The earliest mention of a sect of robbers, who murdered their victims in obedience to a religious vow, is found in the account of the 7th-century Chinese pilgrim Hsuen Tsang. The *Thags* maintained that their sect originated from the goddess Bhavani herself, who taught them how to use their cord. The victims were normally attacked from behind, garrotted and buried in graves dug with a pickaxe, a sacred implement of the *Thags'* trade and upon which oaths were sworn, and which were used for divinatory practices. The pickaxe was gifted to a *Thag* as a token of initiation on being accepted into the fraternity.

Strangulation, however, was not the only method they employed, as there was also poisoning with the toxin extracted from the DATURA plant; some bands of *Thags* operating on RIVERS, especially on the Ganges between VARANASI and Calcutta, drowned their unsuspecting victims. The sect flourished along the main trade and PILGRIMAGE routes in Uttar Pradesh and Madhya Pradesh, where they joined groups of travellers. Some bands were active to a lesser degree in the Deccan. *Thags* were both Hindu and Muslims who, especially around Delhi, had an organization of their own. In 1799 the attention of British authorities was drawn to the *Thags* and a special department was later set up to combat them. However, the systematic search for members of the band only started in 1831 and by the mid-1830s all the larger gangs had been eliminated, thanks to the uncommon skills of Major General W. H. Sleeman and Colonel P. Meadows-

General view of the Mukteshvara temple, with the characteristic intricately worked tower, or *rekha-deul*, surmounted by a ribbed *amalaka* and *amrita-kalasha*. The pyramidal stepped roof of the hall, or *jagamohan*, is as profusely decorated as the tower. Bhubaneshvar, Orissa, Sandstone, 10th century

Taylor, both of whom studied the rituals, secret language, and organization of the *Thags* in great depth. By 1861, the lesser groups were disbanded and in 1882 the last of the known *Thags* was hanged. Sleeman, W. H., 1915

tilaka or **pundra** A sectarian mark, either white, red or black, worn on the forehead. A red mark is drawn on particular occasions, such as at the beginning of a journey or after a visit to a TEMPLE. The significance of the red mark worn on the forehead by women has been generally interpreted as an indication of married status. The significance, however, varies from community to community.

time *see* CALENDAR; JYOTISHA; KALPA; YUGA

tirtha 'ford, passage, road'. The term designates a TEMPLE or holy place on a RIVER, a 'crossing place' where men and gods meet. A *tirtha* can also be a place where particular landscape elements are found, such as rocks, trees, caves and pools. The term can also be used for any place associated with mythological events. To bathe and to drink water at a *tirtha* purifies and fortifies, and dying at a *tirtha* is especially meritorious. Most of these places are of great antiquity and were originally connected to local gods and heroes, later substituted by Pauranic deities. The localities connected exclusively with goddesses are called PITHAS or 'seats of the goddess'. *See also* SATI

tirthankara 'ford maker'. *See* JAINISM

Tirujnanasambandar *see* SAMBANDAR

Tirumala 'holy hill'. One of the most famous and the wealthiest VAISHNAVA places of PILGRIMAGE,

Tirumala (Chittoor district, Andhra Pradesh) is part of a small range of seven hills, Saptagiri or Sheshachalam, rising dramatically seven hundred metres above the town of Tirupati. The TEMPLE, nestled among the densely forested 'seven hills', said to represent the hoods of SHESHA, is dedicated to VENKATESHVARA, an aspect of VISHNU, known in the north of the country as Balaji. The oldest part of the temple dates back to the 9th or 10th century, but was substantially enlarged in the 16th and 17th centuries by the Vijayanagara kings when they chose Venkateshvara as the patron deity of the royal family. Thereafter, the fame of the temple steadily increased. At present, the daily number of pilgrims visiting the temple is in excess of ten thousand. They generally offer their hair, and considerable amounts of cash, silver and gold. The gross income of the temple in 1996 was of *c.* 1.3 billion rupees, and *c.* 340 kilogrammes of gold.

Tiruttontarpuranam *see* PERIYA PURANAM

Tiruvanaikkaval 'seat of the water LINGA'. *See* SRIRANGAM

Tiruvannamalai Among the five Tamil TEMPLES enshrining the elemental LINGAS, the Arunachaleshvara at Tiruvannamalai is the seat of the FIRE *linga*. Situated in the North Arcot district of Tamil Nadu, Tiruvannamalai is also a PILGRIMAGE place, famous for its temple (one of the largest in Tamil Nadu) dedicated to SHIVA as the lord of the Arunachala, the hill that rises steeply to the west of the town. The great event of the year is a ten-day FESTIVAL that takes place in the month of *Karttika* (November–December) and ends with a huge bonfire on the summit of the hill which is visible from a great distance. This fire is said to be the

Left: Shiva on his magical chariot aims at the three converging fortresses of the *asuras*. Panel from the Kumbeshvara chariot. Kumbakonam, Tamil Nadu. Wood, 19th–20th century.

trishula

tangible manifestation of the fiery *linga* enshrined in the temple below.
L'Hernault, F., 1993

tithi 'day'. The thirtieth part of the lunar month, *c.* 29½ solar days. The basic unit of the Hindu calendar. *See also* CALENDAR

torana 'arch, doorway, portal'. An arch, either of branches, foliage, or other materials, decorated with cloths and tinsel and erected at FESTIVAL times. In ARCHITECTURE it refers to a gateway marking the entry to a BUDDHIST STUPA, but in SCULPTURE it is the arch of flames under which bronze IMAGES, especially NATARAJA, are kept. A MAKARA-*torana* is an arch originating from the mouth of *makaras*.

tree *see* VRIKSHA

treta 'triad'. The side of the dice marked with three dots. The third of the four YUGAS.

tribhanga 'three bends'. A stance common to the majority of figures, in which the body has three bends: from feet to hip, from hip to shoulder, and from shoulder to crown.

trikona 'equilateral triangle'. One of the most frequent geometrical symbols used as an aid to meditation in YANTRAS. The upward pointing triangle denotes, among other things, FIRE, the LINGA and the PURUSHA; the downward pointing triangle, water, the YONI and SHAKTI or PRAKRITI. The two interpenetrating triangles respectively pointing upwards and downwards represent *purusha* and *prakriti*. When united to form a six-pointed star, they represent the quality of RAJAS (activity) from which springs the universe. A circle surrounding the

hexagon signifies the revolving of time in which this manifestation of *purusha* and *prakriti* takes place. When the triangles are disjointed the principles constituting the universe are separated, time and the universe cease to exist. The hexagon symbolizes also the SHAKTA cult.

trimurti 'having three forms'. The Vedic *trimurti* consisted of AGNI, INDRA (or VAYU) and SURYA. Later, these were replaced by BRAHMA, VISHNU and SHIVA with their specific functions: Brahma as the point of equilibrium between the two opposing centripetal (Vishnu: preservation and renewal) and centrifugal (Shiva: destruction and disintegration) forces. The *trimurti* has other symbolic meanings: the three ages of man, childhood, youth and old age, or morning, noon and night, and also the three fundamental principles (GUNAS) of the universe, namely *sattva*, *rajas* and *tamas*.

tripundra 'three *pundra*'. SHAIVA sectarian mark. Three horizontal lines drawn on the forehead and on the chest with sacred ash.

Tripurantakamurti 'form (as) destroyer of the three cities'. Form of SHIVA in the act of destroying the three fortresses of the ASURAS. According to the myth, BRAHMA gifted an aerial city to each one of the three sons of the *asura* Taraka. They became very proud and harassed the gods who eventually approached Shiva for help. The three cities revolved in the sky for hundreds of years, and would converge only occasionally. The way to destroy them was to wait until they converged, and then hit them with a single arrow. Shiva waited for the appropriate moment, mounted on a magical chariot and shot them down. Shiva as Tripurantaka is generally depicted with four arms: in the upper pair are

Vishnu as Trivikrama, with one foot raised and the other resting on the head of King Bali; in the upper pair of hands are the *chakra* (discus) and *shankha* (conch), while the lower are in *abhaya-* and *varadamudra*. Caption in Telugu. Probably Thanjavur, *c.* 1830. From an album of paintings on European paper watermarked 1820.

the axe and the antelope, and the lower pair hold the bow and the arrow.

Tripuri-purnima *see* FESTIVALS

trishula or **shula** 'trident, spike'. The typical emblem of SHIVA symbolizing his functions of creator, preserver and destroyer. The three prongs of the *trishula* represent also the three GUNAS, or fundamental principles of the universe. Among the YOGA adepts, it represents the three subtle channels of the body, *ida*, *pingala* and *sushumna*, which ascend from the base of the spinal cord to the thousand-petalled lotus at the top of the skull. The *trishula* is believed to have great magical powers; it is an independent cult object and is an attribute of a number of deities, including AGNI, BHADRAKALI, CHAMUNDA, DEVI, GANESHA and KALI.

Trivikrama 'taking three steps'. Epithet of VISHNU in his VAMANA AVATARA. The name probably refers to the solar origin of Vishnu and indicated east, zenith and west, the three outer points of the solar orbit. Later, in the Vamana myth, Vishnu is said to have measured the universe (heaven, earth and the nether world) with three steps.

Tukaram(a) (1608–49) One of the most famous poet saints from Maharashtra, born in a SHUDRA family at Dehu near Pune. A number of legends have been woven around his eventful life, full of miraculous occurrences. He is known for his *abhangas*, or hymns devoted to VITHOBA or Vitthala of PANDHARPUR, of whom he was a great devotee and for whom he neglected his business and family life. Eventually he became a SANNYASI. His songs are regularly sung by the *Varkaris*, devotees of Vithoba.
Abbott, J. E., 1926–34

tulasi or ***tulsi*** (*Ocymum sanctum*). The basil shrub, believed to be the vegetal aspect of VISHNU. The plant is regularly worshipped in VAISHNAVA households and TEMPLES, as it contains the essence of both Vishnu and LAKSHMI, personified as the goddess Tulasidevi. A necklace of *tulasi* seeds (*tulasimala*) is worn by devout VAISHNAVAS.

Tulsidas or **Tulsidasa** 'servant of the TULASI' (1543–1623). Poet, native of Awadh and author of the celebrated version of the RAMAYANA, the *Ramacharitamanasa* (The Lake of RAMA's Deeds) composed in Awadhi, a dialect of Hindi. This poem is the most renowned religious text in northern India, continually referred to and quoted, though little is known of Tulsidas himself. The traditional account of his life states that he was a BRAHMIN, abandoned by his parents at birth because he was born with teeth, and brought up by a wandering ascetic. He was happily married, but his son died very young, and he eventually embraced the life of a SANNYASI. He wrote a number of works, among which is the *Kavitavali*, produced in his mature years, which contains some of his most profound expressions of faith in Rama. His fame, however, rests on the *Ramacharitamanasa*.
Growse, F. S. 1978 ed.

Tumburu The leader of the GANDHARVAS and associate of NARADA. Tumburu, often depicted with a horse's head, carries a lute. He is said to be the personification of the TAMBURA.

Tvashtri 'carpenter'. The divine craftsman who can fashion anything. It is believed that, apart from various ritual ladles and drinking cups, he also made INDRA's VAJRA, heaven, earth and all creatures, for whose well-being and prosperity he is responsible.

Uchchaihshravas 'long-eared' or 'neighing aloud'. Name of the mythical king of the horses, the prototype of all equines, which emerged from the CHURNING OF THE OCEAN. It is said to be white with a black tail. Associated with INDRA and the solar gods, the horse is one of the ANIMALS connected with royalty.

udarabandha 'band, girdle around the stomach'. A broad band, generally decorated, which is worn between the chest and abdomen. It is the ORNAMENT of various male deities, including NATARAJA, VISHNU and GANESHA, whose *udarabandha* is a snake.

udumbara (*Ficus glomerata*). The wild fig tree is regarded as sacred and its wood is used to fashion a number of amulets and ritual implements. The *udumbara* also symbolizes fertility and abundance. It is sacred to Kaumari, one of the SAPTAMATRIKAS.

ugramurti(s) 'terrible, powerful form'. The basic meaning of *ugra* is 'powerful', in a good or a bad sense, usually referring to violent representations of a deity, such as SHIVA'S SAMHARAMURTIS, or to *ugra* NARASIMHA, i.e Narasimha in the act of disemboweling HIRANYAKASHIPU.

Ugrasena King of MATHURA, deposed by KAMSA, but, after the latter's death, re-instated by KRISHNA.

Ujjain or **Ujjaini** One of the seven sacred cities and an important political, commercial and cultural centre of ancient India. It was the seat of an influential school of astronomy from 5th to 7th centuries, as well as being the point from which longitude was measured in traditional Hindu GEOGRAPHY. Known to the Greeks as Ozene, this town is situated on the

Sipra RIVER in Madhya Pradesh at the junction of important trade routes leading from Broach, on the Arabian Sea, to the Gangetic plain in the east. It is celebrated as one of the most refined cities, a thriving centre of learning and new ideas. The semi-legendary king of Ujjain, Vikramaditya, is said to have held a court celebrated for its poets and scholars, and to have introduced the Vikrama Samvat or Vikrama ERA commencing in 58 BCE. In the 4th and 5th centuries CE, the town was a significant centre of the Gupta rulers; it later became the capital of the Paramaras, but in 1235 the city was sacked by the Muslims. It flourished again in the early 18th century under the rule of Jai Singh of Jaipur. Ujjain is the seat of a renowned SHIVA TEMPLE, the Mahakala, destroyed in the 13th century and substantially rebuilt in the 20th. It is one of the four places where, in the course of the fight between gods and ASURAS, some drops of AMRITA fell to the ground. This event is commemorated by a KUMBHAMELA festival at regular intervals.

uluka 'owl'. The owl has been regarded as ill-omened since Vedic times. It is associated with a number of deities, including CHAMUNDA, RAHU, VARAHI and, especially in Bengal, with LAKSHMI, who is often depicted seated on an owl. Owls formed part of the sacrificial offerings to NIRRITI, in the course of the RAJASUYA and the ASHVAMEDHA ceremonies, to avert evil from the king.

Uma 'light'. Name of SHIVA'S wife, daughter of HIMAVAT and Mena. Uma is originally a non-Vedic goddess, who gradually assimilated the characteristics of other local goddesses whose names she adopted: AMBIKA, DURGA, GAURI, PARVATI among others. Uma is said to be the nourisher and sustainer of the world.

Two brahmins in the Ramasvami temple, Kumbakonam, Tamil Nadu. The one to the right displays a prominent Y-shaped *urdhvapundra*, which proclaims his affiliation to the Tengalai Shrivaishnavas.

Uma-maheshvara An aspect of Shiva, shown sitting with the goddess Uma on his left thigh. He may be represented with two or four arms.

upachara(s) 'service, act'. *See* PUJA

upanayana 'initiation'. One of the SAMSKARAS, the ceremony by which a GURU initiates a boy into his CASTE. This ceremony, during which the boy receives the sacred thread (YAJNOPAVITA), takes place between the ages of eight and twelve and it is called 'second birth'. The three classes that celebrate this ceremony, BRAHMINS, KSHATRIYAS and VAISHYAS, are termed *dvija* or 'twice-born'. This *samskara* does not apply to SHUDRAS.

Upanishad(s) The term derives from *upa*, 'near to', and *ni-shad*, 'sitting down' (at the feet of a teacher who imparts secret knowledge). It indicates a corpus of philosophical works, the concluding part of the divinely inspired Vedic literature. Apart from thirteen *Upanishads*, or according to some authorities, fourteen, most of the works – which total over two hundred – do not contain secret or esoteric knowledge; the rest, generally of late composition, expose the doctrinal views of SHAIVAS, SHAKTAS and VAISHNAVAS. The dating of the thirteen or fourteen classic *Upanishads* has been established between *c.* 700 and 300 BCE, though some texts were revised over the centuries. The teachings of the classic *Upanishads* centre on four points: the identity of BRAHMAN, the divine source of the universe, the divine source of ATMAN and the essence of man. As long as man is unaware of this essential identity, he is subject to endless series of rebirths according to his KARMA. When he realizes the identity of *brahman* and *atman*, he will find the path to liberation (MOKSHA), but to gain this insight, he must discard all worldly concerns and embark on a path of meditation (DHYANA) and discipline (YOGA).

Upapurana(s) Minor PURANAS.

Upaveda(s) 'supplementary knowledge'. Texts dealing with different arts and sciences, which have no connection with the four VEDAS: AYURVEDA (medicine), *Gandharvaveda* (music and dancing), *Dhanurveda* (archery and military science), *Stapatyaveda* (ARCHITECTURE).

urdhvapundra Vertical mark in the form of a U or a Y worn on the forehead respectively by the followers of the Vadagalai and Tengalai branches of the SHRIVAISHNAVAS. *See also* NAMAM; TILAKA

urdhvatandava or **lalatatilakam** A DANCE pose of Shiva, in which his left foot crushes the back of APASMARA, while the right is lifted with the heel level with his forehead. This pose is also called scorpion (VRISHCHIKA) as it imitates the scorpion's tail. In this aspect, Shiva can have eight or sixteen arms.

Urvashi 'born from the thigh'. A ravishing APSARA, who, according to one account, was born from a drawing traced by the sage NARAYANA on his thigh. Once, at the mere sight of her, the gods MITRA and VARUNA, engaged in a sacrifice, spilled their seed. Mitra and Varuna cursed Urvashi to be banished to the earth. She met the famous King Pururavas, who fell in love with her and asked her to marry him. She agreed on condition that her two pet rams could sleep beside her, and that the king never showed himself naked before her. In the meantime, the gods were waiting eagerly for the return of their favourite *apsara*. To speed her return, they sent a GANDHARVA to earth to steal her two rams during the night.

As expected, Urvashi cried out for help, and Pururavas, in a state of undress, came to her aid; but at that moment the gods sent a flash of lightning, which lit up the naked king. The promise was broken and Urvashi returned to the world of the gods. The heartbroken Pururavas wandered for many months until he finally found her. She told him that she was pregnant, and requested him to come back after a year, when she would hand over their son, and he would lie with her once again. In vain the king pleaded with her, but Urvashi remained adamant. She met with him annually and bore him a number of sons, the first of which was Ayu. This myth is connected with the lighting of FIRE: the two fire sticks are named Urvashi and Pururavas, and the ensuing fire is called Ayu.

Usha *see* ANIRUDDHA

Ushas 'dawn'. One of the oldest Vedic deities, Ushas is the goddess of dawn, daughter of the sky, Dayus.

ushnisha 'row of small curls fringing the forehead'. In early Indian SCULPTURE, the term designates either a band, turban or fillet worn around the head. In iconography, especially in the BUDDHIST tradition, the *ushnisha* is the cranial protuberance, covered by curls, which is emblematic of BUDDHA's superhuman knowledge.

utkutikasana 'sitting upon the hams'. A yogic posture, in which the adept squats on his heels with his back slightly curved. His raised knees are held in position by a YOGAPATTA or band. The term *utkutikasana*, however, also refers to a different position, in which the right leg is bent and rests on the plinth, while the left hangs down.

utsavabera, *utsavamurti* or *utsavavigraha* 'festive, ceremonial image'. The three terms refer to the moveable images, generally bronzes, that are carried out of the TEMPLES during FESTIVALS and processions.

Uttara A daughter of Virata, king of the Matsya, an ally of the PANDAVAS. Uttara was married to ABHIMANYU, one of the sons of ARJUNA. He died in the great war of the MAHABHARATA, and she bore his posthumous son, PARIKSHIT, who eventually became a famous king.

Opposite: Devotees with flags, pennants, umbrellas and torches, process bearing icons of Ganesha, Subrahmanya and consorts, Shiva and Parvati on Nandikeshvara, the human form of Nandi. Thanjavur or Tiruchirappalli. Pen-and-ink drawing on European paper, *c.* 1820.

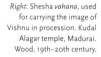

V

Right: Shesha *vahana*, used for carrying the image of Vishnu in procession. Kudal Alagar temple, Madurai. Wood, 19th–20th century.

Vach 'speech'. Originally a Vedic goddess, Vach is the 'mother of the VEDAS' and the origin of the universe; she was later regarded as one of the daughters of DAKSHA, wife of KASHYAPA, and mother of the APSARAS and GANDHARVAS, and is occasionally identified with the goddess of learning, SARASVATI.

Vadagalai *see* SHRIVAISHNAVISM

vahana 'vehicle, mount' of a BUDDHIST, JAINA or Hindu deity. Each animal *vahana*, generally typical of only one deity, is the most reliable clue to its identification and can be interpreted as an emanation of the deity's personality. It can also indicate a seat or a throne on which a particular deity is seated.

Vaikuntha 'the land of no hindrance'. An epithet of VISHNU and the name of his heavenly sphere.

Vaishnavism, Vaishnava 'related to VISHNU'. The cult of Vishnu, one of the three major cults of modern Hinduism along with SHAIVAS and SHAKTAS. Originally, Vaishnavism was connected with Vishnu, the 'Pervader' of Vedic solar mythology, but the god was later associated with NARAYANA, the cosmic energy. Eventually, when the hero KRISHNA-VASUDEVA was elevated to divine status, these three persons merged into one. Vaishnava doctrine had a wide appeal because of its tolerance, non-violence, self-discipline, as well as for its AVATARA doctrine, according to which, in times of need, Vishnu would descend to earth in one of his forms to redress the balance between good and evil. The most famous movements within Vaishnavism were the devotional ones, initiated by the ALVARS (*c.* 6th–9th centuries) in the south and by the *sants* or poet saints (*c.* 12th–16th centuries) in the north. In the 14th

century the Vaishnavas split into four major sects (*sampradaya*): 1. the SHRIVAISHNAVAS founded by the thinkers of SRIRANGAM, among whom the most important is RAMANUJA. Their major centres of activity are Srirangam and Tirupati-TIRUMALA. 2. the followers of MADHVA, the Madhvas, whose centre is in Udupi, on the western coast of Karnataka. 3. the Nimbarka school founded by Narada, but named after its most famous exponent, Nimbarka (1125–62), which is based in GOVARDHANA; 4. the Rudra-*sampradaya* at GOKULA, founded by Vishnusvamin, but known as Vallabhas from their most famous master, VALLABHA. There are two other important *sampradayas*: the followers of CHAITANYA, the Gaudiya (Bengali) Vaishnavas, with its headquarters in Nabadvip (Bengal), and the Shri-*sampradaya*, founded by RAMANANDA, based in AYODHYA. A number of minor sects also exist. Vaishnavism had a great influence in cultural life, especially in the literary output both in SANSKRIT and local languages, as well as in the ARTS.

vaishya(s) The third of the four communities constituting traditional Indian society, the *vaishyas* were generally traders, accountants, cattle-raisers, agriculturalists. Their duties were to bestow gifts upon the BRAHMINS, to offer sacrifices and to study the VEDAS.

vajra 'lightning, thunderbolt, diamond'. Fashioned in metal by the divine craftsman, TVASHTRI, the *vajra* was the favoured weapon of INDRA. Generally depicted as a double-ended trident, it is held in the middle. This weapon gradually assumed many functions, including the driving away of evil spirits. It symbolizes strength and vigour, and in TANTRISM is stands for the LINGA. The *vajra* is an attribute of a number of deities such as AGNI, KALI, KARTTIKEYA

Shri Nathji, the aspect of Krishna worshipped by the followers of Vallabhacharya, in evening robes. Nathdvara, Udaipur (Rajsthan). Gouache on paper, 19th century.

and SHIVA. The word *vajra*, in the sense of 'diamond', represents enlightenment and plays an important role in the Tantric school of BUDDHISM, the *Vajrayana* or 'diamond vehicle'.

vakula *see* BAKULA

Vali(n) or **Bali(n)** 'tailed'. One of the characters of the RAMAYANA, Vali is the son of INDRA, reputedly born from his mother's hair (*bala*), hence his name. He was king of the monkey kingdom of Kishkindha, but was killed by RAMA and succeeded by his younger brother SUGRIVA, an ally of Rama.

Vallabha or **Vallabhacharya** (1479–1531). Vallabha, founder of the Vallabhacharya-*sampradaya* or sect, was born near Raipur (Madhya Pradesh). His family were originally BRAHMINS from Andhra. Soon after his father's death, when he was eleven years old, he started on the first of three extended PILGRIMAGES over India. During his first pilgrimage, KRISHNA directed Vallabha to a place near MATHURA, where he discovered an IMAGE of the god in the act of lifting the GOVARDHANA. There, Krishna revealed to him the doctrine of *pushti marga*, or 'way of grace'. Thereafter, on the instructions of VITHOBA of PANDHARPUR, Vallabha married and had two sons. Apart from preaching, Vallabha wrote commentaries on the BHAGAVATA PURANA, a crucial text for his doctrine, and on the *Brahmasutra*. Vitthalnath, his second son, who succeeded his brother in the leadership of the *sampradaya* in 1543, is credited with the organization of the Vallabhacharya sect and gathered around him poets and artists. The seven sons of Vitthalnath divided the leadership of the sect between them. Their followers adopted the title of *Maharaja*, lived in luxury, and proclaimed to be the living embodiment of Krishna, especially in relations

with female devotees. This ended in a court case in which the Bombay Supreme Court in 1862 found one of the *Maharajas* guilty of gross profligacy.

The doctrine of Vallabha, *pushti marga*, sees the unlimited grace of God as the means of salvation. To renounce well-being and pleasure would be an offence to Krishna. The devotee is enjoined to enter a mood of 'playful enjoyment', to participate mystically in the 'pleasures of Krishna', to enjoy the ceremonies connected with him and to surrender himself completely to God's grace. According to Vallabha, this is the highest form of BHAKTI, entailing the unreserved surrender of oneself and one's own to the GURU. There are four ways to express *bhakti*: the devotee sees himself as servant, parent, companion or lover of Krishna, the most popular being the parental and the erotic moods. The devotee was encouraged to concentrate all his attention on the service of Krishna, which takes place in the sect's own shrines, called *havelis* ('mansions'). The most important of them is at NATHDWARA, near Udaipur (Rajasthan), where the image of Krishna lifting the Govardhana is worshipped as Shri Nathji, 'the auspicious Lord of Shri'. The image is regarded as the deity himself and, in the course of the day and the year, the worship follows the main events in Krishna's life. There are eight daily services (*upacharas*) in which the image is dressed differently; appurtenances, flower decoration, singing, poetry and food offerings are all appropriately selected, creating a unique blend of worship and aesthetic experience. The *Vallabhacharyas* have been a source of inspiration for the ARTS of western India and Rajasthan.
Jindel, R.,1976

Valli 'earth'. The second and favourite wife of SUBRAHMANYA, generally represented wearing a

Sugriva enthroned and the court of the *vanaras* (forest dwellers) in Kishkindha. Leaf from a *Ramayana* manuscript. Nalagarh (Hindur), Panjab Hills. Opaque watercolour on paper, *c.* 1820.

breast-band and standing or sitting on the right of the god. She is greatly revered in Tamil Nadu.

Valmiki 'anthill'. The mythical sage and reputed author of the RAMAYANA. He was a bandit and lived by robbery until NARADA discovered him and, sensing his potential as a great poet, persuaded him to change his lifestyle. Valmiki lived in a hermitage visited repeatedly by RAMA and SITA during their exile. Later, when banished from Rama's kingdom, Sita sought shelter there and gave birth to her twins. KUSHA and LAVA were educated by the sage, who taught them their father's story.

vama 'left'. The left is believed to be inauspicious, therefore weapons and other attributes of destruction are carried in the left. *Vama*, however, also signifies the female principle, and the left side is not inauspicious for the female sex: goddesses are often shown either standing to the left of their consort or sitting on his left thigh, and in SHIVA's aspect as ARDHANARISHVARA, the female part is on the left. In the HARI-HARA image, VISHNU, the opposite of Shiva, is shown on the left side. *Vama* or *vamachara* ('left-hand practice') also indicates the SHAKTA cult. Finally, in the offerings to the PITRIS, all rituals that are usually performed with the right hand, are switched to the left, to indicate the difference between the sphere of the living and that of the dead.

Vamadeva 'left-hand deity'. *See* PANCHANANA

Vamana *avatara* 'dwarf incarnation'. VISHNU assumed the form of Vamana to help the gods who had been deprived of the offerings, prayers and sacrifices due to them, as well as of their abode, by the extraordinary spiritual power of King BALI. This virtuous king was celebrating a sacrifice when

Vamana appeared and asked him for three paces of land, on which to build his hut. The king, despite the reservations of his PUROHITA, agreed and immediately the deed was sealed; Vamana transformed himself into the gigantic TRIVIKRAMA and encompassed the whole universe in two paces. His third step rested on the king's head, pushing him down into the nether world, of which he became the ruler in recognition of his past good deeds. In the depictions of this *avatara* Vishnu is shown either as Vamana, dressed as a BRAHMACHARI, carrying in his hands a KAMANDALU, a book and an umbrella, in the act of requesting the land from the king, or as Trivikrama, with one leg raised to the sky and the other resting on earth.

Vamana Purana see PURANA(S)

vanaprashtha 'forest dweller'. The third of the four stages (ASHRAMAS) in the life of a devout Hindu, when he retires to the forest to meditate.

vanara(s) 'monkeys, forest dwellers'. The proud forest dwellers of the southern part of the subcontinent and renowned fighters, disparagingly called 'monkeys'. In the RAMAYANA the *vanaras*, led by their king SUGRIVA and by the famous hero HANUMAN, help RAMA in the conquest of LANKA.

varadamudra 'gesture of the granting of wishes'. A hand pose that indicates the dispensing of favours. The left hand is held out, palm uppermost with the fingers pointing downwards. VARADA- and ABHAYAMUDRA are the two most common MUDRAS seen on Hindu and BUDDHIST icons.

Varadaraja 'King among the bestower of wishes'. Name of one of the most important TEMPLES of

Left: Varadaraja seated on Garuda's shoulders. Carving on a pillar of the 17th century *kalyana-mandapa* (marriage hall) of the Varadaraja temple. Kanchipuram, Tamil Nadu. Granite.

KANCHIPURAM, the headquarters of the followers of the Vadagalai or northern branch of SHRIVAISHNAVISM. In iconography the term indicates the eight-armed VISHNU riding on GARUDA.

Varaha *avatara* 'boar incarnation'. Third AVATARA of VISHNU, in which he appeared as a boar to retrieve the earth goddess BHUMIDEVI from the depths of the waters. The story probably originates from an ancient cosmogonic myth; in Vedic literature PRAJAPATI assumed the form of a black boar to raise the earth from the cosmic waters. According to the puranic legend, Vishnu assumed the form of Varaha when the DAITYA HIRANYAKSHA threw the earth into the ocean; he killed the *daitya*, dived into the waters and lifted the earth with his tusks. Varaha is generally depicted as a male figure with a boar's head carrying Bhumidevi on his shoulder or his arm. However, Varaha can be also shown as a huge boar, with rows of sages, ascetics, deities and other figures carved on his body, symbolizing his cosmic aspect.

Varahi Aspect of DEVI and one of the SAPTAMATRIKAS, consort of VARAHA. She is generally represented as a woman with a boar's head. Her attributes are a plough and a spear, occasionally a fish, and her mount may be an ELEPHANT, a buffalo or a boar.

Varanasi The holiest of the holy cities of India is situated between the Varana and the Asi RIVERS. The earliest name by which this city was known was Kashi, derived either from the name of the first chieftain (Kashi), or of the people living in the area. According to one legend, Kashi is the name of a species of grass, *kasha* (*Saccharum spontaneum*), which grew on the site where the city was built. The name Varanasi is also ancient and appears both in BUDDHIST literature and in the MAHABHARATA. For a long time the town was known as Banaras or Benares, but in 1947 it reverted to its original name Varanasi. From the 6th century BCE, the city became a prominent centre of learning and played an important role in the history and politics of the northern part of the subcontinent. Its situation on the river Ganges enhanced its religious prestige, and it became a PILGRIMAGE centre for Buddhist, JAINAS, SHAIVAS, VAISHNAVAS and SHAKTAS. It was at Sarnath, near Varanasi, that BUDDHA delivered his first sermon. The historical spot is marked by a huge STUPA, commemorating the event. To the Shaivas, Kashi is the city of SHIVA, whose epithets include *Kashinatha*, 'the Lord of Kashi'.
Eck, D., 1982

varna 'colour, caste', the original four castes.
See CASTES

Varuna One of the earliest and most prominent of Vedic deities. His name derived from the root *vri* ('to cover, encompass'), suggesting his connection with the sky. He is one of the ADITYAS and is associated with cosmic and worldly law and order (*rita*). The responsibility for maintaining the universal order also extended to the holy sacrificial rules and the seasonal rhythms of agriculture. In this, he shared his duty with AGNI, INDRA and MITRA. Later, *rita* was mainly associated with ethics, which also fell under Varuna's control. When the priestly class became guardians of law and order, the position of Varuna was diminished. As was the case with Agni and Indra, Varuna became one of the ASHTADIKPALAS, the guardian of the west. He is the overlord of the waters and his VAHANA is the MAKARA. He is associated with rain, water and fertility, and his generative powers are equated to that of the stallion, his favourite sacrificial ANIMAL.

Opposite: One of the *saptamatrikas*, Varahi seated on a bull, with a child on her lap. The goddess carries in her right hands a skull cup and a fish. In her upper left hand there was probably a lotus, and the lower left holds the child. Madhya Pradesh. Sandstone, 9th century.

Right: Varuna, guardian of the west on his *makara* mount. Caption in Telugu. Probably Thanjavur, *c.* 1830. From an album of paintings on European paper watermarked 1820.

Varunani or **Varuni** Either the wife or the daughter of Varuna, who emerged from the Churning of the Ocean. According to the *Vishnu* Purana she is the goddess of wine and inebriation. She is depicted seated in a boat; her attributes are a wine goblet, a lotus and the flowers of the parijata tree.

Vasishtha 'owner of wealth'. A famous Vedic rishi, who reputedly composed the seventh book (*mandala*) of the Rigveda, as well as a number of other hymns. He is a son of Brahma, the epitome of the orthodox brahmin, and owner of Kamadhenu, the mythical cow of plenty. In later mythology he became one of the *saptarishis*, i.e. the stars of the Great Bear. His wife is Arundhati.

Vastunara or **Vastupurusha** 'man of the building'. Name of an undefined creature, whose huge body blocked the earth and the sky. The gods seized it and pressed it face to the ground. Each of them sat on one of its limbs, and became the presiding deity of that limb. This myth, suggesting a sacrificial dismemberment, is symbolically re-enacted each time a building is constructed. First of all, the Vastunara believed to inhabit the chosen piece of land, is honoured with prayers and food. The ground on to which the building is to be erected is then divided into a number of squares, sixty-four in the case of a temple, which are again subdivided. Each square is dedicated to a deity, a planet or an asterism. The central and the largest one, where the diagonals meet, is reserved for Brahma. This grid, called *vastumandala* ('house-circle, plan of a building') schematically recreates the structure of the universe, ensuring that the building is correctly aligned with the cosmic powers.

vastuvidya 'science of architecture'. *See* ARCHITECTURE

vasu(s) 'good, bountiful, wealthy'. The eight *vasus* constitute a class of divine beings connected with the atmospheric powers, often associated with Agni and Indra, and frequently invoked in the Vedas, especially for aid or material benefits. In the Mahabharata they appear in connection with the rishi Vasishtha, who, disturbed by them, cursed them to be born as humans. They requested the Ganga to be born as her sons, fathered by some famous king, who would not object to seven of them being killed at birth, and letting the last survive on condition of not begetting offspring. Eventually, the goddess Ganga married Shantanu, who accepted the condition of not objecting to any of her actions. She thus drowned her first eight sons and the ninth lived to be the famous hero Bhishma.

Vasudeva Husband of Devaki and chief minister of Kamsa, king of Mathura. When Kamsa heard that one of Devaki's sons would kill him, she and Vasudeva were imprisoned. However, by a ruse, Balarama and Krishna, the seventh and eighth sons, were saved, and eventually the prediction was fulfilled.

Vasudeva 'good, beneficient divine (being)'. Patronymic of Krishna, son of Vasudeva. Early tradition does not mention his name, but only his mother's, Devaki. However, there was a god, Vasudeva, who enjoyed great popularity, especially in western India. An important inscription on the famous Heliodorus pillar at Besnagar (Vidisha, Madhya Pradesh) shows that by the 2nd century BCE, the cult of Vasudeva had followers among the ruling classes. The cult was later assimilated with that of Vishnu. The Krishna-Vasudeva cult seems to have originated as a reform movement against the overpowering supremacy of the brahmins. Krishna,

Left: Vatapattrashayi floating on the primeval waters. Caption in Telugu. Probably Thanjavur, *c.* 1830. From an album of paintings on European paper watermarked 1820.

Opposite: The image of Venkateshvara in the temple on Tirumala hill. The stump-like figure carries in the upper hands the *chakra* (discus) and *shanka* (conch), the lower right is in *varadamudra* and the left rests on the hip. On its face is a conspicuous *namam*. Colour print, *c.* 1975.

a widely recognized figure, was regarded as a full manifestation (*purna avatara*) of Vishnu. However, the assimilation of the Krishna-Vasudeva cult with the VAISHNAVA religious system was a long and complex process, and eventually led to the creation of different currents of thought, such as the mystical PANCHARATRA or BHAGAVATA.

Vasuki 'one who clothes(?)'. A king of the NAGAS, Vasuki is the son of KADRU. He acted as the churning rope during the CHURNING OF THE OCEAN. Some PURANAS identify him with SHESHA.

vata (*Ficus indica*). The Indian fig tree, symbol of the universe, is sacred to SHIVA – who is also known as Vateshvara or 'Lord of the *vata*' – as well as to other deities, such as CHAMUNDA and VISHNU who, at the end of every cosmic cycle, rests on the *vata* leaf in his form as NARAYANA.

Vatapattrashayi(n) 'lying on the VATA leaf'. Aspect of KRISHNA shown as an infant reclining on the leaf of the *vata* tree (Indian fig tree) and floating on the primeval waters.

Vatsyayana or **Mallanaga** Author of the *Kamasutra*. *See* EROTICS

Vayu 'wind, air'. In the VEDAS, Vayu is depicted as the god of the wind, originated by the breath of the cosmic PURUSHA, or identified with the breath of Purusha. Closely associated with INDRA, he possesses purifying powers and frees from misfortune. In later mythology, Vayu became one of the five ELEMENTS, one of the eight VASUS and one of the ASHTADIKPALAS, the guardian of the north-west. He is shown as a handsome, dark-complexioned youth, either with two or four arms.

In his right hand he carries a banner or a goad and in his left, a staff. His conveyance is an antelope, or occasionally, a lion.

Vayu Purana *see* PURANA(S)

Veda(s) 'knowledge'. This term designates the 'sacred knowledge' consisting of the collections (*samhitas*) of prayers and hymns contained in the four *Vedas*: RIGVEDA, SAMAVEDA, YAJURVEDA and ATHARVAVEDA. Part of this supreme knowledge are the BRAHMANAS, treatises on ritual appended to the four *Vedas*, the ARANYAKAS and the UPANISHADS, philosophical and metaphysical treatises. The Vedic hymns were probably collected before 1000 BCE and orally transmitted with great precision through the centuries. Although the language changed, and difficulties exist in decoding the original meaning of the hymns, the basic thought permeating the *Vedas* is that there is one Reality expressed in a diversity of manifestations.

Vedanta 'the end of the VEDAS' or complete knowledge of the *Vedas*. This term indicates the interpretation of the basic truth expressed in the *Vedas* in the light of the philosophy taught by the UPANISHADS. One of the six major schools (DARSHANAS) of Hindu philosophy.

Vedavyasa *see* VYASA

vedi 'altar'. Generally an elevated, and occasionally an excavated, piece of ground with pits for the sacrificial FIRE. In Vedic tradition, the *vedi* was identified with the centre or navel of the earth.

Venkateshvara or **Venkatesha** 'Lord of Venkata'. Form of VISHNU worshipped at TIRUMALA, near

Right: Four-armed Krishna playing the flute. His upper arms carry the *chakra* (discus) and *shankha* (conch). The youthful god is flanked by cows and two five-hooded *nagas*. Panel from a processional chariot. Tamil Nadu. Wood, 19th century.

Tirupati in Andhra Pradesh. Although VAISHNAVAS claim that the icon worshipped is that of Vishnu, SHAIVAS say that it represents SHIVA. It is impossible to examine the IMAGE closely without its dress, jewelry, flowers and other decorations. It has been suggested that it depicts HARI-HARA, Shiva on the right side, and Vishnu on the left. In the upper hands it carries the SHANKHA and the CHAKRA, the lower right hand is in ABHAYAMUDRA and the left rests on the hip. Among his other names are Balaji ('beloved child') and Shrinivasan ('abode of Shri').
Krishna, N., 2000

Venugopala 'cowherd with the flute'. A form of KRISHNA playing the flute. He is shown planted on one leg, with the other crossed in front. In the lower arms he holds the flute. When shown with four arms, the upper pair carries the VAISHNAVA emblems. He is flanked by COWS and, occasionally, by GOPIS.

vetala(s) 'demon, ghost, vampire'. A category of ghouls who inhabit dead bodies and are said to dwell in the burial grounds. Occasionally, a *vetala* is an attribute of AGHORAMURTI.

Vibhishana 'frightful, terrifying'. One of RAVANA'S brothers, to whom, according to the RAMAYANA, BRAHMA granted the boon of never committing a sinful action. He strongly opposed Ravana's war against RAMA and was therefore banished. He joined Rama's forces and was eventually consecrated king of LANKA.

vibhuti 'pervading; superhuman power'. 1. Name of a group of eight attendants of VISHNU. 2. Special faculties attributed to SHIVA. 3. 'ashes' with which Shiva smeared his body, hence its white colour; the practice of rubbing cow dung ashes on the forehead and on other parts of the body is commonly followed by SHAIVAS. Ashes are believed to have fecundating powers and to avert evil.

vidya 'wisdom, knowledge'. According to the UPANISHADS, *vidya* is the highest aim of life. It is the recognition of the ultimate reality, dispelling ignorance (*avidya*), and eventually leading to emancipation from the endless cycle of rebirths.

vidyadhara(s) 'bearers of knowledge'. Semi-divine beings of great beauty, who can assume any shape at will, sometimes appearing human, sometimes half-human and half-bird. They fly through the sky bearing either a sword, representing knowledge cutting through ignorance, or floral garlands, symbolizing victory.

Vighneshvara 'Lord of obstacles'. Epithet of GANESHA.

vijaya see BHANG(A)

vimana 'chariot of the gods'. 1. A divine, self-moving, aerial conveyance; an aerial palace. 2. The designation of the TEMPLE as a whole, complete with sanctuary, porches and halls.

vina A string instrument reputedly invented by the seer NARADA. The term designates a seven-stringed bamboo lute with a resonance gourd placed at one or both ends. There are many different types of *vina*. It is the attribute of a number of deities, such as SHIVA, as master of music, SARASVATI and NARADA.

Vinata 'bent, curved'. One of the wives of the mythical seer KASHYAPA and sister of KADRU. Vinata was mother of GARUDA.

Left: Virabhadra stands between the ram-headed Daksha and his own consort Bhadrakali. The god carries in the upper hands arrow and bow. In the lower right he brandishes a sword, while the left rests on his shield. Panel from a processional chariot. Tamil Nadu. Wood, 19th century (?).

Right: Hero stone in the old fortress of Kummata Durga, near Hospet, Karnataka. In the lower panel a hero on foot fights against a group of horsemen. In the second, the hero is transported to heaven, and in the third he worships a *linga*. Granite (?), early 14th century.

Vinadhara Dakshinamurti 'representation [of SHIVA], carrying the VINA'. Aspect of Shiva as the supreme teacher of music, represented standing with the left foot planted on APASMARA's head and the right placed on the ground. The lower pair of hands hold the *vina*, which, in the case of metal IMAGES, was separately cast. The upper hands hold the axe and the leaping antelope.

Vinayaka 'removing, remover'. Epithet of GANESHA, the 'remover of obstacles'.

vira 'hero, leader'. A title applied to various deities, including INDRA and VISHNU, and also to the BUDDHA, the JAINA prophet Mahavira, and to any other eminent sages whose spiritual powers transcend all earthly bonds.

Virabhadra 'distinguished hero'. Name of the personified wrath of SHIVA, created expressly to destroy DAKSHA's sacrifice, to which the god was not invited. Virabhadra is shown with three EYES, small protruding tusks and four arms in which he carries bow and arrow, sword and shield. His hair is dressed in a *jatamukuta* and he wears sandals. He is occasionally flanked by his consort, BHADRAKALI and by the ram-headed Daksha. Virabhadra is worshipped especially in southern Maharashtra and Karnataka.

virakal 'hero stone'. Memorial slab set up to commemorate a person who performed a heroic deed, or a warrior who died a glorious death in battle. The slab is carved usually with three scenes, which represent, in ascending order, the cause of the death of the hero (battle, cattle raid), the hero transported to SVARGA by the APSARAS, the hero at worship in the 'heaven of heroes' (*virasvarga*).

virasana 'hero's posture'. A sitting posture in which the left foot is placed on the right thigh and the right foot on the left thigh. There is another description of *virasana*, in which one foot is placed on the ground with the other leg resting on the knee of the first leg.

Virashaiva(s) A southern Indian SHAIVA religious group, also known as Lingayats, founded in the 12th century by BASAVA. This movement abolished CASTE distinctions and the authority of the BRAHMINS, and recognized the equality of the sexes. According to its doctrine, SHIVA, in his unmanifested state, is the sole reality (*shiva-tattva*). When activated by his SHAKTI, he becomes manifest both as Shiva the Lord and as each individual being. Thus, the individual is essentially identical with Shiva, but this identity is clouded by ignorance. By meditating on the personal Shiva LINGA, which every Virashaiva wears in a container around their neck, the devotee realizes his essential identity with the universe and with Shiva in his unmanifested state. The Virashaiva teachings are collected in thousands of *vachanas*, or brief literary works, composed by BASAVA and a number of other poets. These short hymns are in simple language and filled with colloquiallisms. A figure of great respect among the Virashaivas are the JANGAMAS or itinerant priests. Virashaivas are strict vegetarians, teetotallers, and bury, rather than cremate, their dead.

Virupaksha 'of misinformed EYES'. Epithet of SHIVA. Virupaksha was the family deity of the rulers of Vijayanagara (1336–1565), who built their capital in the immediate proximity of Virupaksha's temple and actively promoted his cult in the 14th and 15th centuries.

Vishaprahara(murti) or **Vishapahara** 'representation destroying the poison'. An aspect of SHIVA referring

Left: Vishapraharamurti. This image refers to the poison, symbolized by the snake in Shiva's left hand, which surfaced from the depths of the ocean and was swallowed by the god to protect the newly commenced creation. Tamil Nadu. Bronze, *c.* 950.

Vishnu, magnificently dressed and bejeweled, stands in a dignified pose with the *chakra* (discus) and *shankha* (conch) in the upper hands. The lower right is in *abhayamudra*, the left rests on his hip. The sacred thread is conspicuously shown across his chest. Tamil Nadu. Bronze, *c.* 1000.

to his holding in his throat the deadly poison which emerged from the ocean, thus saving from certain death all living beings. He is generally represented with three EYES, carrying in the lower pair of arms a cup in the right hand and a snake in the left. In the upper pair of hands are an axe and antelope.

vismayahasta A gesture expressing either astonishment or praise. The forearm is bent at the elbow and the palm of the slightly raised hand faces the image. The fingers point upwards.

Vishnu 'All Pervader, or taking various forms'. Originally a minor Vedic deity, personifying solar energy, described as encompassing the whole universe in three strides, Vishnu acquired new attributes and slowly became one of the most important Hindu deities, along with SHIVA and BRAHMA. He is the sustainer of the universe and occasionally descends to earth assuming various forms (AVATARAS) to redress the balance between good and evil, and is hence known as the Preserver. In due course, Vishnu came to represent the traditional order of society, ever mindful of maintaining orthodox standards of behaviour, especially against pollution on the part of intruders. Carefully avoiding all extremes, this god stands for law and order.

To his followers, he is the supreme deity, the embodiment of goodness and compassion, the sole source of manifestation. This is exemplified in his form as ANANTASHAYANA, reclining on the coils of ANANTA, the symbol of eternity, and floating on the waters of the ocean, representing the unmanifested state of the cosmos before creation. The lotus growing out of Vishnu's navel signals his creative force and lordship over the universe, while BRAHMA seated in the lotus, preparing to execute Vishnu's

orders, is reduced to a secondary figure. Vishnu's vehicle is the eagle GARUDA, a solar symbol. His wives are LAKSHMI and BHUDEVI. Occasionally, especially in eastern India, SARASVATI takes the place of Bhudevi. At the end of a creative cycle, Vishnu destroys the universe and returns to a period of quiescence in which he floats on the waters of the ocean reclining on Ananta's coils, united with the goddess YOGANIDRA.

Vishnu's usual attributes are the SHANKHA (conch), symbol of the five existential ELEMENTS, the CHAKRA (discus), symbol of the speed of thought, the PADMA (lotus), symbol of the powers of illusion from which the universe originates and the impulse towards liberation, and the GADA (mace), symbol of knowledge and power. His typical hand pose is ABHAYAMUDRA. On his chest sparkles the brilliant gem KAUSTUBHA, which represents consciousness manifested in all that shines, e.g. the sun, moon, FIRE and power of speech. The *shrivatsa* ('beloved of SHRI'), a lock of golden hair representing the source of the natural world, glows on his left breast. His dark hue symbolizes the infinite substance constituting the universe. He is clad in a thin yellow cloth, the *pitambara*, draped around his hips, which is said to represent the VEDAS, through which the divine nature emanates. The deity wears a KIRITAMAKUTA, the YAJNOPAVITA and the usual ORNAMENTS. His other names include Anantashayana ('reclining on Ananta'), Hari ('tawny'), Narayana ('moving in the waters'), Padmanabha ('lotus-navelled'), Perumal (Tamil, 'distinguished, illustrious'), Ranganatha ('lord of the assembly hall'), Venkatachala ('moving upon the hills') and VITHOBA ('standing on a brick').

Vishnudharmottara Purana An important text on the ARTS, dated between the 7th and the 10th centuries and appended to the *Vishnu* PURANA.

Worship of Vishvakarman. The god is seated on an elephant, surrounded by various tools. Andhra Pradesh. Colour print, late 1980s.

Vishnu Purana *see* PURANA(S)

Vishvakarma(n) 'all-maker'. The architect of the universe, Vishvakarma represents the supreme creative power, knowledge and wisdom. He is believed to be the founder of *vastuvidya* (science of ARCHITECTURE), and can be identified with TVASHTRI.

Vishvamitra 'universal friend'. One of the most distinguished Vedic RISHIS, author of a section of the RIGVEDA and of a number of hymns of the ATHARVAVEDA. In the post-Vedic period Vishvamitra became the hero of a number of myths, the most important being his long-standing rivalry with *rishi* VASISHTHA, who had replaced him as royal priest. The feud between the descendants of the two *rishis* continued for many generations.

Vishvanatha 'Lord of the universe'. Epithet of SHIVA. He is the patron deity of VARANASI and the famous Kashi Vishvanatha TEMPLE is dedicated to him.

vishvarupa 'encompassing all forms'. This term refers to the cosmic form of any god or goddess. In particular, it refers to VISHNU who, in the famous episode described in the BHAGAVADGITA, manifests himself in his universal form to ARJUNA. In the *vishvarupa* aspect, any deity is said to represent the whole universe and to be the embodiment of every conceivable manifested form.
Maxwell, T. S., 1988

vitarkamudra A gesture assumed while discussing. *See* CHINMUDRA

Vithoba or **Vitthala** 'standing on a brick' or **Pandarinatha** 'Lord of PANDHARPUR'. An aspect of VISHNU or KRISHNA, whose main shrine is in Pandharpur, Maharashtra. The god, as the name states, is generally depicted standing on a brick, with hands resting on the hips. This peculiar iconography is explained by a legend, according to which NARADA and Krishna, wanting to see the extraordinary devotion of Pundalika for his aged parents, paid him a visit. They arrived while the boy was busy attending to his parents. Without interrupting his activity, he tossed a brick towards Krishna and asked him to wait. The cult of Vitthala is most popular in Maharashtra and parts of Karnataka.

vivaha 'marriage'. *See* MARRIAGE

vrata 'vow'. A religious practice performed by individuals to fulfil an obligation towards a deity. A *vrata* can consist of fasting on certain days, PILGRIMAGES to a particular TEMPLE or recitation of special prayers. Performing a *vrata* is believed to help in difficult times, restore a sick person to health, etc. *Vratas* play an important role in everyday religious life.

vriksha 'tree'. The term designates either a tree or its wood. From time immemorial, trees have played an important role in Indian mythology and folklore. The evidence of tree worship has been found in the remains of the Harappan civilization (*c.* 3000–1700 BCE) and the custom is still observed even now. According to Hindu belief, trees and plants possess a latent consciousness that enables them to feel pleasure and pain. Trees are a symbol of reproduction and continuity of life and old or large trees in particular are worshipped as the vital power that sustains a community. Tree MARRIAGES are still practised, in which trees such as the ASHVATTHA and the NIM are planted together and trained in such a way that the stems and branches become

Vitthoba stands straight with his arms resting on the hips. In one hand he carries a pouch with pebbles, in the other, a conch. Maharashtra, perhaps Pandharpur. Bronze, 19th century.

intertwined. On these occasions, a full wedding ceremony takes place. Trees are consulted as oracles in time of crisis and are believed to dispense wealth, prosperity and offspring. The BUDDHA attained enlightenment beneath a tree and religious personalities meditate in their proximity.

However the most important powers, in or near trees, groves or forests are the *vriksha-devatas* (tree spirits), NAGAS and YAKSHAS who dwell in them. They play a prominent part in popular religion, and a number of them have been absorbed into the major religious systems. Their regular appearance in the sculptural programme on religious buildings testifies to their enduring protective powers. Tree spirits are worshipped by circumambulating the tree, decorating its stem and branches with garlands, bangles and other items, and offering prayers, perfumed pastes and, in some cases, sacrificing small ANIMALS. Before felling a tree, prayers are addressed to the *vriksha-devata* to encourage it to move to another tree, without harming the cutter. Particular trees are associated with specific deities: AGNI with the SHAMI tree, VISHNU with the *ashvattha*, BANYAN and UDUMBARA, SHIVA with the BAKULA and the BILVA. INDRA's paradise is graced by the PARIJATA. The wood of certain trees was used to feed the sacrificial FIRE, to fashion the kindling sticks (*aranis*) and other implements, such as the various ritual ladles.

Vrindavan(a) or **Brindavana** The region near MATHURA, where KRISHNA spent his early life.

vrishabha 'bull'. *See* RISHABHA

Vrishavahana(murti) or **Vrishabharudha(murti)** 'having the bull as mount' or 'sitting on a bull'. Aspect of SHIVA standing by, or seated on, NANDI.

vrishchika 'scorpion'. 1. Name of a DANCE posture in which one leg is lifted up to the forehead. 2. The scorpion is an attribute of various deities, such as CHAMUNDA. SHIVA in his aspect as VISHAPRAHARAMURTI ('destroyer of poison') wears a *vrishchikamala*, a garland of scorpions symbolizing poison.

Vritra 'to hold back, to obstruct'. The power of obstruction personified. In Vedic mythology, Vritra, a dragon or a giant snake, symbolizes the primeval chaos potentially containing the whole cosmos. Vritra was responsible for holding back creation, having captured the waters of life. INDRA attacked him and pierced him with his VAJRA, releasing the waters and initiating the process of creation.

Vyaghrapada 'having tiger feet'. Name of a sage, devotee of NATARAJA of CHIDAMBARAM. According to tradition, Vyaghrapada was a young RISHI, whose duty it was to pick flowers for Nataraja. To prevent the thorns from hurting him while engaged in this task, SHIVA bestowed tiger's feet on him. This also enabled him to climb trees and to gather blossoms early in the morning, before the bees could defile them. Vyaghrapada is depicted as a man with the legs and tail of a tiger. In southern Indian iconography he is shown paying homage to Shiva Nataraja, in the company of the sage PATANJALI.

Vyakhyana Dakshinamurti 'form (of SHIVA) explaining'. Aspect of Shiva in the act of teaching the different sciences. He is shown seated under a tree, in his upper right hand he carries the AKSHAMALA, in his left, the FIRE or a snake. His lower right hand is in JNANAMUDRA and the left, either in VARADAMUDRA or DANDAHASTAMUDRA. A DATURA flower, a snake and the crescent moon adorn his matted hair.

vyakhyanamudra see CHINMUDRA

vyala see YALI

Vyasa or **Vedavyasa** 'arranger, editor, compiler'. A title given to an editor or compiler of literary works. This title was given to the editor(s) of the VEDAS, and later to other prominent personalities. Among them is Krishna Dvaipayana Vyasa, the mythical author of the MAHABHARATA.

vyuha 'manifestation, appearance, emanation'. This term is used in PANCHARATRA theology to indicate the four manifestations of VISHNU on earth as the Supreme Being. They have been identified with VASUDEVA, SAMKARSHANA, Pradyumna and ANIRUDDHA, out of whom emanate three further *vyuhas*. The latter twelve preside over the months of the year.

Yadava(s) 'descended from YADU'. The line founded by Yadu, who had among his descendants VASUDEVA, father of KRISHNA and his sister KUNTI, who became the mother of the PANDAVAS. A contemporary of Vasudeva was KAMSA, the tyrannical king of MATHURA who deposed his father UGRASENA and was eventually killed by Krishna. The latter restored Ugrasena and, shortly afterwards, Jarasandha, Kamsa's father-in-law and king of Magadha, waged war on the Yadavas to avenge his death. The Yadavas were forced to retreat, migrating to the western coast of India, where they settled in DWARKA. At the end of Krishna's life, a war broke out among them in which practically all perished.

Yadu Name of one of the five Aryan clans mentioned in the RIGVEDA. In the MAHABHARATA and the PURANAS, the name Yadu refers to the elder son of King Yayati. It is not certain where Yadu settled, but it has been suggested that he inherited the region to the south-west of the Gangetic plain, between the RIVERS Chambal, Betwa and Ken, roughly corresponding to the border area between Uttar and Madhya Pradesh. There he founded the YADAVA dynasty, the first of the CHANDRAVAMSA, or Lunar dynasties, to become famous in Indian history.

yajna or *yaga* 'sacrifice, oblation'. The aim of the sacrifice was magical rather than religious. A *yajna* was celebrated to maintain the well-being and prosperity of the *yajamana*, the person celebrating the sacrifice, his family and the community in which he lived. Moreover, the *yajna* was necessary to restore the power of the gods, who were invoked to partake of the offerings, and to give them the necessary strength to protect the world and sustain all the various forms of life on it. Some *yajnas* were celebrated by priests on behalf of an individual,

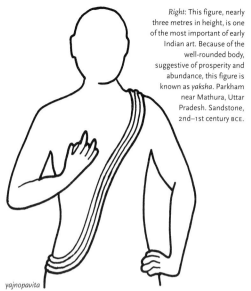

Right: This figure, nearly three metres in height, is one of the most important of early Indian art. Because of the well-rounded body, suggestive of prosperity and abundance, this figure is known as *yaksha*. Parkham near Mathura, Uttar Pradesh. Sandstone, 2nd–1st century BCE.

yajnopavita

while the householder was expected to conduct the domestic sacrifice. The rules to be observed on such occasions were subsequently described in the GRIHYA-SUTRAS.

yajnopavita 'sacred thread'. The *yajnopavita* is conferred on boys of the three upper CASTES during the UPANAYANA ceremony. It symbolizes a second (spiritual) birth. The *yajnopavita* is worn on the left shoulder, across the chest, to hang under the right arm. It usually consists of three cotton strings, symbolizing the three GUNAS informing the primeval matter (PRAKRITI). It is also a reminder to the wearer that he must observe the rules of DHARMA.

Yajurveda 'the VEDA of the *Yajus*'. The *yajus* are particular MANTRAS uttered in the course of a sacrifice. The *Yajurveda* contains the rules to be observed by the priest in charge of the performance of the YAJNA. The work consists of two separate collections (*samhitas*), the *Taittiriya* (Black *Yajurveda*) and the *Vajasaneyi* (White *Yajurveda*). The date of the completion of the *Taittiriya Samhita* has been estimated to *c.* 600 BCE, while that of the *Vajasaneyi Samhita* somewhat later.

yaksha(s), yakshi(s) or **yakshini(s)** 'ghost'. The term, whose etymology is uncertain, indicated a creator-god, such as PRAJAPATI, and was later used simply to designate a deity. It eventually became a collective noun for mysterious semi-divine beings, who can assume any form at will, living in forests, trees, caves and jungles and play a prominent role in Indian mythology and folklore. They were said to inhabit the sacred tree in each village and to protect the prosperity and well-being of the community. Trees, NAGAS, *yakshas* and *yakshis* were connected to the fertility cult. The *yakshis*, in particular, were

associated with the tree's life-sap and energy, and barren women who worshipped the tree were believed to become fertile. However, *Yakshas* could also be malevolent and cause several ailments, especially nervous illnesses. They were originally the godlings of the village and rural communities. Although ignored in most of the Vedic lore, they surface again in various passages of the ATHARVAVEDA. Eventually, they were absorbed into BUDDHISM, where they appear in numerous legends, and play a prominent role in JAINISM where they are among the attendants of the twenty-four TIRTHANKARAS. The PURANAS contain numerous references to *yakshas*. Many of these beings found a place among the attendants of KUBERA, their chief, whose mount is occasionally a *yaksha*, whereas others were assimilated into main deities, such as SHIVA, as exemplified by his epithet VIRUPAKSHA, which originally was the name of a *yaksha*. In time, Hindu mythology provided them with parents and they are believed to be either the offspring of KASHYAPA and Khasa, or to have been created by BRAHMA. They are depicted as handsome, strongly built men, the embodiment of prosperity and well-being, and as beautiful women. In the development of Indian iconography the *yaksha* IMAGES were crucial in providing the basis for the development of cult icons such as Shiva, probably GANESHA, and others. Among the goddesses, the SAPTAMATRIKAS, sixty-four YOGINIS, SHALABHANJIKAS and the *alasa-kanyas* (creeper girls), are all derived from the *yakshis*.
Coomaraswamy, A. K., 1971

Yakshagana 'Song of the YAKSHAS'. A colourful DANCE drama that originated in the early 16th century and is typical of the South Kanara district of Karnataka. Like the KATHAKALI, it is performed by an all-male cast consisting of about twenty actors and

Left: A warrior rides on a rearing *yali*, whose hind legs rest on a *makara*. Pier in the *kalyana-mandapa* (marriage hall), Jalakanteshvara temple, Vellore, Tamil Nadu. Granite, late 16th century.

Right: Yama, the guardian of the south, armed with noose and mace, rides on his buffalo mount. Caption in Telugu. Probably Thanjavur, *c*. 1830. From an album of paintings on European paper watermarked 1830.

musicians. The repertoire of the *Yakshagana* plays is mainly inspired by episodes from the epics, especially the MAHABHARATA. The all-night performances are organized at the behest of a wealthy patron, for special occasions, such as thanksgiving, or the consecration of a new house. These take place in the open air and no particular props are needed. Its spectacular costumes are enhanced by tall, dramatic headgear, a profusion of ORNAMENTS and elaborate makeup.
Ashton, M. B., and B. Christie, 1977

yali or *vyala* 'leogryph, fabulous ANIMAL'. A mythical lion-faced animal that appears in carved friezes on TEMPLE walls. In southern Indian SCULPTURE from the 16th century onwards, figures of rearing, almost three-dimensional *yalis* bearing heads either of horned lions or ELEPHANTS and feline bodies, standing on the back of a MAKARA or other fabulous beasts, guard the entrances of temples and line the approaches leading to sanctuaries.

Yama 'the Restrainer'. The ruler of the dead. Since he was the first man to die, he accompanies the deceased to the *pitriloka*, the sphere of the ancestors. Eventually, he became the judge of the dead and performs this duty assisted by CHITRAGUPTA. He is one of the ASHTADIKPALAS, the regent of the south, where *yamaloka*, the realm of Yama, is located. He is of dark complexion with bloodshot EYES, protruding fangs and wears a garland of red flowers. In his arms he generally carries a noose and a staff. His VAHANA is a buffalo. Occasionally, he is flanked by Chitragupta, KALA and a host of goblins. He is the twin of YAMI, later identified with the river YAMUNA (Jumna).

Yami Twin sister of YAMA, occasionally identified with the river YAMUNA (Jumna). Yami is one of the seven or eight MATRIKAS. She carries a KAPALA (skull cup).

Yamuna or **Jumna** A RIVER that descends from the Himalayas and joins the Ganges at PRAYAGA (Allahabad). She is worshipped as a goddess, the twin sister of YAMA. Although she flows through a number of sacred places, for instance MATHURA and VRINDAVAN, her sanctity cannot be compared with that of the GANGA. The Yamuna and the Ganga are often depicted at the entrance of sacred precincts or on sanctuary door jambs, to ensure that the visitor is symbolically purified before entering. The Yamuna, portrayed as a handsome woman, carries in her hands, a blue lotus, a fly-whisk and a water pot. Her mount is a tortoise, because a great number of them live in her waters.

yantra 'instrument, tool'. A geometrical diagram believed to possess mystical powers and employed as a tool to help meditation. All deities have their specific *yantra*, into which they 'descend' when it is used in meditation. *Yantras* can represent the universe and be used as magical charms to ward off evil. They can be drawn on the ground with coloured powders or be written on paper or other materials, sealed in a metal case and worn as an amulet. Alternatively, they can be engraved on a thin sheet of copper and worshipped along with other deities in the daily domestic PUJA. The most famous among them is the *Shri Yantra*, or 'illustrious *yantra*', which consists of nine superimposed triangles, five pointing upwards, four downwards, symbolizing the successive stages of creation. They converge on the BINDU, or central dot, the source of the universe.

Yashoda 'conferring fame'. The foster-mother of KRISHNA and wife of NANDA, the chief of the

Left: The river goddess Yamuna rides on her tortoise mount, flanked by female attendants. Carving on a pilaster on the porch of the Lad Khan temple, Aihole, Karnataka. Sandstone, *c.* 7th century.

Right: Narasimha sits in *utkutikasana*, with a *yogapatta* firmly tied around his legs. In his upper right hand is the *chakra* (discus) and the *shanka* (conch) would have been in his left. Tamil Nadu. Bronze, *c.* 13th century.

cowherds, to whom VASUDEVA brought the infant to save him from being killed by KAMSA.

yatra *see* PILGRIMAGE

Yavana(s) 'Greeks'. The term referred to the Greeks, in particular the Ionians from Asia Minor who, in the 6th century BCE settled in Bactria, as well as on the southern shores of the Black Sea and the north-western borders of India.

Yellamma A folk goddess whose main centre of PILGRIMAGE is Saundatti (Belgaum district, Karnataka). There are two traditions regarding her origin. According to one, she is RENUKA, the mother of PARASHURAMA, who was ordered by his father JAMADAGNI to cut off his mother's head for her unchaste thoughts. To seek comfort, Renuka embraced an outcaste woman, and Parashurama cut off both their heads. For having obeyed his command, Jamadagni granted his son a favour. The latter wanted his mother's life restored, but in his haste, Parashurama stuck the wrong heads on the wrong bodies. Thus, the woman with a BRAHMIN body and the outcaste's head became Yellamma, while the other is worshipped as MARIAMMAN. According to another version of the story, Yellamma is the virgin mother born from the earth.

yoga 'the act of yoking'. A discipline combining physical training to improve the health of the body (*hatha yoga*) and a technique of intellectual discipline to achieve final liberation. There are a number of different *yoga* schools such as KUNDALINI *yoga*, in which the various CHAKRAS of the subtle body are awakened by sophisticated *hatha yoga* methods, BHAKTI *yoga*, where the final aim is achieved by devotion to God, KARMA *yoga*, where disinterested action is stressed, and JNANA *yoga*, focusing on direct experience of inner knowledge. Among the other schools is TANTRA *yoga*. Despite their differences, all of them require discipline, extreme concentration and their aim is elimination of ignorance.

Yoga Dakshinamurti 'form (of SHIVA) as teacher of yoga'. Four-armed representation of Shiva, seated in PADMASANA posture. In his upper right hand he carries a trident and in his upper left a skull cup. The lower right hand is in CHINMUDRA, while the left is raised to the chest. Yoga Dakshinamurti can also be represented seated beneath a BANYAN tree with one leg resting on the ground, and the other on his thigh, kept in place by a YOGAPATTA. In his upper right hand he carries an AKSHAMALA, in the left FIRE; the lower right hand is in DHYANAMUDRA, and the lower left in ABHAYAMUDRA. Two deer crouching beneath his seat and a cobra wound around his right arm look towards him.

Yoga-Narasimha Aspect of VISHNU's incarnation as NARASIMHA, in which he is shown almost squatting (UTKUTIKASANA), with one or both knees held in position by a YOGAPATTA.

Yoganidra 'meditation-sleep'. A form of inner withdrawal, in which the YOGI is unaware of the outer world, but has full control over his mental faculties. Yoganidra has been personified as a form of DEVI, and is identical with Mahamaya. The term Yoganidra applies to the sleep of VISHNU in the interval between creations.

yogapatta 'cloth, band'. The band that keeps the knees of a meditating YOGI firmly in position.

yogasana *see* PADMASANA

One of the sixty-four *yoginis* in the Chaunsath Yogini temple at Hirapur, Bhubaneshvar, Orissa. Crowned by a flame, this *yogini* stands proudly on her bird mount. Schist(?), 9th century.

yogi(n) A person who practises YOGA. One who has bridged the opposition between self and non-self, and has achieved a state of unity with all things animate and inanimate.

yogini(s) 'demoness, sorceress'. 1. A woman possessing supernatural powers. Eight *yoginis* emanated from DURGA to help her in exploits. Later their number increased to sixty-four. They represent the forces of fertility, vegetation, illness, death, magic and YOGA. They are worshipped together, each enshrined in an individual niche, generally in circular TEMPLES open to the sky. One of the most impressive *yogini* temples is the 9th-century Chaunsath Yogini, ('sixty-four *Yogini*') temple at Hirapur, Bhubaneshvar district, Orissa. Other important *yogini* temples are the 10th-century monuments at Khajuraho, near Chhattarpur and Bheragat, near Jabalpur, both in Madhya Pradesh. 2. A female attendant of DURGA. 3. In Tantric cults, the term designates an initiated female sexual partner.
Dehejia, V., 1986

yoni 'holder, receptacle, vagina'. Among the finds of the Harappan civilization (*c.* 3000–1700 BCE) are a number of so-called ring-stones, fashioned out of stone, shell, etc. which have been identified as *yoni*. There are no references to a *yoni* cult in the VEDAS, although it probably existed continuously in rural communities then, as it does today. It emerged in the post-Vedic period along with SHAKTI worship and the SHIVA cult. The *yoni*, generally shown in conjunction with the LINGA, represents the divine generative force.

Yudhishthira 'firm, steady in battle'. The eldest of the five PANDAVAS, son of KUNTI and DHARMARAJA, one

of the heroes of the MAHABHARATA. He represents the ideal of justice and truthfulness. He was selected by his uncle DHRITARASHTRA to succeed him on the throne of HASTINAPURA, in preference to his own son DURYODHANA, and this caused the old feud between the KAURAVAS and Pandavas to flare up.

yuga(s) 'age of the world'. There are four *yugas* in each cycle of creation. These are the KRITA or *satya yuga*, the TRETA *yuga*, the DVAPARA *yuga* and the present KALI *yuga*, or age of Kali, at the end of which the universe will disappear in an enormous conflagration; after a period of rest, the cycle will recommence. After the first *yuga*, which is a 'golden age', progressive deterioration sets in: the *yugas* become shorter, as does human life, and moral standards decline. The sum total of the human years constituting a complete cycle, or *mahayuga*, is 4.32 million. One thousand *mahayugas* make up a KALPA.

yupa 'peg, post, pillar'. The term refers particularly to the sacrificial stake to which the victim was tied. It symbolizes INDRA'S VAJRA, the thunderbolt with which he tranfixed VRITRA and propped up the heaven, separating it from the earth. From this mythological incident was derived the association of the *yupa* with the cosmic pillar, the cosmic tree connecting heaven and earth, and the cosmic phallus. The octagonal-shaped *yupa*, fashioned from different kinds of wood, was among the deified objects used in Vedic sacrifice. The octagonal pillar, one of the most common in Indian ARCHITECTURE, possibly took its shape from the *yupa*. In the course of time, the *yupa* became the *dhvajastambha*, or flagpole, outside TEMPLES.

Principal Dynasties and Empires in alphabetical order

Chandella This dynasty ruled central India between the 9th and *c.* 11th centuries, and their power peaked in the 10th and 11th centuries, though Chandella rulers can be traced up to 1540. Among its most noteworthy achievements are the magnificent group of temples at Khajuraho (Madhya Pradesh), begun in 925 CE.

Chola The Chola dynasty, whose power temporarily extended to the island of Sri Lanka, was the paramount force in southern India between the 9th and 13th centuries. The Cholas patronized a number of imposing temples, such as the Rajarajeshvara (also known as Brihadeshvara) at Thanjavur. During this period, bronze casting attained an unparelleled degree of excellence.

Eastern Ganga Between the early 12th and the 15th centuries this dynasty ruled eastern India. The celebrated Surya temple at Konarak (Orissa) was built during the reign of one of its most distinguished rulers, Narasimhadeva (1238–1264).

East India Company and the **British Empire** The British established the first trading post for the East India Company in 1613 at Surat on the west coast. By the beginning of the 19th century, the East India Company ruled a substantial part of India, but in 1858 the British Crown supplanted the Company and assumed direct control over Indian affairs. The building activity, commencing in the early 19th century, gained momentum, culminating in the construction of the new capital, New Delhi, inaugurated in 1931. In 1947 the British handed over India to the first prime minister, Jawaharlal Nehru, and Pakistan to Muhammed Ali Jinnah, its first governor general.

Gupta The Imperial Guptas ruled most of northern India between *c.* 320 and *c.* 500 CE, and their successors ruled until 647 CE. This was the so-called 'classic' period of Indian Culture during which literature, astronomy, mathematics and the arts reached great heights. The earliest Hindu temples date from this age, as well as the Buddha image, which became the model for sculptors throughout the Buddhist world.

Hoysala The Hoysala carved out a small kingdom around Belur (Karnataka) in the 10th century. In the following century, they expanded their territory, establishing a new capital at Dorasamudra, now Halebid. Their power reached its climax in the 12th century, but by the beginning of the 14th century they had succumbed to the forces of the Delhi sultan. They left a splendid artistic legacy in the elaborately carved temples at Belur, Halebid and Somnathpur (Karnataka).

Kalachuri This dynasty ruled the western coast of India during the 6th century. Hindu rock-cut architecture started in this period and the Shiva cave temple at Elephanta was probably built under their patronage.

Kushana Of central Asian origin, the Kushanas ruled over the territory that extended from the Oxus river to their capital Mathura, from the middle of the 1st century to the 3rd century. They sponsored both Buddhism and Hinduism. Under their patronage, two distinct Buddha types were created: the Hellenistic image, in the north-western region of Gandhara, and the indigenous one at Mathura.

Maurya Shortly after Alexander the Great began to withdraw from India in 326 BCE, Chandragupta

Maurya established the Maurya dynasty, which ruled over the whole of India except for its southernmost regions. Emperor Ashoka, who held the power from *c.* 268–233 BCE, converted to Buddhism. His edicts, propagating the Buddhist ethos, were engraved on free-standing stone columns, the first example of monumental art in stone. He was also responsible for the first rock-cut caves, in the Barabar Hills, near Gaya (Bihar).

Mughal This Islamic dynasty of Mongol origin ruled over northern India from 1526 to 1858, when the British exiled the last of the Mughal emperors. The dynasty is famous for a number of magnificent buildings, painted manuscripts and albums, and jewelry.

Nayaks Originally, the Nayaks were provincial governors of the Vijayanagara kings, but they eventually severed their allegiance to the central government and founded independent states. One of the most important was that of the Nayaks of Madurai (1526–1736). They refurbished and added exuberant sculptures to various temples throughout southern India.

Pala-Senas These two dynasties successively ruled a substantial part of eastern India between *c.* 750 and 1200. They patronized both Hinduism and Buddhism.

Pallava One of the most important dynasties of southern India, the Pallavas ruled from *c.* 550 to 728. Under their patronage rock-cut architecture, large-scale stone sculpture and the Dravidian style of temple architecture evolved at Mamallapuram and Kanchipuram.

Portuguese The Portuguese presence in India commenced in 1498, when Vasco da Gama landed near Kozhikode (Calicut) on the Malabar coast. From 1510 to 1961, the Portuguese Estado da India (State of India) was based in Goa. Magnificent mansions, churches, monasteries and religious objects bear witness to its splendour.

Rashtrakuta This dynasty ruled over the northern part of the Deccan between the 7th and the 10th centuries. One of their great artistic achievements, under the patronage of Krishna I (757–783), is the majestic rock-cut Kailasanatha temple at Ellora, a monolithic structure hewn out of a hill.

Satavahana Between the 1st century BCE and the 2nd century CE, parts of the Deccan were under Satavahana rule. One of the most notable artistic projects of this period is the great *stupa* at Amaravati, completed *c.* 200 CE, and a number of rock-cut Buddhist monasteries.

Shunga When the Mauryan empire fell, the Shungas (*c.* 185–75 BCE) and their successors, the Kanvas, ruled over central India until *c.* 25 CE. Under their patronage, Buddhist art flourished at Bharhut and Sanchi.

Sisodia One of the most important among the Rajput clans, the Sisodias established themselves in the 14th century. They ruled from Chitorgarh fort for some time, but after its sacking, settled in Udaipur, where they sponsored the construction of beautiful palaces and encouraged the art of painting.

Solanki The Solanki dynasty ruled western India between *c.* 950 and 1304. Among the important building projects of that time are the Jain temples on Mount Abu. The first surviving illustrated Jain manuscripts on palm leaf date from this period.

Sultanate Collective name given to separate dynasties of Turkish origin: the 'Slave', Khalji, Thuglak, Sayyid and Lodi, which ruled over northern India from 1206 until the advent of the Mughals in 1526. In the Deccan, the Bahmani sultans ruled from 1347 to 1538, when their territory was divided into five sultanates: Bijapur, Ahmadnagar, Bidar, Berar and Golconda. In 1686 they were conquered by the Mughals. Muslim sultans were in power in Gujarat and Bengal.

Vakataka Central India and the Deccan were under Vakataka rule during the 4th and the 5th centuries CE. One of the most famous of the Vakataka rulers is Harisena (*c.* 462–91) in whose reign the rock-cut Buddhist monasteries at Ajanta were embellished with paintings.

Vijayanagara Three separate dynasties ruled over a part of the Deccan and southern India from 1336 to 1565. They were responsible for a number of magnificent sacred and civic buildings in the capital Vijayanagara, as well as for additions and refurbishments of earlier temples in various parts of the empire. Their sculptural style paved the way for the flamboyant 17th-century Nayaka style.

Subjects and Sanskrit equivalents

A

actions and consequences of   *karma(n)*
ages, of the world   *kalpa*; *yuga* (*dvapara*, *kali*,
   treta, *krita*)
altar   *vedi*
ambrosia   *amrita*
   vessel   *amritakalasha*
amulet   *raksha*
ancestors   *pitri(s)*
animals
   antelope   *mriga*
   boar   *varaha avatara*
   buffalo   **Mahisha**
   bull of Shiva   **Nandi**
   cat   *marjara*
   cow   *go, gomata*
   dog   *shvan*
   elephant   *gaja*
   fish   *matsya*
   horse   *ashva*
   lion   *simha*
   mongoose   *nakula*
   monkeys   *vanara(s)*
   rat, mouse   *musha*
   scorpion   *vrishchika*
   serpent, snake   *naga*
   tortoise   *kurma*
animals and birds (mythical)   *gandabherunda*;
   Garuda; *makara*; **Nandini**; **Narasimha**; **Sharabha**;
   Surabhi; **Uchchaihshravas**; *yali*
architect, sculptor (divine)   **Vishvakarma(n)**
architecture, science of   *vastuvidya*
   ideal plan   **Vastunara**
art, treatise   *shilpashastra*
arts, practice of   *shilpa*

asceticism   *tapas*
ashes   *vibhuti*
astronomy, astrology   *jyotisha*
auspicious objects (eight)   *ashtamangala*

B

band
   between the chest and abdomen   *udarabandha*
   to support the knees   *yogapatta*
banner, flag   *dhvaja*
being, self-existent   *brahman* (neuter)
bell   *ghanta*
birds
   cock   *kukkuta*
   crow   *kaka*
   gander, goose   *hamsa*
   owl   *uluka*
   parrot   *shuka*
   peacock   *mayura*
body, positions of   *dvibhanga*; *lalitasana*;
   padmasana; *tribhanga*; *virasana*;
   utkutikasana
bowl   *patra*
breath or vital air   *prana*
butter (clarified)   *ghee*

C

caste, social class   **brahmin**, *kshatriya(s)*,
   vaishya(s), *shudra(s)*
cattle and other domesticated animals *pashu*
chariot   *ratha*
Churning of the Ocean   *Samudramanthana*
circles, mystical, of the body   *chakra*
circumambulation   *pradakshina*

cities, the seven sacred **Ayodhya, Dwarka, Hardwar, Varanasi, Kanchipuram, Mathura, Ujjain**
   three cities, destruction of **Tripurantakamurti**
club, mace, of Vishnu **Kaumodaki**
concentration, meditation *dhyana*
   last stage of *samadhi*
conch *shankha*
consecration *abhisheka*
   royal *rajasuya*
corpse as seat *pretasana*
cow
   of plenty **Surabhi**
   wish-fulfilling **Kamadhenu**
cowherd, cowherdesses *gopa, gopi*
craftsman of the gods **Tvashtri**
creation, myths **Hiranyagarbha; Prajapati**
crown *karandamakuta; kiritamakuta*
cup
   skull cup *kapala*

D

dance
   circular of Krishna *rasa-lila*
   cosmic of Shiva *tandava*
   Lord of **Nataraja**
   Parvati's *lasya*
   Shiva's *talasamsphotitam*
   treatise on *Bharatanatyashastra*
dance drama *Kathakali; Yakshagana*
dawn, goddess of **Ushas**
death
   personification **Mrityu**
demons, demigods *asura(s); bhuta(s); Bhairava(s); daitya(s); danava(s); gandharva(s); kinnara(s); rakshasa(s)*
   causing eclipses **Rahu**
   dwarf **Apasmara**
   flesh-eating *pishacha(s)*
devotion *bhakti*
diagram, symbolic
   for meditation *mandala; yantra*
donation *dakshina*
door (arch) *torana*
door (portal) *dvara*
   guardians of *dvarapala(s)*
drum *damaru, mridanga(m)*
duty, civil, religious, etc. *dharma*

E

earring *kundala*
earth, the **Bhudevi**
   personified **Prithvi**
editor, arranger, compiler, **Vyasa**
egg, cosmic **Hiranyagarbha**

elements *bhuta(s)*
elephant *gaja*
   goad *ankusha*
   mythical **Airavata**; *diggaja*
emotion, taste, essence *rasa*
energy, divine, cosmic, personified **Shakti**, *shakti*
extinction *nirvana*

F

face of glory **Kirtimukha**
faces (the five-faced, epithet of Shiva) **Panchanana**
female organ *yoni*
festivals *ashvamedha; Divali; Ganesh Chaturthi; Holi; Janmashtami; Makara Sankranti; Naga-panchami; Navaratri; Rama-navami; Shivaratri; Shravani-purnima; Tripuri-purnima*
fire, god of **Agni**
fish form of Vishnu **Matsya** *avatara*
   auspicious pair *matsyayugma*
fish-eyed goddess **Minakshi**
fly-whisk *chamara*
food, goddess of **Annapurna**
form, shape *murti; rupa*
   benevolent *anugrahamurti(s)*
   destructive *samharamurti(s)*
furrow, personified **Sita**

G

Ganges **Ganga**
garland *mala*
gems *ratna*
   the nine *navaratna*
gesture, ritual *mudra(s)*
ghosts, spirits of the dead *preta(s); vetala(s)*
gifts, to priests *dakshina*
god *deva; devata(s)*
   aspects of
   peaceful **Saumya**
   destructive *ugra*
   chosen *ishtadevata*
   folk *gramadevata(s)*
   household *kuladevata(s)*
   all-encompassing *vishvarupa*
goddess *devi*
   groups of goddesses *navadurgas; saptamatrikas*
   the Great Goddess **Devi**
   of villages *gramadevata(s)*
   protective *yaksha(s); yogini*
grace, divine *prasada*
grasses, sacred *darbha; kusha; munja*
guardians, the eight *ashtadikpala(s); lokapala(s)*
guild *shreni*

H

hair, hairstyle
    curls, matted *jata(s)*; *jatabhara*; *jatamakuta*
hands, arms, position of *mudra(s)*; *hasta*;
    abhayamudra; *anjalimudra*; *chinmudra*;
    dandahastamudra; *dhyanamudra*; *jnanamudra*;
    lolahastamudra; *mushtimudra*; *namaskaramudra*;
    patakahasta; *suchihasta*; *tarjanimudra*;
    varadamudra; *vismayahasta*; *vyakhyanamudra*
heaven, paradise *svarga*
    of Krishna **Goloka**
    of Vishnu **Vaikuntha**
hell *naraka*
hermitage *ashrama*
hero, leader *vira*
    hero stone *virakal*
holy man *sannyasi(n)*
horse sacrifice *ashvamedha*
horsewhip *chentu* (Tamil)
house, ideal design **Vastunara**

I

iconometry *talamana*
illusion *maya*
images *murti*
    processional *utsavabera*
incarnation, 'descent' *avatara*
    complete *purna avatara*
incarnations, the ten *dashavatara(s)*
initiation *diksha*; *upanayana*
island *dvipa*
    rose-apple **Jambudvipa**

J

jewels, **gems** *ratna*
    Vishnu's *kaustubha*
    the nine *navaratna*
judge of the dead **Yama**

K

king *raja(n)*
knowledge *vidya*
Krishna, child aspect of **Balakrishna**

L

lamp *dipa*
law, custom, duty, justice. *dharma*
left *vama*
legends, ancient **Purana(s)**
leogryph *yali*
liberation *moksha*

life, principle of *atman*
life, stages of *ashrama(s)*: *brahmachari(n)*;
    grihastha; *vanaprashtha*; *sannyasi(n)*
lord **Ishvara**
luck, riches, lord of **Lakshmi**
lunar dynasty **Chandravamsha**

M

magic powers *siddhi(s)*
man **Manu**; *nara*
manifestation, incarnation *avatara*
    four manifestations of Vishnu *vyuha*
mark, sign, characteristic *lakshana*; *linga(m)*
    sectarian *tilaka*; *tripundra*
    Vaishnava *urdhvapundra*; *namam*
marriage *vivaha*
    ceremony to choose a husband *svayamvara*
medicine, work on; system of **Ayurveda**
meditation *yoga*; *samadhi*
mendicant *sannyasi*
mind *manas*
moon god **Chandra**
moon-crested **Chandrashekharamurti**
Mothers, the divine *matrika(s)*
    the seven *saptamatrika(s)*
    the eight *ashtamatrika(s)*
mountains
    gold **Meru**
    mythical **Kailasa**; **Mandara**
music, teacher of (Shiva)
    Vinadhara Dakshinamurti
musical instruments
    cymbal *tala*
    lute *vina*
musicians, celestial *gandharva(s)*
    leader of **Narada**; **Tumburu**
mystical diagram *yantra*

N

naked (Jainism) **Digambara(s)**
navel *nabha*
    lotus **Padmanabha**
nether world *patala*
noose, fetter *pasha*
nymph *apsara(s)*; *gandharvi(s)*; **Urvashi**

O

objects, eight auspicious *ashthamangala*
oblation *homa*
obstacles, lord of **Vighneshvara**
offering *bali*
ornaments
    anklet with bells *nupura*

bracelet *valaya*
breast band *kuchabandha*
chain *chhannavira*
crown **karandamakuta**
diadem *chudamani*
finger ring *pavitram*
garland **mala**
hair band *keshabandha*
necklace *hara*
shoulder ornaments *skandhamala*
torque *kanthi*
outcaste **chandala(s)**; **dalit(s)**; **harijan(s)**

P

pair, couple **mithuna**
parasol, ceremonial **chhattra**
perfected person **siddha(s)**
pestle **mushala**
phallus **linga(m)**
  aniconic **banalinga**
  five-faced *panchamukhalinga*
  fundamental **mulavigraha**
  of light **jyotirlinga**
philosophical works **Upanishad(s)**
pillar, post **yupa**
  cosmic **skambha**
planets, the nine **navagrahas**
  Jupiter **Brihashpati**
  Mars **Mangala**
  Mercury **Budha**
  Moon **Soma**
   ascending node of **Rahu**
   descending node of **Ketu**
  Saturn **Shani**
  Sun **Ravi**; **Surya**
  Venus **Shukra**
plants
  basil, holy **tulasi**
  berries for prayer beads **rudraksha**
  grasses **darbha**; **kusha**; *munja*
  hemp **bhang(a)**
  lime **nimbu** (Hindi)
  lotus **padma**
  magical, medicinal plants **oshadhi**
  turmeric **haridra**
play, sport **lila**
plough **hala**
poet saints **alvar(s)**; **nayanmar(s)**
poison, remover of **Vishaprahara(murti)**
pole star **Dhruva**
pot, vessel, pitcher **kumbha**; **kamandalu**
  symbol of universe **kalasha**
power(s)
  creative **maya**; **shakti**
  gained by austerity **tapas**

prayer **japa**
prayer beads **akshamala**
priest, priestly class **brahmin**
prosperity, fame, glory
  goddess of **Shri**

Q

quality, characteristic **guna**

R

release, liberation **moksha**
ritual
  ladle, spoon **sruk**; **sruva**
rivers personified; goddesses of **Ganga**; **Kaveri**;
  Narmada; **Sarasvati**; **Yamuna**
ruler, universal **chakravartin**

S

sacred knowledge **Veda(s)**
  bearers of **vidyadhara(s)**
sacred thread **yajnopavita**
sacrifice **yajna**
saint **sadhu**
sandals, slipper **paduka**
seat, throne **asana**; **pitha**
seed-syllable **bija**; **mantra**
seer, sage **rishi**; **Narada**
  seven great *sapta maharishi(s)*
  tiger-footed **Vyaghrapada**
  vedic **Vasishtha**; **Vishvamitra**
serpents, cult of **naga**
  goddess of **Manasa**
  king of **Kaliya**; **Shesha**; **Vasuki**
  votive stones **nagakal(s)**
shell, fossilized **shalagrama**
  of Vishnu **shankha**
shrine, place of pilgrimage **tirtha**
skull carrier **kapalika**
sky, eight guardians of **ashtadikpala(s)**
solar dynasty **Suryavamsha**
sound **nada**
  sacred **om**
south, right hand **dakshina**
speech **Vach**
spirits
  forces of vegetation **yaksha(s)**; **gandharva(s)**
  troop, multitude of **gana(s)**
  malevolent **bhuta(s)**
staff **danda**
student, of religion **brahmachari(n)**
Subrahmanya, child aspect of **Balasubrahmanya**
sun **Savitar**; **Surya**
sweetmeat **laddu**; **modaka**

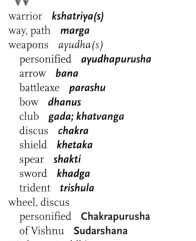

Chronology *c.* 3000 BCE–2001 CE

To piece together an approximate chronology of Indian history from its earliest known beginnings until at least the common era, and even until the 13th century CE, is a difficult task, due to inadequate sources and the various calendars used, which render the conversion into the Gregorian calendar problematical. Moreover, a number of Indian scholars assert that the *Rigveda* was composed in 4000 BCE, thus rejecting the theory of the Aryan migration. The majority of Western scholars, however, maintain the theory of the Aryan migration and set the date of the composition of the *Rigveda* to *c.* 1700–1300 BCE. While there are still unresolved questions, such as the dates of Mahavira, the Buddha and the regnal years of some kings, this concise chronology intends to provide an approximate framework in which to place historical, religious and cultural events discussed in the book.

BCE

c. 3000–1700	Harappan civilization. A refined culture flourished in cities, such as Mohenjo Daro on the Indus and Harappa on the Ravi, now in Pakistan. Numerous seals, statuettes and other artifacts were found at these sites.
c. 2000–1000	Arrival of the Aryans.
c. 1500–600	Composition of the *Vedas* and *Brahmanas*.
c. 700–300	Composition of the *Upanishads*.
c. 527 or 526	Death of Mahavira, the historical founder of Jainism (according to Jaina sources).
late 6th century	Darius, the Persian king, conquers part of Pakistan.
c. 486	Death of the Buddha, Indian tradition. Chinese record 483 BCE.
c. 400	Composition of the first Sanskrit grammar, Panini's *Ashtadhyayi*.
4th century BCE–4th century CE	Period of composition of the *Ramayana* and the *Mahabharata*.

327–25 BCE	Alexander the Great invades northern India.
c. 321–181	Maurya dynasty founded by Chandragupta.
c. 300	Megasthenes, Greek ambassador, visits the Maurya king.
c. 300	Suggested date of the *Arthashastra*. Some scholars, however, date the work to 100 CE.
c. 268–233	Reign of Ashoka, the Maurya emperor who embraced Buddhism. Beginning of rock-cut architecture.
c. 185–75	Shunga dynasty rules over central India.
2nd century BCE–3rd century CE	Buddhist and Jaina influence in India reaches its peak.
1st century BCE–1st century CE	Shakas, Parthians and Kushanas invade India.
1st century BCE–2nd century CE	Satavahana rule.
58–57 BCE	Vikrama Samvat era begins.

CE

78 CE	Beginning of the Shaka era.

1st–3rd century	Reign of the Kushana dynasty. First depictions of Jaina *tirthankaras* and multi-armed Hindu deities.		14th century	The Sisodias establish themselves.
			14th–15th century	Life of Ramananda.
			c. 1450?–1547?	Life of Mirabai.
4th–5th century	Vakataka rule over central India and the Deccan.		1440?–1518?	Life of Kabir.
			c. 1469	Birth of Guru Nanak, the founder of Sikhism.

1st–3rd century   Reign of the Kushana dynasty. First depictions of Jaina *tirthankaras* and multi-armed Hindu deities.

4th–5th century   Vakataka rule over central India and the Deccan.

4th–6th century   Gupta period in northern and central India.

c. 500   Completion of the rock-cut Buddhist temples at Ajanta. First free-standing stone temples, e.g. Dashavatara temple at Deogarh (Madhya Pradesh).

c. 5th–7th century   Spread of Vaishnavism, especially of the Krishna cult. Worship of local deities. Emergence of Tantrism.

5th–6th century   Invasion and supremacy of the Hunas (Huns).

6th century   Kalachuri dynasty rules the western coast of India.

6th–8th century   Pallava dynasty in southern India. Rock-cut architecture begins in the south; temple building flourishes at Mamallapuram and Kanchipuram.

6th–10th century   Tamil devotional poetry.

7th–8th century   Decline of Buddhism in northern India. Hindu revival.

7th–10th century   Rashtrakuta dynasty rules over northern part of the Deccan.

early 8th century   Arab merchants settle on the coast of Sindh, Pakistan, and Gujarat.

8th–12th century   Pala dynasty rules in Bihar, Bengal and large part of eastern India.

788–820   Life of Shankaracharya.

8th–13th century   Eastern Ganga dynasty.

9th–11th century   Chandella dynasty rules central India.

9th–13th century   Chola dynasty becomes the paramount force in southern India.

10th–14th century   Hoysala dynasty.

10th–14th century   Solanki dynasty governs western India.

999–1026   Raids of Mahmud of Ghazni in the north of India.

1192   Muhammad of Ghor invades India.

11th–12th century   Life of Ramanuja.

12th–15th century   Eastern Ganga dynasty rules Orissa.

12th–13th century   Buddhism disappears from India.

13th century   Life of Madhva.

1211–1526   The Delhi Sultanate is established.

1336   Founding of the city of Vijayanagara.

14th century   The Sisodias establish themselves.

14th–15th century   Life of Ramananda.

c. 1450?–1547?   Life of Mirabai.

1440?–1518?   Life of Kabir.

c. 1469   Birth of Guru Nanak, the founder of Sikhism.

1479–1531   Life of Vallabha.

c. 1485–1533   Life of Chaitanya.

1498   Vasco da Gama lands on the Malabar coast near Kozhikode (Calicut).

1510   Goa proclaimed capital of the Portuguese Estado da India (until 1961).

1526   Babur founds the Mughal dynasty.

1526–1736   Rule of the Nayaks of Madurai.

1543–1623   Life of Tulsidas.

1556–1605   Reign of Akbar. In this period the Mughal territory includes the whole of northern India.

1565   The rulers of Vijayanagara are defeated by a confederacy of the Deccan sultanates.

1605   The Mughal emperor Jahangir comes to power (until 1627).

1608–49   Life of Tukaram.

1613   British trading post established at Surat.

1627   The Mughal emperor Shah Jahan rises to power (to 1657). Expansion of the Mughal empire to the Deccan.

1650   The British East India Company establishes a factory on the Hugli (West Bengal).

1662   Bombay becomes a British possession through the marriage of Catherine of Braganza to Charles II.

1686   Annexation of the sultanates of the Deccan to the Mughal empire.

1690   The British East India Company establishes a trading post at Calcutta.

1757   Robert Clive defeats the Nawab of Bengal at Plassey. British power in India commences.

1772   Warren Hastings first Governor General of India.

1784   Sir William Jones founds the Asiatic Society in Calcutta.

1828   Ram Mohan Roy founds the reformist movement Brahmo Samaj.

1829   Law against *sati*.

1831–37   Campaign against the *Thags*.

1835   Introduction of English school system.

1840	Introduction of photography in India.	1955	Untouchability Offences Act.
1857	Indian uprising.	1956	Reorganization of the states (formerly provinces) on linguistic principles.
1858	The British Crown exiles the last Mughal emperor and rules India directly through a viceroy.	1961	Indian troops reclaim Goa from Portugal.
1875	Svami Dayananda Sarasvati founds the reformist movement Arya Samaj.	1964	Death of Jawaharlal Nehru. Lal Bahadur Sastri succeeds him as prime minister.
1877	Queen Victoria proclaimed Empress of India.	1965	Conflict with Pakistan (West); Indira Gandhi succeeds Sastri as prime minister.
1885	The Indian National Congress is founded in Bombay.	1984	The Sikhs agitate for an independent state, Khalistan. Indira Gandhi is assassinated by two Sikh guards.
1911	George V, the first British monarch to visit India. The capital is shifted from Calcutta to Delhi.	1985	Indira Gandhi's eldest son, Rajiv, is elected prime minister.
1920	Mahatma Gandhi begins the first All-India Civil Disobedience Movement.	1991	Tamil extremists assassinate Rajiv Gandhi in Sriperumbudur.
1931	Inauguration of New Delhi.	1992	Destruction of the Babri mosque in Ayodhya by extremist Hindus.
1947	Independence is granted to India and Pakistan. Caste system officially abolished.	1997	Kocheril Raman Narayanan, a *dalit*, is elected President of India.
1948	Assassination of Mahatma Gandhi. Pandit Nehru elected prime minister of the Indian Union.	1998	Hindu parties win the election. Atul Behari Vajpayee nominated prime minister.
1950	The Indian Republic is declared. Indian constitution accepted. Migration of Indians to the West.	2001	Mahakumbhamela celebrated at Allahabad in January.

Bibliography

Art and iconography

Auboyer, J. and M.-Th. de Mallmann, 'Sitala-la-Froide', in *Artibus Asiae*, vol. 13 (1950), pp. 207–27

Barrett, D., and D. Gray, *Indian Painting* (Geneva, 1963, reprint New York, 1978)

Begley, W. E., *Visnu's Flaming Wheel: The Iconography of the Sudarsana-Cakra* (New York, 1973)

Binney, E., and W. G. Archer, *Rajput Miniatures from the Collection of Edwin Binney 3rd* (Portland, Oreg., 1968)

Blurton, T. R., *Hindu Art* (London, 1992)

Coomaraswamy, A. K., *Yaksas,* 2 vols. (Washington, D.C., 1928)

—, *The Dance of Shiva* (London, 1958)

Dallapiccola, A. L., (ed.), *Krishna the Divine Lover: Myth and Legend Through Indian Art* (London, 1982)

Dallapiccola, A. L. and S. Zingel-Avé Lallemant (eds), *The Stupa, Its Religious Historical and Artistic Significance* (Wiesbaden, 1980)

Dehejia, V., *Yogini Cult and Temples. A Tantric Tradition* (New Delhi, 1986)

—, *Indian Art* (London, 1997)

—, *Devi, the Great Goddess* (exh. cat., Arthur M. Sackler Gallery, Washington, D.C., 1999)

Desai, D., *Erotic Sculpture of India: A Socio-Cultural Study* (New Delhi, 1975)

Eck, D., *Darshan: Seeing the Divine Image in India* (2nd edition, Chambersburg, Penn., 1985)

Gopinatha Rao, T. G., *Elements of Hindu Iconography*, 4 vols. (Madras, 1914, reprint New York, 1968)

Goswamy, B. N., and E. Fischer, *Pahari Masters, Court Painters of Northern India* (exh. cat., Rietberg Museum, Zurich, 1992)

Harle, J. C., *The Art and Architecture of the Indian Subcontinent* (Harmondsworth and New York, 1986)

Hudson, D., 'Kanchipuram', in *Temple Towns of Tamil Nadu*, (Mumbai, 1993), pp. 18–39

Huntington, S., *The Art of Ancient India: Buddhist, Hindu, Jain* (New York and Tokyo, 1985)

Jain, J., *Kalighat Painting: Images from a Changing World* (Ahmedabad and Middletown, N. J., 1999)

Knox, R., *Amaravati, Buddhist Sculpture from the Great Stupa* (London, 1992)

L'Hernault, F., 'Tiruvannamalai', in *Temple Towns of Tamil Nadu* (Mumbai, 1993), pp. 40–57

Liebert, G., *Iconographic Dictionary of the Indian Religions: Hinduism, Buddhism, Jainism* (Leiden, 1976)

Mallebrein, C., (ed.), *Die anderen Götter: Volks- und Stammesbronzen aus Indien* (Cologne, 1993)

Maxwell, T. S., *Vishvarupa* (New Delhi, 1988)

—, *The Gods of Asia: Image, Text, and Meaning* (New Delhi, 1997)

Michell, G., *The Hindu Temple: An Introduction to Its Meaning and Forms* (London, 1977)

—, (ed.), *Living Wood: Sculptural Traditions of Southern India* (London, 1992)

—, (ed.), *Temple Towns of Tamil Nadu* (Mumbai, 1993)

—, *Architecture and Art of Southern India. Vijayanagara and the Successor States* (Cambridge and New York, 1995)

—, (ed.), *Eternal Kaveri* (Mumbai, 1999)

—, *Hindu Art and Architecture* (London and New York, 2000)

Pal, P., (ed.), *The Peaceful Liberators: Jain Art from India* (exh. cat., Los Angeles County Museum of Art, Los Angeles, 1995)

Rawson, P., *The Art of Tantra* (exh. cat., Hayward Gallery, London, 1973)

Sivapriyananda, *Astrology and Religion in Indian Art* (New Delhi, 1990)

Sivaramamurti, C., *South Indian Painting* (New Delhi, 1968)

Skelton, R., *Rajasthani Temple Hangings of the Krishna Cult, from the Collection of Karl Mann, New York* (New York, 1973)

Spink, W., *Krishnamandala* (Ann Arbor, Mich., 1971)

Srinivasan, K. R., *Temples of South India* (reprint New Delhi, 1991)

Stronge, S., (ed.), *The Arts of the Sikh Kingdoms* (exh. cat., Victoria and Albert Museum, London, 1999)

Stutley, M., *The Illustrated Dictionary of Hindu Iconography* (Boston, Mass., and London, 1985)

Vogel, J. Ph., *The Goose in Indian Literature and Art* (Leiden, 1962)

—, *Indian Serpent Lore or the Nagas in Hindu Legend and Art* (London, 1926, reprint Varanasi, 1972)

Material culture

Achaya, K. T., *Indian Food. A Historical Companion* (New Delhi, 1994)

Jagdisha Ayyar, P. V., *South Indian Customs* (Madras, 1925, 2nd reprint, New Delhi, 1989)

Jain-Neubauer, J., *Foot & Footwear in Indian Culture* (Ahmedabad and Middletown, N. J., 2000)

Patnaik, N., *The Garden of Life: An Introduction to the Healing Plants of India* (New York, 1993)

Prakash, O., *Food and Drink in Ancient India* (Delhi, 1961)

Untracht, O., *Traditional Jewellery of India* (London, 1997)

Hinduism, Buddhism, Jainism, Sikhism

Abbott, J. E., *The Poet-Saints of Maharashtra*, 12 vols (Poona, 1926–1934)

Bhandarkar, R. G., *Vaisnavism, Saivism and Minor Religious Systems* (Strasbourg, 1913, reprint Poona, 1982)

Bharati, A., *The Tantric Tradition* (London, 1965)

Bhardwaj, S. M., *Hindu Places of Pilgrimage in India: A Study in Cultural Geography* (Berkeley and Los Angeles, Calif., and London ,1973)

Brand, M., 'A New Hindu Goddess', in *Hemisphere*, vol. 26, no.6 (May–June, 1982), pp. 380–84

Briggs, G. W., *Gorakhnath and the Kanphata Yogis* (Calcutta, London and New York, 1938, reprint Delhi, 1973)

Brockington, J. L., *The Sacred Thread: Hinduism in Its Continuity and Diversity* (Edinburgh, 1981)

Coburn, T. B., *Devi Mahatmya: The Crystallization of the Goddess Tradition* (Delhi, 1984)

Conze, E., *A Short History of Buddhism* (London, 1980)

Courtright, P., *Ganesa: Lord of Obstacles, Lord of the Beginnings* (London and New York, 1985)

Dehejia, V., *Slaves of the Lord: The Path of the Tamil Saints* (New Delhi, 1988)

Dowson, J., *A Classical Dictionary of Hindu Mythology* (10th edition, London, 1961)

Dundas, P., *The Jains* (London and New York, 1992)

Eck, D., *Banaras, City of Light* (New York, 1982)

Eschmann, A., H. Kulke and G. C. Tripathi, *The Cult of Jagannath and the Regional Tradition of Orissa* (New Delhi, 1978)

Fuller, C., *The Camphor Flame: Popular Hinduism and Society in India* (Princeton, N. J., 1993)

Gonda, J., *Visnuism and Saivism: A Comparison* (London, 1970)

Heesterman, J. C., *The Ancient Indian Royal Consecration* (The Hague, 1957)

Hiltebeitel, A., *The Cult of Draupadi*, 2 vols (Chicago, Ill., 1988)

Huyler, S. P., *Meeting God: Elements of Hindu Devotion* (London and New Haven, Conn., 1999)

Jagdisha Ayyar, P. V., *South Indian Festivities* (Madras, 1921, reprint New Delhi, 1982)

Kersenboom-Story, S. C., *Nityasumangali-Devadasi Tradition in South India* (Delhi, 1987)

Kinsley, D., *Hindu Goddesses: Visions of the Divine Feminine in the Hindu Religious Tradition* (Berkeley, Calif., 1986)

Klostermaier, K. K., *A Concise Encyclopedia of Hinduism* (Oxford, 1998)

Knott, K., *Hinduism: A Very Short Introduction* (Oxford, 1998)

König, D., *Das Tor zur Unterwelt* (Stuttgart and Wiesbaden, 1984)

Krishna, N., *Balaji, Venkateshwara, Lord of Tirumala-Tirupati – An Introduction* (Mumbai, 2000)

MacLeod, W. H., *Sikhism* (London, 1997)

Maity, P. K., *Historical Studies in the Cult of the Goddess Manasa* (Calcutta, 1966)

Mokashi, D. B., *Palkhi. An Indian Pilgrimage*, trans. P. C. Engblom (Albany, N. Y., 1987)

Ravindran Nair, G., *Snake Worship in India* (New Delhi, 1993)

Sontheimer, G. D., and S. Settar, (eds), *Memorial Stones: A Study in Their Origin, Significance and Variety* (Dharwad and Heidelberg, 1982)

Stutley, M. and J., *Dictionary of Hinduism: Its Mythology, Folklore and Development, 1500 BC–AD 1500* (London, 1977)

Vettam Mani, *Puranic Encyclopaedia* (Delhi, 1975, reprint 1979)

Walker, B., *Hindu World: An Encyclopedic Survey of Hinduism*, 2 vols (London, 1968)

Werner, K., *A Popular Dictionary of Hinduism* (London, 1994)

Whitehead, H., *The Village Gods of South India* (London, 1921)

Zimmer, H., *Myths and Symbols in Indian Art and Civilization* (New York, 1953, reprint Princeton, N. J., 1972)

Zysk, K. G., *Religious Medicine: The History and Evolution of Indian Medicine* (London and New Brunswick, N. J., 1993)

History, languages

Keay, J., *A History of India* (London, 2000)

Keith, A. B., *History of Sanskrit Literature* (Oxford, 1928, reprint London, 1966)

Majumdar, R. C., et al., *The History and Culture of the Indian People*, 11 vols (Bombay, 1950–)

Shastri, K. A. Nilakantha, *A History of South India from Prehistoric Times to the Fall of Vijayanagar* (Madras 1955, reprint Delhi, 1965)

Sleeman, W. H., *Rambles and Recollections of an Indian Official* (revised edition, London, 1915)

Spear. P., *A History of India*, vol. 2 (Harmondsworth, 1966)

Thapar, R., *A History of India*, vol. 1 (Harmondsworth, 1966)

Tod, J., W. Crooke (ed.), *Annals and Antiquities of Rajasthan, or the Central and Western Rajput States of India*, 3 vols (London, 1829–36, revised edition, 1920)

Yule, H., and A. C. Burnell, *Hobson-Jobson, A Glossary of Colloquial Anglo-Indian Words and Phrases* (London, 1886, reprint 1985)

Zvelebil, K. V., *Lexikon of Tamil Literature* (Leiden, 1995)

Performing arts

Ashton, M. B., and B. Christie, *Yaksagana – A Dance Drama of India* (New Delhi, 1977)

Bharata Iyer, K., *Kathakali, the Sacred Dance Drama of Malabar* (London, 1955)

Classical and Folk Dances of India (Bombay, 1963)

Vatsyayan, K., *Classical Indian Dance in Literature and the Arts* (New Delhi, 1968)

Primary sources in translation

Bharata, *The Natyasastra*, trans. M. Ghosh, 2 vols (Calcutta, 1950–61)

Bühler, G., (trans.), *The Laws of Manu*, 2 vols (2nd edition, New York, 1969)

Dehejia, V., *Antal and Her Path of Love: Poems of a Woman Saint from South India* (Albany, N. Y., 1990)

Dimmit, C., and J. A. B. van Buitenen (trans. and eds), *Classical Hindu Mythology. A Reader in the Sanskrit Puranas* (Philadelphia, Penn., 1978)

Karavelane, *Karaikkalammeiyar. Oeuvres editées et Traduites* (Pondichery, 1956)

Kautilya, *The Arthashastra*, ed., rearranged, trans. L. N. Rangarajan (New Delhi and New York, 1992)

Kokkoka, *The Koka Shastra, and Other Medieval Indian Writings on Love*, trans. A. Comfort (London, 1964)

The Mahabharata of Krishna-Dwaipayana Vyasa, trans. P. C. Roy, 12 vols (2nd edition, Calcutta, 1952–62)

O'Flaherty, W., *Hindu Myths. A Sourcebook translated from the Sanskrit* (Harmondsworth, 1975)

Pandey, S. M., and N. Zide, *Poems of Mira Bai* (Chicago, Ill., 1964)

Ramanujan, A. K., *Speaking of Siva* (Harmondsworth, 1973)

—, *Hymns for the Drowning: Poems for Visnu by Nammalvar* (Princeton, N. J., 1981)

The Ramayana of Valmiki, trans. M. L. Sen, 3 vols (Calcutta, n.d.)

The Ramayana of Tulasidas, trans. F. S. Growse (revised edition, Delhi, 1978)

Stoler Miller, B., *Jayadeva's Gita Govinda* (Indian reprint, Bombay and Delhi, 1978)

Vatsyayana, *Kama Sutra of Vatsyayana*, trans. Sir R. Burton and F. F. Arbuthnot (London, 1963)

—, *Kamasutra: A New Translation*, W. Doniger and S. Kakar (Oxford, 2002)

Vaudeville, C., *Kabir* (Oxford, 1974)

Sources of illustrations

The following abbreviations are used to identify
illustrations and sources:-
c centre; l left; r right

All maps and artwork by Graham Reed 17, 18, 20,
22l, 25l, 25c, 30, 31, 35, 41l, 48r, 50r, 51r, 55l, 57l, 57r,
60, 62, 90, 91l, 102l, 105, 110r, 113l, 114l, 115l, 115c,
115r, 116l, 137, 141r, 145, 147, 152r, 153r, 154, 159, 161r,
172, 174r, 186, 188, 190r, 207l

Photographs
Archaeological Museum, Alampur 122

Clare Arni 82, 86r, 88, 109r, 124l, 130, 165l, 166,
170, 185l, 195, 198l, 208l

C. L. Bharany Collection, New Delhi 59

T. R. Blurton 167

Crispin Branfoot 180

Courtesy, Cambridge-Kumbakonam Project 190l

Bhuri Singh Museum, Chamba 24

Government Museum and Art Gallery, Chandigarh
103, 123l

Anna L. Dallapiccola 21l, 25r, 32, 38r, 39, 40, 45l, 55r,
56, 58, 79, 86l, 108r, 112, 116r, 117r, 127, 132, 135, 150,
151, 155, 158, 168r, 176, 179, 197, 201l, 210

University of Durham, Oriental Museum 126

Musée d'Ethnographie, Geneva 52

Archaeological Museum, Halebid, Karnataka 87

Site Museum, Khajuraho 139

Mr A. Korner 45r, 61, 68, 71, 74, 84, 95, 96–97, 193

Copyright British Museum, London 21r, 22r, 26, 33,
36, 38l, 41r, 42, 43, 49l, 54, 80, 81, 83, 92r, 94, 97,

98, 99, 100, 107l, 107r, 106, 107, 109l, 110l, 111l,
114r, 118, 119l, 120, 121, 123r, 125, 128, 129l, 129r, 134,
138l, 138r, 140r, 142l, 143, 146, 148, 152l, 160, 161l,
162l, 164, 165r, 168l, 169, 171l, 171r, 173, 174l, 178,
182l, 182r, 183l, 183r, 184, 191, 194, 198r, 199, 200,
203l, 203r, 204, 205r, 208r

India Office Library, London 75, 140, 163

Private Collection, London 85l, 157, 205l

Los Angeles County Museum of Art 37, 51l, 53, 104,
117l, 124r

Madras Government Museum 48l

Archaeological Museum, Mathura 207r

George Michell 49r, 202r

Ajit Mookerjee Collection 47, 69, 72, 76, 77, 93,
196

Cleveland Museum of Art, Ohio 28, 181, 209r

Musée Guimet, Paris 201r

Courtesy J.u.E. von Portheim-Stiftung, Heidelberg
108l

Courtesy Gordon Reece Gallery, Knaresborough
202l

Russek Collection 141l

Courtesy Dr. Sivapriyananda 64, 92

Edwin Smith 131

Museum and Art Gallery, Tiruvananthapuram 66

V&A Picture Library, London 2–3, 23l, 46, 102r, 111r,
162r, 185

Courtesy Vijayanagara Resarch Project 29, 133

Rietberg Museum, Zurich 50l, 144, 153l